Urban Politics in America

Urban Politics
IN AMERICA

John H. Baker

Southern Illinois University

Charles Scribner's Sons
NEW YORK

3 5 7 9 11 13 15 17 19 C/P 20 18 16 14 12 10 8 6 4

Printed in the United States of America

ISBN 0–684–13910–3 (pbk)
Library of Congress Catalog Card Number 79–135389

To my Wife,
   DOROTHY WEKALL BAKER,
Whose support and encouragement have
made this a partnership effort.

preface

It is virtually impossible for an author to complete a task as large as this one without incurring a number of intellectual debts which must be acknowledged. It is unfortunate that space will not permit a full listing of all those whose assistance made this book possible. However, the contributions of a few were so great that they must be noted.

My colleague, Professor Stephen L. Wasby, provided the initial encouragement and advice which brought the book into focus. It is safe to say that without his support it would never have been written. In addition, Hassan Nejad and Kenzie Phelps provided valuable research assistance in the early stages of writing.

I owe a particular debt to my students in Urban Politics over the past several years. Many of the ideas presented in this work were first tried in the classroom. The searching questions and comments of these students saved me from many of the errors which I might otherwise have committed. They also served to help me identify some of the ambiguities which plague my writing.

The intellectual and moral support provided by my colleagues in the Department of Government at Southern Illinois University, Carbondale has been invaluable. In many ways this book is as much theirs as it is mine.

JOHN H. BAKER

Carbondale, Illinois,
1970

contents

**Part Two
The Politics and Structure
of Urban Government**

Contents

Part Three
The Functions of
Urban Government

Part Four
Prognosis and
Conclusions

Part One
The Context of Urban Government

The government and politics of urban areas are complex phenomena which are not amenable to the simple, straightforward approach that both students and teachers of the subject would prefer. The basic contention of this book, and especially of the first four chapters, is that the study of urban politics must be both interdisciplinary and intergovernmental. Chapter 1 will focus on the interdisciplinary study of the process of urbanization and the relationship that this process bears to political questions. The remaining three chapters will detail the complex intergovernmental web in which cities, towns, and other urban places must operate in their effort to satisfy both the basic service needs of urban citizens and the political criteria of democratic systems.

The chapters will also introduce the concepts and problems that will be necessary to an undertanding of subsequent parts of the book, and therefore will help students to avoid some of the pitfalls of oversimplification which in the past have plagued those who have insisted upon studying city or municipal government out of context.

chapter 1
The City
and Urbanization

⟨Seen from above, the modern city edges imperceptibly out of its setting. There are no clear boundaries. Just now the white trace of the superhighway passed through cultivated fields; now it is lost in an asphalt maze of streets and buildings. As one drives in from the airport or looks out from the train window, clumps of suburban housing, industrial complexes, and occasional green spaces flash by; it is hard to tell where city begins and country ends. Our difficulties with nomenclature reflect the indeterminacy of these limits; we reach for some vague concept of metropolis to describe the release of urban potential from its recognized ambit.[1]

The City: A Problem in Definition

For some years a popular television program opened with a panoramic view of Los Angeles at night and the statement, "This is the city." Few, if any, of the people watching the program stopped to examine the meaning of this statement. Of course it was the city. Many had driven up into the mountains or foothills on a clear evening to enjoy just such a spectacular view of "the city." But what the television audience and the Southern California sightseers were enjoying was in reality the lights of many cities, one city, or a portion of a city, depending upon the definition of city that the observer wanted to use.

---

[1] Oscar Handlin, "The Modern City as a Field of Historical Study," in *The Historian and the City*, ed. Oscar Handlin and John Burchard (Cambridge, Mass., 1963), p. 1.

In the not too distant past, the student of government had no difficulty giving a definition of the city. The standard approach to the study of city government was to examine the institutions and processes of the municipal corporation. The corporation had a legal definition included in the statutes of the state in which it was located and a set of geographic boundaries clearly indicated on official maps. It seemed clear that the relevant governmental activity would take place within these clearly defined limits and according to the legal terms of the statutes under which the government was incorporated.

In the last thirty years, however, an increasing number of political scientists have become aware of changes taking place on the periphery of many of our larger cities, changes that call into question the usefulness of the traditional governmental definition of the city. The blurring of the geographic boundaries described by Oscar Handlin in the opening quotation of this chapter has had political effects as well. The rapid growth of our metropolitan areas and the well-publicized "flight" of many city residents to suburbs on the edges of the old city have injected into the study of the city new political questions that have reduced the importance of purely municipal studies. Those concerned with the study of the decision-making process must now consider an increasingly complex number of intergovernmental relationships. At least in metropolitan areas, the scope of concern must now include intermunicipal, county-municipal, and special purpose district-municipal contacts and ties to a much greater degree than older definitions of the city would allow.

While the definition of the city has become broader, the span of attention of at least some political scientists studying the city has narrowed. As a result of the closer intellectual ties that have developed between some students of government and the urban sociologists, a great deal more attention has been given in recent years to the operation of subcommunities or subsystems within municipal boundaries. It has become increasingly clear that many important decisions are made outside of the structure provided by the municipal corporation but within the physical boundaries of that corporation. This knowledge has further encouraged some political scientists to abandon the traditional definition of the city.

As a result of these two tendencies, it has obviously become necessary to develop a new definition of the city. However, necessity has not yet become the mother of invention. We have not found a definition general enough to include all of the new problems in the political study of the city. Throughout this book, the discussion will be centered upon "urban government," a concept that is so general that it covers a multitude of sins, and yet so vague that it cannot be considered a truly satisfactory definition.

Even this obvious effort to avoid a definition leaves us in some difficulty. Clearly some definition must be offered for "urban" in order that governments in this category might be distinguished from those that could legitimately be called "rural." It is safe to say that there is no universally accepted definition of this term that can be adopted. Even so worthy an institution as the United States government cannot seem to arrive at a definition that satisfies its officials. The Bureau of the Census since 1950 has classed as urban any place, incorporated or unincorporated, having a population of 2,500 or over and certain other areas with a population density of 1,500 people per square mile. However, at least some members of Congress have found this to be too all-inclusive and have suggested another definition which would include:

1. Geographic areas within a unit of general local government, excluding counties and parishes, with a population of 10,000 or more;
2. The portion of the geographic area within a county, town, township, etc., with no incorporated unit of general local government but with a population density of 1,500 per square mile; and
3. The portion of the geographic area with a population density of 1,500 per square mile which is adjacent to an incorporated unit of general government with a population of 10,000 or more.[2]

At least two criteria are suggested in these definitions—population within an identifiable governmental unit, and population density. Students of urban areas often add a third criterion in order to avoid including a relatively densely populated rural settlement in the definition. This third criterion is a devotion to nonagricultural activities.[3] As the discussion in Chapter 4 will indicate, this standard is also used by the Census Bureau in its definition of the territory to be included within the metropolitan area. While this attention to the realities of the economic differences between urban and rural areas may be quite helpful in one respect, it creates certain problems in others. As Max Weber has pointed out, it is entirely possible for a population concentration to have the economic characteristics of urbanism and yet not possess the density of population suggested in definitions like the one outlined above.[4]

The City in History

We have established enough criteria at this point to pause and consider the historical development of urban areas. In the centuries that man has

---

[2] Title VIII of the proposed Intergovernmental Cooperation Act of 1967, Section 806 (b), *Congressional Record* (Washington, Jan. 26, 1967), p. S958.

[3] See Leo F. Schnore, "The City as a Social Organism," *Urban Affairs Quarterly* 1 (1966): 59.

[4] Max Weber, "The Nature of the City," in *Perspectives on the American Community*, ed. Roland L. Warren (Chicago, 1966), pp. 10–12.

been talking and writing about cities, he has had in mind at the very least some combination of the three criteria suggested earlier: (1) gathering of people, (2) relatively dense settlements, and (3) some economic differentiation between these aggregations and the predominantly rural countryside. While considering the history of the city in these terms, we will be able to discern other criteria of urbanism which will be important in a later discussion of the process of urbanization in its broadest sense.

The urban environment is a relatively recent experience for man. "The 6,000 years of man's urban existence represent only slightly more than one percent of his total existence on earth and only about 10 percent of his existence as physically modern man." [5] The process can be traced back to the stage, sometime in the Mesolithic era, when man ceased being a wanderer and began to settle in one spot and to raise food for his sustenance. It was not until the Neolithic era that settlements able to support the sort of population that might later become a city began to develop. Among the oldest of these settlements unearthed and dated by archaeologists were those in Jarmo (Iraq) and Jericho (Jordan), which were established by 6500 B.C.[6]

These farming villages could hardly be dignified by the term "city" at this point. While they were indeed population aggregates of some significance and relatively dense for their time, they were most assuredly lacking the economic characteristics that would differentiate them from the surrounding countryside. It was not until the fourth millennium B.C. that the process had progressed to the point where one could identify what Gideon Sjoberg has called the "preindustrial city." Although the population aggregates of this period were not large by modern standards, a few of these cities had more than 100,000 inhabitants, with a good many remaining below the 10,000 level. These early cities were characterized by their ability to support religious and government officials as well as craftsmen out of the community storehouse. The city was divided into occupational sectors with the center of the city reserved for religion, government, and the upper classes who held the power in the community through religious and governmental office. There was a rigid class system, and the entire fabric of society—religion, education, the extended family —was devoted to the maintenance of the status quo. This was not only a city as an identifiable geographic entity but also a new and different social system.[7]

These cities obviously did not spring full grown from the soil. There had to be a slow evolutionary process by which man reached the point

---

[5] Noel P. Gist and Sylvia Fleis Fava, *Urban Society*, 5th ed. (New York, 1964), p. 3.
[6] Gist and Fava, *Urban Society*, p. 6.
[7] Gideon Sjoberg, *The Preindustrial City: Past and Present* (Glencoe, 1960), pp. 323–328.

at which he could live in this sort of environment. The key to this process was technology. Man had to develop the ability to master at least a portion of his environment with relative efficiency before he could afford the luxury of urban living. "The very emergence of cities is functionally related to society's ability to produce a sizeable surplus; and the orientation, quite late in history, to an industrial base made possible a kind of city never before imagined." [8] Once this surplus had been achieved, the social organization outlined above was necessary for the distribution of the surplus among the rest of the population. This organization could indeed be called the essence of "civilization." Its introduction meant functional specialization, which in turn meant an increasing number of indirect associations and a variety of interdependences that would eventually become more important than kinship in ordering men's lives.[9]

However, if the process were as simple as all this, cities would have developed much more rapidly than they did, and the Industrial Revolution would have begun centuries earlier than it did. The rigid class structures and the orientation toward the traditional that were part of the pre-industrial city described by Sjoberg retarded the impact of technology and the process of specialization within the city. These factors, combined with the predominant ruralism of the Middle Ages, helped to slow the evolutionary process to a snail's pace for centuries. The commercial aspects of the Renaissance were needed to shatter the chains of the rigid class structure that bound the cities, and to lay the foundation for their reappearance as dominant social forces and their full participation in the Industrial Revolution.[10]

Another phenomenon then gave added impetus to the rise of the cities, a phenomenon all too often ignored as a contributor to the Industrial Revolution. The emergence of the national state had, at least in part, the effect of undermining the old loyalties to family, guild, and Church, and of encouraging the development of a more individualistic spirit that would be essential for the rapid development of functional specialization.[11] It is surely somewhat ironic that the growth of nationalism and centralization of power should have been so vital in the realization of the full potential of the city, since many now view national power and centralization as major threats to the continued meaningful existence of our cities.

The central element in the development of the modern city was the impact of the Industrial Revolution. Technological developments in the

---

[8] Sjoberg, *The Preindustrial City,* p. 329.
[9] Gist and Fava, *Urban Society,* pp. 9–11.
[10] Gist and Fava, *Urban Society,* pp. 11–24.
[11] Handlin, *The Historian and the City,* p. 9, and Gist and Fava, *Urban Society,* p. 31.

harnessing of energy led to the development of the machine, which in turn made possible the utilization of the factory system of production. This required even heavier concentrations of population in order that the labor necessary for a system of mass production might be close at hand. Further technological developments in agriculture resulted in greater surpluses of labor, thus freeing many agricultural workers for employment in the factories of the city. Along with these economic factors came the cultural growth in the arts and in education inspired by the Renaissance, which demanded the concentration of even more specialized talent in the cities. The Renaissance also encouraged the rapid development of scientific inquiry. The results of scientific inquiry were quickly turned into the technology that further fed the development of the new economy of the cities.

The rise of Protestantism clearly played a role in the process as well. In the course of seriously fragmenting the religious order of its time, emergent Protestantism helped to change the entire social fabric of those societies in which it played an important role. The role that its emphasis on worldly labor and its toleration if not encouragement of the accumulation of wealth played in the development of the capitalist system has often been detailed.[12] While no one would suggest that either industrialization or urban development is dependent for its existence upon a strong Protestant movement, the contribution of such movements, especially in England, Western Europe, and the United States, is difficult to ignore. It is particularly important to note the differences in the roles played by Protestantism in this period and by religion in general during the preindustrial period. Such a comparison suggests strongly that religion is one of the important independent variables in urban development.

There are in the world today some cities of great size and significance that obviously do not fit neatly into the pattern suggested by this brief analysis. The cities of the economically emergent nations of Asia, Africa, and Latin America cannot trace their growth immediately to the industrialization of their nation's economy for, in many cases, this process is just beginning. Many of these cities drew the impetus for their growth from nations that were experiencing industrial and commercial expansion and that were at the same time expanding their influence abroad as colonial or imperial powers. The colonial system needed administrative and economic centers to control the utilization of the resources in the commercial and industrial economies of the dominant world powers. It may not be stretching the point too far to claim that these cities are also

---

[12] See for examples R. H. Tawney, *Religion and the Rise of Capitalism* (New York, 1926), and Max Weber, *The Protestant Ethic and the Spirit of Capitalism*, trans. Talcott Parsons (London, 1930).

the products of the forces of industrialization, albeit indirectly. Gist and Fava have suggested that the separation of these cities from the economies of their former colonial masters might well create serious social problems.[13] Great Britain has recognized this by granting Commonwealth status to former colonies, thus assuring them of a continued tie to the economy of the mother country, which should be beneficial to all concerned.

The existence throughout history of relatively dense population aggregates without commensurate industrial or commercial development raises the problem of definition again. Clearly a nation with a limited land mass and a high birthrate, such as Japan, must have developed such population aggregates long before these aggregates were touched by the process of industrialization. Some students of urban history would rule them out altogether as not being sufficiently urban in character to be classed as cities. However, it may make more sense to recognize that urban development and industrial development have both been distributed somewhat unevenly on the earth's surface. This allows identification of preindustrial cities of Sjoberg's variety in a world that is in general postindustrial. When, as in the case of Japan, industrialization does catch up with these areas, the development of the fully industrial city appears to be much more rapid than was the case with cities that became industrialized as much as 200 years earlier. Urban growth is much more predictable than it was; it is characterized by certain results that will be discussed later in this chapter.

The City in American History

In many respects, America has been almost the ideal breeding ground for the city. A study of the conditions present in this country throughout its history shows that it is not accidental that the United States has produced so many major urban areas in such a short time. Temperate climate, amazingly varied natural resources, and ideal geographic location combined to provide an excellent environment for urban growth. The social structure of the country, characterized by the absence of rigid class structures, by the small family, and to a degree by the Protestant ethic combined with a spirit of intense individualism and an energetic population to make it almost inevitable that the favorable environment would be used to develop an industrial economy.[14]

"Although the American experiment began in a wilderness and was sustained through agriculture, there was recognition on the part of those engaged in colonial ventures that cities and towns were both culturally

[13] Gist and Fava, *Urban Society*, pp. 36 and 37.
[14] Gist and Fava, *Urban Society*, p. 39.

and economically essential." [15] Being part of the British mercantile system, the colonies had to develop port facilities in order to engage in trade with the mother country. Even the stalwart Jeffersonian agrarians of the post-Revolutionary era were dependent upon the export trade for marketing their goods and were, therefore, dependent upon the cities that grew and thrived on this trade. The rapid development of the domestic economy under the watchful eye of practical men such as Alexander Hamilton guaranteed not only the adequate support of existing cities but also their development at a rapid rate. Once more it is interesting to note the importance of the development of a national government in the growth of the cities. Had the Constitutional Convention of 1787 failed to provide a central government of adequate strength, the expansion of urban America would certainly have been seriously retarded.

Quite often analysts of American urban history pass rapidly over the first half of the nineteenth century without noting the spectacular growth in both the size and number of cities during this period. Using the Census Bureau figure of 2,500 as the basis for urban population, one can see an increase of 797 percent in the urban population between 1820 and 1860, while the total population was increased 226 percent. Much of this growth took place in the larger cities; as a result, eight cities had populations over 100,000 in 1860, while there had been only one in 1810. Eighty-nine additional cities of over 10,000 appeared between 1820 and 1860. Since manufacturing had not yet really taken hold of the economy at this time, most of the growth can be traced to commercial activity. This commerce was, of course, facilitated by the expansion of the domestic transportation system, especially the railroads, over the eastern half of the country. The impact of the transportation system was particularly significant in the growth of such cities as New Orleans, Cincinnati, St. Louis, and Chicago, which acted as a series of gates to the vast resources of the American West. The only part of the country that remained largely untouched by these developments was the South, where a primarily agrarian orientation prevailed.[16]

Between 1860 and 1910, the city really came into its own as a dominant feature of American life. The completion of the transcontinental railroad, the mechanization of agriculture, and the many technological advances that went along with the industrialization of the economy stimulated the growth of the cities to such a degree that, by the end of this period, they clearly dominated the American scene. New York, Philadelphia, and Chicago each passed the one million mark; New York reached five million. In the Midwest, the major agricultural marketing centers began

---

[15] Charles N. Glaab, *The American City: A Documentary History* (Homewood, Ill., 1963), p. 5.

[16] Glaab, *The American City*, pp. 65–68.

their boom, and Omaha, Kansas City, Wichita, Duluth, and Minneapolis all became major cities. Attracted by the promise of economic growth and the dream of the new freedom to be found in a democracy, wave upon wave of immigrants reached our shores to be absorbed in the growing labor market found primarily in the cities of the eastern seaboard. While this immigration factor is undoubtedly of central importance to the growth of American cities, it is easy to overemphasize it. Too few demographers have taken note of the migration of rural residents to the cities. This migration reached major proportions at this time; it may well have been more important than immigration as a source of industrial labor. The tremendous productivity of American farms, stimulated by technological advances in agriculture, was already pushing the marginal farmer toward the city. Because the great demand for unskilled labor in the cities could easily accommodate most of these migrants, the process escaped the notice of most social observers of the time, and its full impact was to be delayed until well into the twentieth century.[17]

Another modern phenomenon of American city growth can be traced to the latter half of the nineteenth century. As early as 1823, enterprising land developers were attempting to lure residents of New York City into the surrounding countryside. As the central cities became more and more congested, and as transportation became more readily available within the urban area, the attraction of the fringes of the city became hard to resist. Satellite settlements sprang up around the city until a suburban area was clearly identifiable, as it was around Chicago by 1873. While the process of suburbanization would not achieve major proportions until after World War II, its inevitability was obvious by the end of the nineteenth century.[18]

Even though the growth patterns of the American city in the twentieth century have been so often discussed in the current popular and professional literature that they are well known, they will be summarized here to complete the picture. This century has been characterized by a continuation of the process of industrialization with its concomitant effects on the urban setting. Technological advances, spurred in part by the military demands of two world wars, two "police actions," and the demands of cold war national defense, have had a continuing impact on the development and form of the American city. Agricultural techniques have been perfected to the point where only a relatively minor proportion of the total population needs to be employed to meet the demands of the nation; in fact, agricultural surpluses have become a major economic problem. Architectural and engineering achievements have enabled

---

[17] Glaab, *The American City*, pp. 173–176.
[18] Glaab, *The American City*, p. 229.

us to build upward in the center of our great cities and to reach population densities which are truly staggering. The addition of the truck and the airplane to rail and water systems as major means of transporting industrial production has facilitated the growth of major population centers in areas once thought inaccessible. The development of mass communications media has contributed to the ability of single governments to control large numbers of people in an urban environment.

However, these factors have not resulted in the simple continued growth of the "city" in the old sense of the word. They have altered old patterns of urban existence, making older concepts of the city obsolete, as was suggested earlier in this chapter. The automobile allowed a far greater number of urban residents to enjoy the surrounding countryside and to reside in this idyllic environment while continuing to answer the city's call for more labor. The nation's system for the distribution of wealth, while far from ideal for many people, did manage to allocate the proceeds of industrial and commercial success to vast numbers of urban residents and thus enable them to purchase automobiles and to make the down payment on their own single-family retreat from the city crowds. As the newly mobile labor force accelerated its move to the suburbs, industry and commerce began to follow, further spreading the urban area across the landscape. The end result was, of course, the metropolis, about which more will be said in Chapter 4. It is sufficient to observe here that the twentieth century American city is geographically far different from its predecessors.

The Urbanization Process

Because the effects of city growth must be considered along with the facts and causes of this growth, we will now examine the process of urbanization as it is defined by scholars from a variety of disciplines.

THE DEMOGRAPHIC APPROACH. The demographer is concerned primarily with the spatial distribution of people on the face of the earth. In urban studies, the concept of population concentration is of major importance to those with a demographic orientation, and questions about the size and density of the population of an area are often the key to the basic differentiation between urban and rural populations. The answers to such questions and the definitions derived from them are in a form particularly amenable to statistical presentation and analysis and, therefore, often deemed most suitable for governmental purposes. The definition used by the Bureau of the Census that was given earlier in this chapter is an excellent example of this type of demographic approach.

In its simplest form, demographic analysis of the city is concerned with "the multiplication of points of concentration" and "the increase in the size of individual concentrations" of population.[19] This approach does not go far enough even for most demographers. The fact that the total number of population concentrations is increasing or that any one or more of these concentrations is becoming larger may not in itself be significant. What of the relationship of these factors to the rest of society? It is in the answer to this question that the demographic approach to urbanization has its greatest value to social science in general. This concern may be expressed in an emphasis on urbanization as the proportion of urban population at a particular time $[U_t/P_t]$ or as the change in that proportion over time $[\Delta U/P]$.[20] (In these formulations, U = the urban population, and P = the total population.) Such an approach enables those who wish to take a demographic view of the subject to comment both upon the extent and the rate of urbanization.

Two examples of these different types of demographic analysis will illustrate the point further. Table 1–1 represents the simplest form of demographic analysis outlined above. Note that the data presented here do not necessarily indicate any changes in the importance of urban areas to society as a whole. All of the data save that on annexations could readily be explained, as indeed much of it is, by shifts within the existing structure of our urban areas. While such data may not offer much information with respect to the extent and rate of urbanization, it does give us a great deal of valuable information with respect to the form that urbanization is taking. The generally larger percentile increases in suburban population when compared to the population of the central cities is obviously a key factor in discovering the process of suburbanization. Although the thorough demographer would want to examine other factors, such as differentials in birth and death rates and differentials in immigration and in-migration rates, before he could make any definite statement, it would appear on the surface from the data presented that a population flow exists from the central cities toward the suburbs. Such an observation seems almost commonplace, but it provides an excellent starting point for the demographer in any attempt to determine the extent and rate of this important subprocess that conventional wisdom has for so long emphasized as crucial to the understanding of the problems of American cities.

Table 1–2 illustrates the second approach to urban demography. With the data presented here, one can speak with some precision about the

---

[19] Philip M. Hauser, "Urbanization: An Overview," in *The Study of Urbanization*, ed. Philip M. Hauser and Leo F. Schnore (New York, 1965), p. 9.

[20] Leo F. Schnore and Eric E. Lampard, "Social Science and the City," in *Urban Research and Policy Planning*, ed. Leo F. Schnore and Henry Fagin (Beverly Hills, 1967), p. 26.

TABLE 1–1. 1960–1965 **Percentage of Population Change by Aggregates and Divisions**
(Data in italics reflect adjustment for annexations)

Region Division	Total	PLACES OVER 10,000					Metro. Areas	Non-metro. Areas
		Cities Central	Suburbs	Non-metro. Places	Metro. Remainders	Non-metro. Remainders		
New England	5.2	-4.0 / -4.0	6.8 / 6.8	4.6 / 2.1	18.0 / 18.0	6.7 / 7.9	5.0	6.0
Middle Atlantic	5.2	1.3 / 1.3	5.1 / 4.9	-0.3 / -0.8	14.6 / 14.7	3.3 / 3.4	5.9	2.5
East North Central	5.7	1.9 / 0.2	14.0 / 12.4	5.4 / 4.0	11.1 / 16.4	1.9 / 2.3	7.2	2.7
West North Central	3.6	3.3 / 0.9	26.7 / 23.3	7.2 / 5.9	6.5 / 17.2	-1.6 / -1.2	8.7	0.4
South Atlantic, upper	6.6	1.2 / 1.1	27.1 / 25.6	1.0 / -0.2	20.3 / 20.4	0.3 / 0.5	10.4	0.4
South Atlantic, lower	11.2	9.8 / 6.9	40.9 / 21.3	13.0 / 8.4	18.4 / 27.4	5.7 / 6.8	16.7	7.1
East South Central	3.3	14.6 / 6.2	9.6 / 5.2	10.2 / 7.1	2.1 / 17.5	-2.1 / -1.5	9.9	-0.0
West South Central	9.4	11.5 / 10.0	31.0 / 28.9	9.1 / 5.6	18.5 / 26.8	3.0 / 4.4	14.7	4.8
Mountain	15.2	12.7 / 10.7	53.3 / 37.9	16.3 / 9.5	40.3 / 51.8	3.5 / 6.4	24.7	7.3
Pacific	14.4	10.5 / 8.2	26.9 / 22.9	22.4 / 15.5	11.3 / 20.3	6.3 / 8.5	15.8	10.3
Northeast	5.2	0.3 / 0.3	5.7 / 5.6	1.5 / 0.3	15.2 / 15.3	4.1 / 4.5	5.7	3.4
North Central	5.1	2.2 / 0.3	16.0 / 14.2	6.1 / 4.8	10.3 / 16.5	0.3 / 0.7	7.5	1.7
South	8.4	10.1 / 7.2	31.6 / 21.9	10.2 / 6.5	15.9 / 24.0	2.4 / 3.4	13.9	4.0
West	14.6	11.0 / 8.8	28.8 / 24.0	19.6 / 12.8	16.3 / 25.7	5.2 / 7.7	17.3	9.1
UNITED STATES	7.6	5.1 / 3.5	16.5 / 13.9	9.1 / 6.0	14.4 / 19.6	2.3 / 3.3	10.1	3.9

SOURCE: Richard L. Farstall, "Population Change in American Cities, 1960–65," *The Municipal Yearbook*, 33 (Chicago, 1966), p. 35. Reprinted by permission of the International City Management Association.

TABLE 1–2.

Region and division	EXTENT OF URBANIZATION [U/P]		RATE OF URBANIZATION 1950–1960	
	1950	1960	Absolute $[\Delta(U/P)]$	Relative $\left[\dfrac{\Delta \frac{U}{P}}{\Delta P} \Big/ \dfrac{U}{P}\right]$
United States	63.9	69.8	5.9	158.8
Northeastern	79.4	80.2	.8	108.1
New England	76.2	76.4	.2	102.0
Middle Atlantic	80.4	81.3	.9	109.8
North Central	64.0	68.7	3.7	152.5
E. North Central	69.6	72.9	3.3	129.4
W. North Central	51.9	58.7	6.8	251.6
The South	48.6	58.5	9.9	243.4
South Atlantic	49.0	57.1	8.1	190.0
E. South Central	39.0	48.3	9.3	602.0
W. South Central	55.5	67.7	12.2	253.5
The West	69.4	77.6	8.2	142.0
Mountain	54.8	67.1	12.3	185.9
Pacific	79.6	81.0	1.4	122.7

SOURCE: Calculated from *The Municipal Yearbook*, 33 (Chicago, 1966), p. 22.

NOTE: *New England:* Maine, N.H., Vt., Mass., R.I., Conn. *Atlantic:* N.Y., N.J., Pa. *E. North Central:* Ohio, Ind., Ill., Mich., Wis. *W. North Central:* Minn., Iowa, Mo., N.Dak., S.Dak., Nebr., Kans. *South Atlantic:* Del., Md., D.C., Va., W.Va., N.C., S.C., Ga., Fla. *E. South Central:* Ky., Tenn., Ala., Miss. *W. South Central:* Ark., La., Okla., Tex. *Mountain:* Mont., Idaho, Wyo., Colo., N. Mex., Ariz., Utah, Nev. *Pacific:* Wash., Oreg., Calif., Alaska, Hawaii.

extent of urbanization, that is, the degree to which people live in urban rather than rural areas, and the rate at which the process of urbanization occurred in the decade between the two censuses. To be sure, this type of analysis is often plagued by problems of definitions. The inability of demographers in the Bureau of the Census to find a lower limit for their definition of "urban" that will last for more than one census might appear to frustrate attempts at longitudinal comparison of census data.

The Census Bureau recognizes this problem, and has calculated the effect of its changing definitions. Only 0.1 percent of the noted increase in urban population could be attributed to change of definitions in 1960.[21]

Other factors also enter into this second type of demographic analysis. Once the phenomenon of urban growth relative to the rest of the population has been noted, it is necessary to ask what the causes of such growth might be in demographic terms. There are three basic sources of growth in the urban population, all of which have been mentioned pre-

[21] Henry D. Sheldon, "Urban Places and Population," in *The Municipal Yearbook*, ed. Orin F. Nolting and David S. Arnold, 33 (Chicago, 1966), pp. 23–24.

viously in this discussion: (1) natural increase, (2) net migration, and (3) reclassification.[22] Natural increase is the excess of births over deaths and must be compared with the same phenomena in rural areas in order to determine its relative importance to urbanization. Historically, the high death rate that went along with the concentration of large numbers of people in the cities worked to the disadvantage of urban areas. Modern medical science in controlling communicable diseases has lowered the death rate from disease and infant mortality in the United States to the point that the rate of natural increase in the cities may well be higher than in rural areas. This factor enters into any explanation of urbanization.

Net migration deals with the movement of rural population to the city, the movement of urban population to rural areas, and immigration to both urban and rural areas from other countries. Any examination of the pattern of immigrant settlement in this country will reveal a marked propensity for locating at least initially in the city. Whether this was a matter of choice or of economic necessity really makes little difference at this point. Subsequent population movements within the country have been largely movements from the farm to the city in the twentieth century. To be sure, there has been the movement out of the central cities noted in Table 1-1, but these migrants have settled in areas that were already considered urban or that rapidly fell within the demographer's definition of an urban place. Net migration, then, also can be considered as a factor strongly favoring an increased degree of demographic urbanization.

Reclassification refers to the process of changing definitions, and also to the process by which new places are added to the urban category given a relatively constant definition of "urban." Natural increase and, to a minor degree, net migration result in population increases in places that were outside the defined limits in one census and within those limits in the next. The annexation by existing urban places of territory that had previously been considered rural also reclassifies the old residents of that territory. In fact, there are instances in which one can find farmers tending their fields within the corporate limits of municipalities almost as if they were engaged in a final effort to prove the folly of Census Bureau definitions of "urban." All of this gives additional impetus to the process of urbanization.

In order for the social scientist to get the most out of the work of the demographers, it is necessary for him to give careful attention to both of the approaches outlined above. If either is neglected, the result will be an incomplete view of urbanization from the demographic point of view. The extent to which an increasing number of Americans are living in

---

[22] Hauser, "Urbanization: An Overview," p. 31.

urban areas, the varying rate at which population patterns are changing, and the changing forms of these population patterns within urban areas are all of vital importance. In fact, it can be claimed with some justification that these demographic factors are central to any study or understanding of the city, regardless of the particular discipline followed by the student.[23]

URBANIZATION AND SOCIOLOGY. For many social scientists the demographic approach is only satisfactory as a beginning to the study of the urbanization process. For many sociologists the relevant questions about urbanization center around what happens to the social environment and structure when large numbers of people are brought together in what we have called urban areas.

Some early students of urbanization chose to adopt what they called the ecological approach. Robert Park, the leading exponent of this particular mode of study, defined the elements of the community that were of interest to him as (1) population, (2) culture, which included artifacts as well as customs and beliefs, and (3) natural resources or habitat.[24] In summarizing Park's approach Peter Orleans has said:

> In effect, Park is asking what characteristics of a population distributed in distinctive spatial enclaves have what kinds of effect on the development of the normative order. The strong implication is that the organization of urban populations is largely a function of the interaction of the differentiated attributes of such populations and their spatial distribution (concentration and segregation).[25]

For some, the main thrust of the effort has been directed toward the spatial distribution aspects of Park's analysis. In these cases, "urban ecology includes the study of such external expressions of ecological interrelationships as the distribution of cities or their internal structure and composition." [26] This has led to the development of general theories concerning the basic ecological patterns of urban growth. In essence, these theories suggest that certain basic patterns of land use characterize the process of urbanization and that these patterns may be represented graphically. For example, Burgess' Concentric Zone Theory viewed the city's land uses as being distributed in concentric circles with the central business district at the core surrounded by rings of residential areas ranging from those of the workingman closest to center city to those of

---

[23] Schnore and Lampard, "Social Science and the City," p. 25.
[24] Robert Park, "Human Ecology," in Warren, *Perspectives*, p. 43.
[25] Peter Orleans, "Robert Park and Social Area Analysis: A Convergence of Traditions in Urban Sociology," *Urban Affairs Quarterly* 1 (1966): 9.
[26] Gist and Fava, *Urban Society*, p. 96.

the upper-income commuter on the urban fringe. Growth resulted from outward pressures by the business district and the workingman which forced the downgrading of land uses in each zone and the addition of new commuter rings on the periphery of the city. On the other hand, Hoyt's Sector Theory posited a more uneven pattern of growth in the city. In this formulation, the major transportation routes exerted a "drag" effect on land uses and "pulled" them out from the central city causing sectors of land use to radiate from the center of the city cutting through the concentric rings of the original settlement. The Harris and Ullman Multiple-Nuclei Theory posits a still more uneven pattern of land use in which scattered centers of commercial and industrial development and their attendant residential areas break up the predictable pattern of city growth. While it is clear that none of these theories has universal application as a picture of urban growth, the pattern of growth in metropolitan areas certainly suggests the highly scattered picture of land uses drawn by the Multiple-Nuclei Theory.[27]

For many social scientists, the ecological approach to urbanization is almost all-inclusive. By emphasizing the elements of population, environment, technology, organization, and social psychology, and by recognizing their essential interrelationships, it is possible to gain a broad overview of the process and its major effects.[28] The major difficulty that the approach seems to have experienced is the paucity of comparative research that it has engendered and the lack of any general theoretical formulations about the nature of urbanization. The natural emphasis of the ecologist seems to have been on the uniqueness of the individual city, since it is highly improbable that so wide a range of variables could be reproduced successfully from one study to another. In fact, for the ecologist, merely moving the attention of a research effort from one city to another changes in a serious way the content of the study, and any attempt to compare the apples of one study with the oranges of another can only be made at such a high level of abstraction as to be almost commonplace.

Other sociologists have chosen to concentrate upon the urbanization process as reflected in changing social structures. For many of these scholars, the urban process is "the community application of the process through which units of organization become more *specialized* (division of labor) and hence more *interdependent,* and the sum of units becomes more *complex.*" [29] The "industrial-automotive process" is viewed as the technological side of urbanization, but, although it encourages and speeds

---

[27] This discussion draws heavily from Gist and Fava, *Urban Society,* pp. 108–116.
[28] Gist and Fava, *Urban Society,* pp. 97–101.
[29] David Popenoe, "On the Meaning of 'Urban' in Urban Studies," *Urban Affairs Quarterly* 1 (1965): 29.

the entire process, it is not considered to be a precondition for urbanization.[30] These changes in institutional structure do take place without industrialization, albeit slowly. It is equally important to recognize that specialization, interdependency, and complexity can and do occur outside of the cities and that this still can be called "urbanization."[31] It should be clear, however, that the extent to which these rural manifestations of urbanization exist is largely dependent upon the extent to which the fabric of the larger society, national or international, is dominated by cities. The urban process as defined above has its beginning in the cities even though its ultimate impact cannot be confined within them. As more effective means of transportation and communication bind the hinterland closer to the cities, the institutional changes pass into rural areas. In spite of the emphasis often placed upon urban-rural differences, the institutions and life styles of the two types of area are becoming increasingly similar, that is, increasingly urban.

Louis Wirth, one of the pioneers in urban sociology, gave a description of urbanization as a social phenomenon that has been standard for much of the work done in this area. Wirth pointed out that increased specialization was the natural outgrowth of the increase in population density in the cities and the necessity for enabling the urban area to support more people. Specialization was further encouraged by social forces such as class, caste, and prejudice which forced the grouping of homogeneous elements within the city. As larger and larger numbers of people were concentrated in a relatively small space, interpersonal and informal means of social control such as the extended family and the clan were no longer adequate, and new formal controls of a more impersonal nature had to be established. Increased specialization also brought with it a heterogeneity of population and a further breakdown of interpersonal relationships between individuals outside of the context of their work functions.[32]

Specialization and impersonal, formal relationships are central concepts in the definition of bureaucracy. It is not unusual, then, that many urbanists should consider bureaucratization as a natural concomitant of urbanization. If this description is accurate, the burgeoning bureaucracy can be expected in every institution undergoing the urbanization process, regardless of the institution's purpose or location.

The increase in heterogeneity and the breakdown of the family (and religious institutions) as a major means of social control have indicated for many the decline of what sociologists call primary groups. In place of these groups, the individual begins to associate himself with secondary

---

[30] Popenoe, "On the Meaning of 'Urban,' " p. 30.

[31] John Friedmann, "Two Concepts of Urbanization," *Urban Affairs Quarterly* 1 (1966): 79–80.

[32] Louis Wirth, "Urbanism as a Way of Life," in Warren, *Perspectives*, pp. 44–53.

groups or voluntary associations. Like the rest of urban society, these associations have tended to be specialized. Therefore, a vast array of them is necessary in order to accommodate the entire spectrum of urban life. The voluntary association is the means through which the individual reestablishes the contact with his fellow man that he lost with the disintegration of the extended family and other primary groups. But the process of shifting from primary to secondary group affiliation is far from complete. There are large numbers of individuals within the urban environment who profess no formal associations.[33] These individuals, at least as far as this particular approach goes, are left to drift in the vast urban sea.

This description of urbanization is not, however, without difficulties. For example, recent empirical investigations have revealed that the family has not disintegrated as a primary group and as an instrument of social control to the degree indicated above. Not only is the conjugal family an important social referent for many urban residents, but also the pattern of contacts with members of the extended family group is sufficiently broad as to indicate that it still may be a potent force in the city. This may be true of other primary groups as well. If so, this alteration of the basic theory of urbanization could have important implications in terms of individual behavior patterns, some of which will be discussed later in connection with the psychology of urban life.

Even those who subscribe heavily to this theory of the urban process have recognized that imposing formal, legalistic controls is a less efficacious method of regulating human behavior than the informal controls of a less complex society.[34] This is nowhere more obvious than in those large cities in the United States where these formal controls essentially broke down during the "long, hot summers" of 1965 and 1967. It is interesting to note that, at least in some instances, these formal controls were replaced with some success by interpersonal controls of the old, preurban variety. This might well indicate that the progression toward increasing formalization of control may not be irreversible. This is particularly so if familial and religious primary groups have indeed continued as relevant factors in the life of urban man.

THE CITY AND THE INDIVIDUAL. Another view of the process of urbanization stresses the impact of urbanization on the individual citizen. "When nonurban persons acquire roles, style of life, symbols, forms of organization, and cultural artifacts characteristic of the city, and when they come to share the meanings, values, and perspectives that are characteristically

---

[33] Gist and Fava, *Urban Society*, pp. 386–388.
[34] Hauser, "Urbanization: An Overview," p. 21.

urban, we can say that they are experiencing the process of urbanization." [35] In fact, it is possible to view all of the organizational changes
noted above as essentially the result of the urbanization of individuals.
Roger Starr has presented the picture of the city as a system whose essential purpose is to transform rural into urban man. The inputs of the system are the impoverished refugees from the farms, and the various
institutions and activities that are devoted to their education when they
reach the city. The output of the system is an urbanized work force capable of contributing to and sharing in the city's products and services.[36]
While this view may be somewhat extreme, there is little doubt that the
individual urban resident is the key factor upon which the process works.
The most obvious shortcoming in Starr's system is its failure to consider
the effects of the process upon those born and bred within the city.
Urbanization's effect on the individual does not stop with the transforma-
tion of a newly arrived migrant into a useful member of the urban work
force.

Although the impact of urbanization on the individual is in a way a
precondition of the social and institutional changes that are part of the
urban process, these changes, to the degree that they have actually taken
place, have themselves had a further effect on the individual in the city.
The specialization of the individual's work task and the relative anonymity and freedom that derive from living in a large population aggregate
free from many of the pressures of primary group association have combined, in the view of some analysts, to modify seriously individual behavior patterns. In the urban situation, the pace of urban life and the
close proximity in which individuals live result in an increase in nervous
stimuli which the individual can reduce by utilizing intellectual rather
than emotional responses as a defense mechanism. These intellectual
responses are based upon the substitution of essentially quantitative values
for qualitative values. The questions "How much does it cost?" and
"What time?" become basic to urban existence. By responding to stimuli
in terms of money and time, the urbanite is able to avoid the dangers
of emotional involvement. When these responses are combined with the
impersonalization that has been said to characterize urban life, they can
result in the blasé attitude that passes for sophistication in many cities.
This essential reserve in contact with other people is quite productive.
In addition to providing a comfortable way of responding to the proliferation of stimuli, it gives the individual even more freedom from social
pressures than he enjoyed before.[37]

---

[35] Gist and Fava, *Urban Society*, p. 271.

[36] Roger Starr, *The Living End: The City and its Critics* (New York, 1966), p. 248.

[37] George Simmel, "The Metropolis and Mental Life," in Warren, *Perspectives*, pp. 13–24.

This freedom may not be free of psychological cost to the individual, however. Wirth sees the "superficiality, anonymity, and the transitory character of urban-social relations" as leading eventually to a loss of self-expression and to a loss of a sense of participation which are equivalent to Emile Durkheim's *anomie* which is so often mentioned as a major psychological concomitant of urban life.[38] The compulsion to join voluntary, formal organizations may be viewed in these terms as an effort on the part of the individual to belong to something and to make his life count for something. The anxiety and fears that are the result of the isolation and anonymity of the individual can obviously result in serious mental illness. In fact, Durkheim's original discussion of *anomie* centered on his famous analysis of the factors contributing to suicide.[39] While it is obvious that most residents of cities react to the pressures of urban living with a response that is short of suicide, the mental health of the urbanite continues to be a matter of particular concern to urban scholars.

The case for an adverse psychological impact of urban life upon the individual can easily be overstated. To the extent that the ties of family, kinship, neighborhood, and community remain strong, these ties provide the resident with an identity and a sense of belonging. Current research indicates that membership in formal organizations is not widespread and that the specialization of work functions seldom affects family relationships and the formation of friendships. In the attempt to identify the variables that directly affect human behavior, such factors as socioeconomic level, age, and marital status appear to have much greater explanatory value than the fact of urban residence. In fact, many of the mental disorders that have been linked so closely with urban life have been discovered in the idealized close, rural community as well. There is some indication that the full psychological impact of the city is centered upon the extremely poor and the downwardly mobile individuals who have lost the hope of participation in society for reasons that may not be directly related to urban residency.[40]

URBANIZATION AND THE ECONOMIST. Much of the discussion of institutional changes that may accompany urbanization deals with alterations in patterns of production and consumption that are intrinsically interesting to economists. In fact, Max Weber refers to his definition of the city as an economic definition because it views the development of a market

---

[38] Wirth, "Urbanization as a Way of Life," p. 47.

[39] Emile Durkheim, *Suicide*, trans. John A. Spaulding and George Simpson, ed. George Simpson (Glencoe, 1951), pp. 241–276. Durkheim's concept of *anomie* as formulated here differs somewhat from that mentioned above, but I have used the concept in its more popular form.

[40] Gist and Fava, *Urban Society*, pp. 441–457.

with the accompanying tradesmen and economic versatility as the essential characteristic of the city.[41] Specialization and division of labor are as important to the economist as they are to the urban sociologist, and the process of industrialization which has been so important in the development of many modern cities is a major factor in any study of the system utilized for the allocation of goods and services.

A great many urban economists have concentrated their efforts upon developing a theory of urban growth which might offer an explanation of the differential growth rate and potential between urban areas.[42] The central concept in this theory has been that of the "export base." That is to say, a city or urban area must have an industry or industries whose products are sold outside the immediate urban area. The mere presence of an export base is not, however, sufficient to guarantee the growth of an urban area. Other factors enter the picture as well. If rising prices result in reduced consumer demand, if new products are developed that may be substituted for those that constitute the export base, or if changes in consumer preference in general severely reduce the demand for the products, urban growth may be retarded or stopped completely. But a reduction in any of the resources—land, labor, capital, and entrepreneurship—necessary to the continued expansion of the export base could have a similar effect upon urban growth.

Other economists are concerned with the spatial distribution of economic activity within the urban area. These analyses detail the decentralization or suburbanization of the major economic activities, manufacturing, wholesaling, retailing, and services.[43] The migration of employment opportunities which has been facilitated by improved means of transportation and communication has been in part a cause of, and in part an effect of, the general movement of the population to the suburbs which has been described by the demographers. However, because a significant portion of the population remains in the central city, because this portion of the population is often poor and most in need of employment, and because these people have benefited to only a small degree from improvements in transportation, serious social problems are raised by this migration. Is it economically feasible to attempt to reverse the flow of economic activity and to locate employment opportunities in the central city once more? Or is it more desirable to provide relatively cheap transportation so that those in the central city may go where the jobs are? Or is it better

---

[41] Weber, "The Nature of the City," pp. 10–11.
[42] The following discussion draws heavily upon Wilbur Thompson, *A Preface to Urban Economics* (Baltimore, 1965), pp. 11–39.
[43] See for example John F. Kain, "The Distribution and Movement of Jobs and Industry," in *The Metropolitan Enigma*, ed. James Q. Wilson (Washington, 1967), pp. 1–31.

still to make the social changes that are necessary to permit the permanent migration of those in need of employment to the residential suburbs closer to the decentralized jobs? These are the basic questions raised in this area of urban economic research.

Another aspect of the changing urban scene which has received attention from the economists is the pattern of changing urban land uses in general. The economist is interested in the process by which the market mechanism operates to encourage and, in some instances, almost force the transition of land use from single-family residential, through multiple-family and commercial, to industrial uses. The process is, of course, not always a complete one. Especially in the central city, the process may go no further than the multiple-family uses if the population density is high enough to enable a large return on the property. Urban land economics is considerably more complicated than this brief presentation indicates. It is sufficient for our purposes here to note that these shifts in land usage are part of the urbanization process for the economist.

URBANIZATION AND THE POLITICAL SCIENTIST. What does urbanization mean to the student of the urban governmental process? In order to answer this question, it is first necessary to recognize the eclectic nature of modern urban studies. Most urbanists are presently attempting to pull together the approaches of planners, political scientists, economists, geographers, and sociologists as mutually supporting concerns.[44] Each particular approach to urbanization contains within it elements that will prove to be of great interest in the further study of decision-making in an urban environment. A few examples will illustrate the point.

The demographer's data on the extent and rate of population concentration can lead us to a fuller appreciation of the magnitude of present urban problems and to the realization that, given the present rate of concentration, these problems are destined to become more rather than less important. We have already reached the point at which most government in this country is urban government. We shall soon reach the point at which nearly all of the governmental process which takes place within the confines of this country is urban, and in several decades we may see a situation develop in which most of the governing in the world is accomplished in an urban setting. If nothing else, these disturbing facts should answer the question, Why study urban government?

The urbanization process suggests other interesting problems for the student of government. If, as Wirth and others claim, urbanization is characterized by the replacement of informal, interpersonal means of social control by formal, impersonal, and legalistic controls, this is a fact of

---

[44] Popenoe, "On the Meaning of 'Urban,'" p. 23.

tremendous significance. The institutions of government are, by definition, the repositories of the means of such formal social control. As the society becomes more and more urban in character, government can be expected to play a larger and larger role in the life of the individual. As more and more problems are met by the public rather than the private sector of society, the process by which decisions are made in the public sector and by which the decision makers are selected achieves greater importance. And if, as was suggested earlier, these formal controls are less effective in ordering human behavior in a mass existence, serious questions can be raised about the ability of government to provide the sort of ordered environment necessary for future urban existence without some major assistance from the informal controls of the primary group whose demise Wirth and others have predicted. To the extent that urbanization has not proved destructive of these informal controls, the picture for government and the future of the cities is far less bleak. The continued and perhaps increased efficacy of these primary groups as agents of social control might well be a matter of particular interest to those whose ideology leads them to view with alarm any increase in the size and scope of governmental activity.

The question of whether primary or secondary group affiliations are dominant in the life of the urban resident raises other interesting and practical problems for the political scientist. Which is more significant in determining the political behavior of urban man, his family and religious ties or his voluntary association with other residents who share his occupational and avocational interests? To the extent that the voluntary association represents the wave of the future in the cities and in urban society in general, one might productively center his attention upon the activities and impact of the interest group in politics and neglect the more traditional variables in the determination of political behavior. If, however, family and religion are still significant factors in the life of urban man, they must be considered as important agents of political socialization. As later chapters will indicate, political scientists have wisely chosen to continue the consideration of both primary and secondary group effects on political behavior in the face of, or perhaps in ignorance of, the fact that many sociologists have considered the former doomed by urbanization.

The psychological impact of urbanization is of major importance to the political scientist as well. If a significant number of urban residents are suffering from *anomie*, it is quite possible that their general feeling of nonparticipation will find itself expressed in a generally poor record of the variety of political participation which is an integral part of the democratic process for some political scientists. The political expression for *anomie* might well be a low sense of efficacy which could lead in turn to a record of nonvoting and general nonparticipation in political action groups. Obviously, either the presence or absence of *anomie* as a factor in urbanization is an important element in the study of political life in an urban environment.

One further example should serve to illustrate the point adequately. The spatial distribution of jobs and industry as analyzed by some economists is directly relevant to some of the major policy questions which face the governments in our urban areas today. The question of employment for the inhabitants of the ghettos of our cities demands an immediate answer, if not on the simple grounds of humanity, then because of the increasing pressure of civil rights advocates, both violent and nonviolent. If economic analysis reveals that attempts to reverse the flow of commerce and industry from the central city to the suburbs are either futile or unwise in the long run, then the policy emphasis must shift from such attempts to the construction of adequate, low-cost transportation, or to the full-scale racial integration of the suburbs, or to both. The current frustration of efforts on the part of government at all levels to deal with the problems of mass transportation and integration of housing illustrates the political problems that would be involved in such a shift of public policy emphasis. Studies' such as these, combined with more general treatments of urban land use, must be considered an integral part of the policy-making process in vital areas of interest to urban governmental agenies such as planning, housing, and urban renewal.

The picture presented by these examples does not portray the political scientist as a jack-of-all-trades. What is clearly indicated is that urbanization is a process that benefits from interdisciplinary analysis. Students of each discipline must be at the very least aware of the contributions of the other disciplines if their own efforts are to fit into the general pattern of modern urban studies. The task that such an approach presents to the political scientist is not an easy one. But the problems of our urban areas are complex and do not lend themselves to simple analysis. The only course of action open is for us to join with other students in an effort to understand just what it is that urban government is attempting to govern. Only by understanding the social, psychological, and economic forces that are peculiar to the urban environment can we hope to understand the political forces that reside there as well. These are the gifts that the political scientist can gratefully receive from scholars in other areas. The contributions that he can make to urban studies—greater understanding of governmental institutions, intergovernmental relations, and the political process—are to be the subjects of consideration in the rest of this book.

Suggested Readings

Chapin, F. Stuart, and Weiss, Shirley F., eds. *Urban Growth Dynamics*. New York, 1962.

Gist, Noel P., and Fava, Sylvia Fleis. *Urban Society*. 5th ed. New York, 1964.

Glaab, Charles N. *The American City: A Documentary History*. Homewood, Ill., 1963.

Handlin, Oscar, and Burchard, John, eds. *The Historian and the City*. Cambridge, Mass., 1963.

Hauser Philip M., and Schnore, Leo F., eds. *The Study of Urbanization*. New York, 1965.

Hirsch, Werner Z., ed. *Urban Life and Form*. New York, 1963.

Meier, Richard. *A Communications Theory of Urban Growth*. Cambridge, Mass., 1962.

Mumford, Lewis. *The City in History*. New York, 1961.

Murphy, R. E. *The American City*. New York, 1966.

Reissman, Leonard. *The Urban Process*. New York, 1964.

Schnore, Leo F. *The Urban Scene: Human Ecology and Demography*. New York, 1965.

Sjoberg, Gideon. *The Preindustrial City: Past and Present*. Glencoe, 1960.

Thompson, Wilbur R. *A Preface to Urban Economics*. Baltimore, 1965.

Wirth, Louis. *Community Life* and *Social Policy*. Chicago, 1956.

chapter 2
City-State Relations

([That local governments are sovereign in any measure will sound blasphemous to purists among professors and practitioners of law. In most statements of the legal status of municipal corporations, one reads that the sovereignty belongs to the state, not to the locality. The latter is a mere "creature," an "agent," an "instrumentality," a "department," or a "subdivision" of the state. It lives and functions by the grace and during the pleasure of its lord and master, its creator, the sovereign state.[1]

Although the approach adopted in Chapter 1 tends to deemphasize the study of the municipal corporation, it does not relieve the student of urban problems of the necessity for examining some aspects of the municipal corporation. The legal status, the powers, and the structure of these corporations are variables that the social scientist must consider even though they do not constitute the whole of urban political science.

The Overall View: Two Basic Positions

A well-known American expert on municipal law, Charles Rhyne, has suggested that much of the difficulty surrounding the nature of the municipal corporation stems from the conflicting meanings present within the term itself. Rhyne points out that in both the Roman and the English

---

[1] Anwar Syed, *The Political Theory of American Local Government* (New York, 1966), p. 53.

traditions "the word municipal connoted local self-government." But, on the other hand, he refers to Supreme Court decisions which hold that a corporation is severely limited in its activities by the powers which are granted in the charter which creates it.[2] In the first case, the emphasis would clearly be placed upon the inherent right to local self-government. In the second case, the emphasis would be placed upon the powers and responsibilities of the creator of the corporation, the state. This apparent contradiction in terms has caused much of the debate over city-state relationships in this country.

THE TRADITIONAL THEORY. Many Americans believe that the emphasis on self-government that prevailed in the concept of the Roman and English municipality is particularly appropriate for this country as well:

> The traditional Jeffersonian theory asserts for localities a right to self-government as an expression of the sovereignty of the individual, derived from the doctrine of the sovereignty of the people, the individual's presumed condition in the state of nature, and a theory of natural rights. The inspiration of this theory was predominantly Lockean. In Alexis de Tocqueville it found a great elucidator, and it still has considerable popular appeal.[3]

The popular appeal of this particular approach to the status of local government in the American system can be traced in many instances to the great ideological appeal of the particular normative theories upon which it appears to be based—popular sovereignty and natural rights. While a cynic might well point out that the average American has no clear conception of the meaning of either of these two terms, the use of such terms as symbols serves to cement popular support of a particular ideological position. For many people, then, the "right" to local self-government has become a part of the sacred, American political tradition.

The traditional theory is not grounded merely in ideology and normative theories, however. It also is based upon experience in the creation and operation of both city and state governments in American history. In Rhode Island and New Hampshire, the community or city not only preceded the state in time but also played a vital role in the creation of the state. The settlements of Providence, Portsmouth, Newport, and Warwick banded together to create the state of Rhode Island which then granted charters to its creators. At least in the case of Providence, the debt of the state was clearly recognized by the issuance of a charter which granted sweeping home rule powers to the municipality. Experiences like this one gave theoreticians such as de Tocqueville some historical basis

---

[2] Charles S. Rhyne, *Municipal Law* (Washington, 1957), p. 1.
[3] Syed, *American Local Government*, p. 5.

for their claims that the local community yielded a portion of its sovereignty to the state rather than receiving sovereignty from the state.[4]

This traditional approach is not exclusively popular in nature; it has some advocates within the judicial systems of various states. Indiana, Iowa, Kentucky, Michigan, and Montana have applied the doctrine of an inherent right of local self-government through their courts at one time or another.[5] The leading exponent of this judicial position was Thomas M. Cooley. Judge Cooley set forth his position initially in *People* v. *Hurlbut* in 1871. He defended local self-government as an inherent and inalienable Anglo-Saxon right that had been clearly established by history. He went on to draw heavily from de Tocqueville in arguing that the state received its sovereignty from the localities rather than the other way around.[6] While it is clear that the Cooley position as outlined here is far from universally accepted, it has provided a certain amount of welcome legal support for the embattled adherents to the traditional theory of local self-government.

THE "MODERN" THEORY. According to Anwar Syed, the "modern" theory of the relationship between the state and its municipalities was derived from the idea of an indivisible sovereignty which led in turn to a concept of an organic community.[7] There are some evident problems in applying such a theory to state-local relations. Clearly, the application is successful only to the extent that one is able to ignore the operation of the states within the federal system. If one does not accept the states as the ultimate repository of sovereignty in the federal system—and few people do so today—then it is necessary either to grant the divisibility of sovereignty or to assign it in its entirety either to the national government or to the people. If sovereignty is divisible or if it ultimately lies in the hands of the people, then there would seem to be little justification for state supremacy in the states' relationships with their municipalities. It is possible, however, to place such arguments aside and to recognize that by some means advocates of state supremacy were able to arrive at the position that enabled them to attribute undivided sovereignty to the states in state-local relations without engaging in a similar attribution with respect to state-federal relations.

Judge John F. Dillon is usually identified as the most articulate spokesman for this point of view among the members of the legal profession. He is credited as the man who most definitively brushed aside Anglo-Saxon tradition and established that municipal corporations were "mere

---

[4] Syed, *American Local Government*, pp. 21–28.
[5] Rhyne, *Municipal Law*, p. 57.
[6] Syed, *American Local Government*, pp. 54–59.
[7] Syed, *American Local Government*, pp. 11–18.

tenants at will of the legislature." [8] Dillon's position became the leading rule of law in the field and was adopted by court after court.

The United States Supreme Court was no exception to this trend. It used reasoning quite similar to Dillon's in several opinions in the late nineteenth and early twentieth centuries. Perhaps the most extreme statement of the position can be found in a portion of the Court's ruling in *Hunter* v. *Pittsburgh*:

> The number, nature, and duration of the powers conferred upon these [municipal] corporations and the territory over which they shall be exercised rests in the absolute discretion of the State. Neither their charters, nor any law conferring governmental powers, or vesting in them property to be used for governmental purposes . . . constitutes a contract with the State within the meaning of the Federal Constitution. The State, therefore, at its pleasure may take without compensation such property, hold it itself, or vest it in other agencies, expand or contract the territorial area, unite the whole or part of it with another municipality, repeal the charter and destroy the corporation. All this may be done, conditionally or unconditionally, with or without the consent of the citizens, or even against their protest. [9]

It is difficult to imagine a more sweeping declaration of state power. To say that the relationship between state and local governments "rests in the absolute discretion of the State" certainly dashes any dreams of an inherent power of local self-government. At least insofar as the federal Constitution was concerned, this appears to be precisely what the Court intended to do.

The *Hunter* decision cannot be treated as an isolated expression of the Court's view of state-local relationships. Later on, in this century, the Court was to quote the above passage once more as the ruling law in the field while it once more denied the possibility of a contractual relationship between state and municipality and further denied to the municipality the protection of the United States Constitution. [10]

This view of the power of the state need not be supported only by a theory of indivisible sovereignty. Another popular approach to the allocation of governmental power that is often used, especially by scholars and reformers, to deny the power of self-government to municipalities, holds essentially that power is allocated according to competence rather than according to some abstract concept of rights:

> In the arena of power, success is the predominant criterion of judgement. Given the necessity for performing certain regulatory and service functions, no other rule is relevant to the problem of dividing governmental power and

---

[8] Quoted in Syed, *American Local Government*, p. 68.
[9] *Hunter* v. *Pittsburgh*, 207 U.S. 161, 178, 179 (1907).
[10] *Trenton* v. *New Jersey*, 262 U.S. 182 (1923).

functions. The tendency of the theory is to accept the proposition that the ends sought justify the means adopted. There is also here the suggestion of an Hegelian twist that what is, is good.[11]

Of course, such an approach raises important questions with respect to standards of judgement. Assuming for the moment that success in the performance of functions is indeed the "predominant criterion," one can quite legitimately ask, What are your criteria for judging success and failure? In spite of the fact that such criteria are rarely, if ever, made satisfactorily explicit, a significant number of scholars continue to deny the existence of a power of local self-government on the basis of the incompetence of the municipal corporation.

THE COOLEY-DILLON ARGUMENT REVISITED. Up to this point we have looked at the traditional view of state-local relations as a battle between those who defend the absolute unitary power of the state and those who defend the concept of local self-government. This view has been presented elsewhere as a battle between the legal philosophies of Cooley and Dillon from which the Dillon position emerged victorious.[12] However, if one goes beyond the legal opinions of these worthy jurists to their more scholarly analyses of the question, it becomes apparent that what seemed to be a fierce battle might be only a minor disagreement. It is quite possible that neither Cooley and Dillon nor those who have followed them really disagree as much as the conventional literature on municipal corporations would have us believe. For example, Cooley's belief in the power of local self-government was not absolute. He recognized that the form and powers of local government were not fixed and that the state could quite properly alter either as long as it did not in the process deny the basic right to self-government.[13]

Dillon's ultimate position was certainly no more extreme. He clearly recognized that the state could not arrogate to itself all authority and that it must provide for some local government while retaining the right to alter its structure and the nature of its powers.[14] Thus the two historic antagonists meet on a middle ground.[15] It may not be pure chance that the states and their municipalities in practice occupy this same middle ground. Sheer practicality and the demands of American political ideology have rendered complete local self-government and the absolute, unitary

---

[11] Syed, *American Local Government*, p. 143.

[12] See for example Syed, *American Local Government*, Chapter 3.

[13] Syed, *American Local Government*, p. 62.

[14] Syed, *American Local Government*, p. 70.

[15] Although this interpretation is not widely followed, other scholars have arrived at similar conclusions. See for example Duane C. Buchholz, "Home Rule: A Solution For Municipal Problems?," *Wyoming Law Journal* 16 (1961): 47–73.

state equally untenable. If both positions are understood as essentially normative, that is, descriptions of ideal types rather than of the world as it presently exists, then it is not surprising to discover that nowhere in the United States does either view prevail. For those who are interested primarily in understanding how government operates, the two positions may best be understood as norms that may alter political behavior but that do not necessarily do so.

A MODIFICATION OF THE SUPREME COURT'S VIEW? . The discussion of the legal view of state-local relations should not be closed without considering the possibility that a new approach might be taken in arguing such cases before the United States Supreme Court. In one consideration of a civil rights case, the Court addressed itself to the problem of the powers of the state with respect to its municipalities. The case (*Gomillion* v. *Lightfoot*, 1960) involved the realigning of the borders of the City of Tuskegee by the State of Alabama. The realignment was designed to remove a large proportion of the eligible Negro voters from the city and thus to insure continued white control of the city government. In defending its action, the attorneys for Alabama depended to a degree upon the "absolute discretion" that had been granted the state by *Hunter* and other cases. In overturning the state's action, the Court commented at length on its modern interpretation of the meaning of *Hunter*:

> Thus, a correct reading of the seemingly unconfined dicta of *Hunter* and kindred cases is not that the State has plenary power to manipulate in every conceivable way, for every conceivable purpose, the affairs of its municipal corporations, but rather that the State's authority is restrained by the particular prohibitions of the Constitution considered in those cases.

> The Hunter opinion itself intimates that a state legislature may not be omnipotent even as to the disposition of some types of property owned by municipal corporations. . . . Further, other cases in this Court have refused to allow a State to abolish a municipality, or alter its boundaries, or merge it with another city, without preserving to the creditors of the old city some effective recourse for the collection of debts owed them . . . .

> . . . The Court has never acknowledged that the States have power to do as they will with municipal corporations regardless of consequences. Legislative control of municipalities, no less than other state power, lies within the scope of relevant limitations imposed by the United States Constitution . . . .[16]

The "relevant limitations" to which the Court refers here are specifically those which are contained in the Fifteenth Amendment. However, the "due process" and "equal protection" clauses of the Fourteenth Amendment do

---

[16] *Gomillion* v. *Lightfoot*, 364 U.S. 339, 342–345 (1960).

not appear to have been exhausted as a possible source of limitations. The important factor to recognize here is that these clauses, as they are applied in *Gomillion,* provide protection for citizens and not directly for the municipality. However, it is quite possible that such protection would be sufficient for the purposes of both the municipality and its citizens. The *Hunter* doctrine holds that the views of the citizens of the municipality are not relevant in terms of the protection provided by the United States Constitution. The *Gomillion* opinion suggests that this may no longer be the prevalent view of the Court. If any citizen or group of citizens can prove a denial of due process of law or of equal protection of the laws in the action of a state relative to a municipality, then it would appear that the present Court is prepared to consider such constitutional issues. While it is not clear at this point how far the Court is willing to carry its argument, the fact that the argument exists could well provide some encouragement for those who seek additional protection for the cities from the arbitrary exercise of state power.

Limitations on State Power

Although the courts have been hesitant to recognize a right to local self-government, the strength of the ideological attachment of large numbers of citizens to this "right" has had its effect on state-local relations. The desire to protect local self-government has frequently been manifest in constitutional provisions in the states. These provisions are intended to establish for municipalities a modicum of protection from the most serious and arbitrary exercises of state power.

One of the earliest of these protective provisions is that which prohibits "special" or "ripper" legislation. Such provisions are designed to prevent the legislature from treating municipalities on an individual basis. During the nineteenth century, it was a common practice for state legislatures to pass legislation that was designed to apply only to one municipality. This practice allowed the legislature to grant special powers and privileges to favored communities and to pass special punitive measures directed at municipalities that were out of favor with the legislative majority. Several reasons could be cited by the municipalities for opposing the continuation of special legislation. The most obvious was the injustice of using the power of the state to impose punishment on entire communities for deviations from the prescribed political orthodoxy. Since the tendency at the time was to view legislative power in this area as absolute, there were obviously no standards by which the severity or propriety of such legislation could be judged. Boundaries, governmental structure, tax and debt limits, etc. could be changed at will. As long as such plenary power was in the hands of the legislature, the only safe course of action for municipal officials and voters was to exercise extreme caution and to avoid any actions or statements that might offend the leadership of the state government.

The other objections to the practice were more practical than moral. In the first place, as long as municipalities had to depend upon the careful rationing of small and particular grants of power by the legislature, the time factor was against them. Since the prevailing practice of the time (as well as many constitutional provisions) dictated short, biennial sessions of the legislature, the cities often had to wait for years to receive legislative approval of powers. In addition to the fact that the legislature only met every other year, the increasing volume of business which it was forced to consider crowded the calendar to such an extent that it was impossible to guarantee consideration of each of the requests which might be submitted by individual municipalities. For the citizen demanding solutions to pressing local problems, and for local officials anxious to provide those solutions, the resulting delay was intolerable.

A second practical objection to special legislation was centered on the contention that the legislature lacked the expertise necessary to deal with the peculiar and complex problems of local government. The defenders of the municipality claimed that it was difficult if not impossible for state legislators to be adequately familiar with the individual conditions in each city and town in the state. Even if the legislators were well-disposed toward the problems of local governments—a proposition seriously questioned by most supporters of these governments—they would lack the knowledge necessary to draft satisfactory legislation. The natural result of this lack of knowledge and of the press for time was a tendency on the part of the legislatures to logroll on special legislation. Each representative would introduce those bills that he thought most appropriate for the municipalities in his district. Votes could then be traded on entire packages of local legislation until the required majority was reached. While this process might result in legislation relatively acceptable to individual municipalities, many reform-oriented citizens considered it a perversion of the legislative process.

As the shortcomings and abuses of the practice of special legislation became apparent to sufficiently large numbers of citizens, state constitutions were amended to require that the legislature treat all municipalities in the same manner. As the discussion of charter forms later on in this chapter will indicate, it became necessary to provide for exceptions to the rigid application of this rule. If problems of a peculiar local nature faced municipalities, it was quite possible that sweeping general legislation could be as damaging to local efforts to solve these problems as the special efforts of the legislature had been.

Another constitutional device that has often been viewed by the cities as a protection against the arbitrary exercise of state power is the referen-

dum. This device permits the people of the state to review specific legislative action and to affirm or overrule it as they will. Thus, if the cities
are faced with a particularly odious piece of legislation, they are given
the opportunity to appeal to the electorate of the state directly for its
repeal. Referenda are permitted in twenty-nine states. In twenty-seven of
these states the provision is constitutional, and in the other two it is statutory. However, in six of the twenty-nine states only those issues submitted by the legislature and/or under a constitutional requirement are
susceptible to referenda. In the remaining twenty-three states the referendum may be conducted upon petition of the requisite number of qualified
voters. Clearly, this is preferable from the point of view of the municipality seeking protection. It provides municipalities with the opportunity
to select the issues considered most important, rather than leaving them
dependent upon the judgment of the legislature or of constitutional drafts-
men who may be a century or more removed from pressing contemporary
problems.

In an era when the vast majority of Americans live within the confines
of municipal corporations, it is relatively easy to overemphasize the importance of the referendum as a protective device. One could reason that,
since in most states the majority of the people live in urban areas and
since a majority is what is required to overturn legislation under the referendum, the cities should be able to use this device quite effectively. However, there are several defects in such reasoning. In the first place, our
urban population is far from politically homogeneous. It is conceivable
that a significant minority of the electorate living within the cities and
towns might well wish to join with those living in rural areas to support
legislative action allegedly "unfavorable" to the cities. In the second
place, legislative action that is viewed as unfavorable by one municipality
may not be so viewed by all or even any of the other municipalities. The
ideological differences between metropolitan center cities and their suburbs are often significant, not to mention those between the "big city
folk" and the inhabitants of the cities and towns of the hinterland. From
the standpoint of delivering votes on referenda, the urban majority can be
constructed only with great difficulty.

One of the more widely acclaimed twentieth century protections for the
municipality has been municipal home rule. Recognition of home rule by
the states has involved an explicit statement either in the constitution or
in a statute that certain municipalities, after meeting stipulated criteria,
were to have their right to local self-government recognized. The provision
may be made in a variety of ways. The self-executing constitutional provision sets up the process by which a municipality can achieve home rule
status, and grants such status to any municipality that follows the prescribed procedures. The mandatory constitutional provision requires the

legislature to establish the necessary procedures for home rule. The permissive constitutional provision allows the legislature to establish the procedures if it wishes. And finally, statutory or legislative home rule is granted by the legislature to those municipalities that meet its requirements, but the legislature is under no constitutional mandate to continue the home rule provision. Municipalities obviously find greater comfort in self-executing constitutional provisions that give the legislature little opportunity to influence the terms of the grant. In the absence of an ideal provision, it would seem that the mandatory variety would serve the purposes of the cities adequately. The other alternatives are viewed with some suspicion, primarily because the cities are unwilling to trust the legislature to provide for home rule on their own.

Administrative Relationships

Much of the discussion up to this point has been devoted to the legislative relationships between the states and their cities. There are, however, other important aspects of state-local relationships. Those who dwell on legal relationships frequently arrive at the conclusion that the states are basically unfriendly toward their municipalities. If one examines the administrative contact between states and their cities, a much more positive picture emerges. The governors of the states are becoming increasingly aware of the importance of urban areas to their political survival. To the extent that an urban majority exists in a meaningful electoral sense, the governor, whose constituency is the entire state, cannot hope to gain re-election without the support of at least some members of that "majority." This does not necessarily entail the development of a coherent and consistent urban policy on his part. Even under the best of circumstances such a policy would be difficult if not impossible to draft, considering the diversity of the urban areas within most states. What is needed as a gesture of political good will in most states today is some indication of concern with the problems of all cities. This gesture frequently takes the form of a state agency for local affairs, charged with monitoring intergovernmental relations within the state, with expediting the local governments' administrative dealings with the state, and with identifying potential and existing problems of local government which can be eased through state action. Such agencies also can provide advice to the cities and other local agencies in meeting statutory requirements such as debt and tax limits. Although these agencies lack the ability to solve many of the problems which they identify, they can provide a better working environment for intergovernmental relations by stressing cooperation rather than the contest for power.

The day-to-day working relations between administrators at the state and local levels provide an additional emphasis on cooperation. The professional administrators at both levels have a strong tendency to share a common outlook. The standards by which the performances of officials at both levels are judged are often those that are developed by their common profession. Civil engineers, for example, find it relatively easy to deal with common engineering problems, whether they are employed by the State Department of Highways or by the street department of a major municipality. The vast majority of intergovernmental contacts are at this level and appear to be characterized by a spirit of cooperation. This is not to suggest, however, that there are not very real limits to the degree to which state administrators can cooperate with their local counterparts. Clearly, they must stay within the policy guidelines and the financial limitations laid down by the legislature.

The Effects of Legislative Apportionment

For many years it has been the practice of such supporters of the city as the National Municipal League to explain the absence of constitutional protections for local self-government and the absence of legislative recognition of serious urban problems by referring to the malapportionment that has been endemic in our state legislatures until very recent years. By demonstrating that the rural areas controlled the legislature in spite of the fact that the majority of the people lived in urban areas, these people were able to argue that the anti-urban bias of the rurally dominated legislature was responsible for their problems. They went on to argue that, if the legislatures were reapportioned strictly according to population, the cities would find themselves blessed with a sympathetic legislature for the first time in history.

The United States Supreme Court in 1964 began a series of cases with its historic *Baker* v. *Carr* [369 U.S. 186 (1964)] decision which were to grant the relief from malapportionment so long sought by the cities. Ultimately, the courts required both houses of the state legislature to be apportioned on a population basis [*Reynolds* v. *Sims,* 377 U.S. 567 (1964)]. These decisions opened the way for the control of the legislature by the "urban majority," and the removal of anti-urban bias. They were the occasion for great rejoicing in the pages of the *National Civic Review* and other journals of urban reform.

The impact of the court-ordered reapportionment was not entirely what these reformers had anticipated. Some students of the apportionment problem had been cautious in their claims for reapportionment as a cure for the cities' problems even before the Supreme Court's decisions. They had pointed out that the urban majority was far from an operational reality since it was clearly comprised of a variety of city types, including central cities, suburbs, and small rural towns and cities. From an ideological point of view, the small town and suburban vote might well prove to be allied with the traditional conservative forces that had previously been identified with the rural areas. If this proved to be the case, the reapportioned legislature might not lead to policy decisions favorable to the large cities.[17] Some evidence of this difficulty was presented prior to the Court's decisions by David Derge, who found that in the Illinois and Missouri legislatures there appeared to be little evidence of an urban-rural split on issues that were of importance to the big cities. Derge did find, however, that there were serious divisions within the urban bloc that appeared to account for the defeat of many bills of importance to the major cities of the two states.[18]

The inescapable demographic fact that the suburbs have been gaining rapidly in population in comparison to the central cities may well have resulted in placing the central cities in a less favorable position after reapportionment than they were before. While it may be an exaggeration to say that the suburbs control legislatures in some of our more urbanized states, it is safe to say that the suburbs in combination with ideological counterparts in some rural areas can marshal sufficient votes to block the type of legislation sought by liberal elements within the central cities. This factor may be a partial explanation for some of the results obtained in postreapportionment research. One such study compared the policies of malapportioned states with those of properly apportioned states on issues considered to be of major importance to the large cities: education, public welfare, revenue and taxation, medical care, right-to-work laws, and the income tax.[19] The results were far from encouraging to the large cities.

In nearly every instance examined we have found the reformers' argument empirically unverifiable and thus untenable. This is not to say that in every instance malapportionment plays no part in determining policy outcomes. It is only to say that in general malapportionment is not as significant a factor as has been posited. We would suggest that those who argue that redistricting will solve the major problems of state governments are incorrect. The political scientist who studies the effects of malapportionment after most

---

[17] See for example Gordon E. Baker, *Rural Versus Urban Political Power* (New York, 1955), p. 4, and his subsequent expansion and revision of this work, *The Reapportionment Revolution* (New York, 1966), p. 64.

[18] David Derge, "Metropolitan and Outstate Alignments in Illinois and Missouri Legislative Delegations," *American Political Science Review* LII (1958): 1051. Although some question Derge's findings on methodological grounds, I find them difficult to discount completely. See Richard Frost, "On Derge's Metropolitan and Outstate Delegations," *American Political Science Review* LIII (1959): 792.

[19] David Brady and Douglas Edmonds, "The Effects of Malapportionment on Policy Output in the American States," *A Report from the Laboratory for Political Research*, No. 3 (Iowa City, 1966).

states have redistricted should not be surprised to find that equal representation alone will not greatly change a state's policy output from conservative to liberal.[20]

Some issues that have concerned the cities find the reapportioned legislature more amenable to reason. The constitutional and statutory protections for local self-government mentioned earlier in this chapter should prove popular with such a legislature. These protections are sought perhaps even more fervently by the suburbs and the towns in the rural areas than they are by the central cities of the metropolitan areas. In fact, the central cities may be losing some of their enthusiasm for these devices for reasons that will be suggested in Chapter 4.

The Municipal Charter

As earlier sections of this chapter have indicated, traditional legal doctrine has held the state to be the repository of all governmental power not delegated to the national government. If the municipality is to exercise any governmental powers at all under this doctrine, then it must somehow receive them from the state. The device by which it exercises control over the structure of the municipal corporation is the municipal charter. This charter serves the same general purpose that is served by the constitution at the state and national level of government. That is, it outlines the basic structure of the governmental institutions and states the extent of and limitations upon the powers to be exercised by the government. Charters come in a variety of forms, each of which may be considered to represent a stage in the struggle of municipalities for local self-government.

THE SPECIAL LAW CHARTER. The earliest municipal charters issued by American states were granted to individual municipalities as they applied for them. When a community desired to have the state recognize its status officially, it applied to the legislature for a charter. The charter was then drawn up specifically for that community and passed as a special act of the legislature. As one might expect, there was considerable variety in the charters granted in this manner. One legislative grant could leave a great number of matters to local discretion, while another might restrict the decision-making authority of the locality to a minimum number of routine matters. Obviously, many of the problems referred to earlier in this chapter with respect to special legislation in general had their origins in the granting of charters by special law. The extent to which a community

---

[20] Brady and Edmonds, "Effects of Malapportionment," p. 18.

received leeway in the exercise of governmental powers was often a function of the degree of favor enjoyed by that community in the legislature. If the members of that body decided at any time that a particular municipality was no longer worthy of their trust—and the reasons for such a decision might not always have been the best—they could alter the nature of the charter of that corporation by passing another special act. This alteration would not in any way affect the status of the other municipal corporations in the state.

As more and more cities joined the campaign against special legislation in the late nineteenth century, it became necessary for the legislature to soften its position on the granting of charters. Because of this factor, along with the constitutional amendments and new constitutional provisions that were added during periods of reform, the practice of granting municipal charters by special act of the legislature was effectively ended in all but a few states.

GENERAL LAW CHARTERS. Special acts granting charters were replaced by legislative enactments which in theory treated all municipalities alike. A single law was passed by the legislature; it detailed the prerequisites to incorporation and the steps that a community had to take to achieve this status. The prerequisites generally involve a minimum population aggregate to be governed by the corporation, a defined geographic area over which the corporation is to exercise the authority granted by the legislature, and a desire on the part of the included population to be incorporated. The steps to be followed usually include:

1. A petition for incorporation as evidence of public support
2. The verification of the petition by a state agency, often a county board or state court
3. A hearing to permit public discussion of the issue
4. A referendum to determine whether a majority of those affected desire incorporation
5. The certification of the results of the election by a competent authority

Once this process has been completed, the new municipality automatically receives the powers granted by the general law and establishes its governmental institutions according to the guidelines contained in that law. This prevented many of the major abuses of legislative authority which were possible under the special law charter, since any action taken to alter the powers or structure of one municipality would automatically affect all of the cities in the state. The political consequences of such a reckless action on the part of the legislature were immediately obvious.

CLASSIFICATION.[21] One major difficulty was immediately apparent in the utilization of the general law charter. While the idea that all municipalities should be treated as equals in the eyes of the law provides protection for the cities against legislative discrimination, it also handicaps the legislature when it is attempting to recognize the very real differences that exist between cities. Circumstances may exist that require a broader grant of power to one community than to another. Peculiar conditions may suggest that one municipality utilize a governmental structure that might be inappropriate elsewhere. If one law is to govern all of the cities in a particular state, how can these problems be resolved? How can the legislature recognize that the powers and structure that are entirely adequate to the task of governing a small town in a rural environment might be horribly inadequate to the task of governing a major metropolitan center?

The answer to these questions lies in classification. If the legislature can somehow group its municipalities into classes that reflect the differences in the nature of the governmental problems which the cities face, then it can provide for powers and structures adequate to the tasks facing the cities. The question that becomes' immediately apparent is, Where does classification end and special legislation begin? The state courts have devoted much time and effort to this question. Their answer can best be summarized as follows:

> . . . a law pertaining to municipalities is special if, by reason of its being made applicable to a particular municipality or group of municipalities, it *arbitrarily* grants privileges or imposes burdens upon less than all the municipalities to which the particular law would naturally apply in the absence of the limitation.[22]

The legislatures have used a variety of criteria for determining the limits of the classes used in their general laws. All of these criteria are designed to avoid the "arbitrariness" that would endanger the classification if and when it is reviewed by the courts. The criterion most frequently used and supported by judicial opinion is that of population. It has been generally conceded that it requires something more in the way of governmental power to handle a city of several million people than it does to govern a town of 5,000. Although population criteria are most easily justified, others have been used successfully. These include physical location, area, debt, and tax base. The most important factor for the legislature to keep in mind in developing a classification scheme, no matter what criterion it selects, is the relevance of that criterion and the scheme as a whole to the basic purposes of the general law, in this case the chartering of a

---

[21] This entire discussion draws heavily upon Rhyne, *Municipal Law*, pp. 279–303.
[22] Rhyne, *Municipal Law*, p. 279.

municipal corporation able to exercise governmental powers adequate to the demands of its people.

The courts have required other things of legislative classification systems for general law charters in order to avoid the charge of "arbitrariness." The classification must be open-ended—municipalities must be able to move freely into another class if, by virtue of their circumstances, they meet the criteria for that class. For example, if the legislatively determined lower limit for a Class I city is a population of 500,000, then any city that reaches that population level must be included in that class. However, the legislature can change, and in some cases has changed, the limits of existing classes, or can create new classes if it wishes to avoid allowing a particular city to achieve the new governmental powers which its higher level of population might demand. As long as the legislature is able to justify this practice in terms of some relevant difference in circumstances between the city in question and cities presently in a higher class, the courts are likely to uphold such maneuvers. If, however, it appears that the legislature is drawing distinctions that are too fine to be rational, then the courts are likely to recognize its action as special legislation rather than legitimate classification.

There are other requirements as well. Although it generally does not matter how many cities are included in a class, the statute must be drawn in such a way as to treat all municipalities within a single class equally. For example, all cities within a single class must receive the same grant of powers, be eligible for the same governmental structures, and be required to follow the same incorporation procedures if the general law charter classification is to be upheld.

STRUCTURAL OPTIONS. In some states the legislature has chosen to add flexibility to its general law charters by allowing the incorporated community to select its own form of government. The statute usually provides that the municipality must select the mayor-council (aldermanic) form, the commission form, or the council-manager form, and it gives the details of each of the basic structures which might be adopted. The cities are restricted to the forms contained in the statute and are not free to develop their own local variations. Such statutes also provide for a procedure by which the municipality may change to one of the other approved structures if the one under which it was originally incorporated proves to be unsatisfactory to the people. This procedure generally is the same as that followed for the original incorporation petition, validation, hearing, referendum, and certification. This additional flexibility has proven to be particularly important to those municipal reformers who have believed the structure of the city's government to be at the heart of good government practices.

HOME RULE CHARTERS. For the advocate of local self-government, the ultimate step in the chartering of municipalities is the home rule charter. As an earlier discussion in this chapter indicated, such charters may be provided for either in the constitution of the state or by statute. They may be either self-executing or dependent upon the legislature for approval. The important factor in this chartering procedure is that the charter is drafted by a commission within the community itself and is approved by the voters of the community in a referendum. Theoretically, this allows the community to tailor the powers and structure of the municipal government to its own peculiar needs as it perceives them. The steps that must be followed are frequently much like those followed in obtaining a general law charter. The exception is that the local charter commission often conducts the hearings and then drafts the charter for approval in a referendum. Under self-executing home rule provisions, the municipality may establish its new government and begin operation as soon as the results of the referendum are certified. If legislative action is required, the community may have to wait until the legislature takes official cognizance of the charter and places its stamp of approval upon it. In most cases, communities adopt home rule charters after having achieved corporate status under general law or, if they are old enough, under special law. It is unusual for a community to incorporate initially under home rule provisions.

Charter Interpretation and Municipal Powers

Neither the general discussion of city-state relationships nor the discussion of charter forms has revealed much information about the powers that are actually exercised by municipal governments. Almost everyone is prepared to admit that some powers are most appropriately held by the municipality. The very fact that the states utilize charters for the purpose of granting powers to municipalities implies that, in the judgment of the legislature, these powers are best exercised at that level of government. Certainly the advocate of municipal home rule bases his entire defense of local self-government on the thesis that some governmental powers are inherently local. Since it makes little sense to claim all governmental power below the national level for either the state or the municipality, some division must be found.

One of the ways most often used to determine the number and degree of powers granted to the municipal corporation has been charter interpretation. State courts have looked to the municipal charter for guidance as to the nature of the delegated powers found therein, much in the same manner as the federal courts have looked to the United States Constitution in order to determine the scope of the powers delegated to the national government. A single judicial rule promulgated by Judge John F. Dillon has dominated the interpretation of these charters for most of the twentieth century:

> It is a general and undisputed proposition of law that a municipal corporation possesses and can exercise the following powers and no others: First, those granted in express words; second, those necessarily or fairly implied in or incident to the powers expressly granted; third, those essential to the accomplishment of the declared objects and purposes of the corporation—not simply convenient, but indispensable. Any fair, reasonable, substantial doubt concerning the existence of power is resolved by the courts against the corporation, and the power is denied.[23]

The tendency on the part of the courts was to construe charters almost exclusively in terms of the powers expressly granted and to experience "substantial doubt" about any powers that went beyond these. The following statement represents the traditional view of the effect of the Dillon Rule upon municipal powers.

> Any vestige of inherent powers or liberality in construing delegated powers was soon swept away by the Dillon Rule. This rule was formulated in an era when farm-dominated legislatures were jealous of their power and when city scandals were notorious.[24]

It is unfortunate that most scholars have tended to blame the Dillon Rule itself for a series of decisions which merely used the rule as a convenient vehicle for the prevailing legal thought of the time. In the early decades of the twentieth century, the courts were also denying inherent powers to the national government through restrictive constitutional interpretation without the benefit of the Dillon Rule. The rule itself does not require a restrictive interpretation of municipal charters. It quite clearly provides for the possibility of inherent powers. The key passage in this as in other rules of constitutional interpretation is that which refers to "fair, reasonable, substantial doubt" in the mind of the judge. Doubts that are fair, reasonable, and substantial for one generation of judges may be quite insignificant for another. There would appear to be nothing to prevent a judge today from recognizing sweeping municipal powers under existing charters and justifying his action through the use of the Dillon Rule. It has been the practice in this country for one judge

---

[23] John F. Dillon, *Commentaries on the Law of Municipal Corporations*, 5th ed., vol. I (Boston, 1911), p. 448. Reprinted in Robert L. Morlan, *Capitol Courthouse and City Hall*, 3rd ed. (Boston, 1966), pp. 51–52.

[24] Advisory Commission on Intergovernmental Relations, *State Constitutional and Statutory Restrictions Upon the Structural, Functional, and Personnel Powers of Local Government* (Washington, 1962), p. 24.

to see "fairly implied" powers where his predecessors saw none. It has also been the practice for one court to view powers as "essential to the accomplishment of the declared objects and purposes" of government when earlier courts have taken a different view. Clearly, times and circumstances change, and the powers that are adequate for the municipal corporation in one decade may be woefully inadequate in the next. In fact, our urban experience in this country seems to indicate that this is an inevitability rather than just a possibility. Charles Rhyne in speaking of the police powers delegated to the municipality to protect public health, welfare, and safety puts the matter quite succinctly.

> Judicial cognizance of existing urban conditions necessitating new and more far reaching applications of the police power will bring police power measures under the protective wing of the law that might yesterday have been invalidated.[25]

The fault lies, then, not with Judge Dillon and his rule, but with those who have followed him as interpreters of municipal charters.

Before proceeding with this discussion, it might be well to reconsider home rule in the context of the nature of the powers actually available to the municipality under such a charter. These charters do not constitute an absolute grant of local self-government to the municipality. The powers granted are only those that pertain to matters of exclusively local concern. To the extent that general law charters already grant such power to municipalities—and many do [26]—the achievement of municipal home rule may prove to be a hollow victory. There is little doubt that most state legislatures are ready to narrowly define the limits of matters of exclusively local concern, even if this often means entering an area previously left to the municipalities.

> Without doubt, court sanctification of . . . state interference into an area recognized as strictly within the province of the municipality erects the ever-menacing threat of complete emasculation of home rule. Admittedly, the judiciary has left intact the organizational structure of home rule, but for the future . . . no city can hope for long to maintain the integrity of the functional aspect of home rule free from state interference.[27]

This factor may account in part for the failure of municipalities in some states to take advantage of existing home rule provisions.[28]

---

[25] Rhyne, *Municipal Law*, p. 530.

[26] For an interesting argument on the adequacy of existing municipal powers, see Terrence Sandalow, "The Limits of Municipal Power Under Home Rule: A Role for the Courts," *Minnesota Law Review* 48 (1964): 643–721, especially pp. 663–665.

[27] Arthur B. Winter, "Home Rule Neglected," *National Municipal Review* 47 (1958): 453.

[28] Winter, "Home Rule Neglected," pp. 454–455.

One of the difficulties inherent in discovering which functions belong to the state and which to municipal governments is that the courts have usually approached such questions on a case by case basis, and there is little pattern to their decisions.[29] These decisions can be examined, however, and a list of functions *usually* descriptive of the division can be made:

> For example, municipal affairs generally include the opening and maintenance of streets, the advertisement of a city's advantages, the administration of local health affairs, and the assessment and collection of street paving costs. On the other hand, "state affairs" have been held to include the administration of justice, the creation of general legal rights, municipal tort liability, the administration of police and pension funds, the care of neglected and delinquent children, the regulation of banks, the mediation of labor disputes, the destruction of public records, and the control of a free public school system.[30]

Attempts to systematize the division of powers by dividing municipal functions into "governmental" and "proprietary" categories have not been generally satisfactory:

> Governmental functions are those conferred or imposed on a municipality as a local agency of limited and prescribed jurisdiction, to be employed in administering the affairs of the state and in promoting the public welfare for all the people of the community. . . . On the other hand, a municipality usually exercises proprietary functions when it promotes the comfort, convenience, safety and happiness of its own inhabitants rather than the welfare of the general public.[31]

Under such a classification scheme, the municipality would be exercising governmental powers to the extent that it acted as an agency of the state in helping to perform functions of state-wide concern, for example education and law enforcement. Functions devoted solely to local comfort and convenience, for example street maintenance, could be deemed proprietary. The distinction between the two types of governmental power appears to be more of a label after the fact than a helpful guide to the division of governmental power.

Since the municipality has a free hand only in matters that affect no one outside of its corporate limits, and since the state's definition of what constitutes an "effect" is likely to be quite broad, the possibility of conflict between municipal ordinances and state statutes is quite great. Although a majority of the courts have held that a local ordinance may

---

[29] Richard B. Dyson, "Ridding Home Rule of the Local Affairs Problem," *University of Kansas Law Review* 12 (1964): 369.

[30] Rhyne, *Municipal Law*, pp. 64–65.

[31] Rhyne, *Municipal Law*, pp. 68–69.

be stricter than the statute unless the legislature prohibits it,[32] many courts have held that the legislature has preempted the field in certain subjects and that further local action is inappropriate. Several examples will illustrate this point. The California courts have been particularly hard on the cities in this respect. A Los Angeles ordinance regulating the flow of pedestrian traffic within the corporate limits of that city was invalidated on the grounds that the provisions of the state motor vehicle code dealing with pedestrian traffic preempted the field.[33] The same city also had its ordinance prohibiting sexual relations between unmarried persons voided because the courts viewed the state laws as sufficient to cover all criminal aspects of sexual activity.[34] Many cities have had zoning ordinances invalidated when applied to public utilities on the grounds that state regulations concerning these utilities preempt the field.[35] The courts have experienced difficulties in deciding these cases, similar to those experienced by the United States Supreme Court in attempting to ascertain whether or not Congress has intended to preempt a field and what degree of leeway is left to the states. Legislatures do not often state their intent clearly. They almost never announce, "This statute is intended to exclusively occupy the legislative area." Only slightly more frequently do they outline the degree to which lower governmental units may add legislation of their own in the field. In fact, it would appear that the courts are frequently placed in the position of having to read legislative intent on problems that never entered the minds of the legislators.

This presents a sad picture of municipal powers. It appears that cities, whether home rule or general law in origin, must live constantly in the shadow of the state legislature. They must be prepared to accept at any time a state statute that supersedes long-standing community ordinances. Certainly it is difficult to conduct a vital local government under these circumstances. At least one suggestion for improving this situation seems to have merit. In order to return some meaning to the time-honored customs of local self-government, the states could give the cities and towns a relatively free hand with respect to all governmental functions except boundaries, private law, judicial administration and procedure, and felonies. To prevent the municipality from abusing this freedom by neglecting essential services, the states could provide minimum standards of municipal conduct in each of the areas, with the added provision that

---

[32] "Conflicts Between State Statute and Municipal Ordinances," *Harvard Law Review* 72 (1959): 749.

[33] *Pipoly v. Benson*, 125 P 2d 482 (1942).

[34] Myron Moskovitz, "Municipal Corporations: Ordinance Invalid Where State Legislature Has Pre-empted the Field—*In re Lane* (Cal. 1962)," *California Law Review* 50 (1962): 740.

[35] C. A. Powell III, "Municipal Corporations—Control Over Public Utilities Through Zoning Ordinances," *North Carolina Law Review* 42 (1964): 762.

these standards are not intended to discourage higher levels of performance by communities that wish to experiment with new methods or that wish to provide better services for their residents.[36] The advantage in such a plan lies in its tendency to prevent the most negative aspect of home rule—the slighting of governmental services which could affect the entire state—and in its tendency to accentuate the positive aspects of local self-government.

Municipal Tort Liability

One of the areas in which subtle distinctions concerning the type of power exercised by municipalities has been particularly important in the past is that of tort liability. The basic question here is, To what extent can the municipal corporation be held responsible for negligent acts that result in a civil wrong being perpetrated upon the life or property of an individual? For example, let us imagine that a local police officer is engaged in a high-speed chase of a reckless driver through the city streets. When he reaches an intersection and attempts to turn, he finds that the brakes of the police car have failed. The car crashes through the window of the corner grocery, causing extensive damage. Subsequent investigation reveals that the city garage had known that the brakes were faulty but had failed to repair them. Can the grocer sue the city and recover for the damage done to his store?

The traditional answer to this question would have been, No. The old approach to such problems was to depend upon the distinction between governmental and proprietary functions mentioned earlier in this chapter. Since law enforcement was almost always considered to be a governmental function, the municipality would enjoy immunity to suit. This immunity would have been derived from the so-called sovereign immunity of the state to suit unless it has given its consent. Since the municipality acts as the agent of the state when it performs governmental functions, it inherits the state's immunity to suit. However, since the city was on its own with respect to proprietary functions, it remained liable for acts of negligence committed in the performance of these functions. In many cases, the city could also be sued for sins of omission, such as failure to repair a street that it knew to be in need of repair. If, however, no one was exactly sure which functions were governmental and which were proprietary, how was it possible to decide when the city could be sued and when it could not be sued? The answer frequently used by the courts was to expand the definition of governmental functions and thereby the extent of immunity to suit in order to be on the safe side. The public

---

[36] Dyson, "Ridding Home Rule," p. 381.

interest of the community which was represented in preventing a large number of tort judgments against the municipal treasury seemed to outweigh the interest of the individual citizen who suffered at the hands of his government. For many people, this represented an intolerable perversion of justice.

The end result of this concern with the apparent injustice of the rule was the gradual deemphasis of the governmental-proprietary distinction even in tort cases.[37] The pendulum slowly swung back to the point where immunity to suit was the exception rather than the rule. In 1945, the New York courts removed acts of commission in governmental functions from immunity.[38] Several years later they went even further when they held New York City liable to suit for active negligence when the police failed to adequately protect Arnold Schuster, the informant who "fingered" the well-known criminal Willie (The Actor) Sutton—a failure that resulted in Mr. Schuster's untimely demise.[39] Ultimately, more and more courts began discarding the distinction completely:

> . . . so far as governmental responsibility for torts is concerned, the rule is liability—the exception is immunity. In determining the tort liability of a municipality it is no longer necessary to divide its operations into those which are proprietary and those which are governmental.[40]

The cost of the increased number of damage claims which the virtual elimination of immunity to tort actions has engendered is a matter of substantial concern to many city officials. Not only must the municipality bear the cost of damages in cases where negligence has been proven, but it also must bear the heavy legal costs of defending itself in tort actions even though it ultimately wins the case. Faced with city treasuries that are already seriously depleted by the performance of normal municipal functions, city officials cannot be expected to accept cheerfully the loss of their immunity to tort action.

Summary

It is difficult to find any order in the confusion of ideology and legal opinion which represents an attempt to deal with the relationship between the state and its municipal corporations. In many ways, the municipality clearly seems to remain the creature of the state. The state constitution and the state legislature establish the rules by which the

---

[37] Advisory Commission on Intergovernmental Relations, *Restrictions*, p. 15.
[38] *Bernardine* v. *City of New York*, 62 N.E. 2d 604 (1945).
[39] *Schuster* v. *City of New York*, 154 N.E. 2d 534 (1958).
[40] *Holytz* v. *City of Milwaukee*, 115 N.W. 2d 618 (1962). See also *Muskopf* v. *Corning Hospital District*, 359 P. 2d 457 (1961).

corporation is created and by which it subsequently must live. The state can and does contract the functional areas over which the municipality may exercise power solely by virtue of local initiative, in spite of the constitutional protections against special legislation, the provisions for referenda, and the existence of home rule. On the other hand, the municipality does retain some "right" to local self-government in functional areas that remain after state action, even though it would appear that these areas are substantially less significant in terms of public policy than those over which the state exercises at least supervisory control. To some observers this situation may seem an intolerable violation of the fundamental bases of American democracy. To others it is the inevitable result of the increasing scale of American society, especially in the urban areas—an increase that renders fewer and fewer functions purely local in their impact. The position taken would appear to depend upon which of two variables is most important to the observer: (1) democratic control of government in the sense of the limitation of governmental power, or (2) the satisfaction of social needs by the government according to the demands of the people. Neither view can be called "right." They are simply two different ways of looking at the role of government in a complex society.

Suggested Readings

Advisory Commission on Intergovernmental Relations. *State Constitutional and Statutory Restrictions Upon the Structural, Functional, and Personnel Powers of Local Government.* Washington, 1962.

———. *State Constitutional and Statutory Restrictions on Local Taxing Powers.* Washington, 1962.

———. *State Constitutional and Statutory Restrictions on Local Government Debt.* Washington, 1961.

Baker, Gordon E. *The Reapportionment Revolution.* New York, 1966. See especially Chapter 4.

Rhyne, Charles S. *Municipal Law.* Washington, 1957.

Syed, Anwar. *The Political Theory of American Local Government.* New York, 1966.

chapter 3
The Cities and the Federal Government

⟨[While the major responsibility for solving metropolitan problems lies with State and local governments, many considerations, including the number and size of interstate meteropolitan areas, make these problems a national issue demanding national action. Economic consideration [sic] alone, and the predominant position of the metropolitan areas in the national economy, are sufficient to make the development of these areas a vital concern of the Federal Government.[1]

The Development of the Relationship

Only in very recent years have either scholars or the general public paid any attention to direct relationships between the cities and the national government. Unfortunately, most of the emphasis has been upon the novelty of such arrangements rather than upon the traditional role that they have played in the performance of urban functions. To be sure, there are more of these programs today than ever before, but their great importance in the early development of American cities should not be ignored. "The cities were practicing partners in many cooperative programs from the early 1800s, and in some they were signatories, so to speak, of the agreement on which cooperation rested." [2]

---

[1] Advisory Commission on Intergovernmental Relations, *Metropolitan America: Challenge to Federalism*, Intergovernmental Relations Subcommittee of the Committee on Government Operations, U.S. House of Representatives (Washington, 1966), p. 119.

[2] Roscoe Martin, *The Cities and the Federal System* (New York, 1965), p. 39.

52

With the very beginnings of our national government in the 1790s there came an effort on the part of many American leaders to focus the attention of the federal government upon the problems of internal improvements. Because it would have been impossible for urban development to occur without the opening of lines of communication, the cities had to support these efforts and to participate in the programs once they were initiated.[3] When these programs were started in the 1820s, formal cooperation often took the form of a joint stock company in which the federal government, the states, and municipalities purchased stock. These companies then undertook the construction of the roads and canals which were so necessary to the opening up of the new nation. Even in areas where there was no formal agreement or jointly held company the municipalities were able to receive technical assistance from federal experts if they could establish that a national interest was involved in their particular local project.[4]

Under the Rivers and Harbors Act of 1826, programs were initiated by a request from a local government, and the work itself was performed by the United States Army Corps of Engineers. These programs were not, however, complete federal "give-aways." The local government was expected to contribute significantly to the project. "The localities contributed financial, material, and technical aid amounting to at least one-fifth of the cost of any Corps of Engineers project."[5] The importance of such programs is difficult to overemphasize. Without these cooperative efforts the facilities that provided—and still provide—the life blood of our major cities in the form of commerce would have been difficult if not impossible to construct. If cities had not eagerly participated in such development, the accumulation of capital necessary to spur the Industrial Revolution and the resultant further urbanization of our society might have been seriously retarded.

Other internal improvement programs were far less restrictive and required less in the way of active participation on the part of the federal government. The Internal Improvements Land Grant Act of 1841 provided both state and local governments with the funds necessary to engage in programs largely of their own design.[6] Tracts of public land were granted to these governments by the national government, and the recipient unit could then dispose of the land at the going market price in order to provide itself with capital. The only major federal requirement was that the proceeds be used for internal improvements.

[3] Daniel J. Elazar, *The American Partnership: Intergovernmental Cooperation in the Nineteenth Century United States* (Chicago, 1962), p. 265.
[4] Elazar, *American Partnership*, p. 34.
[5] Elazar, *American Partnership*, pp. 266, 269, and 300. Quotation at p. 300.
[6] W. Brooke Graves, *American Intergovernmental Relations* (New York, 1964), p. 512.

The federal government also took an early interest in other areas. The Northwest Ordinances of 1785 and 1787, which were passed while the nation was still governed by the Articles of Confederation, are the earliest examples of federal aid to education. These acts provided a section in each township to be used to support the common schools. While the original acts provided grants directly to the township, subsequent policy was to grant the land to the state to be used for local educational purposes.[7] During the early part of the nineteenth century, the federal government indirectly provided other assistance to local educational efforts. Some particularly progressive states used the money given them by the federal government as compensation for defense expenditures during the War of 1812 or their share of the federal surplus from land sales and tariffs to set up trust funds for the public schools. This money was redistributed to the local governments with few requirements or strings attached.[8] The fact that this money was viewed as compensation or revenue sharing did not prevent it from being a federal-local program. And the fact that these funds were to be used for federally approved projects appears to have greatly facilitated appropriation of the funds in Washington. The national government used these devices to provide funds for activities considered to be of national importance but inadequately supported by state and local taxpayers. Certainly the distribution of the federal surplus can be interpreted as using the national government's superior revenue-producing capability to give aid in some cases ultimately to local governments, and this concept is central to modern federal-local programs.

In summarizing the early experience with federal-state and federal-local programs in this country, Daniel Elazar has said:

> Wherever strict adherence to the separatist theory of federalism was maintained in a major area of governmental concern, there followed a centralization of power in the hands of the federal government because no smaller unit of government could properly deal with the problems that arose. In most cases, however, the desire for local control over the effects of government locally, coupled with a realization of the need for some type of participation on the part of the federal government (usually fiscal or standard-setting), led to the emergence of a federalism based on the sharing principle.[9]

While this may be a somewhat extreme statement, there is little reason to doubt that the sharing of governmental functional responsibilities was not unusual even in the earliest periods of American history. These programs provided a firm foundation for the developments of the twentieth century in federal-local relations. This does not mean, of course, that these

---

[7] Elazar, *American Partnership*, p. 131.

[8] Elazar, *American Partnership*, pp. 100–102 and 205.

[9] Elazar, *American Partnership*, p. 324.

efforts were widely recognized nor that they were well integrated into the public view of the American political system. In fact, it was not until the 1960s that the late Morton Grodzins and Elazar were able to weave the existence of these programs into a workable theory of the American federal system.[10]

Although the early twentieth century was not a period of rapid growth for federal-local programs, some of the old programs continued and several new ones were developed. The Army Corps of Engineers continued with its program of improving and developing rivers and harbors. A program of federal aid to local schools for vocational education programs was initiated in 1917 and administered through the states. In another somewhat less highly structured effort, President Coolidge—not usually considered a defender of federal power—commissioned local law enforcement officers with powers to enforce national prohibition.[11] The development that was to prove most important to federal-local relations in the long run was not the initiation of any new program but the adoption of the Sixteenth Amendment to the United States Constitution. In 1913, the ratification of this amendment granted to the national government the power to levy an income tax. The end result was a tremendous increase in the ability of the national government to raise revenue. The income tax was able to reach wealth that had been largely immune to the general property tax that formed the backbone of state and local revenue-producing ability at the time. Since states and municipalities were largely unwilling or unable to use this type of tax effectively, the federal government was felt by many to have preempted the field.

We should also note at this point the development of the cash grant-in-aid. Most of the early grants to local governments were in the form of services (for example the Corps of Engineers), technical advice, or land. There were several problems inherent in assistance of this type. The provision of services and technical advice on a large scale to the cities would have required a much larger federal bureaucracy than nineteenth and twentieth century Americans were willing to support or tolerate. The land grant was a happy solution as long as public lands were plentiful and there was no demand for conservation policies to restrict their further disposition. But by the end of the nineteenth century it was clear that there was no longer sufficient land to support the necessary intergovernmental programs. The only answer was to overcome the long-standing legal prejudice against cash grants. This prejudice had not prevented early development of cash grants, however, in the one area in which an overwhelming federal interest demanded them, the support of the state

---

[10] See particularly Morton Grodzins, *The American System*, ed. Daniel J. Elazar (Chicago, 1966).

[11] Grodzins, *The American System*, p. 39.

militia. Throughout the nineteenth century, beginning in 1808, the national government had supported the states' military efforts by means of cash grants.[12] This effort provided the precedent for the establishment of such grants in the twentieth century.

The advantages of the grant system are particularly significant. In the first place, grants tend to minimize the growth of the federal bureaucracy. This is particularly important in a country in which the public tends to fear "big" government as a positive evil in itself. In the second place, they provide for a maximum degree of flexibility and local administration of public services, which fits in well with the home rule ideology.[13]

Contacts between the national government and the cities multiplied rapidly after the onset of the depression of the 1930s. Like many individuals and private corporations, the cities of America found themselves nearly if not entirely insolvent. Because they were heavily dependent upon the property tax, the cities experienced a serious shrinkage in their tax base with the decline in real estate values and the drastic reduction in inventories, machinery, and other taxable personal property. To make matters worse, the public was unable to pay even the taxes that were levied on the reduced value of their property. The issuance of bonds was out of the question since there was little money available in the market to lend to anyone and since it would not have been prudent to purchase municipal bonds at a time when the assets and taxing power necessary to back them was at an all time low. The cities naturally looked to the states for help.

> States, however, were not in a much better position. Only the federal government, with its unlimited borrowing power and its ability to act and tax nationally, could deal with this "local" problem.[14]

It was not only the broader tax base and the greater ability to borrow that made the national government the logical source of aid for the stricken cities. By virtue of the economic theories of John Maynard Keynes, national leaders discovered that they could actually "create" money by manipulation of national monetary policies. This discovery enabled the New Deal to answer the cry of the cities with immediate and direct cash relief. Direct payment of municipal salaries enabled the cities to provide essential services such as police and fire protection at adequate levels.[15] Federal agencies such as the Public Works Administration and the Works Progress Administration sponsored large-scale

---

[12] Graves, *American Intergovernmental Relations*, p. 512.
[13] Advisory Commission on Intergovernmental Relations, *Metropolitan America*, p. 121 and Grodzins, *The American System*, p. 363.
[14] Jeanne R. Lowe, *Cities in a Race With Time* (New York, 1967), p. 23.
[15] Lowe, *Cities*, p. 24.

construction projects that provided not only much-needed public facilities but also jobs for many of the unemployed. Federal contributions to welfare programs helped to reduce the tremendous burden on state and local facilities and to reduce the human misery that resulted from prolonged unemployment. The grants for unemployment compensation and the Social Security Act of 1935 were particularly helpful in this respect. But the value of federal assistance did not lie solely in its ability to bring local governments back to their previous levels of performance. "In the process, the new national leadership and federal funds led cities into accepting responsibilities they had long ignored." [16] The cities found that they were able to use federal money in conjunction with local funds to provide expanded services for their citizens and that this, in many cases, served to strengthen the ideological commitment to home rule that was so important to local politics. An example of this expanded approach to municipal functions can be found in the public housing effort. The Housing Act of 1937 provided for long-term loans for up to 80 percent of the cost of constructing public housing units.[17]

In addition to the development of cash grants and the depression of the 1930s, Roscoe Martin finds that two other forces modified federal-city relations: (1) the emergence of a metro-urban society, and (2) the demonstrated incapacity of the states to play an effective role in solving urban problems.[18] The first factor focuses upon the fact that by the end of World War II over 50 percent of the population of the United States lived in areas defined as "urban" by the Census Bureau. The 1960 census revealed that this figure had increased rapidly until nearly seven out of every ten people lived in an urban environment. This fact is important for several reasons. First, it has increased the severity and scale of urban problems until even their symptomatic treatment is clearly beyond the financial means of the cities acting alone. Second, it has increased the political importance of the cities to our national governmental officials, especially the President. To the extent that the cities—or even the very large central cities of our metropolitan areas alone—are able to mount concerted pressure for assistance in meeting their problems, the President cannot afford to ignore them. If he did so, he could conceivably be defeated by an urban-oriented opponent at the next election on the basis of the big city vote.

The metro-urban society also implies an economy that is dependent upon the city. The strength of the economy, which is to a large extent the strength of the nation, is dependent upon the maintenance of a favorable environment for commerce and industry in the city. In its

---

[16] Lowe, *Cities*, p. 24.
[17] Graves, *American Intergovernmental Relations*, p. 535.
[18] Martin, *Cities and the Federal System*, p. 111.

efforts to deal with difficult economic problems such as unemployment, the federal government finds itself perforce dealing with predominantly urban problems. The economy cannot be separated from its urban setting.

The last force listed by Martin is highly controversial. The central question of this argument is whether the states have shown themselves to be incapable of dealing with modern urban problems or merely unwilling to do so. Because there are facts to support both sides of the argument, the position that one takes in this argument is based largely upon whether or not one is fond of state government. Unlike the federal government, the states clearly do not have the monetary and fiscal powers that would enable them to marshal extraordinary resources in times of severe economic crisis. State governmental officials are also to a great degree prisoners of outmoded revenue systems which restrict them even in the best of times. However, the states are not merely helpless victims of circumstance. It is possible to identify at least five areas in which they might have improved their capacity to assist the cities in meeting urban problems.[19] The electorate can certainly change outmoded and inflexible constitutions in order to permit a greater response by both state and local governments to urban conditions. Voluntary reapportionment could help the state legislature to more accurately reflect the needs of an urban society to the extent that such needs are clearly agreed upon by those living in the cities. It also is clear that the states are not adequately exploiting their existing resources in an effort to raise funds for the cities. For example, some states still refuse to levy an income tax, and many of the existing state income taxes do not adequately reach the resources of the state. The argument that the federal tax has preempted the field is singularly unpersuasive when one examines the untaxed resources remaining after federal collections. Finally, it is possible to combine Martin's last two sins into one single negative attribute. The states have displayed a tendency to say "No" all too quickly when any help is requested. Part of this may be attributed to the inherent conservatism of many state legislators which makes them hostile to any new program simply because it is new. And part of this negativism may be explained by the fact that the states have been told for so long that they are archaic and helpless in the face of modern problems that they have begun to believe it themselves. The specific contributions that might be made by the states in the policy areas now covered by federal-local programs will be suggested later in this chapter. It is sufficient at this point to understand that they might have done more in the past and that their failure to do so contributed to some degree to the increased interest of the national government in urban problems.

---

[19] Martin, *Cities and the Federal System*, pp. 79–80.

The Nature of the Relationship

In an attempt to increase our understanding of the operation of the federal system of government in the United States, Morton Grodzins found a particularly helpful simile. He claims that our system has never been a governmental layer cake in which the functions are clearly allocated to one level of government rather than to another. Grodzins sees the system as a marble cake in which some functions are primarily national, some primarily state, and some primarily local, but in which a large number of functions are shared by government at several levels.[20] Applying this simile to current federal-local relations in urban areas emphasizes the sharing of common functions. According to Grodzins, there are three essential types of functional sharing: (1) by design, (2) by politics, and (3) by professionalization.[21] The federal grant programs to the cities are examples of sharing by design. The programs are planned with their impact on the cities firmly in mind. The rivers and harbors program is, on the other hand, largely sharing by politics since the program was not designed solely for the cities. Specific projects are obtained by the city not because the national government intended them to be used to solve urban problems but because of the political influence which the cities can exercise over the process of allocation. A wide variety of programs experience sharing of functions by virtue of professionalization—by virtue of technical advice and assistance which is passed through professional channels rather than through structured intergovernmental programs. This is the same type of sharing and cooperation which was described earlier in Chapter 2 with respect to state-local relations.

> The tendency of professional workers at each level of government to identify themselves with the function to be performed, rather than with the particular government served, has become more pronounced as the number of workers at the several levels who are products of the same professional training increases.[22]

"The number and size of federal-aid programs have been growing at a striking rate: there are now more than 70 Federal-aid programs that directly support urban development, as well as a number of other kinds

---

[20] Morton Grodzins, "The Federal System," in The President's Commission on National Goals, *Goals For Americans* (New York, 1960), pp. 265–282, and "Centralization and Decentralization in the American Federal System," in *A Nation of States*, ed. Robert A. Goldwin (Chicago, 1963), pp. 1–23.

[21] Grodzins, *The American System*, p. 11.

[22] Grodzins, *The American System*, p. 71.

of Federal aid available to local governments in metropolitan areas." [23]
The variety of these federal programs is often amazing to those who have
adopted the simplest view of intergovernmental relations. As Table 3–1
indicates, there are a variety of channels through which these programs
can be developed.

TABLE 3–1: Channels of Federal Activity on the Local Scene

Mode of Activity	Examples
1. Federal direct-to-people activities	Old Age and Survivors Insurance Veterans' benefits Mail delivery Taxation Licensing
2. Federally engineered local governments, relatively independent of state or local governments.	Soil Conservation Agricultural Stabilization and Conservation Grazing Service Advisory Board
3. Federally engineered local governments, relatively dependent on state or local governments	Selective Service Civil Defense Rationing during World War II Public housing and urban redevelopment (in some states)
4. Federal grants channeled through states	Welfare, highways, employment security, forestry, vocational education, public health, etc.
5. Federal grants and other aid directly to local governments	Airports (in some states) Public housing and urban redevelopment (in some states) Flood control School construction (in some states) Disaster relief (in some cases) Technical assistance in many fields Services by contract

SOURCE: Morton Grodzins, *The American System*, ed. Daniel J. Elazar (Chicago, 1966),
p. 191. © 1966 by Rand McNally and Company, Chicago. Reprinted by permission.

Of the direct federal aid programs, nineteen receive particular emphasis
because they are administered by the Department of Housing and Urban
Development as part of its more or less concerted effort to attack the
problems of American cities. This cabinet level agency was created by
the national government in 1965 in response to the growing demand for
recognition on the part of urban America. It was designed to provide the
cities with an official outlet in the executive branch of government, to
develop new programs of assistance for the cities, and to urge these new
programs upon Congress. The nineteen programs listed in Table 3–2
represent the efforts of the existing agencies which were merged into the

---

[23] Advisory Commission on Intergovernmental Relations, *Metropolitan America*, p. 8.

TABLE 3–2

Program	Content
1. Workable Program for Community Improvement	Requirements for planning and coordination as a condition of receiving federal grants
2. Urban Renewal	Individual projects to renew blighted areas
3. Community Renewal	Planning for community-wide renewal
4. Low-rent Public Housing	Inexpensive housing for the poor
5. Rent Supplement Program	Grants for the difference between what the poor can afford for rent and the market rent for housing
6. FHA Section 221 (d) (3)	Insurance for low interest loans for the construction of housing for those above the public housing level but too poor to afford regular housing
7. Low-income Housing Demonstration Program	Experiments with rent supplements and purchase of homes by low-income families
8. Housing for the Elderly and the Handicapped	Public housing, FHA insured loans for low-rent units, and Federal loans to non-profit corporations
9. Neighborhood Facilities Program	Youth centers, health centers, community buildings, etc., for large and medium-sized cities
10. Urban Mass Transportation	Grants for demonstration projects and loans for equipment and facilities
11. Open Space and Beautification	Grants for purchase of land and for improvements
12. Metropolitan Planning	Grants for area-wide planning
13. Urban Planning Assistance	Grants for individual city planning
14. Public Facility Loans	Water and sewer systems, storm sewers, health clinics, municipal buildings, etc.; Mostly used for small towns
15. Basic Water and Sewer Grants	Provide up to half the cost of construction
16. Advances for Public Works Planning	
17. College Housing	Aid to education, but it relieves some burden on the housing market
18. Housing for the General Market	FHA loan insurance for middle income homes (Average: $17,000)
19. Mortgage Credit, Federal National Mortgage Association	Purchase of federally-insured loans to expand credit supply

SOURCE: Department of Housing and Urban Development, "Summary: HUD: 1961–66," *The Federal Role in Urban Affairs*, Subcommittee on Executive Reorganization of the Committee on Government Operations of the U.S. Senate, vol. 1 (Washington, 1966), pp. 229–234.

new department as well as the new programs successfully added by the department since 1965.

One can appreciate the increasing importance of some of these older HUD programs as well as the grant programs of other federal agencies by examining the trends in intergovernmental payments. Between 1932 and 1963 federal-local payments increased ninety-four times as compared to thirty-seven times for payments to the states, and fourteen times for state-local payments. However, state-local payments were still ten times as great as the federal-local variety in 1963, and in that year federal-local payments were less than 12 percent of the federal-state and local total and less than one-third of the amount given to the states for highways alone.[24] It is easy to see that, while they have increased dramatically in importance, federal-local grants can hardly be said to have attained equal status among intergovernmental payments. This is particularly true when one is concerned primarily with the urban impact of such grants and discounts that portion of the federal-local effort which is directed to rural areas. State and local financial efforts are obviously still far more important in providing the funds for solutions to urban problems than those of the national government.

It is all too easy to emphasize the sharing of functions by design in Grodzin's typology and to neglect the important sharing by professionalization. Although it is not a "pure" type, the example used by Grodzins for this kind of sharing is particularly impressive:

> There is hardly a local police force, however small and parochial it may be, that does not depend upon federal assistance in its day-to-day activities; and hardly a federal police activity that is not dependent upon local aid.[25]

> .   .   .   .

> FBI technical services are given freely to local governments without regard to the issue of formal jurisdiction.[26]

> .   .   .   .

> Perhaps the most significant federal laws in direct aid of state and local police work are those covering fugitive felons and witnesses, and persons attempting to avoid custody or confinement after conviction.[27]

The local police department depends upon the skill and expertise of a variety of federal law enforcement agencies to provide it with investigatory assistance and instructors for training programs. Fingerprint and records checks as well as sophisticated laboratory analyses that are beyond the capability of local officials are frequently performed by the FBI. Agents of the FBI and the Treasury Department conduct in-service training programs for local police in current detection and crime prevention methods. The FBI Academy provides training facilities for senior

---

[24] Martin, *Cities and the Federal System*, pp. 112–114.
[25] Grodzins, *The American System*, p. 89.
[26] Grodzins, *The American System*, p. 91.
[27] Grodzins, *The American System*, p. 98.

local police officers so that they might return to their communities and operate more efficient departments.

In many areas, the responsibilities of federal and local officials overlap and cooperation is the rule. Bank robbery, narcotics, mail fraud, kidnapping, and auto theft are only some of the areas in which a criminal may violate both state and federal law with a single act and thereby bring intergovernmental enforcement machinery to bear upon his capture. Neither constitutions nor statutes dictate how such cooperative ventures are to be handled. The cooperative effort is largely an ad hoc arrangement between the officers in the field unencumbered by sophisticated theories of intergovernmental relations. Petty jealousies do interfere with the cooperative effort, but in most cases the relationship is amicable. Current national concern with law enforcement and an increasing crime rate have led the federal government to consider expanding its role in this functional area. One of the major proposals has been the creation of a National Academy for the training of police officers. This would enable the federal government to greatly expand the present training program conducted at the FBI Academy. While this is only one area of professional sharing of functions, it is an excellent example of what can be accomplished without large-scale grants-in-aid.

Constitutional Interpretations of the Relationship

Most of the functions shared by the federal and local governments are in areas in which the local government has traditionally exercised some powers under state constitutional and statutory grants. In these cases there is little doubt that both levels of government can fully participate in these programs without running afoul of any constitutional provisions. There are, however, some programs that encourage municipal participation in activities that are not only not covered in their general grant of power but also are directly in conflict with some existing state program. If, as Chapter 2 indicates, the cities are for the most part creatures of the state and subject to its legislative will, how can they participate in such programs?

The question is important. The Supreme Court of the United States found itself dealing with just this problem. In an effort to provide additional electric power for its citizens, the City of Tacoma, Washington, applied for a license from the Federal Power Commission to construct two dams with generating facilities on a nearby river. Unfortunately the project ran afoul of the State of Washington's conservation policies—it would disturb the fish in the river, flood the land occupied by a state fish hatchery, and create dams larger than those permitted under existing state law. The question was then raised as to whether the city could perform acts as a federal licensee that it obviously could not perform on its own as a municipal corporation in the State of Washington. By virtue of a rather complex process, the case [*City of Tacoma* v. *Taxpayers of Tacoma*, 357 U.S. 320 (1958)] ultimately reached the Supreme Court.[28]

The Court held that the power to regulate the construction of generating facilities on navigable waterways in the United States belongs to the Federal Power Commission by virtue of the Commerce Clause of the Federal Constitution and the Federal Power Act. The governmental powers under which the project was to be constructed were those of the national government and thus took precedence over the otherwise legitimate conservation activities of the state. The fact that a municipal corporaton, a creature of the state, was the licensee did not alter the situation. The state could not bar one of its own subdivisions from acting under a federal license even though this action meant, among other things, the exercise of the right of eminent domain over state property—the fish hatchery. The Court did not, however, satisfactorily deal with the question of whether or not debt limits imposed upon the city by virtue of its charter might effectively limit its participation in the program.

Although this decision avoids a direct confrontation with the *Trenton* v. *New Jersey* and *Hunter* v. *Pittsburgh* decisions discussed in the last chapter, it obviously suggests another source of power for the municipality. To the problem-bound urban government faced with a recalcitrant state legislature, the federal government can provide not only funds but also the governmental authority needed to expend these funds. Given the current tendency to adopt an extremely broad view of the Commerce Clause as a source of constitutional authority for national government action, it is entirely possible that the federal government could enact legislation granting powers to local governments which would exercise these powers not as a matter of home rule but as agents of Washington. While such action would indeed seem possible under the *Tacoma* decision, there are compelling political reasons for the failure of the federal government to seriously consider such an approach. Such a policy would run headlong into three strongly held positions in American political ideology. The first two of these positions are the contradictory views of the role of local government in our system detailed in the last chapter. In the first place, the *Trenton* v. *New Jersey* doctrine that the cities are pawns of the states is attractive to large numbers of Americans even if it does not accurately describe existing relationships. In the second place, the advocates of home rule could hardly be expected to look with favor

---

[28] G. Theodore Mitau and Harold W. Chase, eds., *Proximate Solutions* (New York, 1964), p. 68.

upon a policy that declared the municipality a mere agent of the national government. Finally, the states' rights advocates would undoubtedly view such action as another attempt to grab power from the states. In spite of the fact that these three positions overlap a great deal, they command sufficient support from the general public to render federal action of the sort described above politically foolhardy.

The Spectre of Federal Control

One of the charges most frequently made against federal-local sharing of functions is that this sharing leads inevitably to federal control of the decision-making apparatus and to further erosion of jealously guarded home rule powers and states' rights. The preceding section indicates that such domination by the federal government is at least possible in some programs under existing constitutional theory. The argument is further strengthened by the array of control measures instituted in federal grant programs. These control measures are designed primarily to insure that federal funds are not used improperly by local officials. The major assumptions behind them would appear to be that local government officials cannot be trusted and that the local electorate cannot be depended upon to monitor the activities of these officials. Unfortunately, there would appear to be a great deal of historical and contemporary evidence that these assumptions are valid, if not in every community, at least in some. Both Congress and the administrative agencies that handle the grant programs appear anxious to prove to the American people that they are diligently guarding the taxpayers' money. This diligence appears to some people to be far more pervasive in intergovernmental grant programs than in programs in which the national government itself is spending the money.

The first type of control measure is designed to guarantee that the project to be funded is properly planned. Planning requirements such as the Workable Program for Community Improvement in the Urban Renewal program are aimed at insuring that the project has been thought through, that it will meet minimal construction standards, that the community has the resources available to pay its share of the cost, that the local agency has the proper personnel resources to supervise the project, and that the project has some public support. Other planning requirements are aimed at obtaining community-wide coordination of efforts and even greater coordination on the regional or metropolitan level.

The voluminous paperwork involved in these grant programs also involves the imposition of controls. From the initial application through the project reports, the local government is required to submit vast quantities of information to feed the federal mill and to provide justification for the project. This information is not only for the benefit of administrative officials with scarce resources to allocate, but it also is for the edification of Congress when that worthy body periodically reviews the progress of federal programs and decides whether to increase or decrease its appropriations or whether to cancel the program altogether. From the federal point of view such requirements are an absolute necessity.

The national government also issues voluminous instructions covering every aspect of its programs from the application for funds to the ultimate expenditure of these funds upon local projects. These instructions usually represent detailed interpretations and expansions of the basic guidance given by Congress in passing the necessary enabling legislation for the program. They cover such diverse matters as forms to be used, channels of communications, timetables for program operation, and accounting procedures and other standards of administrative performance. Federal officials take these policies and procedures seriously, and any deviation from them is likely to result in a severe setback for the community's program. Many, if not most, of the cities now participating in federal grant programs must have experienced the frustration of receiving a voluminous application, report, or other communication back from Washington or a federal regional office because the appropriate forms and procedures were not observed.

Because they are not satisfied with paper promises of good conduct and adequate performance, the federal agencies and Congress also require inspections and audits by federal personnel who check on the accuracy of the reports filed by the local agency. Inspections are conducted at every stage of a project's operation to insure that everything is proceeding according to plan and that all reports accurately reflect the status of the project. Periodic audits of the funds expended and on hand are conducted by agency auditors and representatives of Congress's General Accounting Office to determine if public funds have been misappropriated by accident or design.

In most programs it is also traditional to include some provision requiring civil service, merit systems, and abstention from political activity for local employees involved in the federal grant project. Such requirements date back to the 1939 amendment to the Social Security Act of 1935 which demanded merit systems in programs receiving federal funds and to the second Hatch Act (1940) which prohibited political activity on the part of state and local employees who received all or part of their salary from federal funds.[29] While such requirements have served to limit

[29] Harry W. Reynolds, Jr., "Merit Controls, the Hatch Acts, and Personnel Standards in Intergovernmental Relations," *The Annals of the American Academy of Political and Social Science* 359 (1965): 82 and 89.

somewhat the use of patronage in federal grant programs, the results have not been completely satisfactory, due in part to a rather casual attitude on the part of national government agencies in enforcing the requirements.

> Invitation rather than coercion; precept and example, rather than compulsory adherence, as a basis for compliance—these have become (and remain) the guidelines, indeed the foundation, upon which federal-state co-operation in the various dimensions of public personnel administration has evolved. . . . Errant practices by recipient levels have never yet been corrected by any actual stoppage of aid funds.[30]

In spite of the rather healthy list of controls exercised by the federal government in the grant programs, there is reason to believe that officials at the national level do not seek to make basic policy decisions in these programs when it can be avoided. This can be traced to several factors. In the first place, such an attitude tends to avoid direct confrontations with local governments and to minimize the opportunity for conflict.[31] For most administrators in the federal agencies, conflict is not productive. It tends to limit their ability to realize program goals, and it tends to draw congressional attention of an unwelcome variety to their programs. Secondly, the federal agencies obviously do not have enough personnel to make many policy decisions.[32] If these agencies were to attempt to make very many policy decisions for the local governments participating in their programs, they would have to vastly increase the number of administrators on the job. Thirdly, federal administrators know that to allow local government to make basic policy decisions is to gain important political allies for their programs in the annual battle before Congress to expand these programs.[33] A relatively happy mayor makes a much more favorable witness than one who feels that his prerogatives have been usurped by the federal government. Finally, the Washington bureaucrat might find it impossible to fight the strong grass roots ideology of the American people even if he were so inclined.[34]

As might be expected, local governmental officials occasionally take a somewhat different view of the effects of federal controls. Before these differences are ennumerated, however, one point should be emphasized. Local governments—especially those in urban areas—are generally quite enthusiastic about federal grant programs:

---

[30] Reynolds, "Merit Controls," pp. 91–92.

[31] Charles R. Adrian, "State and Local Government Participation in the Design and Administration of Intergovernmental Programs," *The Annals of the American Academy of Political and Social Science* 359 (1965): 38.

[32] Adrian, "Government Participation," p. 38.

[33] Adrian, "Government Participation," p. 38.

[34] Adrian, "Government Participation," p. 38.

These federal activities in their community are not viewed as the forcible intrusion of a distant central government but almost invariably, as the successful consequences of local efforts to secure federal benefits to serve local ends. These benefits are considered to be good for community and nation both.[35]

Those who do complain do so for the most part with a view toward improving an expanded federal-local partnership rather than toward abolishing existing grant programs.

Roscoe Martin details three basic types of objections to grant program controls: (1) objections to planning requirements, (2) objections to policies and procedural requirements, and (3) objections to audits.[36] Some local officials view planning requirements such as those included in the Workable Program for Community Improvement as unnecessary chores rather than as opportunities to provide for the orderly redevelopment of their urban environment. This is particularly the case in communities that consider planning suspect, the first step down the path to the perdition of a socialist state. Fortunately for the federal grant programs and for the general development of urban America, this attitude is not particularly widespread. The objections to the policies and procedures are centered upon delay, red tape, and inflexibility. A. V. Sorensen, mayor of Omaha, has particularly criticized the nit-picking on applications which tends to frustrate the cities.[37] Jerome P. Cavanagh, mayor of Detroit, echoes the sentiments of many urban administrators when he says:

And some of these programs appear to be wrapped in complex rules and regulations that at times at least to some of us seem to be designed more for the convenience and protection of some distant administrators than for flexibility at a point of use right out in the city. . . . Aside from the veritable crush of paperwork, the delays and lack of funding, the urban renewal program, for example, allows little local discretion.[38]

The third source of irritation, the audit, is perhaps the most serious. The participating local governments find that they are exposed to audits from several federal agencies in addition to those required by state law and local practice. The end result is that some of these local programs are "audited to death." The frequent appearance of auditors so disrupts normal office routines that little progress is made on the program itself. Most local

---

[35] Daniel J. Elazar, "Local Government in Intergovernmental Perspective," *Illinois Local Government: University of Illinois Bulletin*, vol. 62, no. 92 (June, 1965), 2d ed., p. 20.

[36] Martin, *Cities and the Federal System*, pp. 151–162.

[37] U.S. Senate Subcommittee on Executive Reorganization of the Committee on Government Operations, *The Federal Role in Urban Affairs* (Washington, 1966), IV, p. 1053.

[38] U.S. Senate Subcommittee on Executive Reorganization, III, pp. 619 and 620.

governments feel that one standardized audit, whether it be at the local level, the federal agency level, or at the level of the General Accounting Office, should be enough to satisfy even the most suspicious person. They fail to see the public purpose served by wasting the taxpayers' money through needless duplication of effort.

This should not be taken to indicate that the cities view all or even most of the federal grant program control measures as unnecessary usurpations of the prerogatives of local decision-makers. Mayor John V. Lindsay of New York sums up this attitude in saying:

> But I do not think we can—nor should we—realistically expect the Congress to make available these vast amounts of money unless our cities demonstrate the willingness and the ability to modernize and streamline their administrative machinery to use Federal resources efficiently and to make the effort from their own resources.[39]

The results of a survey of state and local officials indicate that two-thirds of the local officials responding thought that state and local failures were the reason for the expansion of federal programs, that one-half of these officials were generally satisfied with existing grant programs, and that three-quarters of them were happy with their relationship with federal agencies.[40]

While many local officials, especially those from the big cities, are vitally interested in seeing program flexibility increased through the use of such devices as the unrestricted block grant, their major goal appears to be a great increase in the amount of funds available in the form of federal grants.[41] The amounts deemed necessary by these officials are often staggering, even to hardened spenders like members of the United States Congress. Mayor Lindsay's casual mention of $50 billion for the next ten years for New York City alone brought incredulous responses from some of the most liberal members of the Senate.[42] Since the figures presented by the mayors of Atlanta, Detroit, and Omaha, and by a top administrative official from Boston are roughly proportional to that given by Mayor Lindsay, it is obvious that many of our major cities are ready to come back to Washington for quite a bit more without much fear of federal controls over the decision-making process.

---

[39] U.S. Senate Subcommittee on Executive Reorganization, III, p. 551.

[40] Robert W. McCulloch, "Intergovernmental Relations as Seen by Public Officials," *The Annals of the American Academy of Political and Social Science* 359 (1965): 131.

[41] See particularly Mayor Cavanagh's testimony in U.S. Senate Subcommittee on Executive Reorganization, III, pp. 618–623.

[42] U.S. Senate Subcommittee on Executive Reorganization, III, p. 582 ff.

CONTROL AND SHARING THROUGH POLITICS. In some programs, the sharing of functions consists mainly of attracting federal projects which benefit the city. Federal control is obviously much more rigid in these programs than it is even in grant programs. For example, in the Rivers and Harbors program the central function has traditionally been considered appropriate to the national level. The projects may be initiated at local request, but they are designed and controlled by Washington. The funding, services, and advice offered by local officials would not appear to be sufficient to shift the center of decision-making authority from the national to the local level. In some instances, the local government may take an even more active role in the planning and construction process, but in many of these projects the local government may be acting as an agent or licensee of the federal government as in the *Tacoma* case.

There is little cause for alarm in these programs, however. They did not represent a very large proportion of the total number of federal-city shared functions in the 1960s. Whenever the national government has chosen to expand its area of interest in urban problems, it has chosen to do so through grant programs or professional channels rather than through an increase in the number of functions in which it holds the preponderant influence and in which the projects are handed out as political plums. Although the number of functions shared in this manner have not increased significantly, the number and dollar value of the specific programs has increased markedly. If the emphasis is placed upon projects and upon their cost rather than functions, then there might be some basis for concern about federal domination in these areas. The major problem is that the only remedy for federal activity of this sort is to remove or erode functional responsibilities that have traditionally been exercised at the national level. For a significant number of Americans such a remedy would be worse than the disease.

CONTROL AND SHARING THROUGH PROFESSIONALIZATION. When functions are shared by virtue of common professional ties or by virtue of informal coordination of activities, formal controls on the part of either level of government are at a minimum. It is quite possible, however, for the professionals at one level to dominate the decision-making process. This can be accomplished through the command of superior professional resources or through effective control of the standards and policies set by the relevant professional group. The absence of research in this area makes it necessary to rely upon highly impressionistic reactions to information presented in the mass media for any statement about effective controls.

The federal government does in some cases command enough in the way of superior professional resources to make its efforts in the decision-making process, at least within limited areas, weigh more heavily than those of even the largest city. This is particularly the case in certain specialized areas of shared functions which demand skilled scientific technicians and elaborate laboratory facilities. To revive the law enforcement example used earlier, it is clear that the Federal Bureau of Investigation is the professional leader in developing new investigatory techniques that call for the scientist more than for the policeman on the beat. By passing these techniques on to local law enforcement agencies, the FBI can heavily influence the kinds of policy decisions these agencies are able to make in performing their duties. This influence is not quite the same thing as control. It serves to expand the decision-making possibilities of the local professional rather than to restrict them as control would.

There does not seem to be any hard evidence at this point that major professional groups involved in shared governmental functions are dominated by those of their membership who are employed by the national government. These groups seem rather to experience a great many values and policy preferences that are shared for the most part by the membership at large. These shared values frequently come from common educational experiences and from exposure later on in the careers of the membership to common literature contributed both by academicians from professional schools and by the practitioners themselves. Even if a content analysis of the professional literature should reveal a disproportionate contribution on the part of federal professionals, this could not be interpreted as proof of federal policy domination. The tendency for specialists to speak as professionals rather than as employees of a particular level of government has already been noted (see p. 38).

CONTROL OF THE RELATIONSHIP BY THE CITIES. One frequently overlooked factor that tends to lay to rest the specter of federal control is the degree of control exercised by the cities over federal urban policies. In the first place, professionalization plays a role in all shared federal-local functions, and this professionalization may work to the advantage of the cities.

> What is commonly considered to be federal supervision of these programs is largely national supervision by mutual accommodation. Leading state and local officials, acting primarily through their professional organizations, are in great measure responsible for formulating the very standards that federal officials then try to implement.[43]

The major problem with this sort of control mechanism is that it may bear very little relationship to the local electorate and to the policy deci-

---

[43] Elazar, "Local Government in Intergovernmental Perspective," p. 21.

sions of local elected officials. While it may be used as a means by which the cities can make their influence felt in Washington, it can also be used as a device through which local professionals establish standards that have proven or might prove to be unacceptable to higher authority in their own city. The fact the federal standards are established through cooperation with local professionals is no guarantee that these are the standards that the cities would establish if given a free hand.

The cities also use their representatives in Congress to influence both the general character of the legislation establishing federal-local relationships and the character of the process by which such legislation is administered by executive agencies.[44] The urban electorate selects to represent it in Washington candidates whose views of the federal role in meeting urban problems coincide most nearly with those of the voting majority. The voters, with the necessary assistance from local officials who monitor the development and administration of federal programs, keep track of the stewardship of their congressmen—a fact that does not escape congressional notice. The result of this process when combined with the population shifts that have made this nation predominantly urban is that "the combined power of all cities in Congress is probably greater than the power of the cities of any single state in that state's legislature." [45] This statement is made notwithstanding the significant amount of malapportionment in congressional districts that continues to result in rural overrepresentation. The real problem is that in Congress, as in state legislatures, urban areas are unable to join frequently enough in a common cause to make full use of this great potential power.

This lack of unity is nowhere more evident than in the efforts of the cities to mount an urban lobby. The big cities use the United States Conference of Mayors as their organized spokesman and frequently maintain a full-time individual lobbyist in Washington as well. The small towns depend upon the American Municipal Association to represent their interests, and occasionally receive valuable assistance from state lobbies such as the Council of State Governments. It is not unusual for these two groups of lobbyists to disagree.[46] When this happens, Congress and the executive agencies concerned frequently are able to play one group against the other and to obtain some insulation from local pressures.

Nongovernmental groups also provide political support for the cities in their attempts to influence federal urban policy. On a national level, alliances with such influential interest groups as the AFL-CIO, the National Association of Home Builders, and the National Association of

---

[44] Grodzins, *The American System*, p. 212.
[45] Grodzins, *The American System*, p. 223.
[46] Grodzins, *The American System*, pp. 224–227.

Manufacturers are often quite productive.[47] Within individual cities, private interests with a stake in the solution of urban problems with federal help, such as the construction industry, private planning firms, and downtown merchants, add to the pressures placed upon the congressional delegation to influence the decision-making process in Washington.

> Local influence on national programs is exercised by bringing to bear on national officers the combined weight of the public and private sectors. Where the public-private linkage is strong and where its strength is utilized, local influence over federal activities on the local scene is maximized.[48]

This influence is particularly effective when it is expressed in the form of congressional pressure on an administrative agency designed to gain favorable consideration for a community within the congressman's district or the senator's state. The frequent result of such pressures is an infinite variation in urban programs that were designed to produce uniformity.[49]

In spite of the fact that the contest between federal and local governments for control of shared functions would seem unequal, the cities are clearly capable of significantly influencing the decision-making process. The argument that the federal government must control the relationship by virtue of its superior size and financial power is based upon the assumption that the federal government is monolithic and has a single, identifiable position that it might force upon the cities. This assumption is clearly not supported by the facts. Intergovernmental relations tend to be characterized by friction between bureaucrats and legislators at all levels rather than by friction between levels.[50] In some cases, faced with competing and conflicting claims from a variety of local governments, the federal government is forced into acting as a mediator and compromiser and thereby prevented from adopting policies of its own which are unrelated to the desires of the local communities.[51] These considerations make it inevitable that the cities play a role in determining urban policy.

> The correct conclusion to be drawn from considerations of local influence on federal . . . programs is not that the local view is controlling. It is rather that the localities can be full and powerful participants in the procession of decision-making.[52]

---

[47] Grodzins, *The American System*, pp. 248–249.
[48] Grodzins, *The American System*, p. 231.
[49] Totten J. Anderson, "Pressure Groups and Intergovernmental Relations," *The Annals of the American Academy of Political and Social Science* 359 (1965): 124.
[50] Adrian, "Government Participation," p. 37.
[51] Grodzins, *The American System*, p. 257.
[52] Grodzins, *The American System*, p. 250.

THE ABSENCE OF CONTROL AT ANY LEVEL. Our discussion of control has centered upon the sharing of individual functions and the determination of policy in these functional areas. This approach does not consider the development of an overall urban policy, or the role played by federal and local governments in determining such a policy. It may well be that control over the decision-making process in functional areas is meaningless in the absence of some sort of control over the entire context of urban decision-making.

Federal grant-in-aid programs have traditionally been oriented toward substantive programs rather than toward governmental units. These grants have gone to special purpose districts, public authorities, and private groups as well as to general purpose units of local government.[53] The result of this grant policy has been a serious fragmentation of governmental responsibility and control in urban areas. No single unit of urban government can develop a coordinated policy for administering all of the aided functions and for coordinating these functions with those not shared with the national government. Under these circumstances, many students of intergovernmental relations have recommended that the federal government revise its grant program in favor of such general purpose units of government as the city and county in order to give them meaningful control over urban policy.[54] In recent years the federal government has responded to this criticism by encouraging the use of multipurpose rather than single-purpose districts to administer federally-aided functions. It has also required the participation of local governmental officials in the decision-making machinery of federally-aided private groups under the Poverty Program.

One of the reasons that the federal government has not done more to correct this situation is that much of the structural fragmentation is outside of its control. There is at least some evidence to indicate that federal grant programs have merely gone along with fragmentation, that they have reflected existing trends in local government rather than caused new fragmentation. Daniel Elazar claims that Anglo-American local government has traditionally been fragmented and that this tendency has been encouraged by special interest groups within the community demanding special governmental recognition of their interests. He further states that any federal requirement for or encouragement of fragmentation has been in response to local administrative patterns and interest group demands.

---

[53] William G. Colman, "The Role of the Federal Government in the Design and Administration of Intergovernmental Programs," *The Annals of the American Academy of Political and Social Science* 359 (1965): 28–29.

[54] Advisory Commission on Intergovernmental Relations, *The Impact of Federal Urban Development Programs on Local Government Organization and Planning*, Intergovernmental Relations Subcommittee of the Committee on Government Operations, U.S. Senate (Washington, 1964), pp. 22–23.

Elazar sees good leadership in the local party organization or power structure as the only practicable solution to the problem of fragmentation.[55] This further illustrates the degree to which the control of shared functions is a burden placed upon local as well as national shoulders.

Another type of fragmentation which occurs within the pattern of shared functions under federal grant programs is a good deal more important in terms of control and policy impact. The federal administrative agencies that administer these grant programs are seriously fragmented and lack anything remotely resembling a common focus. This factor adds to the cities' ability to mold policy in individual functional areas, but it detracts from their ability to develop an overall urban policy. There is a need for interagency coordination of programs at the federal level so that both the national government and the cities can avoid working at cross purposes with each other and with themselves.[56] In some cases the federal program may have an almost unconscious effect on the cities; in other cases the effects may be planned, but the results of two programs may be mutually inconsistent.[57] An example of the latter effect can be found in the Federal Aid Highway and Urban Renewal programs. Urban renewal is designed to increase the supply of adequate housing for urban Americans while the highway program often reduces this supply in urban areas through subsidizing the purchase of rights-of-way for new expressways. The end result in some areas is that the federal government is subsidizing the removal of adequate housing at a greater rate than it is subsidizing the construction of adequate units. Under such circumstances neither federal nor local governments can really be said to control the decision-making process. Once again a part of this fragmentation can be attributed to local governments and interest groups themselves. Because there is a great deal of conflict between governments and between interests with respect to the emphasis placed on urban development, the tendency is for the federal government to resolve this conflict by giving something to everyone.[58]

While it might not be politically feasible to resolve this problem by developing a single, consistent, long-range national policy, it certainly would be possible to develop a mechanism by which the national government could recognize the effects of its urban programs and could make sure that these programs are not cancelling one another.[59] In order to achieve this goal, President Johnson in 1966 directed the Secretary of the

---

[55] Daniel J. Elazar, " 'Fragmentation' and Local Organizational Response to Federal-City Programs," *Urban Affairs Quarterly* 2 (1967) : 30–46.

[56] Advisory Commission on Intergovernmental Relations, *Metropolitan America*, p. 10.

[57] Martin Meyerson, "National Urban Policy Appropriate to the American Pattern," in *Goals for Urban America*, ed. Brian J. Berry and Jack Meltzer (Englewood Cliffs, N.J., 1967), pp. 69–70.

[58] Meyerson, "National Urban Policy," p. 71.

[59] Meyerson, "National Urban Policy," p. 72.

Department of Housing and Urban Development to take responsibility for coordinating federal programs by cooperative consultation with other federal agencies, for cooperating with state and local governments in urban programs, for providing an urban information clearinghouse, for encouraging comprehensive planning, and for identifying urban problems that need intergovernmental or interagency coordination.[60] The fact that HUD has been given this responsibility does not mean that it will be able to exercise it effectively. The pressures of interagency rivalries may make coordination impossible. The department could, however, at least identify the inconsistencies in federal programs in order that Congress and the President might take the appropriate action. Fragmentation is not likely to be seriously reduced under such a program, but many of its more unpleasant effects could be eliminated.

The Role of the State in Federal-Urban Programs

Earlier discussion emphasized the inability or unwillingness of the states to offer the cities much in the way of assistance in solving urban problems. The states themselves have contributed to the downgrading of their role in urban problems by claiming far too frequently that the federal government has preempted the resources and functions necessary for the states to act.[61] As indicated earlier in this chapter, this is not necessarily the case. A variety of roles might be played by the states in conjunction with federal and local governments in the sharing of urban functions in a federal system. Roscoe Martin has listed five of these positive steps:

1. The creation of state program agencies in problem areas
2. Passage of enabling legislation to give cities the power to act and to help them to participate in federal-local programs
3. Providing leadership and technical assistance
4. Assist localities in developing and enforcing standards
5. Providing financial assistance to localities [62]

According to Martin, the states have only been active in the second of these recommended roles. Most of them have made it possible for their cities to participate at least minimally in federal aid programs. Lack of progress in the other areas cannot in most instances be traced to a lack of ability. "When states choose to become active participants in any pro-

---

[60] Lyndon B. Johnson, Executive Order of August 11, 1966, reprinted in U.S. Senate Subcommittee on Executive Reorganization, I, pp. 164–165.

[61] Martin, *Cities and the Federal System*, pp. 164–165.

[62] Martin, *Cities and the Federal System*, p. 163.

gram carried on within their borders that directly affects their citizens, they are invariably able to do so." [63]

Many state officials feel that there is a role for the states in acting as a channel for federal funds, thus eliminating or drastically reducing the direct federal-local contacts in the sharing of functions by design through grants-in-aid.[64] This attitude has had a serious effect on the character of grant programs, and nearly one-half of these programs require some sort of state supervision or involvement in the expenditure of funds.[65] However, the Advisory Commission on Intergovernmental Relations, although for the most part sympathetic to the states' position, has expressed serious doubts that such channeling of federal funds through the states will work effectively if the states do not first establish program agencies and policies as suggested above.[66]

Summary

There is every reason to believe that the number of contacts between the national government and local governments will continue to increase as the severity and complexity of urban problems continue to tax the talent and resources of our cities. These contacts generally take the form of the sharing of functions by design, politics, professionalization, or some combination of these three factors. In the process of sharing functions, neither the national nor the local governments can totally dominate the decision-making process, but officials and groups at both levels contribute significantly to the determination of urban policy. Serious problems of structural and policy fragmentation may inhibit the ability of any or all levels of government to control the thrust of urban policy, especially under federal grant programs, but concerted efforts at coordination and evaluation of these programs may well lead to significant improvements. As long as the states are willing to make a positive contribution to this functional sharing, there is a role for them to play in policy-making as well as in administration.

Suggested Readings

Advisory Commission on Intergovernmental Relations. *The Impact of Federal Urban Development Programs on Local Government Organization and Planning.* Subcommittee on Intergovernmental Relations of the Committee on Government Operations, U.S. Senate. Washington, 1964.

---

[63] Grodzins, *The American System,* p. 194.

[64] Martin, *Cities and the Federal System,* p. 167.

[65] Advisory Commission on Intergovernmental Relations, *Impact of Federal Urban Development Programs,* p. 13.

[66] Advisory Commission on Intergovernmental Relations, *Impact of Federal Urban Development Programs,* p. 30.

———. *Metropolitan America: Challenge to Federalism*. Intergovernmental Relations Subcommittee of the Committee on Government Operations, U.S. House of Representatives. Washington, 1966.

———. *Intergovernmental Relations in the Poverty Program*. Washington, 1966.

Berry, Brian J., and Meltzer, Jack, eds. *Goals for Urban America*. Englewood Cliffs, N.J., 1967.

Connery, Robert H., and Leach, Richard H. *The Federal Government and Metropolitan Areas*. Cambridge, Mass., 1960.

Elazar, Daniel J. *The American Partnership: Intergovernmental Cooperation in the Nineteenth Century United States*. Chicago, 1962.

Grodzins, Morton. *The American System*. Edited by Daniel J. Elazar. Chicago, 1966.

Graves, W. Brooke. *American Intergovernmental Relations*. New York, 1964.

Martin, Roscoe. *The Cities and the Federal System*. New York, 1965.

Lowe, Jeanne R. *Cities in a Race With Time*. New York, 1967.

U.S. Senate, Subcommittee on Executive Reorganization of the Committee on Government Operations. *The Federal Role in Urban Affairs*. 17 vols. Washington, 1966.

chapter **4**
Metropolitan
Problems

❴[The words "metropolis" and "metropolitan" have different meanings to different individuals. To an expanding number of people, they mean a major problem or series of problems that need solution. To some others they bring forth such epithets of fear as "supergovernment" and "un-American." To others they are only words of idle and polite conversation ... And to still other people, they are nebulous and at times troublesome words that, like democracy and foreign policy and peace and automation, need to be brought into focus.[1]

The Problem of Definition

Chapter 1 indicated some of the problems involved in developing a concise and manageable definition of the city. One of the difficulties identified was the fact that the city frequently exists in a larger context in which social, economic, and political interaction may affect the decision-making process in important ways. This chapter will deal with this larger context. Those interested in the study of urban problems have experienced some frustration in their attempts to arrive at a definition of this broader area usually called "metropolitan." In general terms this area:

> consists of heavily populated land whose central and other portions have a high degree of economic and social interaction. The central portion is gen-

---

[1] John C. Bollens and Henry J. Schmandt, *The Metropolis: Its People, Politics, and Economic Life* (New York, 1965), pp. 1–2.

erally called the central city (or cities). It is the major population, economic, social, and governmental center of the area, but it is not necessarily central in spatial terms; that is, at the geographical center of the area. The other portions are usually called the suburban or outlying parts.[2]

While this definition is accurate to a degree, it is far too broad to serve as a basis for research into the political processes of the metropolis.

THE CENSUS BUREAU DEFINITION. Since 1910 the Bureau of the Census has attempted in each decennial census to establish criteria for classifying particular areas as metropolitan. The criteria presently used were developed in 1958 as the Standard Metropolitan Statistical Area (frequently abbreviated SMSA). This definition attempts to answer two basic questions: (1) what constitutes a central city for a metropolitan area? (2) what territory should be included as suburban once the central city has been defined?

In answer to the first question, the Census Bureau has declared cities with a population of 50,000 or more or twin cities with a combined population of 50,000 or more to be central cities in an SMSA unless, of course, such cities are already included within the area of another SMSA. As far as the second question is concerned, the bureau includes as a minimum all of the territory within the county that the central city is located in. If two or more adjacent counties have cities of 50,000, and if these cities are within twenty miles of one another, the counties are considered as one SMSA.

Other contiguous counties are included in the SMSA if they are metropolitan in character and if they are socially and economically integrated with the county containing the central city. The metropolitan character of a county is determined primarily by the number of people in its labor force who are engaged in nonagricultural occupations and, in some cases, by population density. Economic and social integration are reflected primarily by the commutation patterns of the workers and residents of the county with respect to the county that contains the central city. If such data produces inconclusive results, the bureau considers a variety of other factors including telephone calls, newspaper circulation, charge accounts in central city stores, store deliveries, traffic flow, public transportation facilities, and cooperative planning efforts. Since the city and the town are more important administrative units in New England, they are used rather than counties to identify SMSA's in that region.

As of July, 1966, the bureau had identified 231 SMSA's throughout the country and in Puerto Rico. As Figure 4–1 indicates, these areas are scattered unevenly across the United States. On the Northeastern sea-

---

[2] Bollens and Schmandt, *Metropolis*, pp. 6–7.

board and in California they are clustered. In other areas, they are widely dispersed. Some states have a great many SMSA's. Texas, for example, has 21. Others (Alaska, Vermont, and Wyoming) have none.

SMSA's vary widely in size. The population ranges from a low of 51,850 in Meriden, Connecticut, to a high of almost 10.7 million in the New York area. Meriden is also the smallest SMSA in terms of geographic area, covering a mere 24 square miles, which is tiny compared to the 27,295 square miles of the San Bernardino-Riverside-Ontario SMSA.

PROBLEMS WITH THE SMSA. Although the Census Bureau has provided us with a clear and understandable, if not always simple, definition of the metropolitan area, some of the characteristics of this definition detract from its utility. The use of the county as a basic definitional unit makes particularly good sense to the federal government whose many agencies frequently use the administrative apparatus of the county and report their data in these terms. However, metropolitan development does not respect arbitrarily drawn lines separating civil subdivisions. In most cases, the county is either too small or too large a unit to use to define the metropolitan area. It is too small when the area has outgrown the confines of a single county but has not grown large enough to effect a change in character of entire contiguous counties or to affect the integration of these counties. It is too large when the inclusion of all of the territory within the county or counties of the central city or cities results in obvious definitional absurdities. The outstanding case in point is that of the largest geographic SMSA, San Bernardino-Riverside-Ontario, which includes thousands of square miles of uninhabited desert because of the unusual size of San Bernardino and Riverside counties. It may make sense someday to talk about the metropolitan problems of the Mojave Desert, but that day has not yet arrived.

The minimum population figure of 50,000 for central cities also creates problems. The metropolis of 50,000 to 75,000 is not only quantitatively but also qualitatively different from the metropolis of eight to ten million. In fact, the differences may be so great as to suggest that it makes no sense whatever to refer to a free-standing city of 50,000 and its environs as a metropolis. This problem is significant enough to lead many scholars to ignore the less-populated SMSA's and to consider only the top hundred or so when conducting metropolitan research.

The SMSA also tends to be a less useful definition as metropolitan areas in the more densely populated regions of the country begin to merge with one another. Figure 4-2 shows several areas in which a series of SMSA's cover all or nearly all of a region. The data on social and economic integration tell us that when SMSA's grow this close together they probably constitute one metropolitan area rather than several. This ten-

Figure 4–1: **Standard Metropolitan Statistical Areas**
     (Areas Defined by United States Bureau of the Budget
     to December 31, 1965)

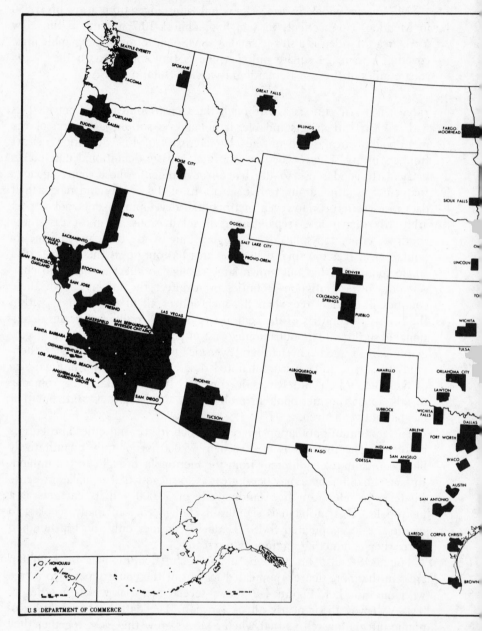

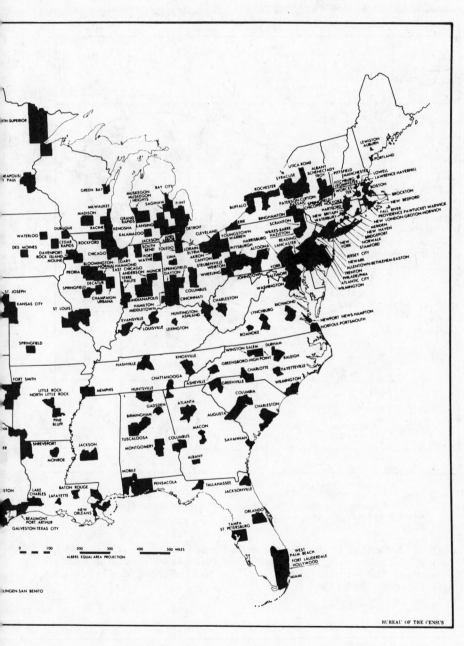

SOURCE: U.S. Bureau of the Census, *County and City Data Book*
(Washington, 1967), p. xii.

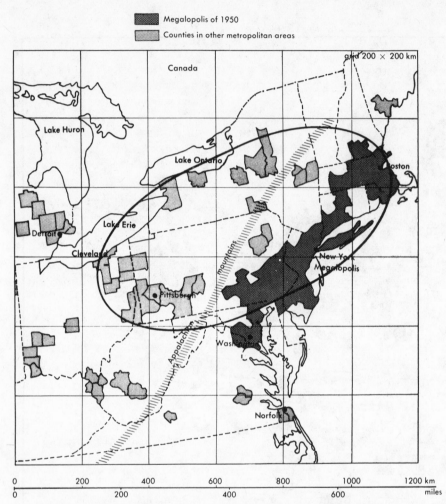

Megalopolis of 1950

Counties in other metropolitan areas

Based on an interim report by Jean Gottmann, "Megalopolis: Some Lessons from a Study of the Urbanization of the Northeastern Seaboard," in Twentieth Century Fund, 1957 **Annual Report** *(New York: 1958), Map 2.*

SOURCE: C. A. Doxiadis, *Urban Renewal and the Future of the American City* (Chicago, 1966), p. 70. The figure originally appeared in the *1957 Annual Report, The Twentieth Century Fund*, The Twentieth Century Fund, New York, 1957. Reprinted by permission of The Twentieth Century Fund.

dency is illustrated particularly well by developments on the Northeastern seaboard, around Chicago, and in Southern California. In recognition of this problem, the Census Bureau has developed a larger unit, the Standard Consolidated Area, which it applies in order to report data for certain large clusters of SMSA's. At present, the bureau uses this unit only in the New York-Northeastern New Jersey and the Chicago-Northwestern Indiana areas. In the case of New York, even the Standard Consolidated Area appears to be too small a definitional unit to comprehend the full area of social and economic integration; and, unless the bureau alters its definitional standards, this appears likely to become a problem with respect to other larger, expanding metropolitan aggregations.

THE MEGALOPOLIS. In order to meet this final problem with the SMSA as a metropolitan definition, the French geographer Jean Gottmann developed a new concept—the megalopolis. Gottmann has applied the term to "the unique cluster of metropolitan areas of the Northeastern seaboard of the United States."[3] Unlike the Standard Consolidated Areas, the megalopolis includes population classed as rural but which is in close proximity to urban areas and is closely tied to the city or cities by interests and work.[4] The megalopolis stresses the time factor as well as spatial propinquity, and this permits the inclusion of areas which are physically separated when developments in transportation and communications forge social and economic links. This is illustrated clearly in Figure 4–2 by the link between the megalopolis of the Northeastern seaboard and Pittsburgh, Cleveland, Buffalo, and other metropolitan areas in the interior. While this concept avoids some of the more serious conceptual pitfalls of the Census Bureau definition, it suffers somewhat from serious limitations of its own. The criteria utilized to determine the degree of social and economic integration within the larger community are understandably somewhat more vague than those used in the SMSA. In the second place, it is quite possible that those areas still classified as rural but within the megalopolis are no more oriented toward the cities than are other rural areas throughout the country. Certainly some of the political viewpoints expressed in these areas indicate that this is the case. In spite of its limitations, the megalopolis does emphasize the uncomfortable fact that our urbanized areas are quite probably outgrowing our definitional ability.

THE ECUMENOPOLIS. Although we tend to find the megalopolis a concept difficult enough to grasp in our attempt to define the broader context of urbanization, particularly visionary students of urban development have

---

[3] Jean Gottmann, *Megalopolis* (New York, 1961), p. 4.
[4] Gottmann, *Megalopolis*, p. 5.

predicted even more difficult concepts for the future. Perhaps the most startling of these is the ecumenopolis or universal city of the Greek planner C. A. Doxiadis. This convincing prognosticator describes the ecumenopolis as a state of development in which "all settlements . . . [are] interconnected into a continuous network that will cover the entire earth." [5] The idea depends heavily upon many of the factors which Gottmann observed in the megalopolis and projects them to their logical conclusion. The conclusion assumes a continued rapid population expansion as well as the continued development of technological advances which will permit proximity in time rather than space to create social and economic integration over even larger areas. If the political problems of the interstate SMSA and the multistate megalopolis seem perplexing to those who attempt to deal with the metropolitan environment of today, the problems of the multinational ecumenopolis appear to be infinitely more troublesome.

ANOTHER VAGUE DEFINITION. What we end up with after considering many definitions of the larger urban environment is less than satisfactory. It seems little more definite for most of us than a sweep of the arm indicating "something out there." Bollens and Schmandt come close to capturing it in its most limited sense:

> The metropolis, as is well recognized, does not designate a legally definable entity as a municipality or county does, although metropolitan boundaries might conceivably be coterminous with the territory of a governmental unit. When people speak of Philadelphia, Chicago, or Seattle, they often mean the sociological or economic city, the larger community that extends out beyond the legal limits of the major municipality and embraces the adjacent population and governments.[6]

We must be content with such a broad statement, for any attempt to form a more specific definition admits to so many exceptions as to render the attempt useless.

Metropolitan Problems: The Standard Case

The concentration of population in metropolitan areas has led to developments which social scientists, businessmen, and some government officials have viewed with increasing alarm. A significant population increase naturally leads to an increase in the demand for the traditional services performed by local governments. This factor, when coupled with an

---

[5] C. A. Doxiadis, *Urban Renewal and the Future of the American City* (Chicago, 1966), p. 75.

[6] Bollens and Schmandt, *Metropolis*, p. 34.

increasing demand for new governmental services in urban areas, has caused many observers to question the adequacy of existing governmental units.[7] The social and economic integration of the metropolis means that the governmental action of some units materially affects other units within the area and that the units and their citizens are mutually dependent. But many metropolitan analysts are even more specific in identifying problems.

PROLIFERATION OF GOVERNMENTAL UNITS. In 1960 there were an estimated 16,967 separate units of government in the 212 SMSA's identified by the Bureau of Census.[8] Many condemn this fragmentation of governmental authority as one of the gravest evils of metropolitan development. Bollens and Schmandt list five serious effects that it has on the political life of the metropolitan "community." [9] In the first place, they allege that public control over policy decisions is weakened because of the disinterest and alienation which develop through voter fatigue when many of the metropolitan governmental units overlap. This overlap is often manifest in frequent elections or extraordinarily long ballots or both; these factors are undoubtedly discouraging to many voters. In the second place, claim Bollens and Schmandt, the presence of many smaller units of government encourages the development and maintenance of local loyalties which undermine the formation of consensus in the wider community. This often forces the establishment of new policy leaders.

> These leaders—politicians, editors, businessmen, labor leaders—operate informally and outside the regular structure of government, as they attempt to prod government into action. They lack the requirements for effective policymaking: an adequate institutional base, legal authority, direct relationships with the metropolitan constituency, and established processes for considering and resolving issues as they emerge.[10]

Bollens and Schmandt also list the tendency of governments within the metropolitan area to adopt conflicting programs in the same or related functional categories. A particularly odious example of this type of conflict can be found in contiguous communities in which highly incompatible land use plans are developed that could result in heavy industry being located immediately adjacent to expensive single-family residences.

---

[7] Bollens and Schmandt, *Metropolis*, p. 29.

[8] Advisory Commission on Intergovernmental Relations, *Governmental Structure, Organization and Planning in Metropolitan Areas* (Washington, 1961), p. 14.

[9] Bollens and Schmandt, *Metropolis*, pp. 177–180.

[10] Advisory Commission on Intergovernmental Relations, *Metropolitan America: Challenge to Federalism*, Intergovernmental Relations Subcommittee of the Committee on Government Operations, U.S. House of Representatives (Washington, 1966), p. 8.

The fourth problem of fragmentation is perhaps the most frequently cited in metropolitan literature. It is often noted that some functions such as transportation, air pollution control, and water supply are no longer purely local in nature, but area-wide. It serves no purpose for one community within the metropolis to control the emission of noxious pollutants by its factories if neighboring governmental units continue to permit their factories to pollute the air with smoke, chemicals, and other harmful industrial residue. The problem, it is claimed, lies in the absence of a single unit of government which can exercise control over the entire area and perform these essentially nonlocal functions.

FINANCIAL PROBLEMS. The standard metropolitan analysis usually reveals a variety of financial problems which plague governments in their attempts to provide services to the public. These are correctly identified by Bollens and Schmandt as a function of the proliferation of units, at least in part. In the first place, all governments in the metropolis, regardless of level, seem to be plagued by inadequate revenue-producing machinery.[11] The taxing and bonding powers of local governments are frequently placed under rather strict limits by the state legislature in order to prevent these units from overtaxing their citizens or from borrowing more than they can repay. Even without these limitations many students believe that the taxes and charges levied by local governments cannot equitably raise the large amounts of money necessary to support the increased service levels required by a growing population with increasing demands for new services.

A second problem is that the taxes levied by governments in the metropolis are frequently not related to the benefits received.[12] The major claim here is that the suburban resident is receiving benefits at his place of employment (usually identified as the central city) and in his travels throughout the area for which he does not pay taxes. This emphasizes the nearly undeniable fact that the direct, individual taxes are most frequently paid in the unit where the citizen lives rather than where he works or travels. Officials of the central city claim that they are forced to provide streets, fire protection, police protection, and other services for commuters who have fled to the suburbs in order to avoid paying for all the benefits they receive.

The final problem related to finances is the existence of discrepancies in the capacity of governmental units to perform necessary services.[13] This is at least partially related to the second problem, in that some units

---

[11] Lyle C. Fitch, "Metropolitan Financial Problems," *The Annals of the American Academy of Political and Social Science* 314 (1957): 67.
[12] Fitch, "Metropolitan Financial Problems," p. 67.
[13] Fitch, "Metropolitan Financial Problems," p. 67.

cannot perform the services demanded of them because they are unable to muster the resources to serve those who do not "pay" taxes in their jurisdictions. But suburban communities suffer as much in this respect as do the central cities. Even though those receiving the benefits pay the taxes, the communities are often too small to bear the cost of providing major service facilities, such as a sewage treatment facility. In other cases, the community may be growing so rapidly that heavy demands for capital construction are placed upon it in a relatively short period of time, and it is unable to tax or borrow at sufficiently high levels to meet these demands. Consider, for example, the residential suburb of 50,000 people that is constructed and occupied practically overnight in a rapidly growing metropolitan area like Southern California. If left to its own devices, it would have to raise staggering amounts of money to construct and equip schools, police and fire stations, libraries, and other public facilities in a short period of time. Under most circumstances this is clearly impossible; the suburb must therefore either require its citizens to accept less than complete service or come up with some alternative plan for obtaining the services without engaging in massive capital construction.

SOCIOECONOMIC DISPARITIES. The standard picture of the metropolis portrays significant social and economic differences between those living in the central city and those living in the suburbs. The central city, seen as the home of the extremely rich and the poor, is characterized by town houses and luxury apartments on one hand and substandard housing and slums on the other. Because the poor outnumber the rich, low status characteristics and problems appear to dominate the central city. Low status occupations, broken families, a high percentage of aged population, high crime rates, a great number of school drop-outs and the resultant lower level of educational attainment, and a concentration of racial minorities are all problems that have become identified with central cities.

Suburbs are depicted as having a decidedly middle-class caste. They are said to be more homogenous both socially and economically. Their general pattern of characteristics appears to be the opposite of the central city's. Suburbanites have the high status occupations, unified families, a lower average age, lower crime rates, a greater degree of educational attainment, and a strong tendency toward White Anglo-Saxon Protestantism.

These socioeconomic disparities are closely related to the problems of proliferation of governments and finances. The increase in the number of suburban governmental units can be interpreted as a flight to the suburbs to avoid unpleasant contact with the social and economic diversity of the city. The suburban municipality can become a protective device designed to keep out the unwanted immigrants from the central city who would attempt to flee their environment without first obtaining the necessary social and economic credentials.[14] Most assuredly the presence of poverty and low status characteristics in the central city contributes to the greater demand for services of certain types in this area and to the relatively low ability of the recipients of these services to pay for them through local taxes.

Metropolitan Reorganization: The Response to the Standard Problems

Once one has accepted the existence of these serious metropolitan problems, it becomes necessary to examine possible solutions to them. In the discussion that follows, many of the categories are arbitrary, and some obviously overlap. This is particularly true with respect to the illustrations provided for some of the responses. Many of these solutions are "ideal types" that metropolitan areas have attempted to modify and combine in order to meet their own particular situations.

EXTRATERRITORIAL POWERS. "Extraterritorial powers are powers that a city is permitted to exercise outside its boundaries to regulate activities there or to assist in providing services to people within its boundaries." [15] These powers can be used in some circumstances to meet at least two of the problems suggested above. When the absence of regulation in adjacent territory poses a threat to policies established by the municipality, extraterritorial powers can enable the city to extend its policy beyond its boundaries and to mitigate the policy conflict attendant upon governmental proliferation. The city may also use such powers to extend its services beyond its corporate limits and thereby reduce the tendency for service areas to fail to conform to the area of existing governmental units. There are some serious limitations inherent in the use of these powers, however. They can only be used if the area beyond the city limits is not yet incorporated, but there is an increasing tendency for incorporations to fill up the gaps in metropolitan areas and to leave very little in the way of eligible territory. When the powers are used to provide services they rarely if ever include the power to tax, and the city can extend only those services that it is able to place on a user fee basis. The states are also somewhat restrictive when granting these powers to municipalities. Subdivision regulation is permitted in only thirty of the fifty states, and few

---

[14] See particularly Robert C. Wood, *Suburbia: Its People and Their Politics* (Boston, 1959).

[15] Advisory Commission on Intergovernmental Relations, *Metropolitan America*, p. 86.

states allow cities to zone outside of their legal limits.[16] Since many of the more serious intergovernmental policy conflicts within the metropolitan area can be traced to planning and land use controls, the inability to use extraterritorial powers in this policy area is a particularly serious limitation.

ANNEXATION. Annexation represents one of the oldest methods of dealing with the problems of urban and metropolitan growth. It consists of expanding existing municipal boundaries to include the adjacent territory that is presently urban or about to become urban. In the early years of American urban history the device proved quite satisfactory. "In the pre-1900 era the expansion of municipal boundaries, principally through annexation, largely kept pace with population expansion." [17] However, annexation practices were seriously crippled at the turn of the century by state legislative changes which shifted the control of the process from the city to the territory to be annexed. In the more liberal era, only the city or its duly elected official body had to approve of the annexation before it could take place. After receiving complaints from rural and suburban residents about the rapid expansion of the cities, the legislatures shifted the burden of approval to the territory alone or in conjunction with approval by referendum in the annexing city before any action could be taken. The rapid expansion of urban population also decreased the value of annexation as a tool. In many cases the cities simply could not annex as fast as they had to in order to keep pace. The new areas, encouraged by the absence of rigorous state laws, frequently incorporated as a defense against the threat of future annexation. As the metropolis became more and more crowded with municipalities, the unincorporated land between them was often sought by more than one city. As a result, annexation battles added to the hostility present in the environment. In an attempt to relieve some of these pressures, some state legislatures have attempted to encourage an orderly annexation process. Antiincorporation laws in Arizona, Idaho, North Carolina, Nebraska, New Mexico, Georgia, Ohio, and Wyoming are designed to reduce the possibility of defensive incorporations.[18] Administrative agencies have been established in Alaska, California, Minnesota, Washington, and Wisconsin to review both incorporations and annexations to insure orderly progress, and annexation proceedings are handled by the courts in Virginia.[19] For example, the Local Agency Formation Commission in California has been established at the county level and has representatives of the county and municipal-

---

[16] Advisory Commission on Intergovernmental Relations, *Metropolitan America*, p. 86.

[17] Bollens and Schmandt, *Metropolis*, p. 403.

[18] Bollens and Schmandt, *Metropolis*, p. 423.

[19] Bollens and Schmandt, *Metropolis*, pp. 422–423.

ities for members. It reviews all applications for incorporation and annexation in order to determine if the best interests of the county are being served. While the LAFC's have not eliminated conflict over annexation, they have provided an orderly framework in which the conflict can be resolved with minimal side effects.

In terms of the problems viewed by metropolitan reformers, the annexation procedure has much to recommend it where it is still possible to use it. It tends to hold at a constant level the number of governmental units within the metropolis. It also represents significant progress toward a single unit of area-wide competence when the central city can annex rapidly without serious competition from the suburbs and without defensive incorporations. The fact remains, however, that in most of our major metropolitan areas governmental congestion has effectively ruled out any serious attempt to solve problems through annexation.

A phenomenon that is closely related to annexation is consolidation, combining two existing units of government into one. Consolidations are highly unpopular since few cities are anxious to lose their identities. Only one-half of the states permit cities to consolidate.[20] Although consolidation has not been frequently used because of this unpopularity, occasional movements have started like that in Rock Island, Moline, and East Moline, Illinois in 1967 with some hope of success.[21] In its extreme form, consolidation is the most drastic measure that could be taken in order to meet metropolitan problems. Many, if not all, of the objections of the reformers could be met if all of the existing governmental units in the metropolitan area were consolidated into a single area-wide unit. Few people would consider such a drastic measure, if only because of its extremely low degree of political feasibility.

CITY-COUNTY SEPARATION. In the last half of the nineteenth century, the city and county of a number of metropolitan areas were separated as a response to metropolitan problems. This movement was generally motivated by the central city residents' belief that they were bearing too heavy a share of the costs of suburban services through the county taxes, and that the existence of both a county and a city government in the central city area resulted in an inefficient duplication of effort. Under this plan the central city is removed entirely from the jurisdiction of the county, and those functions and services formerly provided by the county are taken over by the city. Outstanding examples of this arrangement can be found in Baltimore, Denver, St. Louis, and San Francisco. Separation is

[20] Advisory Commission on Intergovernmental Relations, *Metropolitan America*, p. 101.
[21] Howard Ferguson, "3-City Consolidation," *National Civic Review* 56 (1967): 255–259.

still used in Virginia where every city (an incorporated place over 5,000 in population) is automatically separated from the county in which it is located. Although the separation of city and county has reduced some of the duplication of services and functions and has simplified the voters' task by reducing the number of offices to which they must elect officials, it has not been a completely satisfactory solution to metropolitan problems. In the first place, the dichotomy created between the city and the county does not fit well with the concept of social and economic integration which lies at the heart of our definition of metropolitan areas. Separation might be appropriate in areas where the county is almost exclusively rural and one central city of over 50,000 gives the area its metropolitan character. However, few of our metropolitan areas fit this picture at this time. In the second place, county officials are not likely to take kindly to the serious reduction in the authority of their offices which is sure to result from separation. This undoubtedly adds to the already considerable friction between the central city and the outlying areas. Finally, not all of the undesirable duplication of services and offices can be eliminated. In St. Louis, for example, a significant number of residual county offices remain in the city although they are directly responsible to the state rather than to city officials. The fact that these offices command a considerable number of patronage positions within the city makes them potent political rivals in the city administration.[22]

CITY-COUNTY CONSOLIDATION. Another remedy for metropolitan problems that was first used in the last century is the consolidation of the county and some or all of the other units of government within the county into a single unit of government. Some of our largest and most important metropolitan centers used this approach in the nineteenth century. In New Orleans and Boston, the central city and the county were merged. In Philadelphia, a large number of local governmental units were merged with the county. The most spectacular consolidation of all was the combination of five counties to create the present City of New York just prior to the turn of the century.

Although there continued to be strong interest in such consolidations in the early twentieth century, the absence of enabling legislation at the state level and of voter approval at the local level effectively prevented any further use of the plan. Not until the establishment of the partially consolidated government of Baton Rouge-East Baton Rouge Parish in 1949 did the plan meet with any success at all in this century. (This was considered to be only a partial consolidation because the constituent units of gov-

---

[22] This section draws heavily upon Advisory Commission on Intergovernmental Relations, *Metropolitan America*, pp. 101–102.

ernment continued to have a legal and functional identity with the parish providing integration for the effort through taxing and service zones.) A further revival of efforts in the late fifties resulted in a string of defeats for the plan in Nashville, Tennessee; Albuquerque, New Mexico; Knoxville, Tennessee; Macon, Georgia; Durham, North Carolina; and Richmond, Virginia.

In the last decade, however, the consolidation plan has met with enough success to revive interest and enthusiasm. The consolidation of Nashville and Davidson County in Tennessee in 1962 and the consolidation of Jacksonville and Duval County in Florida in 1967 have been considered as major victories for metropolitan reform. Supporters of the plan have been particularly encouraged by the progress that has been made in Nashville in accomplishing the goals set forth for reform. The following list indicates clearly that these goals coincide closely with the problem areas identified earlier in this chapter:

1. Fix responsibility for governmental decisions
2. Economy through the elimination of duplication of services
3. Specialization and professionalization of personnel
4. Equalization of services in urban and suburban areas
5. Planned development of suburban and rural fringe areas
6. Elimination of city-county financial inequalities
7. New suburban services on a pay-as-you-go basis

After studying the first few years of Nashville's operation, Professor Daniel Grant has concluded that progress is being made in most of these areas.[23] The biggest difficulty appears to be in the area of economy in government where demands for additional services and improved service levels have more than offset the economies obtained through the elimination of the duplication of services. Although this is not a surprising development, it does provide additional ammunition for those who oppose metropolitan structural reforms on the grounds that these reforms inevitably result in increased taxes, especially in the suburban areas. However, other claims of disaster in both politics and functional performance have not been substantiated by the Nashville consolidation, and Grant was able to conclude that "Nashville's metro is living up to most of the predictions of its supporters and is moving in the direction of proving incorrect most of the predictions of its opponents." [24]

In spite of the enthusiasm generated by successful consolidations of county and city, some general problems remain to raise questions as to

---

[23] Daniel Grant, "A Comparison of Predictions and Experience with Nashville 'Metro,' " *Urban Affairs Quarterly* 1 (1965): 35–54.

[24] Grant, "Comparison," p. 54.

the general value of the device. In the first place, it is only 100 percent effective in broadening the governmental base of the area to meet area-wide problems in cases where the metropolitan area is confined within the limits of a single county. If the trend is toward more and more inter-county, interstate, or even international metropolitan areas, the city-county consolidation movement may already belong to past metropolitan eras rather than to the future. Under such circumstances, this approach could only be considered appropriate by reformers in those few metropolitan areas that are static, or as a first step toward a more comprehensive future reform. A second difficulty lies in the problems that attend the plan's adoption. Less than half of the states permit such consolidations either by general or special law. Many of the states that do permit city-county consolidation have initiated special requirements for popular approval, similar to those mentioned earlier with respect to annexation. In these states, it is necessary for consolidation plans to receive approval by a majority of citizens voting in each of the affected political subdivisions, including all of the cities as well as unincorporated areas within the county. Such restrictions obviously make it necessary to obtain an extraordinary majority of the total popular vote if the consolidation is to be approved. Such problems as these have led many metropolitan areas to look elsewhere for a scheme of structural reform which will aid in solving metropolitan problems.

THE URBAN COUNTY. A somewhat less radical approach to metropolitan problems would leave the existing governmental structure untouched and shift functions from one level to another within the area. The urban county plan centers upon using the county as the governmental unit for the performance of area-wide functions, while local functions continue to be performed by the municipalities. Area-wide functions become the responsibility of the county in a variety of ways. The most obvious of these is the direct transfer of functions from municipalities and special purpose districts to the county. The county may also assume responsibility for the performance of some functions in unincorporated areas and continue to perform these functions after the area incorporates or is annexed. Finally, the state legislature may delegate sufficient legislative powers to the county government to enable it to develop new functional and service responsibilities of an area-wide nature which have not previously been handled by other local units.

Two widely publicized variants of this approach are presently in use in this country. The first of these is the Miami-Dade County Metro in Florida. By establishing a new charter for the county, residents of the Miami area were able to transfer certain functions to the county, while retaining the local units of government for local purposes. These functional arrangements are relatively inflexible because they are generalized throughout the county and because a charter amendment is necessary to change the allocation or mix of functions in the area. In spite of strong initial opposition to the plan and persistent attempts to weaken the county government after the plan was established, Miami Metro has been relatively well accepted by the citizens of the area and has made some progress in dealing with area-wide problems.[25]

Another type of urban county approach is used by many counties in California. This plan is commonly known as the Lakewood Plan in honor of the community in Los Angeles County which first adopted its benefits on a grand scale. The essence of this approach is the provision by the county of a variety of services and the performance of a variety of functions both local and area-wide in nature. The individual municipalities within that county may then contract for any or all of these services on a fee basis. For example, a relatively new city that is too small to provide a full complement of urban services might contract with the county for police and fire protection, building inspection, and other services at a mutually agreed upon price per unit of service provided. Table 4-1 illustrates the wide variety of services available under such a plan. The political practicality and the major shortcoming of this plan compared to that of Dade County lie in the same characteristic. Each community is able to determine for itself just how much or how little in the way of services it will receive from the county. Functions can only be performed on an area-wide basis if every community elects to have them performed at that level. Should a particular municipality find itself unhappy with the county's performance of a particular function, it is free to discontinue purchasing from the county and to establish its own agency to perform the function. This maintenance of local option disqualifies the Lakewood Plan as a true urban county plan in the eyes of many students of metropolitan problems.

TABLE 4-1: Descriptions of Major Services Available to Cities in Los Angeles County, 1961

Service	Description	Department
Assessment and Tax Collection	Assesses annually all taxable property in the County.	Assessor
	Prepares assessment roll including all taxable land, improvements and personal property in the County.	
	Collects and distributes taxes. Collects business and regulatory license fees.	Tax Collector

[25] See particularly Edward Sofen, *The Miami Metropolitan Experiment*, 2d ed. (New York, 1966).

TABLE 4–1 (*continued*)

Service	Description	Department
Basic Health Services	Provides basic health services required by State law; for example, communicable disease control, public health nursing service, public health education, environmental sanitation services, tuberculosis control, and Health Officer's clinics.	Health
Bicycle License Enforcement	Conducts bicycle licensing programs and inspections.	Sheriff
Building and Safety Code Enforcement	Enforces cities' building, plumbing and electrical codes; makes all inspections and issues all permits and orders required by such enforcement.	Engineer
Business Licenses	Insures that all individuals and companies doing business within the city have obtained applicable licenses.	Tax Collector
	Investigates licensed businesses for conformance with business license ordinances.	Sheriff
	Investigates applications for licenses.	
Consolidation of Elections	Adds city or special district measures to primary or general election ballots.	Registrar of Voters
Emergency Ambulance Service	Answers police calls for emergency ambulance service; administers emergency medical aid. (County contracts with ambulance agencies and medical facilities for these services.)	General Hospital
Enforcement of City Health Ordinances	Enforces city's special health and sanitation ordinances.	Health
	Provides rodent control service.	
Fire Protection	Conducts fire prevention program including: Inspections of dwellings, commercial and industrial buildings, and special fire hazards such as oil fields and weed growths. Educational programs in schools and for the general public.	Fire Department
	Operates fire fighting services including: Fire stations and related facilities with specialized equipment and professionally trained personnel. Central communications and dispatching service.	
	Analyzes fire causes and conducts research on methods and problems of fire fighting.	
	Issues permits and licenses; for example, oil truck safety factors.	
	Provides auxiliary service including postfire investigations for cause, rescue work, consultant services.	
Industrial Waste Regulation	Controls commercial and industrial discharge of waste into sewers.	Engineer
	Guards against pollution of surface and underground waters by industrial waste.	
	Regulates rubbish and refuse disposal.	

TABLE 4–1 (*continued*)

Service	Description	Department
Law Enforcement	Provides general 24-hour patrol service. Enforces traffic laws and maintains traffic flow. Conducts crime detection and prevention program. Furnishes auxiliary services including a basic criminal index and other records and statistics, two-way radio system, interlocking teletype system with other police agencies throughout California and adjoining states, photography and fingerprinting, and recruitment and training. Provides presentence and postsentence detention facilities, and auxiliary services such as booking, hospitalization, feeding, rehabilitation, and paroling of prisoners.	Sheriff
Library Services	Renders complete service to the adult and juvenile reading public, including selection, order and purchase of books, a central book stock, readers' advisory service, teachers' library, cataloging of all books, etc.	Library
Microfilm Record Storage	Provides underground storage for microfilmed city records.	Sheriff
Park Services	Furnishes complete maintenance service for park facilities including craft maintenance of equipment and facilities, and installation of special events facilities. Offers park planning consultant services.	Parks and Recreation
Personnel Services	Offers complete personnel services including: Classification of positions Recruitment programs Examinations Consultant services	Civil Service Commission
Planning and Zoning (Staff Services)	Processes tentative subdivision maps, requests for zone changes, zone exceptions, and special permits. Investigates zoning violations. Attends council meetings on zoning as staff consultant. Prepares new record maps. Revises record maps.	Regional Planning Commission Engineer
Pound Service	Licenses dogs; enforces dog leashing ordinances. Impounds stray and unwanted animals. Investigates cases involving inhumane treatment of animals. Removes dead animals from public streets and private property.	Poundmaster
Prosecution of City Ordinance Violations	Furnishes services in connection with filing and prosecuting violations of city ordinances.	District Attorney

TABLE 4–1 (*continued*)

Service	Description	Department
Recreation Services	Plans and provides supervision and leadership for athletic events, cultural activities, and various social events for all age groups. Provides lifeguard and beach maintenance services. Provides in-service training in recreation leadership. Offers consultant services of staff specialists to community upon request.	Parks and Recreation
Roadside Tree Service	Provides complete services including issuance of permits, planting, tree maintenance, and removal of dead and hazardous trees.	Parks and Recreation
Sample Ballots	Addresses, inserts, and mails sample ballots to registered voters for elections in cities and special districts.	Registrar of Voters
School Crossing Guard Service	Administers school crossing guard services.	Sheriff
Sewer Construction	Makes survey, drafts plans, prepares specifications, etc. in connection with sanitary sewer improvements.	Engineer
Sewer Maintenance	Conducts preventive maintenance against sewer stoppages and damages.	Engineer
Street Construction— Work other than ordinary maintenance and repairs	Includes: Construction and/or installation of streets, bridges, traffic signals, signs, markings, striping, and permanent sidewalk repairs; major street reconstruction or alterations; storm and flood relief measures; cleaning and sweeping of streets; engineering services in connection with traffic and lighting, road construction, construction permits and inspection, and subdivisions; roadside weed abatement.	Road
Street Maintenance— Ordinary maintenance and repairs	Maintains and/or repairs streets, bridges, traffic signals, warning and regulating signs and devices, traffic striping and street marking, and emergency sidewalk damage.	Road
Street Lighting	Designs, installs and maintains street lights.	Road
Subdivision Map Checking	Checks the accuracy of survey and mathematical details of final subdivision maps.	Engineer

SOURCE: Report to the Legislature by the Senate Fact Finding Committee on Local Government, 1961 Regular Session, Sacramento: Senate of the State of California, 1961, pp. 58–59.

The urban county approach has its difficulties, many of which are shared with some of the structural reforms discussed earlier. Voter approval of the more rigid plans of the Miami-Dade County variety is hard to come by. Such plans have been turned down by the voters in recent years in Cleveland, Pittsburgh, Houston, and Dayton.[26] In the second place, the entire plan is based upon the assumption that county government is adequate to the task of providing a vast range of additional services. In the case of most metropolitan counties this assumption is incorrect. Most of these counties have few legislative powers, are without elected or professional executive leadership, and are faced with a tax base inadequate for the purposes which it is presently designed to serve. Thirdly, this plan does not meet previous objections that the county is an insufficiently large base upon which to rest area-wide services in most metropolitan areas. Finally, plans of the Miami-Dade County type require some sort of judgment as to which services are local and which are area-wide. Current research indicates that even the professionals who perform these services do not agree as to which service belongs where. The only statement that can be made with any degree of certainty is that many local administrators tend to view nearly all functions as local and very few functions as of area-wide importance.[27]

THE METROPOLITAN FEDERATION. After some study of metropolitan problems, particularly in large metropolitan areas, Dr. Arthur Bromage came to the conclusion that "only federation of governments and the building of an upper-tier metropolitan council with legislative powers and administrative processes will suffice." [28] Like the strong urban county plans, the federation is based upon the idea that area-wide functions should be performed by area-wide units. The major difference lies in the fact that the area-wide unit in the federation is a new unit created specifically for the purpose of performing metropolitan functions. Frequently, such plans call for the enlargement of municipal boundaries within the federation in order that the entire territory of the metropolis might be covered by appropriate units for the performance of local functions.

There are no true metropolitan federations in the United States today. However, we have been fortunate in being able to observe the plan in operation in Canada, especially in Toronto and Winnipeg, and to evaluate its contributions there. These efforts appear to enjoy some success and popularity with the residents of the areas, even though they have not

---

[26] Bollens and Schmandt, *Metropolis*, p. 453.

[27] David Mars, "Localism and Regionalism in Southern California, *Urban Affairs Quarterly* 2 (1967): 47–74.

[28] Arthur W. Bromage, "Political Representation in Metropolitan Areas," *American Political Science Review* 52 (1958): 407.

proved to be a panacea.[29] Problems with state legislative authorization and popular opposition, especially in the suburbs, make the creation of federations extremely difficult if not impossible in this country. Strong pressures from the counties and from the suburbs make legislative authorization difficult, and the frequent requirement of multiple majorities once state authorization has been obtained gives suburban areas an effective veto over the plan. Between 1896 and 1931 federation plans were defeated in Boston twice and in Oakland, Pittsburgh, St. Louis, and San Francisco once each.[30]

One of the major emphases in metropolitan federations is upon the adequacy of the system of representation. The Metropolitan Council must be constituted in such a manner as to be responsible and responsive to the wishes of the electorate. The usual effort is to have the council made up of directly elected officials who represent the various municipalities that constitute the federation. Equality of representation is attempted by permitting greater representation from the more populous municipalities. Although this is an imperfect scheme in many respects, it conforms to the realities of the perceived split between the central cities and the suburbs.

SPECIAL DISTRICTS AND AUTHORITIES. One of the most frequently used governmental devices in metropolitan areas is the special purpose district. These districts are governments designed to perform only certain limited functions and services rather than the whole range of services provided by general purpose units such as municipalities. For the most part such districts have been single-purpose in nature. When functional and service area boundaries are discovered that do not coincide with those of an existing governmental unit, a special district can be created to perform that function or service, and the boundaries of that district can be specifically designed to fit the area in question. These single-purpose districts have had much to recommend them over the years. They have been able to borrow money, frequently against anticipated revenue from user fees, when existing units have exhausted their powers under the state's limitations on indebtedness. Districts that have been granted the power to levy property taxes have been able to raise money beyond the limits on that tax which have been imposed on counties and municipalities by the states.

The data on the following tables indicate the extent and the variety of uses to which the special purpose district may be put. Table 4–2 indicates the variety of types of authorization for special districts which may be passed by state legislatures, and the degree to which each type has been utilized by local units. Table 4–3 illustrates the ability of the special

---

[29] Frank Smallwood, *Metro Toronto: A Decade Later* (Toronto, 1963).
[30] Bollens and Schmandt, *Metropolis*, pp. 472–473.

district to cross the boundaries of existing political subdivisions to provide needed area-wide services. Not all of the districts listed in the two tables address themselves to urban or metropolitan problems. However, Table 4–4 indicates the number and variety of such districts within SMSA's.

TABLE 4–2: Statutory Authorizations for Types of Special Districts, by State, 1962

| | | NUMBER OF TYPES OF DISTRICTS AUTHORIZED | | | | |
| | | By General Statute | | | By Special Act | |
State	Total	Two or More Districts Organized	One District Organized	No District Organized	Active	Inactive
Northeast:						
Maine	112	2			106	4
New Hampshire	4	3			1	
Vermont	3	2		1		
Massachusetts	97	3	1	1	90	2
Rhode Island	51	2			49	
Connecticut	83	3		7	78	1
New York	9	3		1	5	
New Jersey	23	9	2	6	3	3
Pennsylvania	5	2		2	1	
Midwest:						
Michigan	7	4	1	1	1	
Ohio	11	8	1	2		
Indiana	12	7	2	3		
Illinois	29	16		3	7	3
Wisconsin	9	4	1	1	1	2
Minnesota	12	5	1	4	2	
Iowa	8	7			1	
Missouri	10	7	1		2	
North Dakota	9	6		2	1	
South Dakota	9	4	1	4		
Nebraska	19	12	2	4	1	
Kansas	19	8	3	2	4	2
South:						
Delaware	3	1	1	1		
Maryland	15	4	1		10	

TABLE 4–2 (*continued*)

| | | By General Statute | | | By Special Act | |
| | | Two or More Districts Organized | One District Organized | No District Organized | Active | Inactive |
State	Total			NUMBER OF TYPES OF DISTRICTS AUTHORIZED		
South (*continued*)						
Virginia	16	5			7	4
West Virginia	7	4		1	2	
Kentucky	13	6	1	5	1	
Tennessee	9	4	1	2	1	1
North Carolina	24	5	2	3	8	6
South Carolina	27	7			18	2
Georgia	16	3		1	11	1
Florida	159	7	1	2	105	44
Alabama	10	4	2	4		
Mississippi	7	4			3	
Louisiana	44	9		4	25	6
Arkansas	20	10		10		
Southwest:						
Oklahoma	9	5	1	1	1	1
Texas	21	10			8	3
New Mexico	5	4		1		
Arizona	12	6		5	1	
West:						
Montana	9	6	2	1		
Idaho	16	13	1	2		
Wyoming	14	9	1	4		
Colorado	20	11		4	5	
Utah	11	10		1		
Washington	22	16	3	3		
Oregon	22	18	1	2	1	
Nevada	17	10	1	4	2	
California	55	22	1	2	27	3
Alaska	1	1				
Hawaii	1	1				
Total	1,146	322	36	101	589	88

SOURCE: U.S. Bureau of the Census, *Census of Governments: 1962, vol. I, Governmental Organization* (U.S. Government Printing Office, Washington, 1963), pp. 243–372.

TABLE 4–3: **Multicounty Special Districts**

United States	Total	Two County	Three County	Four County	Five or More Counties
Northeast:					
Maine	6	6			
New Hampshire	4	4			
Vermont	4	2	1	1	
Massachusetts	5	3	2		
Rhode Island	2	2			
Connecticut	3	3			
New York	57	51	2		4
New Jersey	14	8	2	2	2
Pennsylvania	73	70	2		1
Midwest:					
Michigan	13	10	2		1
Ohio	13	4	2		7
Indiana	14	10	3	1	
Illinois	321	261	53	6	1
Wisconsin	6	4	1	1	
Minnesota	13	7	2	1	3
Iowa	18	13	2	1	2
Missouri	47	35	8	3	1
North Dakota	23	16	4	2	1
South Dakota	12	10	1		1
Nebraska	192	108	49	14	21
Kansas	127	99	16	11	1
South:					
Delaware	1	1			
Maryland	5	4	1		
District of Columbia					
Virginia	30	7	9	5	9
West Virginia	17	4	5	3	5
Kentucky	12	11	1		

TABLE 4–3 (*continued*)

United States	Total	Two County	Three County	Four County	Five or More Counties
Tennessee	42	28	11	1	2
North Carolina	22	10	1	4	7
South Carolina	12	9	2		1
Georgia	54	17	6	6	25
Florida	28	17	3	1	7
Alabama	17	7	5		5
Mississippi	49	29	9	3	8
Louisiana	16	9	3	1	3
Arkansas	22	13	8		1
Southwest:					
Oklahoma	33	20	8	5	
Texas	168	88	38	24	18
New Mexico	36	18	12	3	3
Arizona	1		1		
West:					
Montana	26	21	4	1	
Idaho	56	49	6		1
Wyoming	17	13	3		1
Colorado	115	70	33	6	6
Utah	15	12	2	1	
Washington	41	35	4	1	1
Oregon	43	35	6	2	
Nevada	15	9	3	2	1
California	149	124	16	5	4
Alaska					
Hawaii					
Total	2,009	1,386	352	117	154

SOURCE: U.S. Bureau of the Census, *Census of Governments: 1962*, *vol. I*, *Governmental Organization* (U.S. Government Printing Office, Washington, 1963), Table 16.

TABLE 4–4: Special Districts Located Within Standard Metropolitan Statistical Areas, 1962

State	Total	Natural Resources	Fire Protection	Housing and Urban Renewal	Sewerage Disposal	Water Supply	Other Single Function	Multifunction
Northeast:								
Maine	8	1		1	3	3		
New Hampshire	3	1		1		1		
Vermont								
Massachusetts	116	6	5	67	1	34	3	
Rhode Island	36	1	27	3		4	1	
Connecticut	98		20	25	2	5	41	5
New York	447	2	406				38	1
New Jersey	175	9	55	31	30	5	42	3
Pennsylvania	879	2		25	161	120	534	37
Midwest:								
Michigan	30	15			1	7	6	1
Ohio	64	24		12	1	1	26	
Indiana	102	13		9	2		78	
Illinois	704	180	261	24	44	27	164	4
Wisconsin	23	14		6	3			
Minnesota	23	9		8	2		4	
Iowa	66	15	8		2	38	3	
Missouri	59	10	27	5	1	5	11	
North Dakota	13	8		1			4	
South Dakota	2	2						
Nebraska	108	11	16	2	75		3	1
Kansas	50	23		1	1	7	14	4
South:								
Delaware	1			1				
Maryland	23	6		3			11	3
Virginia	10	4			1		5	
West Virginia	18	2		4	4	4	3	1
Kentucky	29	6	8		3	11		1
Tennessee	37	6	1	6		17	1	6
North Carolina	18	4		7	1	1	3	2
South Carolina	38	6	4	5	2	11	5	5
Georgia	42	5		21		1	15	
Florida	78	31	10	16	2		19	
Alabama	20	6		14				
Mississippi	2	7				1		
Louisiana	34	11	1	7	3	4	8	
Arkansas	64	15	2	4	13	28	2	
Southwest:								
Oklahoma	19	10			2	6		1
Texas	214	70	3	39	2	56	14	30
New Mexico	7	3					4	
Arizona	31	25				2	3	1
West:								
Montana	28	23		1		1	3	
Idaho								
Wyoming								

TABLE 4–4 (*continued*)

State	Total	Natural Resources	Fire Protection	Housing and Urban Renewal	Sewerage Disposal	Water Supply	Other Single Function	Multifunction
Colorado	194	17	43	2	53	53	14	12
Utah	44	15			4	10	11	4
Washington	289	56	101	6	30	73	19	4
Oregon	247	22	55	3	27	64	72	4
Nevada	19	7	1	3	2	2	3	1
California	894	245	120	27	90	164	201	47
Alaska								
Hawaii	4	4						
Total	5,410	946	1,174	390	570	764	1,388	178

SOURCE: U.S. Bureau of the Census, *Census of Governments: 1962, vol. I, Governmental Organization* (U.S. Government Printing Office, Washington, 1963), Table 13.

Most of these districts and authorities are single-purpose, that is, governments established for the purpose of performing only one function. As the number of area-wide functions in a metropolitan area increases, it is not unusual for the number of special purpose districts to increase at the same rate. The end result, of course, is an even greater proliferation of governments in an area where the number of governments is already considered one of the major problems. To reduce this difficulty, many students of metropolitan problems have recommended the use of multi-purpose districts. Some have even recommended a single district or authority to handle all area-wide functions. These recommendations have largely fallen on deaf ears, however. The few multipurpose districts that have been created are frequently limited to two closely related functions such as water supply and sewage treatment.[31]

Two other problems have been identified that have tended to discredit the special purpose district among metropolitan reformers. Some scholars are particularly concerned about the absence of an adequate system of representation.[32] The governing board of most districts other than school districts is appointed rather than elected, and in many cases this appointment is made by officials other than those in the area to be served. Critics feel that the end result is a government that is neither responsive nor responsible to the will of the people. The second problem is one of coordination with other units of government. In most metropolitan areas

[31] Advisory Commission on Intergovernmental Relations, *The Problem of Special Districts in American Government* (Washington, 1964), pp. 22–28.
[32] Bromage, "Political Representation," pp. 408–409.

TABLE 4–5: Number of Units Which Participate in Interlocal Cooperation in the Detroit Metropolitan Areas, by Function, 1964

| | NUMBER OF UNITS WHICH: | | | |
Function	Contract To Provide Service	Contract To Receive Service	Are Involved In Joint Agreements	Informally Cooperate
I. GENERAL GOVERNMENT				
Assessing Functions, All				47
Assessing, Part	4	94		39
Elections	14		1	12
Other, Finance		1		2
Personnel, General				11
Purchasing				3
Other General Government Functions	2	1		2
II. POLICE SERVICES				
All Police Services	1	1		6
Animal Control	5	11	8	22
Communications, Police	11	74	31	65
Criminal Investigation			13	65
Jail	9	89		22
Juvenile Activities			31	48
Patrol Service	5	11	16	36
Personnel, Police			43	4
Traffic	3		17	26
Other Police Services	1		23	1
III. FIRE SERVICES				
All Fire Services	28	45	10	6
Buildings and Equipment, Fire	3	3	6	5
Communications, Fire	3	23	13	11
Fire Fighting— Running Card Response			24	
Fire Fighting—Other	4	13	53	31
Fire Prevention	1			9
Personnel, Fire			19	6
Other Fire Services	1	1		3
IV. CIVIL DEFENSE			24	47
V. PUBLIC WORKS AND UTILITIES				
Public Transportation	1			11
Public Works Inspection	3	31	9	9
Other Engineering and Inspection	1	23		3

TABLE 4–5 (*continued*)

	NUMBER OF UNITS WHICH:			
Function	Contract To Provide Service	Contract To Receive Service	Are Involved In Joint Agreements	Informally Cooperate
Reciprocal Licensing of Building Trades			116	1
Refuse Collection	1	1		1
Refuse Disposal	10	14	33	6
Sewerage, Sanitary	9	69	4	
Sewerage, Storm	6	46	4	
Sewage Treatment	13	88	6	3
Streets and Highways	19	74	22	23
Water Distribution System	8	25		2
Water Supply	19	77	21	9
Other Public Works	5	9		2
VI. PARKS AND RECREATION				
Parks	5	6	23	14
Recreation	3	3	12	9
VII. PUBLIC HEALTH, HOSPITALS AND WELFARE				
All Public Health Services			4	4
Public Health Services, Part	4	16	11	10
Hospitals	5	52	37	2
Welfare	2	2	9	11
VIII. LIBRARIES				
All Library Services	8	38	3	10
Library Services, Part	8	35	39	19
IX. PLANNING, URBAN RENEWAL AND HOUSING				
Planning	1	1	10	24
Urban Redevelopment				5
Other Planning, Urban Renewal and Housing Services			22	1
Other Services Not Included in Above			4	1

SOURCE: Metropolitan Fund, Inc., *Regional Organization, Part One* (Detroit, Michigan, 1965), p. 46. Reprinted by permission of the Metropolitan Fund, Inc.

the mechanism for planning and coordination of activities between governmental units has been complicated. The special purpose district is frequently viewed as adding unnecessarily to this complication. Although it is possible to provide for coordination of efforts when establishing districts, such provisions are too infrequent to satisfy most critics.[33]

INTERGOVERNMENTAL AGREEMENTS. The Advisory Commission on Intergovernmental Relations has offered the best available description of this answer to metropolitan problems:

> Intergovernmental contracts and agreements are the most widely used formal method of accommodating governmental problems to geographic boundaries. They provide a formal yet flexible and adaptable method for public jurisdictions of all types and at all levels to cooperate and share responsibility for providing public services and facilities. They constitute a method of adaptation which by-passes basic structural and organizational problems and the issue of allocating responsibility among levels of government. Finally, they stress consolidation of services rather than consolidation of governments.[34]

One such arrangement has already been discussed as an urban county plan for dealing with metropolitan problems. The list of functions provided by Los Angeles County under contractual agreement that is presented in Table 4–1 is an excellent illustration of the variety of agreements which can be utilized when a single governmental unit provides services. Table 4–5 indicates the range of services which can be obtained when the full range of intergovernmental agreements is explored by all of the governments in the metropolitan area. These services can be provided either by a larger unit of government, such as the county or central city, which has expandable facilities, or they may be provided by special units created when two units band together to obtain services that neither unit can afford to provide by itself. In either case, agreements and contracts provide a flexible and politically attractive manner of providing urban services. The major benefit that accompanies this approach is the economy obtained by the avoidance of needless duplication of expensive capital assets such as buildings and equipment.

One of the major drawbacks to the full utilization of agreements and contracts in the past has been the absence of necessary state authorization for such action. However, as Table 4–6 indicates, thirty-two states have now passed legislation which in varying degrees permits their local governments to participate in such contracts and agreements. It can still be

---

[33] Advisory Commission on Intergovernmental Relations, *Problem of Special Districts*, pp. 46–47.

[34] Advisory Commission on Intergovernmental Relations, A *Handbook for Interlocal Agreements and Contracts* (Washington, 1967), p. 18.

TABLE 4–6: General Interlocal Cooperation Acts in the States

CITATIONS AND DATES OF ORIGINAL ENACTMENT

State	Citation	Original Enactment
California	Calif. Government Code, Sec. 51300-51335 (service contracts), Sec. 6500-6578 (agreements)	1921
Colorado	Colo. Rev. Stat. Ann., Sec. 88-2-1	1949
Connecticut	Conn. Gen. Stat. Ann., Sec. 7-339a to 7-339 1	1961
Illinois	Ill. Mun. Code, Art. 1, Div. 1, Ch. 24, Sec. 1-1-5	1961
Indiana	Interlocal Cooperation Act, Ind. Ann. Stat., Sec. 53:1101–07	1957
Iowa	H.B. 188, 1965	1965
Kentucky	Interlocal Cooperation Act, Ky. Rev. Stat., Sec. 65.210–.300	1962
Louisiana	Local Services Law, La. Rev. Stat., Tit. 33, Sec. 1321–32	1942
Maine	Interlocal Cooperation Act, Me. Rev. Stat., Ch. 90-A, Sec. 80B	1963
Maryland	Md. Ann. Code, Art. 23B, Sec. 22	1955
Massachusetts	Mass. Ann. Laws, Tit. 7, Ch. 40, Sec. 4 A	1945
Michigan	Mich. Stat. Ann., Sec. 5.4081–.4084	1951
Minnesota	Joint Exercise of Powers Act, Minn. Stat. Ann., Sec. 471.59	1943
Missouri	Mo. Stat. Ann., Sec. 70.210–.325	1947
Nebraska	Interlocal Cooperation Act, Neb. Rev. Stat., Art. 22, Sec. 23:2201–07	1963
Nevada	A.B. 462, 1965	1951
New Hampshire	N. H. Laws 1963, Ch. 275:14 adding new Ch. 53-A	1963
New Jersey	Consolidated Municipal Services Act, N. J. Stat. Ann., 40:48B	1952
New Mexico	Joint Powers Agreement Act, N. M. Stat. Ann., Sec. 4-22-(1–7)	1961
New York	N. Y. Gen. Mun. Law, Art. 5-6, Sec. 119 (m–o)	1960
North Carolina	N. C. Gen. Stat., Sec. 153-246	1933
North Dakota	N. D. Cent. Code, Sec. 54-4001	1963
Ohio	Joint Municipal Improvement Act, Ohio Rev. Code, Tit. 7, Sec. 715-02	1965
Oklahoma	S.B. 343, 1965	1965
Oregon	Ore. Rev. Stat., Sec. 190-010-.220	1933
Pennsylvania	Pa. Stat. Ann., Tit. 53, Sec. 53-471 to 476	1943
South Dakota	S. B. 20, 1964	1964
Utah	Interlocal Cooperation Act, H.B. 85, Sec. 1-22	1965
Vermont	Vt. Stat. Ann., Sec. 24-4101	1963
Virginia	Va. Code Ann., Sec. 15.1-.21	1958
West Virginia	W. Va. Code, Sec. 8A-4-31	1937
Wisconsin	Wis. Stat. Ann., Sec. 66.30	1939

NOTE: Not all of these State statutes are equally broad either as to powers which may be exercised jointly or units of governments which may participate, nor do they all authorize both agreements and service contracts. A detailed analysis and comparison is contained in Leigh E. Grosenick, "A Comparative Analysis of Joint Exercise of Powers Legislation in the United States" (unpublished master's thesis, University of Minnesota, 1965).

SOURCE: Advisory Commission on Intergovernmental Relations, A Handbook for Interlocal Agreements and Contracts (Washington, 1967), p. 23.

considered a major shortcoming of the states that all of them have not permitted full interlocal cooperation through such devices.

While stressing formal agreements and contracts, one should not neglect the large number of highly effective informal interlocal agreements used to coordinate governmental action in the metropolis. Neighboring public officials faced with common problems often compare notes and reach agreement on a common professional solution. In many of these cases professional bonds are stronger than the divisions of geography and governmental boundaries. For example, police departments in metropolitan areas frequently cooperate in the apprehension of criminals even though hard and fast procedures have not been established for them to follow. A telephone call or a call over a common police radio frequency (established by the Federal Communications Commission because of a shortage of available frequencies) will often result in coordinated pursuit and roadblocks designed to stop the criminal suspect.

Critics of this approach tend to emphasize that such contracts and agreements usually encompass only one of the many functions which are beyond the capabilities of the single local unit and in many cases fall short of covering the entire functional area. They also emphasize the ad hoc nature of the informal agreement—these agreements are concluded as individual problems arise and are intended only to provide a solution to the case at hand, rather than providing a long-range solution to all similar problems in the particular functional or service area.

METROPOLITAN COUNCILS OF GOVERNMENTS. By 1967, eleven metropolitan areas had responded to the need for joint planning and cooperation by forming metropolitan councils of governments. These councils are associations of public officials representing the governments within the metropolitan area. Their purpose is to encourage coordination and cooperation in planning and research on common problems. Table 4–7 illustrates the degree and level of participation in the councils of eight metropolitan areas. The table clearly shows that participation is less than ideal and that full cooperation would be difficult at best without greater participation. However, participation in such councils is increasing, and more councils are being created across the country every year. This increase in activity can be traced directly to the action of the federal government which was aimed at encouraging area-wide planning. In the first place, current legislation makes it impossible for a community to receive federal aid for many projects unless the plans have been approved by an area-wide body such as a metropolitan council of governments. Under the Housing Act of 1965, the federal government will also pay two-thirds of the costs of establishing and operating such councils. These two factors

TABLE 4–7: **Membership in Metropolitan Councils of Governments**

	ORGANIZATION							
	ABAG	MACLOG	MWCOG	M-WVCOG	PSGC	RCEO	SCAG	SICC
Total number of municipalities and counties in region	100	60	70	4	74	388	148	386
Total, member governments:	86	32	13	5	8	59	90	6
Municipalities	78	26	7	1	4	53	84	
Counties	8	6	6	2	4	6	6	6
State				1				
School Districts				1				
Total number of member public officials	86	32	138	5	24	59	90	42

SOURCE: Advisory Commission on Intergovernmental Relations, *Metropolitan Councils of Governments* (Washington, 1966), p. 17.

KEY: ABAG: Association of Bay Area Governments (San Francisco)
MACLOG: Metropolitan Atlanta Council of Local Governments
MWCOG: Metropolitan Washington Council of Governments
M-WVCOG: Mid-Willamette Valley Council of Governments (Salem, Ore.)
PSGC: Puget Sound Regional Governmental Conference (Seattle-Tacoma)
RCEO: Regional Conference of Elected Officials (Philadelphia)
SCAG: Southern California Association of Governments (Los Angeles)
SICC: Supervisors Inter-County Committee (Detroit)

greatly encourage development of and participation in metropolitan councils.

These councils are faced with a variety of problems which serve to limit their effectiveness. In many cases, the need to achieve unanimity or consensus and the desire to avoid conflict limit the areas in which the council can act. If the council enjoys the participation of all of the units of government within the metropolitan area, there are few issues upon which such a large number of governments can be expected to unanimously agree. Some councils can operate by majority rule, but these are a minority, and very few councils can be expected to move in this direction in the future since it would involve a serious surrender of the powers of local government which so many of the participants hold dear. The councils are also limited in that the participants have limited interest, power, and time to devote to council activities. This second limitation underscores the need for adequate staff support to provide for the continuous operation of the council and the conduct of research on a long-term basis. This staff support may either be provided by a full-time staff hired by the council itself or by the professional staffs of the constituent governments on a cooperative basis. The third limitation is in the area of participation. There is a need for greater involvement in the decisions of the council by nonmember public officials and by the public in general. This could be provided by public hearings and discussions of plans and proposals before the council.[35]

STATE ACTION. One of the more drastic solutions to metropolitan problems is the transferal of all area-wide functions to the state government. Few reformers would go this far, since there are at least some area-wide functions and services that can be adequately performed within the metropolis. However, a more moderate transferal of functions can and does take place when the state has the resources to do the job, when the function is not performed within the area, when local performance does not meet state minimum standards, or when the failure to perform the function satisfactorily will seriously affect the rest of the state. In most of these cases, the local governments continue to share in the administration of the function. This response has the advantage of broadening the base of support for the function, enjoying economies of scale, avoiding duplication of effort, and relieving local financial burdens.[36]

There are many opportunities for state action in metropolitan areas short of the assumption of the responsibility for the performance of functions. Because of the degree to which state statutes and constitutions circumscribe local governmental powers, almost all of the responses to metropolitan problems mentioned so far require some state enabling action in the form of legislation or constitutional amendment. The states may also use grants-in-aid to enable local governments to more effectively meet their responsibilities and to equalize the uneven distribution of resources in the metropolitan area. The state agency for local affairs suggested in Chapter 2 can be a major contributor of advice and assistance to governments within the metropolis and can act as a coordinator of local efforts in the absence of a single unit of metropolitan government. The states have been quite slow in recognizing these challenges and opportunities. Authorizations for local governments to act are slow in coming and limited in scope. Grants-in-aid outside of the educational functional area are few and far between. And most state departments of local affairs are not adequately prepared for massive participation in metropolitan problems.[37]

---

[35] Advisory Commission on Intergovernmental Relations, *Metropolitan Councils of Governments* (Washington, 1966), pp. 33–34.
[36] Advisory Commission on Intergovernmental Relations, *Metropolitan America*, pp. 93–94.
[37] See for example the recommendations in Luther Gulick, "Metropolitan Organization," *The Annals of the American Academy of Political and Social Science* 314 (1957): 61.

The Politics of Reform

Responses to metropolitan problems that call for serious structural modification of local government require voter approval; this in turn requires a great deal of political activity in organizing campaigns for and against the proposed structural changes. These campaigns are particularly important with respect to such responses as annexation, city-county consolidation, Dade County Metro, and Toronto Metro.

The Advisory Commission on Intergovernmental Relations conducted a study of eighteen efforts at structural reform in order to identify the issues, groups, and techniques that were relevant to the outcome of the reform effort.[38] The commission was able to make some general statements about the approach taken in these cases. For the most part, the proponents of reform stressed the inadequacy and weakness of the existing local governmental structures, the need for urban services in the outlying areas, and the need to achieve an area-wide allocation of the costs of metropolitan services through area-wide taxes. On the other hand, the opponents stressed the tendency to allocate costs more heavily to suburban areas, the "drastic" nature of the proposals, the possibility of lost jobs for local officials and employees, and the dilution of minority group influence in the central city. The proponents of reform represented a strange combination of interest groups. They included the League of Women Voters, the Chamber of Commerce, metropolitan newspapers, commercial and real estate interests, radio and television outlets, banks, central city officials, academicians, manufacturing industries, public utilities, and central city home owners. The opposition included farmers, rural home owners, county employees, suburban newspapers, suburban officials and employees, and suburban commercial interests. Labor unions, taxpayers' groups, neighborhood improvement groups, and racial minorities were either neutral or adopted widely different positions.

The commission found that certain techniques appeared to contribute to the success of the reform movement in the eight out of eighteen areas in which it did succeed. These techniques were state legislative support, careful staff preparation for the campaign, and the extensive use of public hearings on the proposed changes. Where the reform efforts failed, a variety of factors appeared to contribute strongly: (1) the failure of the general public to perceive a crisis, (2) the fear of higher taxes, (3) low voter participation, (4) competition with other reform approaches and efforts, and (5) overemphasis on efficiency and "good government" and

---

[38] This discussion draws from the summary of the study presented in Advisory Commission on Intergovernmental Relations, *Metropolitan America*, pp. 107–109.

underemphasis on the political realities and interests of the metropolis. This final point has been emphasized by other scholars as well. In speaking of metropolitan reform efforts, Charles Adrian remarked that "a more serious cause of rejection centered in their almost total lack of concern with the political process." [39]

The Critics of Reform

OVEREMPHASIS ON PROBLEMS. Many of the critics and some of the friends of metropolitan reform have pointed out that some problems that reformers have identified are facile oversimplifications of exceedingly complex phenomena. For example, the frequently cited problem of the unequal distribution of wealth between the rich suburbs and the central cities, and the concomitant tendency of suburbanites who work and shop in the central city to enjoy services and facilities for which they pay no taxes, is overdrawn at best. "Services rendered to individuals in their capacity of workers, shoppers, and other economic functionaries may in some instances be properly treated as a charge upon the business firm involved rather than upon the individual." [40] The central city does not suffer appreciably from the influx of suburbanites who work and shop in the city, since both the working and shopping are tax-generating activities. It is precisely when the suburbanite no longer comes to the city to shop and to work because of the economic decentralization of the metropolis that the central city suffers most from an economic point of view. In spite of much of the rhetoric of metropolitan reform, the inherent truth of this statement is recognized by most central cities in their often futile attempts to renew the central business district in order to generate more tax revenue.

Another central city-suburban difference that is frequently misunderstood as a metropolitan problem is the social and economic gap between the residents of the two areas. Current research into the characteristics of our SMSA's indicates that many of the social, economic, and educational differences between the city dweller and suburbanite are overdrawn. *"The fact is that for the majority of metropolitan areas in the United States there is not a ten percent difference between central cities and suburbs in their respective proportions of undereducated adults, high school dropouts, and families with low income."* [41] These findings lead us to believe that the sources of social problems are more evenly dis-

---

[39] Charles Adrian, "Metropology: Folklore and Field Research," *Public Administration Review* 21 (1961): 148.

[40] Fitch, "Metropolitan Financial Problems," p. 73.

[41] Advisory Commission on Intergovernmental Relations, *Metropolitan Social and Economic Disparities* (Washington, 1965), p. 26.

tributed in the metropolitan area than the standard reform literature has claimed. This does not mean the resources are adequate for the solution of social problems within the metropolis, but it does lead one to place greater emphasis on the resources of the total area rather than on differences within the area. For if resources and problems are in fact distributed fairly evenly throughout the area, then no amount of consolidation will magically produce additional resources with which to meet social problems.

THE ADEQUACY OF EXISTING STRUCTURES. "Reform ideology has assumed that a *multinucleated* governmental structure, characterized by a number of formally autonomous units, would result in either a breakdown in public services or such poor performance that popular dissatisfaction would make integration unavoidable. Neither of these events has occurred, in spite of great population growth and increased service demands." [42] By utilizing special districts, intergovernmental agreements, and cooperation through metropolitan councils of governments, metropolitan areas have met many of their problems without resorting to the more drastic forms of structural integration recommended by reformers. There is little empirical evidence that structural considerations are of major significance in determining the ability of the metropolis to meet its current problems. In fact the data on the performance of the larger urban units in performing services within their areal competence is far from encouraging. [43]

It has been suggested that the reason for this relatively effective performance by fragmented governments within the metropolis lies in their ability to cooperate in spite of their diversity of interests.

The assumption that each unit of local government acts independently without regard for other public interests in the metropolitan community has only a limited validity. . . . Contrary to the frequent assertion about the lack of a "metropolitan framework" for dealing with metropolitan problems, most metropolitan areas have a very rich and intricate "framework" for negotiating, adjudicating and deciding questions that affect their diverse public interests. [44]

The problem with this "rich and intricate framework" is that we know so little about its structure and the way in which it operates. Only the most cautious first steps have been taken toward finding a solution to this

---

[42] Robert Warren, "Political Form and Metropolitan Reform," *Public Administration Review* 24 (1964): 180. See also Robert Wood, "Metropolitan Government 1975: An Extrapolation of Trends," *American Political Science Review* 52 (1958): 112.

[43] H. Paul Friesma, "The Metropolis and the Maze of Local Government," *Urban Affairs Quarterly* 2 (1966): 85–89.

[44] Vincent Ostrom, Charles M. Tiebout, and Robert Warren, "The Organization of Government in Metropolitan Areas: A Theoretical Inquiry," *American Political Science Review* 55 (1961): 831 and 842.

problem. The most productive of these is Matthew Holden's suggestion of a parallel between international politics and metropolitan politics as diplomatic systems.[45] Holden suggests that the rich theoretical literature in international politics can provide us with a series of hypotheses which, when tested, might better enable us to understand the process of conflict resolution and consensus in the metropolis. As political scientists follow Holden's lead, we will be able to offer more satisfactory explanations of the ability of local governments to deal with their metropolitan problems in the absence of successful structural integration.

Summary

The fact that an increasing number of modern American cities find themselves in a metropolitan environment has raised a variety of challenges to local government with respect to performing old functions and services and responding to new service needs. Those metropolitan reformers who sought to meet these challenges through the structural integration of the governmental units within the metropolis have had few successes. Instead, the greatest emphasis has been placed upon intergovernmental cooperation, which allows individual local units to maintain their integrity but which also results in a service performance level which is acceptable if not optimal. Such developments may be considered realistic, even if they are not fully satisfactory to the reform-oriented. As the problem area ceases to be the metropolis and moves on through the megalopolis to the ecumenopolis, the difficulties in integrating constituent governmental units into a single unit that includes the entire problem area become staggering. If the political problems involved in merging municipalities, counties, and special districts into a single unit are great, how much greater are the problems of merging states or portions of states or of merging nations or portions of nations, given the prevailing ideologies in the United States and the world? It is quite possible that urban society could not survive if it were forced to wait for these ideologies to change before it could take any action to meet the problems of greater urban concentration. Intergovernmental cooperation has at least enabled us to survive, and it has done so without disturbing too many of the ideologies which govern our attitudes toward local government.

Suggested Readings

Advisory Commission on Intergovernmental Relations. A Handbook for Interlocal Agreements and Contracts. Washington, 1967.

---

[45] Matthew Holden, Jr., "The Governance of the Metropolis as a Problem in Diplomacy," The Journal of Politics 26 (1964): 627–647.

————. *Metropolitan America: Challenge to Federalism.* Intergovernmental Relations Subcommittee of the Committee on Government Operations, U.S. House of Representatives. Washington, 1966.

————. *Metropolitan Councils of Governments.* Washington, 1966.

Bollens, John C., ed. *Exploring the Metropolitan Community.* Berkeley, 1961.

Bollens, John C., and Schmandt, Henry J. *The Metropolis: Its People, Politics, and Economic Life.* New York, 1965.

Booth, David A. *Metropolitics: The Nashville Consolidation.* East Lansing, 1963.

Bromage, Arthur W. *Political Representation in Metropolitan Agencies.* Ann Arbor, 1962.

Crouch, Winston, and Dinerman, Beatrice. *Southern California Metropolis: A Study in Development of Government for a Metropolitan Area.* Berkeley and Los Angeles, 1964.

Eldredge, H. Wentworth. *Taming Megalopolis.* 2 vols. New York, 1967.

Gottmann, Jean. *Megalopolis.* New York, 1961.

Greer, Scott. *Governing the Metropolis.* New York, 1962.

————. *Metropolitics: A Study of Political Culture.* New York, 1963.

Gulick, Luther. *The Metropolitan Problem and American Ideas.* New York, 1962.

Kaplan, Harold. *Urban Political Systems: A Functional Analysis of Metro Toronto.* New York, 1968.

Martin, Roscoe. *Metropolis in Transition: Local Government Adaptation to Changing Urban Needs.* Washington, 1963.

Schmandt, Henry J.; Steinbecker, Paul G.; and Wendel, George D. *Metropolitan Reform in St. Louis.* New York, 1961.

Schmandt, Henry J., and Standing, William H. *The Milwaukee Metropolitan Study Commission.* Bloomington, Ind., 1965.

Sofen, Edward. *The Miami Metropolitan Experiment.* 2d ed. New York, 1966.

Warren, Robert O. *Government in Metropolitan Regions: A Reappraisal of Fractionated Political Organization.* Davis, Calif., 1966.

Wood, Robert. *1400 Governments.* Cambridge, Mass., 1961.

Part Two
The Politics
and Structure of Urban
Government

The six chapters of this part will present a general picture of how urban political systems operate. As many of the relevant decision-making factors as space permits will be introduced. Unfortunately, the relationships between these factors will not always be clear. Far too little is known about the ways in which forms of political participation and structural variables affect decisions in our cities. The emphasis in these chapters is upon raising the appropriate questions for the study of the urban political process, rather than upon providing many answers. A study of this part will make it abundantly clear that those who have developed the easiest prescriptions—both structural and procedural—have focused their attention on questions that were at best too narrow and at worst wholly irrelevant.

chapter 5

Parties
and the Electoral
Process

❡The policy-making activities of local government rest ultimately, if somewhat indirectly, on the consent of an electorate which periodically registers its preferences for candidates and parties in local elections. Centered on the influencing of this consent are the organized political parties.[1]

This declaration of the importance of political parties to the decision-making process in urban government must, unfortunately, be shown to be too absolute; the real world rarely admits to the application of such declarations. The rest of this chapter will be devoted to explaining and modifying the statement in order to offer a better description of the nature and importance of the electoral process in our cities.

The Politics of Nonpartisanship

The first qualification that must be offered is that elections in the majority of our cities have been identified as "nonpartisan." The perceptive reader might well wonder how it is possible for parties to be at the center of the influencing of consent in urban politics if most elections in our cities are nonpartisan. The answer lies in the definition of "party" and of "nonpartisan" which one accepts. Professor Charles Adrian has suggested

---

[1] Peter H. Rossi and Phillips Cutright, "The Impact of Party Organization in an Industrial Setting," in *Community Political Systems*, ed. Morris Janowitz (Glencoe, 1961), p. 81.

that, in America, nonpartisanship is that state in which public offices are filled without placing a party designation on the ballot and in which the ballot is long enough that the affiliation of the individual office-seeker is not obvious.[2] In some areas, it is enough that no national party labels appear on the ballot, while in other jurisdictions local party labels are banned as well.

Such definitions of nonpartisanship are satisfactory only to those who think of parties and politics in terms of groups such as the Republicans and the Democrats that label themselves as parties. Most political scientists, however, would use a much broader definition of party and, therefore, would adopt a much narrower view of true nonpartisanship. It makes a great deal of sense to claim that "any . . . association which backs candidates, raises money for and conducts a campaign, and espouses a platform functions as a party in the local political arena."[3] The most extreme form of this position is that taken by Adrian when he claims that "all elections are partisan in the sense that people and groups take sides and struggle against one another for victory."[4] We can stop short of such an extreme statement and simply say that any group that recruits candidates for public office, mobilizes electoral support for those candidates in elections, and attempts to focus the attention of successful candidates upon particular governmental programs while they are in office possesses the major attributes of a political party, whether it chooses to label itself as such or not. This definition clearly indicates that the mere absence of national party designations on the official ballot does not make an election truly nonpartisan.

In an effort to introduce a more meaningful classification than the usual partisan-nonpartisan dichotomy, Professor Adrian examined the electoral patterns of many of our major cities which had "nonpartisan" elections and developed a new typology of nonpartisanship which permits more accurate description.[5] In the first type, at least one party is still active in local elections, and only those candidates supported by the majority party have any hope of getting elected. The outstanding current example is the City of Chicago, where Democratic dominance of the city's nonpartisan aldermanic elections is well known. Adrian selected cities such as Omaha, Minneapolis, and Cincinnati as examples of his second type. Here slates of candidates are supported by various groups including political parties. In the third and most common type, groups support slates

---

[2] Charles R. Adrian, "Some General Characteristics of Nonpartisan Elections," *American Political Science Review* 46 (1952): 767.

[3] J. Leiper Freeman, "Local Party Systems: Theoretical Considerations and a Case Analysis," *The American Journal of Sociology* 64 (1958): 283.

[4] Adrian, "General Characteristics of Nonpartisan Elections," p. 767.

[5] Charles R. Adrian, "A Typology of Nonpartisan Elections," *Western Political Quarterly* 12 (1959): 449–458.

of candidates, but parties rarely if ever participate. Cities with weak local party organizations, such as Los Angeles and San Francisco, are frequently-cited examples of this type. In the fourth type, the election is a grab bag in which neither slates nor parties are used to mobilize voter support. Throughout the typology Adrian uses the party designation to refer to major, national parties, not in the broad manner suggested earlier. When this typology is applied to the better than 60 percent of our cities over 5,000 that claim to be nonpartisan, most of them would probably fall in the last two categories. This indicates that in most of our cities national political parties play no overt role in mobilizing electoral support for candidates.

THE GOALS OF NONPARTISANSHIP. The early twentieth century reformers who were responsible for the initiation of nonpartisan local government developed a rationale for their recommendations; this rationale is accepted by large numbers of people today in their defense of nonpartisanship. To these reform elements, city government is largely as a matter of business. It can and should be separate from "politics," which they believe consists largely of efforts to accommodate public policy to the selfish interests of individuals and groups in the community, while the "business" of government concerns itself with the economic and efficient administration of the best interests of the entire community. The early reformers also saw little connection between national and local issues. They felt that the operation of national parties on the local level diverted the attention of the electorate from important local issues and, at the same time, bogged down national parties in local minutiae. Nonpartisanship was designed to free both levels of government to work effectively on their own problems, and to make these problems more visible to the voter.

The destruction of the party organization or machine was central to nonpartisanship. The organization was held responsible for the accommodation of public policy to individual and group interests and had to be destroyed if this accommodation was to yield to a more "rational" pursuit of the common good. The reform element further held that more talented and honest men could be attracted to public office once the necessity for dealing with the corruption of political parties was removed.[6]

THE IMPACT OF NONPARTISANSHIP. Although insufficient data exist to pass final judgment on the effects of nonpartisanship, a tentative evaluation can be offered. In the first place, as the Adrian typology suggests, where party organizations were strong and where the electorate had identified

---

[6] This section draws heavily from Eugene C. Lee, *The Politics of Nonpartisanship: A Study of California Cities* (Berkeley and Los Angeles, 1960), pp. 22–30.

them as important agents of public policy, these organizations continued to function much as they had before, even though official party designations had been eliminated. In most of these cities, the same selfish interests continued to express themselves, and, if public officials had been dishonest before, they continued to be so. The infamous Hague Machine operated quite comfortably under a nonpartisan ballot in Jersey City, New Jersey.

In other cities where conflicting social and economic interests led to conflicting views of the public interest, the use of local parties and slates of candidates replaced national party designations when the ties to national parties were too weak to resist nonpartisanship. Such obviously "political" activities clearly frustrated the efforts of reformers to remove "politics" from the "business" of local government. A series of studies has indicated that the cleavages that manifest themselves in nonpartisan electoral conflict reflect the basic social cleavages in the community. To the extent that earlier partisan divisions reflected the same cleavages, there is little difference in the electoral outcome of partisan and nonpartisan elections.[7]

The attempt to focus the attention of the electorate on local issues has been largely unsuccessful. City politics has remained largely a politics of personality rather than of issues. Critics claim that this can be traced to the absence of political parties to formulate issues and platforms. However, the defenders of nonpartisanship hurry to point out that political parties have done little if any better in centering urban election campaigns on the issues rather than on candidate personality.[8] The most serious failure of the nonpartisan reformer with respect to issues rested in his attempt to separate national and local issues, especially in the big cities. By the 1930s it was clear to many urban Americans that the major policy decisions of urban governments and the domestic and foreign policy decisions of the national government were bound closely together.[9] A look at the platform of either major party in the 1960s will demonstrate that these ties have been strengthened over the years. Any attempt to separate the issues of central importance to our cities from those of central im-

---

[7] Oliver P. Williams and Charles R. Adrian, "The Insulation of Local Politics Under the Nonpartisan Ballot," *American Political Science Review* 53 (1959): 1052–1063; Robert H. Salisbury and Gordon Black, "Class and Party in Partisan and Nonpartisan Elections," in *Political Behavior in America*, ed. Heinz Eulau (New York, 1966), pp. 158–175; Gerald M. Pomper, "Ethnic and Group Voting in Nonpartisan Municipal Elections," *Public Opinion Quarterly* 30 (1966): 79–97; and Freeman, "Local Party Systems."

[8] Lee, *Politics of Nonpartisanship*, pp. 168–169.

[9] Charles E. Gilbert, "National Political Alignments and the Politics of Large Cities," *Political Science Quarterly* 79 (1964): 49.

portance to the nation as a whole has been rendered futile by the urbanization process discussed in Chapter 1.

The effect of nonpartisanship upon the recruitment of candidates has not been adequately studied. The reformer operates on the questionable assumption that inefficiency and dishonesty on the part of holders of public office is related causally to their affiliation with a political party. Even a casual observer of urban politics can easily find enough examples of inefficiency and corruption which have survived in a truly nonpartisan environment to cast doubt upon such an assumption. The major difficulty with any comparison of partisan and nonpartisan officeholders lies in our inability to find criteria and standards that are relevant to the comparison. If we say that nonpartisan city A has managed to recruit better city councilmen than partisan city B, on what have we based our evaluation? Education? Socioeconomic status? Voting record? In most cases, it is some combination of factors, including at least those mentioned above. It is commonly held that a college-educated, upper middle-class business or professional man with a record of supporting civic improvement projects of the slum clearance and urban renewal type is a "good" councilman. This implies a theory of representation somewhat akin to that of Edmund Burke, who felt that the representative was elected to exercise his own best judgment, responsible but not responsive to the people. Generally, those attempting to evaluate the performance of democratic institutions prefer to consider both responsiveness and responsibility although, once again, the criteria and standards used are more than a little vague. The end result is a somewhat impressionistic judgement that the public officials selected on a nonpartisan ballot are not demonstrably worse than those selected on a partisan ballot.[10]

Dr. Charles Adrian has pointed out another recruitment problem that is raised by nonpartisanship.[11] To the extent that the device is successful in eliminating the national parties from local political contests, it separates the recruitment channels for partisan and nonpartisan office and permits movement from one political arena to the other only with great difficulty. Each system theoretically must maintain its own pool of candidates. In practice, however, the separation has not been as complete as theory demands. Even in California, where nonpartisanship in local government has been zealously pursued, candidates have moved from partisan to nonpartisan office and vice versa with relative ease.

Perhaps the most serious criticism of nonpartisanship is the charge that

---

[10] See Lee, *Politics of Nonpartisanship*, pp. 170–171 for the strongest possible statement.

[11] Adrian, "General Characteristics of Nonpartisan Elections," pp. 769–771.

TABLE 5–1: Competition and Incumbency in Council Elections
in Cities over 25,000

	No. of Cities Reporting	No. of Candidates per Office	Percent of Incumbents Seeking Reelection	Percent of Running Incumbents Reelected	Percent of Offices Filled by Incumbents
Form of Election					
Partisan	157	2.0	62	76	47
Nonpartisan	414	2.2	61	75	46
Form of Government					
Mayor-council	186	2.0	63	78	49
Commission	58	2.6	71	74	52
Council-manager	322	2.6	63	73	46
Population Group					
Over 500,000	19	2.5	77	88	67
250,000 to 500,000	26	3.0	66	76	50
100,000 to 250,000	72	2.0	59	78	46
50,000 to 100,000	150	2.3	60	71	43
25,000 to 50,000	307	2.0	61	76	46
All cities over 25,000	574	2.2	61	76	46

SOURCE: Eugene C. Lee, "City Elections: A Statistical Profile," *Municipal Yearbook*, 1963 (Chicago, 1963), p. 77. Reprinted by permission of the International City Management Association.

it favors the White, Anglo-Saxon, Protestant middle class.[12] On balance, the existing empirical evidence appears to support such a charge. After studying nonpartisan elections in Des Moines, Iowa, Salisbury and Black concluded that "nonpartisanship gives some additional weight to class by means of a differential turnout, and this in turn gives upper income groups relatively greater power in the local community."[13] In other words, when they are deprived of the vital cues of party affiliation and the stimulus of party organization, the lower income groups tend to vote less frequently. A study of California nonpartisan elections revealed the same phenomenon in cities that had enough social and economic divisions to have a competitive political climate. In such cities, the Republican party was found to have an advantage when no special effort was made to mobilize normally Democratic voters.[14] Although the absence of party labels occasionally allows a Democrat to slip into office in a city dominated by the

---

[12] See for example Robert Lane, *Political Life* (Glencoe, 1959), pp. 269–271.

[13] Salisbury and Black, "Class and Party," p. 169.

[14] Heinz Eulau, Betty H. Zisk, and Kenneth Prewitt, "Latent Partisanship in Nonpartisan Elections: Effects of Political Milieu and Mobilization," in *The Electoral Process*, eds. M. Kent Jennings and L. Harmon Ziegler (Englewood Cliffs, N.J., 1966), p. 215.

TABLE 5–2: **Competition and Incumbency in Mayoralty Elections in Cities over 25,000**

	No. of Cities Report- ing	No. of Candidates per Office	Percent of Incum- bents Seeking Reelection	Percent of Running Incum- bents Reelected	Percent of Offices Filled by Incumbents
Form of Election					
Partisan	94	2.3	63	78	46
Nonpartisan	173	2.5	68	64	44
Form of Government					
Mayor-council	125	2.5	74	66	49
Commission	32	2.5	100	53	53
Council manager	107	2.4	47	74	35
Population Group					
Over 500,000	10	2.7	80	63	50
250,000 to 500,000	15	3.8	60	56	33
100,000 to 250,000	32	2.8	56	83	47
50,000 to 100,000	62	2.4	69	74	52
25,000 to 50,000	148	2.3	67	62	41
All cities over 25,000	267	2.5	66	67	44

SOURCE: Eugene C. Lee, "City Elections: A Statistical Profile," *Municipal Yearbook*, 1963 (Chicago, 1963), p. 77. Reprinted by permission of the International City Management Association.

Republican party,[15] such cases are few in number compared to those in which Republicans are elected in normally Democratic cities. But let us note that Republican and Democratic party labels have been used in many studies as if they were synonymous with certain socioeconomic groups. While such identification is accurate on a national, general scale, regional differences in party affiliation may dictate that the upper income groups that tend to dominate the nonpartisan cities are affiliated with the national Democratic party. In most of these cases, however, competitive politics are unusual.

The upper middle-class bias of nonpartisanship is expressed by some as a natural conservatism that results from the return of a high percentage of incumbents to office. Tables 5–1 and 5–2 show clearly that in both councilmanic and mayoral elections the percentage of offices filled by incumbents is lower in nonpartisan than in partisan elections. These data are the result of a nation-wide survey of cities over 25,000, taken by the International City Managers' Association. They represent the best hard data available at present on the subject and point to factors other than a high rate of incumbency for an explanation of any conservative tendencies in nonpartisan governments.

---

[15] Williams and Adrian, "Insulation of Local Politics," p. 1063.

Another charge that has been leveled against nonpartisan elections is that they prevent the electorate from holding the groups that control government collectively responsible for their acts.[16] The emphasis is on the performance of individual elected officials rather than controlling groups. Defenders of nonpartisanship have pointed out quite correctly that this criticism presumes that parties operate effectively as agents of collective responsibility. Even at the local level, where party discipline and control are at their strongest, they are not sufficiently potent to provide truly responsible party government in most instances. Where party organizations have been strong enough to provide "responsible" government, they have also been strong enough to resist erosion of their control by institutional nonpartisanship. Even in partisan systems the voter must direct his attention to the performance of individual officeholders if he is to effectively assess their performance.

Where a true separation of national parties from the local electoral process has been achieved, special problems are raised in financing both partisan and nonpartisan campaigns.[17] Partisan and nonpartisan candidates become competitors for scarce resources. There is nothing inherently wrong in such competition if it does not raise the total cost of elections in the long run. However, maintaining local campaign organizations for the national parties as well as organizations for nonpartisan slates, or worse yet for individual nonpartisan candidates, undoubtedly results in a great deal of expensive duplication of effort. In this sense, nonpartisanship can be accused of defeating its own avowed purpose of greater economy and efficiency by promoting greater expense and inefficiency.

NONPARTISANSHIP EVALUATED. If nonpartisan politics operated according to the prescriptions of civic reformers, and if all of the cues provided by parties and special interests were in fact removed, the result would undoubtedly be chaos. Robert Wood has pointed out the weakest point in nonpartisan reform ideology:

> Inescapably, there is a belief that the individual can and should arrive at his political convictions untutored and unled; an expectation that in the formal process of election and decision-making a consensus will emerge through the process of right reason and by the higher call to the common good.[18]

Fortunately for those of us who must exercise the often unpleasant task of selecting government officials at the polls, political education and political leadership continue in a nonpartisan environment. This education and leadership inevitably express a particular view of the common good. To the

---

[16] Adrian, "General Characteristics of Nonpartisan Elections," p. 775.

[17] Adrian, "General Characteristics of Nonpartisan Elections," pp. 771–772.

[18] Robert Wood, *Suburbia: Its People and Their Politics* (Boston, 1959), p. 157.

extent that this view is shared by the rest of the relevant community, it may in fact approximate some sort of justifiable concept of the common good. However, to the extent that competing views of the common good exist, the special interests supporting each view will have to battle for public support of their positions.

In his treatment of nonpartisan politics, Dr. Eugene Lee points to tension between consensus or agreement on the common good and conflict as basic to any evaluation of the political life of a community.[19] A number of community characteristics are considered helpful in determining whether a particular city will emphasize conflict or consensus. These characteristics include size, character of the population (both social and economic), the quality of the city's institutions, and the nature of the community press, to name a few. Once these characteristics have been evaluated, Lee suggests that it would be possible to determine the suitability of nonpartisanship to community politics. The general thesis is that the more homogeneous the community, the more consensus-oriented its politics, and the more fruitful nonpartisan politics will be. However, in such communities there appears to be no real difference between nonpartisanship and one party dominance.[20] In the heterogeneous, conflict-oriented community, the abolition of parties will simply result in the formation of local parties or slates which will perform the function previously performed by the national parties. Since the conflict-resolution function must be performed if such communities are to continue as operative political entities, true nonpartisanship is illusory.

The Urban Political Party

Political parties, therefore, continue to play an important role in many of our cities. This is true in the nominally nonpartisan cities as well as in the more than one-third of the cities which still maintain overtly partisan elections. But even in cities that have remained relatively "unreformed" by the wave of nonpartisanship, our century has seen significant changes in the form and style of politics.

THE BOSS AND THE MACHINE. The terms *boss* and *machine* have become two of the most common perjoratives in urban politics. The muckraking cartoonist's portrayal of the urban party leader as a fat, cigar-smoking, greedy crook manipulating urban government to serve his own selfish ends is familiar. This stereotype, like many half-truths, misleads more than it informs:

---

[19] Lee, *Politics of Nonpartisanship,* p. 184.
[20] Eulau, Zisk, and Prewitt, "Latent Partisanship," p. 211.

The boss and his machine we now recognize to have been functional for the newly industrial city; a growing army of public job-holders was recruited, a vast immigration was socialized and provided means of advancement in the urban society, welfare needs were at least minimally provided for, further extensions of public improvement programs were constructed, albeit expensively, and specific services were rendered to the economic elites as well.[21]

It is clear that the great majority of the residents of our largest cities in the late nineteenth and early twentieth centuries found a government controlled by bosses and machines at least minimally satisfactory according to their criteria. Otherwise, those worthy institutions would have been unable to survive, for ultimately they were responsible to the electorate. Pointing out that the machine effectively controlled the opposition party and thus made protest voting difficult is not enough. There appear to be no indications that a majority of big city residents would have exercised such a protest had it been available. Certainly the events of the 1960s present clear evidence of the ability of even significant minorities to register their dissatisfaction with urban government when they consider the polls to be ineffective in guaranteeing responsibility and responsiveness. The machine was remarkably efficient in providing the employment and municipal and personal services necessary to sustain its constituents. That the corruption of the machine rendered such jobs and services inordinately expensive to the community at large was of little concern to the average citizen who bore little of the cost directly. All that he really knew or cared about was that his city government and the party that ran it were there when he needed them.

An interesting study of the 1946 mayoral election in Boston revealed some of the factors which contributed to the success of the boss and the machine.[22] This election was particularly notable since the boss, James Curley, was himself a candidate for mayor and was, during the campaign, under indictment for fraud. In spite of the fact that his personal honesty had been publicly questioned in the fraud indictment, Curley won the election. He drew his support primarily from the lower classes. The Democratic party organization was held solidly behind Curley by virtue of the close identification of the voters with their ward captains and the maintenance of support from the Irish, Italian, and Jewish minorities, all of which had members high up in machine echelons. The Republicans, on the other hand, were divided in their support of Curley's opponents. Another advantage that Curley enjoyed was the fact that many voters were familiar with him and felt that they knew him personally. This

---

[21] Robert H. Salisbury, "Urban Politics: The New Convergence of Power," *The Journal of Politics* 26 (1964): 782.

[22] Jerome S. Bruner and Sheldon J. Korchin, "The Boss and the Vote: Case Study in City Politics," *Public Opinion Quarterly* 10 (1946): 1–23.

familiarity manifested itself either in violent dislike of Curley or in votes for him. How is it possible that the people of Boston could support a man who seemed to make no secret of his dishonesty? The study revealed a series of rationalizations used by Curley supporters to justify their votes. Many viewed the boss as a modern Robin Hood who robbed the rich and gave to the poor. The costs of machine dishonesty appeared remote to these people, while the benefits were real and immediate. This led to the further rationalization that whatever else the machine did, it gave the little man a break. A third justification was the efficiency of the machine. This was not efficiency in the cost-benefits sense but in the sense that demands were met quickly and effectively by ward politicians. The final rationalization was that all politicians were crooks and that Curley was no worse in that respect than were his opponents.

> Finally, in summing up Curley's appeal, one should end on the note of the comparative stimulus value of the personalities involved in the campaign. Rather than diminishing it, the anonymity of life in a great city has intensified the appeal of the colorful personality.[23]

This study is illustrative of the basis for support of bosses and machines elsewhere. Many of these same attitudes manifest themselves among the members of low income minorities in our big cities today. While most big cities no longer have a strong political party organization to take advantage of these attitudes, occasionally a strong personal organization like that of Congressman Adam Clayton Powell of New York can demonstrate its reality in contemporary urban politics.

Political scientists disagree over the characteristics that can be identified as differentiating the urban political party in its newer forms from the machine. In spite of their disagreements, it is possible to make four statements about the old-style machine that indicate its peculiar nature: [24]

1. The party was organized in a disciplined hierarchy led by a single executive or a unified board.
2. Public officials were controlled by the party by virtue of the fact that the party controlled the nomination process.
3. The party leadership was often lower class in origin and did not usually hold office.
4. Support from party workers and a core of voters was maintained by a mixture of material rewards and nonideological psychic rewards, such as the camaraderie of the political club.

---

[23] Bruner and Korchin, "The Boss and the Vote," p. 23.
[24] Fred I. Greenstein, "The Changing Pattern of Urban Party Politics," in *American Party Politics: Essays and Readings*, eds. Donald G. Herzberg and Gerald M. Pomper (New York, 1966), pp. 253–263.

Any political party that possesses these characteristics can accurately be called a machine. But these factors really constitute an ideal machine that existed in its pure form in few cities. Most of these things are matters of degree, and parties could be effectively machine dominated without having all of the characteristics in their most extreme form.

The decline of the boss and the machine in urban politics can be traced more to social and economic developments within the cities themselves than to the efforts of middle-class reform elements. Reformers worried the bosses very little. Civic virtue and reform were a hobby for their practitioners, but machine politics was a way of life for the boss. Reformers generally lacked the staying power necessary to take advantage of their short-run successes. The boss was willing to lose an occasional election as long as he could maintain control of the machine and its patronage mechanism which would guarantee his success in the long pull.[25] On the other hand, reform movements were quite likely to disintegrate immediately following any electoral failure to unseat the boss, and they had to be reconstituted with each new election.

The social and economic factors that led to the decline of the machine were varied. Although they developed over several decades, they came to a head in the 1930s in most cities. In the first place, a generally nativist sentiment in the country encouraged the adoption of a restrictive immigration policy which choked off the flow of ethnic minorities to our great cities. Although existing minorities were not assimilated rapidly enough to cause an immediate sharp decline in the political base of the machine, the freeze on immigration did result in the stagnation of that base. Second, the onset of a serious depression revealed the welfare system of the machine to be woefully inadequate for handling unemployment, sickness, and hunger on a large scale. As the national government established programs that responded to the needs of the disadvantaged in the cities, it effectively cut the ground out from under the machine. Even when the economy returned to normal these federal programs would continue to provide for health, welfare, and employment on a much grander scale than could the machine.

To give reformers their due, however, two successful reforms did contribute to the decline of the machine. The first of these was the establishment of civil service. Civil service drastically reduced the number of jobs which were available to the party machine for distribution as patronage. The second, the development of professional purchasing and accounting systems in our largest cities, seriously reduced the opportunity for graft. The material rewards that had contributed so heavily to the main-

---

[25] See James Q. Wilson, "The Economy of Patronage," *Journal of Political Economy* 69 (1961): 369–380.

tenance of support for the machine either dried up or were replaced by more productive sources. The nonideological psychic rewards of fun and good fellowship were inadequate for the maintenance of anything but a small core of the party faithful.

In some cities, machine politics of the old style continue to exist in a modified form in spite of these changes. Primarily in the industrial cities of the East, where fewer barriers have been erected to machine operation and the needs of the population are great enough that the social welfare programs of the New Deal and subsequent eras have not satisfied people, parties have been able to maintain the old patterns of politics.[26] In the rest of the country, however, a new style of partisan politics has emerged.

THE ORGANIZATION AND THE LEADER. Professor Samuel Eldersveld suggests that one of the major characteristics of the new style of urban party politics is a change in the nature of the leadership.[27] He sees this leadership exercised through a "stratarchy" rather than through a unified hierarchy as it was in the machine. In the stratarchy, political power is diffused at each level in the party structure, and the heterogeneity of the party makes unified control both difficult and unwise. The elite leadership structure is pluralistic in nature, and there is a high turnover of leaders.

While the machine was primarily a lower-class organization, the new style political party draws its cadre from the middle and upper classes. The new "grey flannel suit" image has replaced that of the fat, cigar-smoking ward heeler. In conjunction with this new image, it is now fashionable for the party leaders to hold office themselves. This change in image has brought with it concomitant changes in the rewards of politics. Party workers and the hard core of supporting voters are attracted primarily through psychic rewards. Additional social status is conferred upon some by virtue of their party activity.[28] For others, the rewards are primarily ideological in the sense that they gain satisfaction from working with their fellows for a "cause." To the extent that the new style politician adopts old techniques of constituent services in order to muster support, the services are centered on the needs of upper- and middle-class constituents who generally reflect his value structure.[29]

The control that the organization does exercise over public officials is still exercised primarily by virtue of some control over the process of nominations. However, the heterogeneity of the party structure and its more pluralistic leadership makes the possibility of a successful challenge to the

---

[26] Greenstein, "Changing Pattern," p. 260.

[27] Samuel J. Eldersveld, *Political Parties: A Behavioral Analysis* (Chicago, 1964), pp. 9–11.

[28] Eldersveld, *Political Parties*, p. 11.

[29] Greenstein, "Changing Pattern," p. 262.

ruling groups somewhat greater. The heterogeneity of the party organization renders the organization dependent upon other groups within the
urban environment—Chambers of Commerce, labor unions, newspapers,
civic groups—whereas these groups used to be dependent upon the machine for their political influence.

The major difficulty with the new style of politics is that it is much less
clear-cut than machine politics. Pluralism and heterogeneity increase the
confusion in urban politics. It is increasingly difficult for the voter to intelligently fix responsibility for the decisions of government. The complex
amalgam of party and interest groups does not lend itself easily to the
sort of simplified analysis that a voter is forced to make. We appear to be
caught on the horns of a serious dilemma. If our urban parties are rendered responsible by virtue of the old-style hierarchical organization and
centralized control, then the voter may be unable to affect the decisions
of his government even though he knows who is responsible for them.
On the other hand, if pluralism and heterogeneity in the party structure
grant much easier access to the various groups in the community and
enable them to influence governmental decisions, then sooner or later the
political process becomes so complicated as to render any discussion of
responsible democratic government meaningless. For most political scientists, the answer lies somewhere between the two extremes. We unsuccess-
fully attempt to beg the question by prescribing political parties that are
centralized enough to be held responsible for governmental actions, yet
heterogeneous and pluralistic enough to admit to the possibility of altering those actions should the public call for changes. The search for a
rational role for political parties in our cities must always be conducted
in full awareness of the tension between these competing values.

ELECTORAL COMPETITION. The discussion so far has avoided the basic question of competition in partisan urban politics. Some students of political
parties have suggested that the chance for meaningful competition between the two major political parties increases with urbanization. For the
most part, this tendency is traced to the greater social and economic
diversity that results from urbanization and industrialization.[30] Urban
electoral competition is frequently viewed as a major aid to democratic
government on the assumption that it facilitates governmental accountability and provides the voter with a choice.[31] Unfortunately such assumptions are not always supported by the evidence. If one uses the closeness
of elections and the frequency of defeat for incumbents as measures of

---

[30] Phillips Cutright, "Urbanization and Competitive Party Politics," *Journal of Politics* 25 (1963): 552–564.
[31] Charles E. Gilbert and Christopher Clague, "Electoral Competition and Electora
Systems in Large Cities," *Journal of Politics* 24 (1962): 347.

competition,[32] it is possible to find competition of a variety which neither facilitates accountability nor provides the voter with a significant choice. If the competition indicated by both accountability and choice is to be democratically productive and not merely a beauty contest, the election must be oriented toward a significant issue. Since the low issue content of both partisan and nonpartisan urban elections was noted earlier, it should be obvious that the democratic value of much of this competition is at least questionable.

One of the major goals of urban reformers was to increase electoral competition through the alteration of the electoral system. The most important such alteration was the institution of nonpartisanship. Research into the impact of such alterations has indicated that they were for the most part unsuccessful:

> In general, such factors as prevailing (national) party preferences, the pattern of local interests, and local traditions of political organization appear to outweigh the influence of electoral systems on electoral competition; this even applies on occasion to the important partisan-nonpartisan distinction.[33]

Political Participation

One of the most frequently cited characteristics of democracy—cited both as a virtue and as a requisite—is the participation of the citizenry in the political process. Participation is particularly stressed in any discussion of local government, on the general assumption that participation increases with the closeness of government to the people and with the greater degree of familiarity with candidates and issues that results. The argument is logical enough. The only problem is that the American people just don't behave that way.

VOTING AS PARTICIPATION. In most instances the discussion of democratic participation centers on the act of voting, the major participatory opportunity for the average citizen. A great deal has been written about the fact of low voter participation in the United States in comparison with other democratic nations. While the turnout in national elections is indeed low, it is not nearly so low as that in local elections. It is unusual for more than 50 percent of the eligible voters to cast their ballots in a local election, and all too frequently the turnout falls to 25 percent or below. What explanation can we offer for this alarming state of affairs?

In the first place, structural changes in the electoral system appear to be related to low turnout. The earlier discussion of nonpartisanship briefly

---

[32] Gilbert and Clague, "Electoral Competition," p. 348.
[33] Gilbert and Clague, "Electoral Competition," pp. 348–349.

referred to the fact that nonpartisan elections are associated with a lower voter turnout than are partisan elections. Table 5–3 indicates the extent of this relationship. While the turnout figures are less than spectacular for either type of election, nonpartisan turnout is significantly lower. While 25 percent of the partisan cities had 57 percent or more of their adults voting, the top 25 percent of the nonpartisan cities had only 43 percent or more of their adults voting. An even greater percentage point spread occurs at the median than occurs at the upper quartile.

TABLE 5–3: Percent of Adults Voting in Cities over 25,000
(Cities holding election independently of any other election)

	ELECTION FOR MAYOR [1]				ELECTION FOR COUNCIL ONLY [2]			
	No. of Cities Reporting	Lower Quartile	Median	Upper Quartile	No. of Cities Reporting	Lower Quartile	Median	Upper Quartile
Form of Election								
Partisan	42	28	43	55	14	22	37	50
Nonpartisan	105	21	32	44	140	17	23	32
Form of Government								
Mayor-council	59	38	47	57	18	24	38	51
Commission	25	28	38	47	7	27	38	51
Council manager	63	19	26	33	130	17	23	31
Population Group								
Over 500,000	3	18	20	34	2	20		43
250,000 to 500,000	12	20	38	41	4	14	19	20
100,000 to 250,000	17	24	31	45	19	17	27	47
50,000 to 100,000	30	22	43	52	52	18	23	35
25,000 to 50,000	85	24	35	47	78	17	25	32
All cities over 25,000	147	23	35	47	155	17	24	34

SOURCE: Eugene C. Lee, "City Elections: A Statistical Profile," *Municipal Yearbook,* 1963 (Chicago, 1963), p. 81. Reprinted by permission of the International City Management Association.

[1] Election for mayor includes cities which also elected councilmen at same election.
[2] Election for council only includes several cities which elected only officers other than mayor or councilmen.

Table 5–3 also gives some indication that the election of a mayor serves to focus the attention of the citizenry on the election and to increase turnout. Although turnout is clearly greater in every election in which a mayor is elected along with councilmen, the improvement is most impressive in nonpartisan elections. Professor Eugene Lee has suggested that this can be traced to the fact that the political party serves to focus attention on the election, and that the direct election of the mayor merely serves to reinforce this focus in partisan cities, while in nonpartisan cities it is the main source of such focus.[34] The effect of the direct election of the mayor appears to be independent of the size or governmental form of the city involved.

Another structural variable that appears to affect turnout is the timing of the election. Urban reformers have long stressed the separation of municipal elections from other elections, particularly national elections, in order to facilitate the identification of local issues. Their efforts have been quite successful. As of 1963, two-thirds of the cities over 25,000 conducted their elections independently of all other elections, while 20 percent conducted them with other local elections, and only 14 percent conducted them with state or national elections.[35] Table 5–4 shows the effect of such separation on voter turnout. In every instance but one the independent elections have a poorer turnout than those conducted with other local elections. Both have a poorer turnout than those conducted with state or national elections. The unexplained exception is the case of the three cities with the commission form of government that hold elections with state or national elections and yet suffer a reduced turnout. It is difficult here as it is with respect to other structural variables to find evidence that the separation of elections causes low voter turnout. However, the two factors appear to be closely enough related on the basis of current research to indicate a strong relationship that cannot be reduced by controlling for governmental form or population size. Other voting studies that reveal the generally greater familiarity of the voter with national issues and candidates than with those at the local level add strength to the argument for maximizing turnout by conducting concurrent elections.

A fourth area of consideration which affects participation is the form and size of the ballot. For most of the twentieth century a short ballot movement has been part and parcel of municipal reform efforts. This movement has assumed that the voter's task is easier if he has only a few offices to vote for, and that there is a greater chance for him to exercise his choice intelligently if he has only a few issues and candidates to learn about. While this assumption appears logical, it has not yet been verified by solid empirical research We do not know enough about the effects of the shortening of the ballot on voting behavior. However, research into another area of ballot reform sheds some light on the question. In partisan elections, the ballot may either be a party column ballot, in which all the candidates of a party are listed under that party's name, or an office block

---

[34] Eugene C. Lee, "City Elections: A Statistical Profile," *Municipal Yearbook 1963* (Chicago, 1963), pp. 80–81.
[35] Lee, "City Elections," p. 82.

TABLE 5–4: Percent of Adults Voting in Cities over 25,000

	No. of Cities Reporting	Lower Quartile	Median	Upper Quartile	No. of Cities Reporting	Lower Quartile	Median	Upper Quartile
	ALL CITY ELECTIONS				HELD CONCURRENTLY WITH STATE OR NATIONAL ELECTIONS			
Form of Election								
Partisan	109	37	50	57	31	47	51	65
Nonpartisan	350	21	30	43	32	31	43	59
Form of Government								
Mayor-council	137	38	50	57	31	47	51	65
Commission	41	29	38	47	3	28	33	61
Council-manager	281	20	27	39	29	29	43	60
Population Group								
Over 500,000	15	26	39	47	2	46		47
250,000 to 500,000	25	21	37	48	4	45	56	76
100,000 to 250,000	54	24	32	50	9	30	50	55
50,000 to 100,000	124	21	33	51	17	20	51	62
25,000 to 50,000	243	23	33	47	31	35	47	64
All cities over 25,000	461	22	33	48	63	35	50	62
	HELD CONCURRENTLY WITH OTHER LOCAL ELECTIONS [1]				HELD INDEPENDENTLY OF ANY OTHER ELECTION			
Form of Election								
Partisan	22	48	53	58	56	26	41	53
Nonpartisan	65	27	35	47	246	19	27	39
Form of Government								
Mayor-council	28	40	50	55	78	34	44	56
Commission	5	28	57	71	32	28	38	47
Council-manager	54	26	35	47	193	18	23	32
Population Group								
Over 500,000	7	33	39	50	5	19	20	39
250,000 to 500,000	5	24	35	54	16	18	34	41
100,000 to 250,000	9	31	46	50	36	21	29	46
50,000 to 100,000	24	30	51	55	82	20	29	44
25,000 to 50,000	42	28	41	50	164	20	29	41
All cities over 25,000	87	29	44	51	303	20	29	41

SOURCE: Eugene C. Lee, "City Elections: A Statistical Profile," *Municipal Yearbook,* 1963 (Chicago, 1963), p. 83. Reprinted by permission of the International City Management Association.

[1] Excluding cities also holding election concurrently with state or national election.

ballot, in which the candidates of both parties are listed under the office for which they are running. The party column ballot permits and encourages the simple act of voting a straight party ticket by placing one mark at the appropriate place on the ballot. A study of the impact of these forms arrived at the conclusion:

> that poorly educated voters, who are presumably also the most apathetic, marginal participants, are the ones most directly affected by complicated ballots. Those with the lowest sense of involvement and personal political efficacy are most likely to neglect possible choices or leave portions of the [office block] ballot blank.[36]

If the complexity of the office ballot proves discouraging to the poorly educated, marginal voter, then it is logical to assume that these same voters would be frustrated by the complexity of the long ballot, especially if it is an office block, nonpartisan ballot.

In many of our cities the outright discrimination of public officials against minorities has reduced or effectively eliminated the ability of these minorities to participate through voting. While the most frequently discussed and quantitatively important discrimination has been that against the Negro, the Puerto Rican and Mexican-American minorities have suffered similar fates in some areas. This discrimination frequently took the form of an outright refusal to allow the minority group member to register or to vote. The passage of federal civil rights legislation, supplemented in some cases by state legislation, made such discrimination illegal and guaranteed the right of every citizen to participate in elections regardless of his race, creed, sex, or place of national origin. But progress toward realizing the goals of this legislation has been slow. In the first place, many members of the majority continue to drag their feet and to exert little effort toward compliance with either the spirit or the letter of the law. In the second place, generations of discrimination have left minority group members, particularly Negroes, with a political subculture that does not view the act of voting as acceptable. Before he will go to the polls, the black citizen must be convinced that he can vote without being penalized by the white majority and that this vote will mean something in terms of controlling governmental decisions. Discriminatory barriers make the education process that much more difficult and frequently serve as further indications of white racism to the frustrated black community. In spite of this, participation by black voters appears to be improving slowly, even in Southern cities. But such gains are small cause for rejoicing:

---

[36] Jack Walker, "Ballot Forms and Voter Fatigue: An Analysis of the Office Block and Party Column Ballots," *Midwest Journal of Political Science* 10 (1966): 462.

Negro participation is probably on the rise almost everywhere and percentage-wise their increases may be greater than those of whites. Yet they begin from such low levels of mass participation that impressive percentage gains may still mean that only a minority of Negro adults vote, at most, and that the whites continue to turn out a higher percentage of their own.[37]

The problem of participation through voting becomes a good deal more complex when considerations of the quality of the participation are added to those of quantity. While democracy anticipates the participation of every eligible citizen, it also assumes that such participation will be free and rational. When a large turnout of voters is achieved by the ruling party through intimidation, it may be little if any better than an extremely low turnout. Reformers have also been legitimately concerned by the apparent irrationality of the voters in "blindly" following party designation and candidate image in their voting. However, the discussion of the reform movement earlier in this chapter clearly indicates that these structural manipulations have not resulted in more rational voting behavior. They have merely lowered the quantity of participation without demonstrably improving its quality. For most purposes the act of voting will remain an essentially nonrational act for the foreseeable future. It will continue to be based upon a set of values and attitudes which may have little to do with the issues or with the candidates' qualifications to hold public office. As long as this is the case, emphasizing the turnout of voters in an election and devoting attention to mechanisms that will maximize turnout appear justifiable. Why should both the quality *and* the quantity of electoral participation be sacrificed if such a sacrifice can be avoided?

ALIENATION. Not all nonvoting can be traced to the simple structural problems discussed above.

A large proportion of the electorate feels politically powerless because it believes that the community is controlled by a small group of powerful and selfish individuals who use public office for personal gain. Many voters assume that this power elite is irresponsible and unaffected by the outcome of elections. Those who embrace this view feel that voting is meaningless because they see the candidates as undesirable and the electoral process as a sham.[38]

This feeling of powerlessness is frequently referred to as alienation. As the discussion in Chapter 1 pointed out, the normlessness and social isolation that accompany urbanization are reputed by many social scientists to increase this feeling of alienation. If this is true, one might reasonably

[37] Harry Holloway and David M. Olson, "Electoral Participation by White and Negro in a Southern City," *Midwest Journal of Political Science* 10 (1966): 121.
[38] Murray B. Levin, *The Alienated Voter* (New York, 1960), p. 58.

expect alienation to be more advanced in cities where the urbanization process is most advanced. However, the data in Table 5–3 relating non-voting to the size of the city clearly gives no support for such an expectation.

There exists at least some research that questions the linkage between powerlessness, normlessness, and social isolation as expressions of aliena-tion and the sort of political apathy which leads to nonvoting.[39] Some scholars have suggested an alternative explanation that holds that most citizens are just not concerned with local government and politics and that this lack of concern, rather than alienation, explains low turnout at the polls.[40] A final denial of the alienation theory of nonvoting, a denial that is most assuredly more popular with those in the seats of urban politi-cal power, is that most people fail to vote because they are basically satis-fied with the manner in which their government is being conducted. This hypothesis views voting primarily as protest rather than as participation. While it makes the low voting turnout in our cities easier to accept, no available empirical evidence supports this hypothesis.

POLITICAL ACTIVISM. Because the level of interest and electoral participa-tion by the general urban population is low, the minority who serve as opinion leaders and as mobilizers of electoral support for decision-makers are particularly significant. The goals, values, and motives of this group are of paramount importance to any evaluation of the urban political sys-tem, since they probably serve to shape the political process. Is the descrip-tion of this group given by the allegedly alienated voter accurate? Are these political activists really self-seeking and power hungry?

These questions are difficult to answer. The surface answers suggested by sociological and economic analyses of common characteristics of activ-ists often do not prove very helpful in reaching the question of motivation. Political psychology has not yet reached the point at which it can give us more than very general statements about the kinds of things which do motivate political activists. Statements about the motivation of particular activists require specific analysis of the individuals involved, and such analy-ses are difficult if not impossible to obtain. As a result, statements about the motives of political activists tend to be more impressionistic than empirical. Still, these educated impressions are better than the unexamined political myths that have ill-served us in the past.

The core of activist supporters for the machine was maintained through a combination of material and nonideological psychic rewards. The pre-cinct captain served the party because he was given a job and because

---

[39] Dwight G. Dean, "Alienation and Political Apathy," *Social Forces* 38 (1960): 185–189.

[40] Clarence Stone, "Local Referendums: An Alternative to the Alienated Voter Model," *Public Opinion Quarterly* 29 (1965): 213–222.

he enjoyed the companionship of other party workers. The position that the party took on the issues facing the community was not significant to him unless it served to threaten the rewards that his party work held for him. The end of political activity for this party worker was the winning of elections and/or the maintenance of the system of rewards—occasionally elections had to be lost to maintain the system and its control mechanism.[41] While it is obvious from the discussion of the decline of the machine that the material rewards available to the party—or to similar nonpartisan organizations—are declining in number, there are still many old-time, professional politicians whose loyalty to the party is maintained for nonideological reasons, and who view the major end of their party activity as the winning of elections.

The political machine had no monopoly on material and nonideological psychic rewards. Clearly many of those who participate in reform politics do so to achieve economic advantage, even if this advantage is merely an escape from the heavy taxes and kickbacks imposed by the machine. Reform politics also provide a socially acceptable outlet for civic participation and provide psychic rewards for the participant that are largely independent of the ideological position taken by the group.

Recent developments in American political life have caused us to focus our attention on another group of political activists who appear to be challenging the traditionalists for control of partisan and nonpartisan reform groups. Among these activists "ideological orientation—more than socio-economic status—is apt to determine the urban activists' political affiliation." [42] This new concern with ideology and issues has led to a type of politics frequently characterized as amateur rather than professional:

> The amateur spirit—the belief that the proper motive for political action is a concern for the ends of politics, that participation in the management of the affairs of the party ought to be widespread and in accord with strictly democratic procedures, and that party leaders and elective officials ought to be directly responsive to the substantive goals of the party activists—is becoming commonplace in our cities and counties.[43]

This type of political activism inevitably leads to frustration for its participants. Since ideological purity is more important for these activists than winning elections, it is difficult to mobilize sufficient popular support to win an election.[44] The end result is that activists either withdraw from the

---

[41] Wilson, "The Economy of Patronage," pp. 369–380.

[42] Robert S. Hirschfield, Bert E. Swanson, and Blanche D. Blank, "A Profile of Political Activists in Manhattan," *Western Political Quarterly* 15 (1963): 505.

[43] James Q. Wilson, *The Amateur Democrat*, 2d printing (Chicago, 1966), pp. vii–viii.

[44] Wilson, *The Amateur Democrat*, p. 347.

activity in frustration or revert to professional status by accepting non-ideological psychic rewards and winning as sufficient motivation to continue their participation.[45] In spite of these frustrations, the number of amateur activists—both on the left and on the right of the political spectrum—continues to increase. The 1950s and 1960s proved to be a particularly productive period for the amateur politician, and more of them than ever before battled against the frustrations of defeat to maintain both their activism and their ideological purity. There is little reason to predict long-term success for the amateurs, however. The diversity of the city is essentially a hostile environment for the ideological simplicity of amateur politics. The continuing urbanization process would seem to guarantee that the compromise and relativism of professional politics must triumph in the long run.

POLITICAL CULTURE AND PARTICIPATION. The attitudes and values that are expressed toward government and the political system constitute the political culture of a particular community. Much of our discussion of participation implied the existence of such a political culture, which provides for the transmission of the various attitudes and values expressed by those who participate in various ways or who fail to participate at all. Obviously, the overarching urban political culture contains within it a variety of attitudes and values that can lead to a variety of expressions. Within this general culture exists a number of subcultures, each one transmitting attitudes and values that support a particular political behavior, such as non-voting because of alienation.

One of the most frequently discussed formulations of the concept of an urban political culture is that of the public-regardingness and private-regardingness value premises, devised by Edward C. Banfield and James Q. Wilson.[46] The basis of this concept is the hypothesis that lower-income groups are inclined to support issues and candidates that deliver most to them personally in terms of their immediate self-interest. On the other hand, upper-income groups are more likely to be motivated by public-regardingness, a concept of the public interest, and to support issues and candidates that do not represent immediate rewards to them. The problem with any such hypothesis is the difficulty that social scientists have in testing it empirically. While Banfield and Wilson have been able to find some evidence of the impact of their hypothesized value premises in bond

---

[45] Wilson, *The Amateur Democrat*, p. 5.
[46] Edward C. Banfield and James Q. Wilson, *City Politics* (New York, 1963), and James Q. Wilson and Edward C. Banfield, "Public-Regardingness as a Value-Premise in Voting Behavior," *American Political Science Review* 58 (1964): 876–887.

elections,[47] there is insufficient evidence to support the use of these hypotheses as general explanations of political behavior. Perhaps the public-regarding rhetoric of middle- and upper-class reform groups is simply a disguise—possibly not conscious—for the long-run private-regarding value premises of economic self-interest. While a sense of *noblesse oblige* on the part of the upper classes in our cities may lead them to support some governmental programs from which they will gain no immediate benefit, there is no evidence that public-regarding value premises lead them to make all or even a majority of their political decisions on this basis. On the contrary, if the White Anglo-Saxon Protestant middle class were not private-regarding in many instances, it would be difficult to explain the absence of progress in many fields of social welfare. The contribution of the Banfield and Wilson hypothesis is that it leads us to recognize that such tendencies do exist and that simple explanations of political culture in terms of class and socioeconomic group are likely to be misleading.

Politics in the Suburbs

It has long been alleged that there are significant differences between urban and suburban politics. For many observers, the suburbs represent an attempt to return to small-town society in an era of urbanization. The suburbanite is supposed to be more community-oriented, more active in the political life of his community. However, empirical research reveals that these suburban differences are largely illusory. One current study concludes:

> we find that there is little or no difference between some urban and suburban attitude and activity patterns and that the nationwide urban-suburban division is the *least* rather than the most influential of the forces used to explain these urban and suburban data patterns.[48]

Other scholars who have examined the effect of moving to the suburbs on party affiliation have predicted that as the urban, central city resident moves to the suburbs he changes his outlook and aspirations. He therefore changes his party affiliation to Republican if he was previously a Democrat in order to adopt the political color of his new environment.[49] More careful analysis of voting data reveals quite a different picture. In fact, the Democratic party has experienced a slow but steady growth in suburban areas in recent years.

---

[47] Wilson and Banfield, "Public-Regardingness," pp. 876–887.

[48] Joseph Zikmund, "A Comparison of Political Attitude and Activity Patterns in Central Cities and Suburbs," *Public Opinion Quarterly* 31 (1967): 74.

[49] Fred I. Greenstein and Raymond C. Wolfinger, "The Suburbs and Shifting Party Loyalties," *Public Opinion Quarterly* 22 (1958): 473–482.

The data merely indicate that the vast bulk of such [suburban] immigrants retain their party allegiance because they are changing merely residential location and not their relative position in our social structure.[50]

The great difficulty in making general statements about the suburbs is that, like any other group of cities, they come in various shapes and sizes and have various social and economic characteristics. For example, the economic function served by the suburb—manufacturing and employing or retail and residential—is closely related to such political variables as the existence of nonpartisanship.[51] Furthermore, the degree of participation in suburbs is closely tied to their degree of social heterogeneity. The more heterogeneous communities experience more conflict and thus more participation by the citizenry.[52] Suburbia cannot be treated as if it were a monolithic social unit. It takes a wide enough variety of forms to insure that the suburbs possess nearly all of the political complexities of the major central cities.

Neighborhood Government

The discussion so far has assumed that the relevant decision-making and electoral participation take place within the traditional urban governmental structures. While this is usually the case, Part Three of this book will show that there are significant movements in contemporary urban politics to decentralize both participation and governmental decision-making. Perhaps the most general and radical of such suggestions is that proposed by Milton Kotler.[53] It is particularly important that we understand the objects of Kotler's proposals as political rather than social. In interpreting the revolutionary doctrine of local control, especially for black neighborhoods in the inner city, Kotler claims that the purpose of such political revolutions "is never social change, but political liberty, which requires local self-rule" and that social equality may well be the opposing force of such political revolutions.[54] Such a doctrine is clearly anti-liberal according to most current understanding of liberalism. In fact, it is another example of the curious blending of traditional, conservative thought with the "new" doctrines of urban radicalism. It is at once the antithesis of the

---

[50] Bernard Lazerwitz, "Suburban Voting Trends: 1948 to 1956," *Social Forces* 39 (1960): 36.

[51] Charles S. Liebman, "Functional Differentiation and Political Characteristics of Suburbs," *American Journal of Sociology* 66 (1961): 485–490.

[52] Herbert J. Gans, *The Levittowners: Ways of Life and Politics in a New Suburban Community* (New York, 1967), p. 142.

[53] This assessment and the following discussion are based upon Milton Kotler, *Neighborhood Government* (Indianapolis, 1969).

[54] Kotler, *Neighborhood Government*, p. 101.

traditional legal doctrine of the role of local government which was discussed in Chapter 2 and of the assumptions of the post-depression welfare state trend which has characterized urban politics for the past thirty-five years. It is a challenging and stimulating doctrine, and it may be the logical conclusion for all arguments which focus on decentralization and participation. However, it is also a statement of dogma, presented as an article of faith. While subject to empirical verification, it has not been tested and certainly not verified. It is the kind of statement which might more clearly be true of the upper middle-class, residential suburb in which participation and local self-rule are not likely in any way to affect the search for some modicum of social equality and for the good life as urban Americans view it.

Perhaps it would make more sense to state Kotler's position in another way. Since decentralization, participation, and local self-rule are not likely to result in the facile making of decisions which will lead to social equality, perhaps it is necessary to posit the emphasis on the neighborhood or the small governmental unit as a more democratic expression of the urban polity and as a value in itself. It is possible to maintain a value system in which the means are more important than the ends or in which they are at least as important as governmental program output.

Kotler views the neighborhood as the natural political order. The neighborhood is ". . .a political settlement of small territory and familiar association, whose absolute property is its capacity for deliberative democracy." [55] He claims that, motivated by a desire to frustrate working class political movements, downtown business interests have combined using annexation, non-partisanship, at-large elections, and the bureaucracy to destroy these natural polities. It has only been in recent years that the combination of inadequate constitutional authority, an inadequate financial base, and the professionalization of municipal officials and the resultant loss of a popular base for government have weakened the dominant interests of the center of the city and have encouraged a resurgence of the neighborhood as a political unit.

Kotler's argument contains some serious weaknesses which appear to be common to many of the advocates of decentralization in urban government. In the first place it is a serious mistake to characterize the growth of our major urban centers entirely in terms of annexation and the absorption of old neighborhoods. Surely incorporations have been as common as annexations if not more so in recent years. These incorporations and the resultant suburbanization have not invariably isolated the working classes in the city where they could be exploited by downtown commercial interests. There are a significant number of working class suburbs, and Kotler's

---

[55] Kotler, *Neighborhood Government*, p. 2.

class argument is clearly an oversimplification. Kotler also advocates "localism" rather than "separatism." In other words, he is attempting to introduce a concept of a federal city. He recognizes that such a concept requires a degree of cooperation among neighborhoods and some sort of formal linkage with the central urban government, but the mechanics of the system are illusive. Critics of Kotler's position must be forgiven for suggesting, like James Q. Wilson, that despite the undeniable homogeneity and sharing of norms which characterize neighborhoods within the city there does not seem to be any very good formula for decentralization and neighborhood control.[56] If such a mechanism did exist, the problems of fragmentation which have bedeviled students of metropolitan government would not have proven to be so difficult.

We shall return to this problem again and again in subsequent chapters. The failures of a more localized participation will be evident. Perhaps even more striking is the fact that we will see the inability of those involved to either separate questions of ends and means in public policy or to follow Kotler's lead and to accept the primacy of political process over policy output.

Suggested Readings

Banfield, Edward C., and Wilson, James Q. *City Politics*. New York, 1963.

Eldersveld, Samuel J. *Political Parties: A Behavioral Analysis*. Chicago, 1964.

Eulau, Heinz, ed. *Political Behavior in America*. New York, 1966.

Gans, Herbert J. *The Levittowners: Ways of Life and Politics in a New Suburban Community*. New York, 1967.

Janowitz, Morris, ed. *Community Political Systems*. Glencoe, 1961.

Jennings, M. Kent, and Zeigler, L. Harmon, eds. *The Electoral Process*. Englewood Cliffs, N.J., 1966.

Lane, Robert. *Political Life*. Glencoe, 1959.

Lee, Eugene C. *The Politics of Nonpartisanship: A Study of California Cities*. Berkeley and Los Angeles, 1960.

Levin, Murray B. *The Alienated Voter*. New York, 1960.

Wilson, James Q. *The Amateur Democrat*. 2d printing. Chicago, 1966.

Wood, Robert. *Suburbia: Its People and Their Politics*. Boston, 1959.

---

[56] James Q. Wilson, "The Urban Unease: Community vs. City," *The Quality of Urban Life*, eds. Warner Bloomberg, Jr. and Henry J. Schmandt (Beverly Hills, 1969), pp. 457–467.

chapter 6
Community
Power and
the Political Process

⟨The political scientists who first directed their attention to urban phenomena were interested primarily in the formal institutions of local government. Over the last three decades, however, the sociologists' community
studies, and the political scientists' own growing interest in noninstitutional
or informal aspects of the political process, produced a shift in orientation.
Not the organization of local government but the distribution of power
in the local community became the focus of analysis. This growing concern
with the social basis of politics was reinforced by the substantive conclusions of early studies, particularly the indications that nongovernmental
actors, like a business elite, sometimes dominated local politics.[1]

This shift in focus should not be interpreted as a justification for the
abandonment of the study of local governmental institutions. These institutions remain important variables in the political process. The emphasis
on the distribution of power merely broadens the scope of the political
scientist's effort so that he might better understand and explain the decision-making process.

Several questions are at the center of this new focus. What is the relationship between the general public and its political leadership? Who
controls whom and how? Are there any relationships between community
officials and groups smaller than the entire public that might render

---

[1] Harold Kaplan, *Urban Political Systems* (New York, 1967), p. 156.

questions of public control moot? The variety of answers put forward to these questions has added to the confusion that plagues the study of community politics.

Many have long considered the existence of some sort of positive connection or "linkage" between the general public and political leaders to be a prime requisite of democracy. The attempt to describe these linkages has supplied much of the recent literature in political science.[2] The literature of earlier periods was often occupied by the ideal of Athenian democracy as implemented in this country by the town meeting. Here the basic idea was that linkage was unnecessary, since each citizen participated directly in each decision made by the community. As the community grew larger and more complex, direct democracy became impossible on every issue, and the idea of representative government was instituted. In its simplest form, representative government can be described as a "rational-activist" model[3] wherein "the individual is expected to be politically informed, involved, rational, and above all, active."[4] It is easy to see that it is just such a model of the political process and its linkages which underlies the movement toward nonpartisan municipal government described in Chapter 5.

The next model of linkage, also discussed in Chapter 5, is one in which the political party is introduced as a device between the public and its leaders in order to simplify the process of representation. Ideally, the citizen selects the party of his choice by virtue of its statements on the issues facing the community, and he then votes for the candidates of that party. The party, in turn, exercises control over its elected candidates to insure that they support the stated party position. However, as the discussion in the preceding chapter indicated, these models do not accurately describe the real world. The citizen has proven to be insufficiently informed, involved, rational, and active to support even the more simplified party model let alone the more demanding nonpartisan or fully participatory models. Since this is so, either some other linkage process must take place to satisfy democratic criteria that demand some semblance of popular control over the decision-making process, or the process may be condemned as essentially undemocratic. The following discussion will explore both of these possibilities in some detail. The result will be a more complete picture of the urban political process, one that considers a large number of variables in addition to the institutionally determined patterns for decision-making.

---

[2] The following discussion draws heavily from Norman R. Luttbeg, "Political Linkage in a Large Society," *Public Opinion and Public Policy*, ed. Norman R. Luttbeg (Homewood, Ill., 1968), pp. 1–9.

[3] Luttbeg, "Political Linkage," pp. 4–5.

[4] Luttbeg, "Political Linkage," p. 4.

The Meaning of Power

Throughout the remainder of this chapter the terms *political power* and *political influence* will be used frequently. For the sake of clarity, and because the sociologists and political scientists who have studied their impact have used them in a wide variety of ways, minimal definitions of the two terms must be given. In the first place, the terms *power* and *influence* will be used here as if they were synonymous. While it is possible to give distinct definitions of the two terms, such a distinction sheds little light on questions of importance to political scientists.

Both power and influence may be viewed as the ability to affect the outcomes of public policy decisions. An individual or group may be said to possess absolute power if he (or it) is able to achieve the desired policy outcome in every instance. Obviously power falls a great deal short of being absolute in most cases. But individuals and groups may possess power even though policy outcomes do not correspond with their goals. The fact that they are defeated in their attempts to alter a policy means that they had insufficient power, not that they had no power at all.[5] When we speak of powerlessness, we are referring to a relative state of affairs rather than to an absolute condition. Everyone has some ability to affect the outcome of policy decisions, no matter what type of decision-making structure exists. While the exercise of power usually requires action on the part of the holder, we shall see later on in the chapter that some power is effective even though it is potential rather than exercised. The possibility of action by an influencer is thus as important as the action itself if the possibility is viewed by decision-makers as a threat.[6]

Another dimension to power is sometimes used to separate it from influence as a social phenomenon.[7] This is the use of power by those in authority as an attempt to mobilize support and achieve social control. Rather than distinguish between influence and social control as aspects of power, we will view power as a two-way relationship between authorities and partisans. In some cases, the emphasis will clearly be on attempts to alter the outcomes of decisions. In others, the stress may be on the attempts of the decision-makers to attain support and legitimation for decisions already made. In either case, power is being exercised, and someone is attempting to influence someone else.

The Role of Interest Groups

In what is perhaps the most widely read statement of the importance of groups to the democratic process, Professor David Truman pointed out

---

[5] William A. Gamson, *Power and Discontent* (Homewood, Ill., 1968), p. 72.

[6] Gamson, *Power and Discontent*, pp. 68–70.

[7] Gamson, *Power and Discontent*, pp. 2–18.

that man is by nature a social animal, and as such belongs to various social groups. On one hand, man tends to join groups that express interests and opinions that he already values. On the other hand, the groups tend to shape the interests and opinions of their members.[8] As these groups become active in the political process, they can then exercise influence over governmental officials on behalf of their membership. The end result—or so the argument goes—is that "power has become more widely distributed through greater participation in voluntary associations."[9] In an urban environment, where voluntary associations are thought to be rapidly replacing such primary groups as the family and the church as social referents for the citizen, such an explanation should be particularly significant—if it is valid.

The voluntary association can and does perform a variety of functions relevant to urban politics.[10] Operating under the often perjorative label of "pressure group," it may directly affect the distribution of power within the community by intervening in the decision-making process and altering to some degree the authorities' decisions. It may serve to orient its membership to the political and social process by educating and informing them as to issues and events that bear upon their shared interests and attitudes. It may act as an agent of social change by challenging the existing pattern of social life in the community in order to benefit itself, its officers, or its membership. By resolving or participating in the resolution of conflicts within the community, it can contribute to social cohesion and stability. It can provide its members with a sense of identity in a complex urban society and thereby rescue them from the terrors of meaninglessness and helplessness that contribute to some degree to low levels of political participation. And finally, it can provide its membership with the means to gain social and economic advancement through collective action—advancement that would be beyond their reach as individuals. These functions are, of course, not mutually exclusive. When an interest group seeks to exert pressure on those in authority, it seldom does so without at the same time attempting to perform one of the other functions—social change, conflict resolution, or social and economic advancement.

While many of these interest groups are the traditional economic groups representing industry, commerce, and labor, there are others whose major purpose is more ideological in nature. Good government groups and civic associations are present in every city. To be sure, much of what passes for "good government" orientation is in fact not-too-carefully-veiled economic interest. However, the motivation of all such groups and their members

---

[8] David E. Truman, *The Governmental Process* (New York, 1951).

[9] Arnold M. Rose, *The Power Structure: Political Process in American Society* (New York, 1967), p. 244.

[10] Rose, *The Power Structure*, pp. 247–250.

must not be interpreted as economic in nature. There are too many cases in which these groups adopt public positions that cannot be explained in terms of their self-interest. Either the policies in question have no immediate bearing upon the economic well-being of the membership, or the positions taken appear to be in direct contrast to such interests. These civic groups are an important part of any consideration of the effect of groups on urban politics. Their high level of political activity and the general acceptability of the "good government" ideology to the general public make them a force to be reckoned with.

Where political parties represent an active force in the community, they are obvious points of impact for the interest groups. In fact, much of the literature on these groups links them to the political parties, to the formulation of party platforms, and to the control of party candidates.[11] If, as Chapter 5 claims, the level of participation in party activity is low, where do the active partisans get the ideas that are promulgated in campaign speeches? Do the politicians invent these policy positions with no clue to which issues most concern the electorate and to which positions on these issues might be most popular? Even considering the low level of electoral participation in urban elections, such an approach would obviously be far too risky for most professional politicians. One apparent answer is that the organized interests of the community either suggest the direction in which policies might move, or they present fully-developed policy statements to the political leadership in the hope that they will be accepted. Drawing upon his extensive study of the political process in Chicago, Professor Edward Banfield aptly sums up the second possibility:

> The preparation of policies and plans will be done mainly within those private organizations having some special stake in the matters involved and by the civic associations.[12]

Clearly not all of this contact with public officials is conducted through political parties. As we have already noted, many communities have no effective party organization either because true nonpartisan government has been achieved or because the existing party structure exercises insufficient control over public officials. In these cases, interest groups obviously must deal directly with the officials. The tactics used may vary from a threat to withhold electoral support to an effort to persuade appointed officials that their professional standards and "good government" call for adoption of the group position.

Two tendencies that have been revealed through sociological research raise serious questions about the ability of interest groups to contribute in a major way to democratic participation in the decision-making pro-

---

[11] Luttbeg, "Political Linkage," p. 6.
[12] Edward C. Banfield, *Political Influence* (New York, 1961), p. 251.

cess. In the first place, members of the upper socioeconomic groups are more likely to join potentially active political groups than are members of groups with lower social status. While the political activity of labor unions and the organization of the poor into community action agencies under the poverty program has greatly increased lower-class participation in group politics, the membership of the great majority of activist groups is not representative of the lower classes. Even if one recognizes that group activity is not based entirely on the self-interest of the membership, the absence of the socioeconomic majority from the membership of most active groups raises serious questions as to how the groups determine the "public good" or the "general welfare" for which they work in community politics. In the second place, it has frequently been noted that the internal politics of interest groups is notoriously undemocratic. A small leadership group within the larger body tends to develop group policy and to lead rather than reflect the opinion of the membership. This tendency serves to further narrow the meaningful participation of group members in the political process. Faced with these two problems, many have concluded that the participation of interest groups in urban politics merely serves to further narrow the field of those who have influence over policy decisions.

This conclusion may indeed be warranted in many communities. But the assumption on which it is based—that there is an identity of interests and attitudes expressed by most of the politically active groups which comes in part from the identity of social and economic background of the group leadership—has proven to be incorrect in others. In some communities, ideology and interest can be separated, and ideology may either serve to reinforce interest or to conflict with it. The group leaders may be "the active spokesmen for the people who wanted interest-based decisional preferences filtered through the proper ideological sieve." [13] Furthermore, there are frequently serious differences in both interest and ideology between groups. For example, the Chamber of Commerce and the Homeowners' Association may draw their memberships from the same socioeconomic background, but the positions of the two groups on the question of industrial development for the community may be quite different, the former favoring expanded economic development, and the latter supporting the continuation of a purely residential community. In still other communities, neither interest nor ideology but the need for a cause to maintain organizational momentum leads interest groups into conflict. For example:

Civic controversies in Chicago are not generated by the efforts of politicians to win votes, by differences of ideology or group interest, or by the behind-the-scenes efforts of a power elite. They arise, instead, out of the maintenance

[13] Robert E. Agger, Daniel Goldrich, and Bert E. Swanson, *The Rulers and the Ruled* (New York, 1964), p. 17.

and enhancement needs of large formal organizations. The heads of an organization see some advantage to be gained by changing the situation. They propose changes. Other large organizations are threatened. They oppose, and a civic controversy takes place.[14]

The end result of conflicts, whether traceable to differences in interest and ideology or to organizational maintenance needs, is the failure of interest groups to provide clear policy direction for public officials. Faced with group conflict, the officials must judge the relative strengths and weaknesses of the conflicting groups in terms of the sanctions which they can apply if their recommendation is not accepted. Frequently no group or combination of groups has a clear advantage, and a compromise is the only solution available. The politician may seek to effect such a compromise himself, but sometimes he finds it more advantageous to sit and wait. Banfield's description of the process in Chicago illustrates this strategy:

> The poltical head, therefore, neither fights for a program of his own making nor endeavors to find a "solution" to the conflicts that are brought before him. Instead, he waits for the community to agree upon a project. When agreement is reached, or when the process of controversy has gone as far as it can, he ratifies the agreement, and carries it into effect.[15]

In most communities it is also important to distinguish the political role of the civic associations from that played by other interest groups. It is unusual for the civic association to initiate public policy. In most cases, these associations are brought into the picture after other organizations have suggested a change. The initial suggestion will come from proftmaking enterprises such as stores and newspapers, free public agencies like the department of welfare, and public and semipublic agencies that sell their services like the university.[16] In many communities, the changes may be suggested by the political leadership, partisan or nonpartisan, before they are presented to civic associations. The major function performed by the civic groups seems to be one of legitimation. The prestige of civic leaders is frequently seen as a crucial factor in determining the fate of policy proposals. If these leaders and the organizations with which they are connected can be enlisted in support of a proposal, the proposal is more likely to be accepted by the community at large as being in the public interest. This does not mean that such endorsements are indispensable. They are, however, highly desirable.

The group leaders who are at the center of any discussion of interest

---

[14] Banfield, *Political Influence*, p. 263.
[15] Banfield, *Political Influence*, p. 253.
[16] Banfield, *Political Influence*, p. 265.

group politics are not nearly as different from the general citizenry as some critics would like to indicate. By virtue of a somewhat better knowledge of how the local political system works and of their greater electoral participation, "group leaders feel somewhat more integrated into the social structure, but their difference from the cross section of citizens is not great." [17] Politically active interest groups, especially the kind that propose policy, are becoming increasingly middle class in their orientation. In many communities the participation of the upper socioeconomic groups seems confined to civic leadership roles whose primary function is legitimation.

This picture of competition between a limited number of interest groups may not be wholly satisfactory for those whose definition of democracy includes high standards of political participation. However, to the extent that interest groups do serve to influence the form and substance of decisions in the public sphere, they increase the channels that are at least in theory available to the citizen who wishes to change governmental decisions. The interest group also has the advantage of being able to mass individual influence as collective power and thereby increase the likelihood of success. The vague and general mandate of the ballot box can be rendered much more specific by active interest groups which at least purport to speak for their memberships as voting citizens.

The Power Elite

A popular theory of recent years posits the existence of a socioeconomic elite which dominates the decision-making process. This theory stresses the absence of linkage between general public opinion and public policy. For most of these theorists, the electoral process is a sham; public officials are merely fronts whose main function is to legitimate the decisions made by an elite outside of the context of formal governmental institutions. The elite theorist sees politically active interest groups as important only when they reflect the prevailing attitudes of the elite and when they act as instruments of the elite in presenting their policy decisions to public officials for legitimation.

> The belief that an "economic elite" controls government and community affairs by means kept hidden from the public, is one that can be traced at least as far back in American history as the political attacks of some Jeffersonians on some Hamiltonians at the end of the eighteenth century. Scarcely any lower-class political movement in the United States has failed to express the theme that the upper classes successfully used non-democratic means to thwart democratic processes.[18]

[17] Rose, *The Power Structure*, p. 171.
[18] Rose, *The Power Structure*, p. 1.

The explanation of political decisions as the machinations of a power elite grew out of sociological studies made in a variety of communities in the United States. Among the earliest and most important of these studies were those carried out by Robert and Helen Lynd.[19] The Lynds found that the community they studied was dominated by a single family that formed the controlling socioeconomic elite. They contended that this family could translate its wishes into public policy any time it chose to do so, and that it frequently did so choose. Other sociologists studying other communities came up with similar findings, although the elite was usually composed of more than just one family. The power theories did not become widely noticed outside of sociological circles, however, until the publication of Floyd Hunter's study of Atlanta [20] and the more generalized statements of C. Wright Mills.[21] Within a few years, the presence or absence of a power elite became a subject of debate among sociologists, political scientists, and those in the general public who were concerned about the political process especially at the community level.

The popularity achieved by theories of elite dominance can be explained in several ways. In the first place, most people academicians or not, could readily observe that there existed social and economic differences that divided communities and the nation. Every American had some conception of his social class and status and of his relationship to others who were higher and lower on the social scale. By the same token, one did not have to be a dyed-in-the-wool Marxist to recognize that these differences in class and status carried with them differences in the resources— mainly economic—that the individual could bring to bear in the political arena. This uneven distribution of economic resources was explained in a variety of ways, none of which were wholly incompatible with elite theory. Many of the more radical elements in American politics have tended to agree with Marx that the wealthy have achieved their advantage by means of the systematic exploitation of the working man. Many of the wealthy, however, viewed their resources as rewards won through the possession of such superior virtues as intelligence, thrift, and hard work, and their political advantage as the natural result of their greater fitness to use political power. In between these two extremes ranged a spectrum of positions, all of which recognized the existence of the unequal distribution of resources and hence of political power. For many people, power elite theory was simply additional verification of what was already common knowledge.

In the second place, the obvious shortcomings of explanations of the

---

[19] Robert and Helen Lynd, *Middletown* (New York, 1929), and *Middletown in Transition* (New York, 1937).

[20] Floyd Hunter, *Community Power Structure* (Chapel Hill, 1953).

[21] C. Wright Mills, *The Power Elite* (New York, 1956).

political process which depended in great degree upon evidence of broad participation made the picture horribly confusing. If neat, traditional, eighteenth century democratic theory was an inadequate explanation of our decision-making process, then some other equally simple and manageable theory was needed to take its place. There was, and is, a strong need on the part of many people to believe that someone is indeed running the show.[22] The contention that that someone was a power elite reestablished an element of certainty in the political process. One knew whom to praise if things appeared to be going right and whom to blame if they appeared to be going wrong. The system was manageable once more.

Many social scientists found the elite theories inadequate for explaining community decision-making. The major criticisms were directed at the research methods that had been used to determine the existence of an elite.[23] In almost every instance, the elite had been identified by asking those who, by position and interest in the community, were thought to be most knowledgeable which of their fellow citizens exercised the most influence over public policy decisions. A list was then compiled. In most instances, it included those people who had received the most votes. The socioeconomic status of those whose names had been listed was then determined, as was the frequency of contact between those on the list. The end result was a picture of a power elite. The criticism of this method has really centered on two main points: (1) the accuracy of the ascriptions of political power, and (2) the degree to which such power was actually exercised when possessed.

The first criticism is particularly important. Is it sufficient proof that an individual possesses political power when he is named by several of his fellow citizens as powerful? This question cannot be answered easily. Obviously, there can be cases in which an individual or group exercises a great deal of political power but remains so far behind the scenes that the influence is all but invisible to the general public. That individual or group could conceivably use a portion of the power to further disguise its operation by insuring that those who know of it will not reveal it to a team of itinerant sociologists. But while such conditions are theoretically possible, we have no evidence to indicate that they are particularly widespread. Unfortunately, too many of the pundits of community power interpret this absence of evidence as proof of a conspiracy. As Arnold Rose has perceptively pointed out, "conspiracy and secrecy theories of power are theories based on inference, with very little fact, and their authors

---

[22] Norton Long, "The Local Community as an Ecology of Games," *American Journal of Sociology* 64 (1959): 251–261.

[23] See for example Nelson W. Polsby, *Community Power and Political Theory* (New Haven, 1963).

justify the absence of facts by stating that the important facts are kept hidden." [24] On the other hand, a good portion of political power is in fact reputational. If a large number of civic leaders and public officials believe that Citizen X has great political power, they will behave accordingly, and their prophecy will be self-fulfilling, even though Citizen X has not chosen to expend any resources in an effort to change the course of public policy or to maintain its present course. An example should serve to illustrate the point. If the Superintendent of Streets believes that Citizen X runs his town, then when Citizen X calls the superintendent to complain of the condition of the street in front of his house, the public official will act accordingly. If the belief is particularly strong, he is quite likely to repave the street immediately even though it is not scheduled for repair for several years. Whether Citizen X could have the superintendent fired or have the annual appropriation of the Street Department reduced is not particularly important as long as the superintendent believes that he has the power to do so. To this extent, reputation is a very important part of any study of community power and the process of influencing public decisions.

Much has been made in the community power literature of the difference between *potential* power and *exercised* power. Critics of the elite theorists have pointed out that the reputational method, at best, identifies those who possess potential power. What guarantee is there that this power will be exercised to alter decision-making in the community? The answer, of course, is that there is no such guarantee. As a matter of fact, some studies have indicated that there is a marked reticence on the part of the reputational leaders in the community. "[The] data . . . strongly suggest that the top players of other games play politics little more than they do the formal governmental games in the community." [25] The reason offered is that the rewards and payoffs of exercising political power appear in many instances to be too small. In some instances, scholars have claimed that this failure of the socioeconomic elite to exercise their power has had disturbing results for the community:

> The economic dominants' abnegation of civic responsibility and accountability has perhaps done more than undermine their own claims to legitimacy. Very possibly, their withdrawal from responsible involvement threatens to subvert the viability of community life as well.[26]

However, it is easy to make too much of this point. In one sense, the only power that is really worth comment by political scientists is potential

---

[24] Rose, *The Power Structure*, p. 4

[25] Paul A. Smith, "The Games of Community Politics," *Midwest Journal of Political Science* 9 (1965): 44.

[26] Robert O. Schulze, "The Bifurcation of Power in a Satellite City," in *Community Political Systems*, ed. Morris Janowitz (Glencoe, 1961), p. 73.

power, power that may be exercised in the future. While there are those who find the past intrinsically interesting, most would study the exercise of power in past decisions in order to be able to make some statements about power and its effect on present and future decisions. The fact that a man or a group has exercised power in the past is merely an indication that he or they may have the potential for exercising power in the future.

Reputational community power research has provided us with a great deal of valuable information. It has found that in some communities there are a limited number of individuals who are identified by other citizens as being particularly influential in matters of public policy. It has also given us an indication that many people believe that socioeconomic status differences result in a differential allocation of political power and that this belief can in some cases prove to be correct. Any discussion of decision-making in our cities that ignores these findings is sadly deficient.

On the other hand, it is easy to claim too much for the results of reputational research. There is no proof that all or even most of our cities are dominated by a socioeconomic power elite. As we shall soon see, there are frequent examples of communities in which the socioeconomic elite plays little, if any, role in many of the important public decisions. The uncritical acceptance of the power elite concept as a satisfactory general theory of community politics has led many frustrated political activists to speak darkly of a "power structure" that thwarts their attempts to achieve noble civic reforms. There is little doubt that something approximating a structure of political power exists in every community. The fact that decisions are made at all should be adequate proof of this contention. However, this structure is not in every instance made up of the rich and the well-born. The successes, however minimal they may seem, of civil rights activists give some indication that the poor minorities when properly organized can exercise economic and political power. The system is not the tightly closed one pictured by the elite theorists. Organizational efforts like the Woodlawn Organization in Chicago encouraged by the training given by perceptive political activists like Saul Alinsky prove that the political power of elite groups is indeed frail when faced with the carefully marshalled political and economic resources of the nonelite mass groups. This leads to the conclusion that, if a socioeconomic power elite dominates the politics of a community, it does so at the sufferance of other groups in the community and not because the social and economic system dictates that it inevitably be so.

Critics of the elite theorists have not limited themselves solely to questions of research methodology. Many of them have gone on to point out that analysts like C. Wright Mills—who, by the way, could not be accused of using anything as systematic as the reputational method—chose to ignore other significant factors that have a great impact on the power exercised by socioeconomic elites. These factors might explain some of the failures of elite theory.[27] In the first place, there is a strong tendency to ignore historical and environmental factors that are essentially beyond the control of any elite group. For example, let us assume for the moment that the Negro in many American communities has been rendered politically impotent by the machinations of a socioeconomic elite. As long as that elite is able to isolate the Negro subcommunity from outside influences it may be able to maintain the sense of political inefficacy which effectively prevents any challenge to its domination. However, if the demands of the larger community—the nation—require that members of the subcommunity be removed from their usual environment and trained in organizational and leadership techniques and then returned to the old environment, it is possible that important changes will occur in the local political situation. One might well presume that Negroes who are trained as effective combat leaders in an integrated military establishment will return to their communities as civilians with a new sense of efficacy which might prove to be a challenge to elite domination of the political process. This is only one illustration of the many changes over which local elites have little or no control.

A second factor frequently ignored by elite theorists is the degree to which cultural values limit political behavior. There are some things that the mass of citizens just will not accept. Even the most absolute rulers are subject to some constraints. The rhetoric of democracy which is accepted by the vast majority of Americans in general terms implies some very severe limitations on political behavior. The frequent exercise of raw, naked political power by an elite in violation of these democratic values and, in some cases, of the laws which have been established as formal statements of such values can obviously result in the violent repudiation of the elite through revolution. If there is a ruling elite, it must exercise its power in such a way as to gain at least minimal acceptance from a significant number of citizens within the community.

Finally, most elite theorists proceed on the assumption that the elite pursues its recognized goals in a rational manner. This assumption is not always correct. "If the economic elite uses its power to make decisions for its own advantage in many instances, it lacks alternatives in other instances, and does not always behave rationally where there are alternatives."[28] This point can be illustrated by returning for a moment to our earlier example of the Negro and national military commitments. If we make a further assumption that the local draft board is controlled by the elite, then it is possible to imagine that elite making decisions that would result in deferments for the sons of the elite and inductions for the sons

---

[27] The following discussion draws heavily from Rose, *The Power Structure*, pp. 18 and 19.

[28] Rose, *The Power Structure*, p. 19.

of the members of lower socioeconomic groups. The gains achieved by such a policy might well be only short-run. If the earlier hypothesis concerning the leadership training of the Negro outside the community is at all supported by the facts, then drafting low-income Negroes and sending them out for such training could result in a net long-term loss for the elite.

Pluralism as an Alternative

The major critics of the power elite theory did not rest with a simple refutation of that theory on the grounds of methodological problems and internal inconsistencies. They went on to develop their own alternative theory of decision-making in the community. The outstanding statement of pluralist research and findings is found in Robert Dahl's *Who Governs?* Dahl sees society as divided essentially into two unequal groups. The larger group is made up of the average citizens or "civic" men who are not by nature political and who only participate in the political process when their goals are threatened by governmental action or inaction. The smaller group consists of the activists or "political" men who devote their time, energies, and resources to attaining political power. If a member of this second group is to succeed in his efforts, he must obtain at least the tacit consent of civic man and he must follow the general norms of political behavior outlined by his society. Failure to obtain consent or to obey the norms frequently results in defeat.[29] Nelson Polsby, an associate of Dahl's in the study of New Haven politics, sums up the pluralist alternative well in his discussion of limited participation in decision-making:

> First, different small groups normally make decisions on different community problems, and, likewise, the personnel of decision-making groups often change, even over the short run. Secondly, the decisions made by small groups are almost always considered routine or otherwise insignificant by most other members of the community. Thirdly, when small groups undertake innovation or decision-making in cases salient or likely to become salient to others in the community they must achieve a special kind of legitimacy or risk the likelihood of failure.[30]

The result is a picture of the political process in which disproportionate power is still in the hands of a relatively few men. However, these men are from a wide variety of social and economic backgrounds, and the pluralist theorists find that the activists or political men are much more likely to come from a solid middle-class environment than they are to come from a socioeconomic elite. This fits in quite well with the earlier point that many of the reputational leaders have abdicated their civic

---

[29] Robert A. Dahl, *Who Governs?* (New Haven, 1961), p. 225.
[30] Polsby, *Community Power*, p. 124.

responsibilities or opportunities. Dahl found the activists in possession of a wide variety of political resources of which economic resources were only one type; furthermore he noted that these resources were unequally distributed, but not all in favor of one man or one group, thus resulting in dispersed inequalities of resources rather than cumulative inequalities.[31] In the final analysis, some linkage between the citizen and public policy-making exists in the pluralist system. The dispersal of resources, the ultimate dependence on popular consent, the activation of passive citizens when their interests are threatened, and the prevailing norms of political behavior all serve as a part of this linkage. It is certainly nowhere near as clear a connection as even the party and interest group theorists have posited, but it does represent for many observers a more hopeful picture of the democratic process than does the elite theory.

One further point has emerged in the course of several studies that might be labeled pluralist—the dependence of the decision-making process on the leadership of elected officials. In Dahl's study of New Haven, the mayor was found to be at the center of each issue area studied. He was the political man par excellence. The various groups that participated in the political process did so primarily at the subleadership level. At this level, the primary task that faced the group members was the marshalling of public support for policy decisions that had already been made by the duly elected or appointed public officials. Other studies resulted in some-what similar findings. In a North Carolina community, Benjamin Walter found that "politicians innovated policy choices and had their accept-ability certified by the visible support of top businessmen."[32] This appears to be quite close to the legitimation function of civic associations. It does not mean, of course, that the elected officials and bureaucrats had the real power while the membership of the various groups had none. On the contrary, the fact that the officials felt it necessary to solicit legitimation and the fact that this legitimation might well result in popular support for the program indicates that the groups in question had some power. However, in a pluralist system such power is far from absolute since the theory holds that different groups are involved in different issue areas. If the politician finds legitimation withheld on one issue, he may well sur-vive on the strength of the support he can garner from other groups on other issues. Thus, while the ability to mobilize authoritative support or to deny such support for public officials is perhaps less immediately sig-nificant than the brute power to initiate or to veto policy, it is neverthe-less of central importance to the political process in many communities.

---

[31] Dahl, *Who Governs?*, pp. 226–228.

[32] Benjamin Walter, "Political Decision Making in Arcadia," *Urban Growth Dynamics*, ed. F. Stuart Chapin and Shirley Weiss (New York, 1962), p. 186.

It is important to reemphasize the fact that pluralist theories see participation in the decision-making process as severely limited. Only a few individuals can hope to successfully operate within such a system to directly affect policy outcomes. The great majority of citizens must be content with an impact on policy which is at best indirect.

> Resources and skill and diligence in exploiting them are three conditions which make for success in influencing community decisions. A fourth [is the] ability to choose goals that do not strain the compliance of others in the system. A fifth condition of successful participation is closely related to the fourth: capacity to form coalitions with other participants in order to achieve one's goals.[33]

It is this characteristic of pluralist theory which has led some of its critics to accuse it of being elitism in another form.[34] The criticism is essentially directed at what appears to be an easy acceptance of a system in which the level of popular participation is low. These critics do not quarrel with the research findings of the pluralists. They are simply disturbed that such findings do not generate moral outrage at the betrayal of democratic principle revealed. The moral outrage of the critics is devoted primarily toward a political system that encourages low participation by virtue of apathy born of the average citizen's general feeling of inefficacy. Such critics are not satisfied with the explanation of low participation which traces it to contentment with the present operation of the political system. The motivating factors for the absence of general participation are unclear. However, feelings of contentment and of low efficacy must both be involved to a degree. The important fact is that such criticisms of the pluralist effort do nothing to negate the contribution that it makes to our understanding of the political systems of many communities.

Although pluralist hypotheses are derived primarily from studies that focus on actual decisions made in particular issue areas, the findings of some reputational studies by sociologists have tended to support these hypotheses. For example, Arnold Rose found in his study of a Minnesota community that top political influence was attributed to governmental and political leaders, while the power elite and business organizations were ranked in second and third positions. He further supported pluralist hypotheses through his finding that "different persons are . . . perceived as influential in different areas of life."[35]

---

[33] Polsby, *Community Power*, p. 137.

[34] Jack L. Walker, "A Critique of the Elitist Theory of Democracy," *American Political Science Review* 60 (1966): 285–295, and "A Reply to 'Further Reflections on the Elitist Theory of Democracy'," *American Political Science Review* 60 (1966): 391–392.

[35] Rose, *The Power Structure*, pp. 350–353; quotation at p. 351.

What is Community Power Really Like?

The views presented so far, most especially the elitist and pluralist approaches, have been developed as a result of case studies in single communities. Very little work of a comparative nature has been attempted. The end result has been a suspicion on the part of many social scientists that our much-talked-about community power studies have usually constituted little more than descriptions of unique situations which have little if any general value. However, there are some beginning comparative studies available which enable us to more carefully evaluate elitist and pluralist hypotheses.

In one of the most interesting of these studies,[36] Robert Presthus found that the communities he studied had both political and economic elites and that each type of elite was particularly influential in its own area. The political elite dominated the public decisions while the economic elite dominated the private decisions. He further noted that these two elites frequently competed with one another. Generally, this picture does not differ too much from that presented by Dahl and other so-called pluralists. The major difference is that the comparative study permits Presthus to note that there appear to be some important variations between communities in the degree to which political and economic dominants compete with one another and to which the system is open to participation by large numbers of citizens. This led to an increasing realization on the part of political scientists that community power structures vary with the type of community.[37]

This point has been emphasized even more clearly in a study of 166 community power studies conducted by Claire Gilbert.[38] Figure 6–1 shows a portion of the results derived from this comparison. In this analysis, communities that appear to be dominated by "informals" correspond most closely to elite typologies, and those dominated by the "politicians" most closely to pluralist theories. The picture is clearly one of community power structures which vary according to population. The socioeconomic elite is most likely to be dominant, according to existing case studies, in communities under 1,000 and in those from 20,000 to 50,000. The political elite, on the other hand, is likely to be dominant in communities from 100,000 to 500,000 and over one million. Even if one bears in mind that sociologists tend to find elites when they study com-

---

[36] Robert Presthus, *Men at the Top* (New York, 1964), especially pp. 405–421.

[37] Rose, *The Power Structure*, p. 297.

[38] Claire Gilbert, "The Study of Community Power: A Summary and a Test," in *The New Urbanization*, ed. Scott Greer, Dennis L. McElrath, David W. Minar, and Peter Orleans (New York, 1968), pp. 222–245.

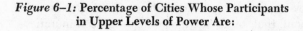

Figure 6–1: **Percentage of Cities Whose Participants
in Upper Levels of Power Are:**

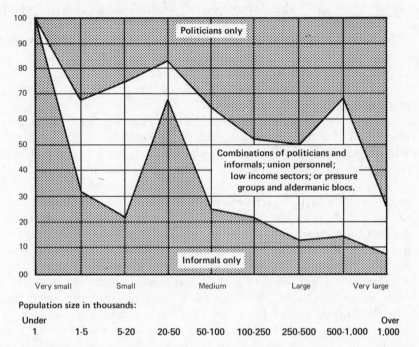

SOURCE: Claire Gilbert, "The Study of Community Power," in *The New Urbanization,* eds. Scott Greer, Dennis L. McElrath, David W. Minar, and Peter Orleans (New York, 1968), p. 230. Reprinted by permission of St. Martin's Press, Inc.

munity power and that they tend to study smaller communities, and the fact that the reverse tendencies appear to be true of political scientists, the population size trends remain.[39] It is important to note that population cannot alone explain variations in the structure of community power. "[Population size] is closely associated with a large number of economic, demographic, and social characteristics that constrain the structure and distribution of community power."[40]

The major point of emphasis should quite probably not be on population at all except as it reflects these other characteristics. What many students seem to be seeking is some measure of political integration, because they assume that political participation increases with that integration.[41] Clearly, one of the central difficulties of our study of community

---

[39] Gilbert, "Study of Community Power," pp. 233–234.
[40] Gilbert, "Study of Community Power," p. 235.
[41] Presthus, *Men at the Top,* p. 412.

power is that we know so little about the nature of integration—that which acts as the cement that binds men together into communities—and its effects upon the distribution of power. This must have priority for future study.[42]

The best general statement that can be made concerning the allocation of political power in our urban communities avoids the pitfalls of specificity and certainly falls a great deal short of being theory. The politics of any particular community may be placed along a continuum ranging from full and complete participation by all citizens to absolute rule by one man. In between the two poles the possibilities range through party competition, interest group competition, competitive elites, and elite domination. The statement is made even more uncertain by the possibility that a particular community may combine these various political styles in such a way as to make its location on the continuum uncertain. It is further possible that the relevant political style might vary from issue to issue as well as from community to community. The perceptive student of urban politics will interpret this confusion over the exercise of power in the political community as a warning to avoid facile statements about the power structure. The absence of a clearly acceptable general theory of community power forces us back to case studies for the communities in which we are interested. We must ask a series of questions which combines the insights gained from all of the various approaches to political linkage. Who is reputed to hold power in the community? What individuals and groups are involved in the making of decisions affecting the public interest? What role do these individuals and groups play in the decision-making process? Once these questions have been answered, it is possible to make a statement about the exercise of political power in a particular community at a particular time. As more and more communities are studied and as the communities that have been examined once are studied again, it should be possible to come closer to identifying the variables that consistently affect the distribution of political power. Once this task is completed, a satisfactory general theory will be possible.

The Character of Community Politics:
Conflict and Consensus

There have been two other traditions of major importance in the study of community politics. One tradition has stressed consensus and agreement as the basic characteristics of politics, while the other has emphasized conflict. Much of the difference between these two emphases can be traced to differences in the ideological presuppositions of their proponents.

---

[42] Gerhard Lenski, *Power and Privilege* (New York, 1966), p. 34.

The sociological functionalists who stress shared values and consensus as the basic cement or integrative force for the community often stem from a conservative tradition. Conflict theorists are much more likely to belong to a radical tradition.[43]

The functionalist begins with the assumption that the community would be by definition impossible if there were not some common element to bind together the individuals who constitute the community. The general position taken by such analysts is that the institutions and processes that add to this consensus are functional, and those that detract from it are dysfunctional. While a statement imputing functionalism to institutions and processes does not necessarily imply a value judgement, in many if not most cases students who accept the functionalist position end up viewing increased consensus as good and conflict as bad. This contributes to their emphasis on the kinds of power which are exercised in such a way as to increase consensus and agreement, that is, the methods of social control. Such an emphasis may lead to concentrating on social control mechanisms as methods of conflict resolution,[44] or it may lead to concentrating on mechanisms of conflict avoidance and suppression. Through the latter mechanisms, the institutions and processes of the community are directed either toward evading any issues that might occasion conflict or toward maintaining a "consensus" by means of forcing agreement with the prevailing social norms.

No matter which form the emphasis on consensus ultimately takes, there are those who view it as basically unhealthy. It obviously does have a certain conservative emphasis on the status quo. Because it views the absence of consensus or discontent as a major contributor to instability and uncertainty within the community, the emphasis on consensus tends to reduce the opportunity for social change. Critics, therefore, see this emphasis on order and stability and on the community and society rather than on the individual as leaning dangerously toward totalitarianism.

The conflict theorists approach the study of community politics from quite a different set of assumptions. While few of them, if any, deny the existence of some sort of rudimentary consensus which serves as the basis for the community, they minimize the importance of such a consensus to the politics of the community. The basic assumptions of this approach appear to stress individual and group differences within the community as the source of political activity. This emphasis leads to a concentration on the kinds of power and influence that are designed primarily to lead to the adoption of one individual's or group's goals and desires as public policy rather than another. This implies at least three further differences

---

[43] Lenski, *Power and Privilege*, p. 15.
[44] Gamson, *Power and Discontent*, pp. 11–16.

between conflict and consensus as focuses in community politics.[45] First, there is a concern with actors rather than with the system as a whole, and with the distributive aspects of power, namely who gains what at whose expense. Second, there is an emphasis on the strategy of conflict rather than on its regulation. And third, discontent is viewed as an opportunity or danger for particular subgroups within the community rather than as a problem of social control.

This last point, the view of discontent as an opportunity, gives conflict analysis whatever radical character it does in fact possess. The stress is clearly laid upon the opportunity for social change rather than upon the status quo. If the conflict theorist views the style of community power as essentially one that embodies conflict through complete participation, party mechanisms, interest group competition, or elite group competition, he sees the end result of the individual, party, or group competition as being a policy different from the one presently being pursued. Even though no one group is likely to have its way in every issue or even at all times on one issue, the resulting compromise is likely to be something more than the same old policy. Even when the community is allegedly dominated by a socioeconomic elite, the conflict theorist looks for some evidence of dissatisfaction on the part of the downtrodden masses. For example, the Marxist clearly expects the masses to rise up and throw off their chains in response to elite-group domination of the policy-making process.

As in most other dichotomies, this contrast between consensus and conflict theories is overdrawn. Much of this can be traced to the excesses of the theorists themselves, but, regardless of the source, the tendency must be combated. After having examined community politics at some length, many scholars are attempting to arrive at a synthesis of functionalist and conflict theory which will provide a better description and explanation of community politics.[46] Competent scholars have come to the conclusion that both conflict and consensus politics are present in our communities, and that the differences between communities may be of degree rather than kind.[47]

Professors Agger, Goldrich, and Swanson have developed a particularly helpful typology of community power structures. This typology helps to place communities in competitive or consensual categories dependent upon the distribution of power among their citizens and upon the ideological agreement among their leaders. Table 6–1 illustrates the typology. The ideological agreement or disagreement between the political

---

[45] Gamson, *Power and Discontent*, p. 10.
[46] Lenski, *Power and Privilege*, pp. 1–23.
[47] Agger, Goldrich, and Swanson, *The Rulers and the Ruled*, pp. 3–4.

TABLE 6–1

Political leadership's Ideology	Distribution of power among citizens	
	Broad	Narrow
Convergent	Consensual Mass	Consensual Elite
Divergent	Competitive Mass	Competitive Elite

SOURCE: Robert E. Agger, Daniel Goldrich, and Bert E. Swanson, *The Rulers and the Ruled* (New York, 1964), p. 73. Reprinted by permission of John Wiley & Sons, Inc.

leadership is used as a primary determinant of the degree of consensus or competition within the community. This approach appropriately emphasizes the importance of leadership and ideology in community politics. Its major shortcoming is that it rather unrealistically continues the dichotomy between consensual and competitive politics and combines it with a sweeping division of the distribution of power into two categories. This shortcoming does not destroy the value of the typology as a heuristic device, but no student of urban politics should be alarmed or disappointed if he discovers that he cannot easily place particular communities into the categories.

Suggested Readings

Agger, Robert E.; Goldrich, Daniel; and Swanson, Bert E. *The Rulers and the Ruled*. New York, 1964.

Banfield, Edward C. *Political Influence*. New York, 1961.

Dahl, Robert A. *Who Governs?* New Haven, 1961.

Gamson, William A. *Power and Discontent*. Homewood, Ill., 1968.

Hunter, Floyd. *Community Power Structure*. Chapel Hill, 1953.

Janowitz, Morris, ed. *Community Political Systems*. Glencoe, 1961.

Lenski, Gerhard. *Power and Privilege*. New York, 1966.

Mills, C. Wright. *The Power Elite*. New York, 1956.

Polsby, Nelson W. *Community Power and Political Theory*. New Haven, 1963.

Presthus, Robert. *Men at the Top*. New York, 1964.

Rose, Arnold M. *The Power Structure: Political Process in American Society*. New York, 1967.

chapter 7
The Structure
of Urban
Governments

([Neither a study of organization charts nor an identification of socio-economic elites is, in itself, a sufficient explanation of urban politics. Neither the formal structure nor the political environment is independent of the other. Studies of legal form and political setting must take into account the influence of the one on the other. Only in this way will we be able to unravel the puzzle of the relationships between them.[1]*

Part of the American political tradition is that the nation's citizens are concerned about the structure of governments. "Constitutionalism" may be one of our most prevalent characteristics as a democratic people. Urban governments have not been immune to this concern. Ever since the chartering of this country's first municipality, governmental architects have been seeking a form or structure that would contribute greatly to the democratic process if not guarantee it. This chapter will deal with these efforts and attempt to assess their impact on the decision-making process. In order to do this, we must examine the basic governmental form, the attempts to reform this structure, and the operation of executive and legislative officials within the various structures. Finally, an evaluation of structural reform must be attempted, as well as some tentative assessment of the role that structure plays in determining the kinds of policies which will be adopted.

---

[1] John H. Kessel, "Governmental Structure and Political Environment: A Statistical Note About American Cities," *American Political Science Review*, 56 (1962): 620.

Mayor-Council Government

Much of the traditional structure of American municipal government was the product of our predominantly English heritage. The institutions of our colonial municipalities were based upon the English concept of the common council which was comprised of a mayor, a recorder, and the councilmen or aldermen. Under this system the mayor wielded considerable influence over the kinds of policy decisions made. His influence was derived from two basic sources. In the first place, the mayor was an appointee of the colonial governor and, as such, bore the authority both of the governor and of the English Crown. The second source of influence was his position in the community. The governor usually selected a man of considerable experience in local government, a man who had already successfully exercised his leadership in community affairs. These mayors exercised little institutional power in the modern sense, however. Although they were permitted to vote on council matters, they had no veto powers and very little in the way of appointment and removal powers.[2]

Following the achievement of independence, the United States entered a period in which distrust of the executive was reflected in institutional arrangements from the national to the local level. This distrust was particularly strong at the local level where the council selected the mayor in most municipalities until after 1820. Even after considerable experience with directly elected executives at the national and state levels indicated that it was probably acceptable, perhaps even appropriate, to elect mayors directly, the municipal chief executive did not gain much in the way of formal powers. The major responsibilities for municipal government remained with the council. This set the stage for the first clearly definable form of American municipal government.[3]

WEAK MAYOR STRUCTURE. In the 1830s and 1840s, an increased emphasis on popular participation in government and the assumption that government required little in the way of professional competency contributed to an increase in the number of directly elected executive officers. These attitudes, usually associated with Jacksonian Democracy, extended the principle of popular control beyond the mayor to include the heads of major administrative agencies as well. Figure 7–1 illustrates the result of this tendency. The institutional powers of the mayor were seriously cir-

---

[2] Jewell Cass Phillips, *Municipal Government and Administration in America* (New York, 1960), p. 261.

[3] Phillips, *Municipal Government*, p. 262.

Figure 7–1: Weak Mayor Structure

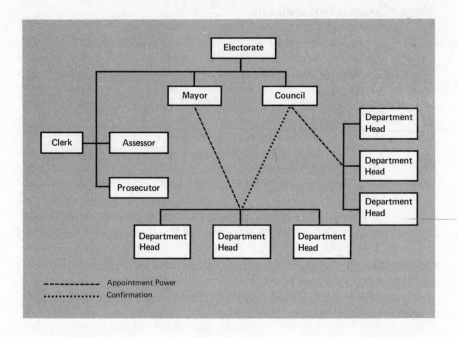

cumscribed. The chief executive had little control over the administration of municipal affairs since his major "subordinates" were responsible either to their own constituencies in the electorate or to the council. The mayor was also in a poor position to deal with the council since he lacked the power to veto council proposals and since the council had direct access to almost all of the other administrative officers. It is particularly interesting to note that the diffusion of executive power at the municipal level occurred at the same time and was supported by many of the same ideological positions as the strengthening of the executive at the national level under the administration of Andrew Jackson. The Era of the Common Man supported the spoils system and the strengthening of executive appointment and removal, as well as a liberal use of the veto at the national level, while rejecting the use of the same devices as dangerous to democracy at the local level.

The fear of executive tyranny at the local level has encouraged the maintenance of the weak mayor form over the years in many of our most important cities. The fragmenting of executive power has not, however, been without serious consequences. Many students of municipal government have pointed out that this form provides no clear-cut institutionalized leadership in the formulation of policy recommendations. They have claimed that this polycentric executive creates too many centers for policy initiation and that the absence of clear lines of executive authority makes it all but impossible to reach the consensus needed for decisions. The result is inaction where action may be desired by the people of the city. New mechanisms were created to fill the power vacuum that inevitably resulted from the weakness of the mayor.

> Disintegrated responsibility invited power to grow up outside the formal structure of government. The boss sought votes at the bottom of the pile to give him control over the nominations and elections, and, in return, he procured at the top councilmen and administrators beholden to him for continuance in office. . . . The executive function was transferred from city hall to the headquarters of the boss, where power, far from providing services at low cost, was utilized to fatten the faithful with patronage.[4]

One must remember that while boss control of the cities was—and still is—morally unacceptable to most Americans, it was not totally evil in its consequences. The price that the boss and the machine paid when "buying" votes was frequently a service price rather than a cash payment. The services rendered for which the grateful working-class majority "sold" their votes were often those that the weakened municipal institutions had failed to provide. The boss filled a service vacuum as well as a power vacuum. Without him, many late nineteenth and early twentieth century immigrants to our shores would not have survived.

The weakness of the weak mayor form has always been a relative matter, and even in the days of greatest distrust of local executives few cities had structures that conformed to the extreme type suggested here. After 1850 there was an increasing tendency to build up the office of mayor as more and more people became dissatisfied with the performance of their municipal government and became less apprehensive about giving additional powers to the chief executive. Perhaps experience with a more traditional system of checks and balances at the national level convinced even the most fearful that such a system might work at the local level as well. Whatever the reason, over the last 120 years we have experienced a gradual strengthening of the mayor's office in mayor-council cities. More and more appointments have been made by the mayor without council approval. Fewer officials are directly elected. More and more mayors are authorized to veto at least some of the ordinances and acts of the city council. Were it not for this factor, the bossism and corruption that so alarmed civic reformers at the turn of the century might possibly have been even more widespread.

---

[4] Arthur W. Bromage, *Municipal Government and Administration* (New York, 1957), p. 264.

Figure 7–2: Strong Mayor Structure

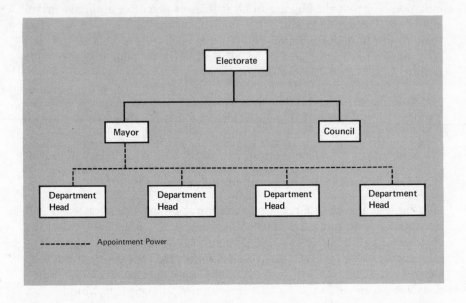

STRONG MAYOR STRUCTURE. As powers are added to the mayor's office, that office eventually reaches a point at which it can no longer be characterized as weak. Figure 7–2 illustrates the extreme type of strong mayor structure in which all administrative powers are concentrated in the hands of the mayor. There are no other elected administrators. The mayor alone appoints and removes the officials in his administration. In addition to the characteristics that can be easily indicated on an organization chart, the mayor also possesses institutional devices that enable him to serve as a check on the activities of the city council. A broad veto power enables him to force the attainment of an extraordinary majority in the council on all measures of which he disapproves. The item veto gives him the ability to delete items added to the budget by the council. Executive control over the budgetary process itself allows the mayor to use his staff to prepare a document that sets the terms of council debate over the level of expenditure for the coming year. In other words, the preparation of the budget gives the executive the initiative in dealing with his legislature.

The powers granted to the strong mayor might have been too broad to be acceptable within the framework of democracy had it not been for two other important developments that accompanied the trend toward the stronger executive. The establishment of a civil service system removed many of the positions in the city administration from the immediate control of the mayor. Although his appointment and removal powers were broadened, the range of offices over which such powers could be exercised was narrowed. Civil service systems also heralded the acceptance of the assumption that the administration of the city required professionals rather than amateurs in the various departments. This, in turn, meant that even those department heads who were still subject to executive appointment had to possess some ability relevant to the job. As strong mayors selected qualified professionals to head the various departments, they found that their appointees were subject to conflicting loyalties. On one hand, they were obviously loyal to the man who had appointed them and who could remove them should their performance prove to be incompatible with the goals he had established for his administration. On the other hand, as professionals they had a loyalty toward the standards and values of their profession which they could compromise only at the jeopardy of their professional future. Faced with such practical limitations, the powers that had been institutionally bestowed upon the mayor were far from absolute.

The strong mayor structure obviously has much in common with the structures established by the Constitution for our national government. This form is particularly attractive to those who admire consistency and neatness in structure and who are fond of that difficult combination of separation of powers and checks and balances which characterizes the national system. The strong mayor, like the President, has become an executive capable of direct confrontation with the legislature and capable of forcing legislative capitulation under some circumstances. However, those who have been particularly alarmed by the growth of executive power at the national level see little cause to rejoice in the development of strong mayors. In most cases, these critics see in the strong executive a commitment to governmental activism that they find unacceptable. Even the most casual examination of the record of the strong mayors in this country would serve to substantiate the charge of activism. Any evaluation of the structure's desirability might well be dependent upon the role one assigns to government in the solving of social problems in a democratic society.

The institutional arrangement that results in a strong mayor presupposes that the man filling the chief executive's position will have various talents. He has two quite different roles to perform by virtue of his position in the structure. In the first place, the mayor is expected to present coherent policy recommendations to the council. The diversity of opinion which was characteristic of the weak mayor form does not disappear when the executive is strengthened. Diverse interest groups and individuals still press for the adoption of their own particular approaches to the problems facing the city. The difference lies in the institutionalized responsibility of the mayor to exercise political leadership and the art of compromise in order to mold these diverse opinions into a single administration policy that will be acceptable to the council and to the electorate. The second role is that of supervising the conduct of the executive branch and insuring that administrative officers are properly carrying out the policies upon which he and the council have agreed. This role requires considerable knowledge of the techniques of public management—skills quite different from those usually employed in the formation of political consensus. Students of American municipal government have suggested that it is almost impossible to find men who combine both of these skills and who are willing to accept the position of mayor, considering the salary and working conditions that usually accompany that office.[5]

REFORM OF THE MAYOR-COUNCIL STRUCTURE. Most of the reformers of the late nineteenth and early twentieth centuries who viewed boss and machine control of many of our cities with alarm did not connect these evils with power and service vacuums created by a weak executive structure. They tended to see the political party as the cause rather than the vehicle of corruption. For this reason the tendency to strengthen the mayor and to concentrate greater political power in the hands of one man was not a satisfactory solution for most reformers to the problems of the cities. In recognition of this fact, many cities that maintained a mayor-council structure instituted electoral reforms of the kinds discussed in Chapter 5. Although the form in its "pure" state would probably still be characterized by partisan, ward elections, there are large numbers of mayor-council cities which have adopted nonpartisan elections, at-large elections, or both.

In recognition of the problem of securing a mayor who possesses both the political and administrative skills necessary to fulfill the expectations of the office in a strong mayor form, many of the larger mayor-council cities have adopted a structural modification that has proven helpful. The mayor has been given the authority to hire an administrative expert to assist him with that part of his responsibilities so that he may devote more of his own time and talents to the political problems of the executive. This assistant has been given many names, such as Deputy Mayor, Chief Administrative Officer, and Administrative Assistant. In spite of loud complaints from supporters of more extreme forms of reform, this modification has been adopted by such major cities as New York, Los Angeles, Philadelphia, San Francisco, and New Orleans with generally good results.[6] The exact powers exercised by the assistant vary widely according to the strength of the mayor, that is, the powers that he can

---

[5] See particularly Charles R. Adrian and Charles Press, *Governing Urban America*, 3d ed. (New York, 1968), p. 195.

[6] For the debate over this modification see Wallace S. Sayre, "The General Manager Idea for Large Cities," *Public Administration Review* 14 (1954): 253–257, and John E. Bebout, "Management For Large Cities," *Public Administration Review* 15 (1955): 188–195.

delegate to his administrator, and to the mayor's personal choice as to the powers he wishes to retain for himself. The crucial characteristic of this modification is that the mayor possesses the appointing authority and that the administrator works for him and with him. Plans that permit the council to appoint the administrator fall somewhere in a never-never land between the mayor-council structure and the council-manager plan that will be discussed later in this chapter.

Another reform movement that has been successful only since 1968 has had an impact on many mayor-council cities. In that year the Supreme Court of the United States applied the principles of previous reapportionment decisions to local governments.[7] Cities that had continued to elect their councils on a ward basis must now devote their attention to insuring that the wards contain sufficiently equal populations to meet the standards of the courts. Although the impact of this court decision is difficult to gauge before many communities have had an opportunity to respond to it, a few tentative guesses as to its importance can be made. Under ideal circumstances, the result of reapportionment would be an increase in the council representatives afforded minority groups. Even though the ward system is more likely to produce minority representation than at-large election, high population densities in minority neighborhoods often result in only token representation which is all out of proportion to the size of the group.[8] However, our experience with the politics of reapportionment indicates that the circumstances are likely to be far from ideal. In the first place, it may be necessary to go through the costly and time-consuming process of initiating legal proceedings in every city in order to force even a minimal effort at reapportionment. In the second place, it is clear that the reapportioned wards may be gerrymandered to eliminate much if not all of the desired effect. Using the "one man, one vote" principle does not eliminate the possibility of other criteria being introduced to aid in the drawing of ward boundaries. The Supreme Court's ruling may make gerrymandering more difficult, but it does not eliminate it entirely as a technique for reducing the impact of "undesirable" elements on legislative bodies.

Commission Government

Civic reform groups reacted so severely to the crime, corruption, and inefficiency that appeared to be endemic in our cities at the close of the nineteenth century that mere "tinkering" with the existing structure of

---

[7] *Avery v. Midland County, Texas, et al.*, 390 U.S. 474 (1968).

[8] Although black Americans constitute a majority or near-majority in many major cities, they have few city councilmen with which they can identify. See for example the *Report of the National Advisory Commission on Civil Disorders* (New York, 1968), pp. 138 and 145.

Figure 7–3: Commission Structure

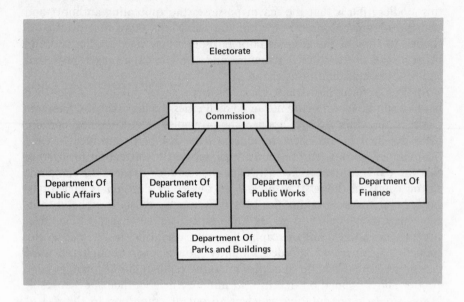

municipal government was not likely to satisfy them. They felt the need for a totally new approach to government, one that would result in honest, efficient, economical government. The answer that they hit upon was to throw out the "politicians" and the "political" structures and to establish a new form of government based upon sound business principles. Most of these reform-minded citizens were products of a middle-class ethic which saw in the success of business procedures in American society the answer to many if not most of our social problems. Their proposal was a commission form of government which combined the executive and legislative branches into a single body that was directly responsible to the people. As Figure 7–3 indicates, each member of the commission was expected to perform a dual function. As a commissioner he was at once a legislator and the administrative officer in charge of a specific division of municipal government. The reform element thought that this plan approximated the business corporation's board of directors system closely enough to guarantee the desired results.

While the reform movement enthusiastically pushed the commission form, it cannot be given credit for developing the form initially. Reformers on a national level later provided the ideological justification for what Professor George Blair has called a "historical accident." [9] In 1900 the city of Galveston, Texas was devastated by a hurricane. When the existing

---

[9] George S. Blair, *American Local Government* (New York, 1964), p. 212.

weak mayor-council government proved inadequate to the task of rebuilding the city, a group of citizens sought help from the state legislature in the form of a new city government. The legislature granted the citizens' request and established a commission to govern the city. When Galveston's five commissioners proved to be dedicated and effective public servants, the results were so spectacular in terms of rebuilding the city and cutting the costs of government that cities all over the country began to consider adopting the commission structure. In the first ten years of its existence the plan was adopted by 108 cities, and by 1917 the number of adoptions had soared to 500.[10] As the change of structure became the rallying cry of reform groups around the country, it was combined with nonpartisan and at-large elections to form a package that would completely separate the new form from the old.

But the commission form shortly ran into trouble. In small communities the burdens of administrative responsibility upon the individual commissioner were not great. Each man found that he could successfully combine the roles of administrator and legislator with those of businessman and family man without too much difficulty. However, as the community grew, it became increasingly apparent that if each commissioner was to administer his department effectively, he would have to devote so much of his time to it that he would no longer be able to pursue successfully his business or professional career. Because of this, some states began to require each commissioner to spend a minimum amount of time on the job in order to guarantee minimal performance of administrative duties.[11] A second difficulty lay in the absence of legislative oversight of administrative operations. Since each legislator was himself an administrator, any criticism directed against the operations supervised by another commissioner invited retribution. Therefore, the only way to preserve any semblance of unity on the commission was to allow each commissioner to run his department without interference from his colleagues except in the most serious matters. This tendency also manifested itself when the time came to prepare the budget for the city. Each commissioner was responsible for his own departmental budget. To question another commissioner's budget left the critic's proposal open to question. The result was a general logrolling of proposals so that the total budget for the city became the sum of the departmental proposals. Such activities tended to offset the economies realized by the change in government forms. The absence of both separation of powers and checks and balances often produced results diametrically opposed to those desired by reform elements. Government was neither efficient nor economical.

---

[10] Blair, *American Local Government*, p. 213.

[11] For example, the state of Illinois requires that commissioners in cities of 20,000 and over devote at least thirty hours per week to their office. *Illinois Revised Statutes*, Chapter 24, Section 4–6–1.

Perhaps the greatest difficulty experienced by the commission form of government was the lack of clear and coherent executive leadership. The structure provided no one man to coordinate the policies of the various departments, and the prevailing practice on most commissions actually discouraged coordination of efforts. In the absence of institutional leadership, the municipality either ran the risk of disorganized and often contradictory programs or was dependent upon leadership developed outside of the official governmental structure and, therefore, not necessarily responsive or responsible to the people of the community. This absence of executive leadership led many reformers to the conclusion that the commission form was not the answer to the sort of business-like government that they sought.

Council-Manager Government

Even before the movement for the adoption of the commission form had begun, there were suggestions that the administration of municipal affairs might best be handled by a professional manager who was, by virtue of his experience and training, particularly well-equipped to handle the administrative problems peculiar to the running of a city.[12] Although Staunton, Virginia experimented with the appointment of a manager as early as 1908, it was not until Sumter, South Carolina adopted a new charter in 1912 that the council-manager form of government was born. This structure provided the reform elements with the vital ingredient that had been missing in the earlier attempts to introduce economy, efficiency, and business procedures in government. Every business has some type of chief executive officer who works for the board of directors and who provides the leadership necessary to make the corporation run. The city manager seemed to be the answer to the need for such an officer in the municipal corporation.

Figure 7-4 indicates the organizational format of council-manager government. The council is usually small and elected on a nonpartisan, at-large basis. The major responsibility of the council is legislative. It is charged with the exercise of the policy-making function. The manager is hired by the council to administer its policies, and, in order to do this, he is given complete control over the administrative personnel of the city. The manager hires and fires all personnel (with the exception of the clerk and the auditor who are frequently viewed as council employees rather than as administrators) subject only to the restraints of the civil service system, where such exists, and to ultimate sanction of the council. This ultimate sanction is, of course, firing the manager. The key to the plan

---

[12] Blair, *American Local Government*, p. 216.

Figure 7–4: Council-Manager Structure

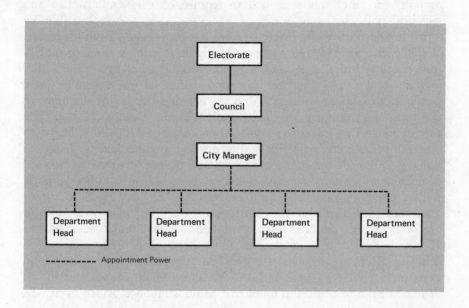

as it was originally conceived was the complete divorce of policy-making and administration. This separation was based upon ideas first developed by Woodrow Wilson and Frank Goodnow in the early part of this century. Although subsequent political scientists found the two activities thoroughly entwined in practice, supporters of the council-manager form such as Leonard White thought that they could be separated under the proper conditions.[13] Increasing experience with council-manager government has led most observers and practitioners to the conclusion that such a separation may be neither possible nor desirable. As Professor Duane Lockard has observed, "the theory of absolute separation of policy and administration, once a key idea of protagonists of the manager system, has been abandoned by nearly all administrative theorists, and even the leading spokesmen of the manager profession have joined in the abandonment."[14] This serves to illustrate that the neatness of organizational charts can be deceiving.

As indicated earlier, a major emphasis of council-manager reform was

[13] Gladys M. Kammerer, Charles D. Farris, John M. DeGrove, and Alfred B. Clubok, *City Managers in Politics: An Analysis of Manager Tenure and Termination* (Gainesville, Fla., 1962), p. 6.

[14] Duane Lockard, "The City Manager, Administrative Theory and Political Power," *Political Science Quarterly* 77 (1962): 224.

that placed upon the professionalism of the manager. The "business" of running our cities was presumed to require certain administrative and technical skills that were not likely to be possessed or exercised fully by a part-time executive officer elected from the community. Even if the best available man were elected, he would rarely be able to do the job. Specialization and technical expertise were a recognized part of twentieth century life, and few people could see any good reason for not extending these principles to local government. With the growing number of adoptions of this form of government an identifiable profession began to develop. The International City Managers' Association, organized in 1914, began to establish professional standards and to develop a curriculum for in-service training to provide communities with administrators who were particularly competent to perform the tasks that face a city manager. Public administration programs in colleges and universities were developed to supply graduates, particularly at the Master's degree level, who were able to accept manager's positions with a minimum of additional training. The ICMA in-service training courses have been particularly effective in bringing current professional standards to large numbers of management personnel. "In 1966 a total of 3,940 municipal employees enrolled in one or more of the 15 courses in municipal administration provided by ICMA through its Institute for Training in Municipal Administration." [15] Many of the employees taking these courses were lower level administrators who were receiving instruction in the latest techniques in order to improve their ability to work with top level managers. If council-manager government accomplished nothing else, its ability to stimulate professional training of municipal employees justified its emphasis on professionalism.

Unfortunately for the movement, the emphasis on professional management has not been uniformly accepted by communities that have adopted the plan. There are still many cities whose councils appoint a manager using quite different criteria. These managers can be called amateurs since neither their education nor their prior administrative experience is extensive enough to assume their professionalism. They are frequently selected locally on the justification that a man who is familiar with the complexities of local problems can better administer the city than can the outsider, no matter how well he is trained. This should not be interpreted as suggesting that the amateur, local manager cannot do a good job by the standards of economy, efficiency, and business-like procedures, but rather that, given the value of education and experience, the amateur is less likely to fulfill the expectations of the reform-oriented than is the fully trained professional.

---

[15] International City Managers' Association, *Municipal Yearbook, 1967,* ed. Orin F. Nolting and David S. Arnold (Chicago, 1967), p. 534.

UTILIZATION OF THE VARIOUS FORMS. Table 7–1 indicates the extent to which the three major forms of municipal government are used by cities in various population categories. The mayor-council form is still the most widely used. Neither this statement nor the table tell the whole picture, however. If one analyzes the data over a period of time, it is apparent that the council-manager form is enjoying more adoptions every year and commands a greater percentage of the total each year. Much of this increase can be traced to the decline of the commission form which is clearly the least popular of the three. As the history of the reform movement indicates, a certain logic can be found in a move from the commission to the council-manager form where the commission form has proven to be unsatisfactory to the city. Note also, however, that mayor-council government has been used in a decreasing percentage of cities over the years. It is reasonable to surmise with the ICMA that the council-manager form will soon be used in over 50 percent of American cities.

TABLE 7–1: Form of Government in Cities over 5,000 Population

Population Group	Total Number of Cities	Total Number of Cities in Table	MAYOR-COUNCIL		COMMISSION		COUNCIL-MANAGER	
			Number	Percent	Number	Percent	Number	Percent
Over 500,000	27	26	20	76.9	1	3.8	5	19.2
250,000 to 500,000	27	27	11	40.7	3	11.1	13	48.1
100,000 to 250,000	96	96	34	35.4	12	12.5	50	52.0
50,000 to 100,000	232	227	84	37.0	22	9.7	121	53.3
25,000 to 50,000	476	462	167	36.1	50	10.8	244	25.8
10,000 to 25,000	1,165	1,105	538	48.7	99	9.0	468	42.4
5,000 to 10,000	1,171	1,146	746	65.1	58	4.9	344	30.0
All cities over 5,000	3,189	3,089 [1]	1,600	51.8	243	7.9	1,245	40.3

SOURCE: International City Managers' Association, *Municipal Yearbook*, 1967 (Chicago, 1967), p. 103. Reprinted by permission of the International City Management Association.

[1] Not included in this table are Washington, D.C., 40 cities with town meeting government, 26 with representative town meeting government, and 33 other cities for which no information was received.

Table 7–1 reveals one further item of interest. The popularity of the mayor-council and council-manager forms appears to be closely related to the population size of the cities concerned. Mayor-council government is most often used in the very large (over 500,000) population group and in the very small (5,000 to 10,000) group. On the other hand, council-manager government is popular in the middle-range cities (10,000 to

500,000) and enjoys a majority in the 25,000 to 250,000 range. While the dominance of mayor-council government in the largest cities can be explained by the need for elected executive leadership in a heterogeneous community, this factor is not a satisfactory explanation for the form's popularity in the smallest cities. Perhaps these small towns choose to retain mayor-council government because they do not perceive the need for full-time professional government. Even in cases where the need for such government might be felt, the small community might have insufficient resources to support professional government of the sort recommended under the manager plan. A more complete explanation awaits further research into the other characteristics of these small cities.

It can reasonably be assumed that council-manager government will continue to grow most rapidly in population categories other than the largest and smallest. Since in the over half a century of its existence the plan has rarely been abandoned once adopted, the ICMA is not being too optimistic in stressing its popularity for the future. This does not mean, however, that council-manager government will sweep the nation. Its rate of adoption has slowed considerably. While it may enjoy the support of the majority of cities, the largest and smallest cities will continue to utilize mayor-council government.

Executive Leadership

In viewing the executive at the state and local levels, some scholars have taken particular note of the changes which have taken place in the attitudes expressed by the reform-oriented.[16] As we have seen, the weak mayor form stressed the idea of representativeness in the executive by proliferating the directly elected executive officers. The switch to neutral competence as a major value in the executive was reflected in the council-manager movement, with its professional administrator who was to be separated from the political process. Finally, the emphasis on the leadership function of the executive has led many to propose a strong-mayor council form in which a single elected official is given the institutional tools he needs to lead both the council and the public. These executive roles should not be seen as mutually exclusive. The development was really a cumulative one in which new roles were added to the old to present a somewhat more accurate picture of the demands placed upon the executive. For example, few reformers would have gone so far as to suggest that the appointed city manager had no obligation to represent the will of the people in his administrative decisions. The only question involved was whether the executive was to be held responsible for the performance of

---

[16] Lockard, "The City Manager," pp. 224–236.

this role directly through the electoral process or indirectly through the city council. In the same manner, few would suggest that the emphasis presently being placed on the leadership function excludes an obligation on the part of the executive to represent the will of the people or to stress professionalism and neutral competence among his administrators. The stress being placed upon leadership today is intended primarily to create a more balanced view of the municipal executive, not to suggest that the executive plays only one role and should be judged by only one set of criteria.

STRUCTURAL VERSUS EMPIRICAL CONSIDERATIONS. In describing the mayor-council form of government, the terms *weak* and *strong* were utilized to distinguish between the different types of institutional structures which could be and are used in American cities. However, the fact that a mayor is institutionally "weak" does not mean that he has little influence over the decision-making process and cannot effectively exercise leadership. Professors Banfield and Wilson point out that the mayor may have resources at his command outside of the formal institutions provided by the city charter.[17] The outstanding example is the city of Chicago. Most observers have placed Chicago in the "weak" mayor category after examining the formal structure of its government. However, the mayor of Chicago has traditionally been an influential if not wholly dominant figure in municipal decision-making when and if he also was the dominant figure in the county Democratic party machinery. Although aldermanic elections in the city are nominally nonpartisan, the partisan affiliation of candidates is obvious to the voters, and Democratic domination of both the Board of Aldermen and the Mayor's Office is traditional. By controlling the nomination process for the party and the dispensing of favors and patronage in the wards, the mayor can exert much pressure on aldermen, individually and collectively, to support his programs. When control of the party lies outside of the Mayor's Office, the executive's leadership abilities conform more to those expected of the structurally weak mayor.[18]

Of course, the political party is not the only device that can be used by a "weak" executive to centralize policy leadership in his office. Even in the absence of influential political parties the mayor can, by virtue of a position of influence in an extragovernmental "power structure" of the sort discussed in Chapter 6, play a dominant role in decision-making. The mayor can also use his ability to capture the public's attention through the focus of the mass media upon his office to solicit direct support from

---

[17] Edward C. Banfield and James Q. Wilson, *City Politics* (New York, 1963), Chapter 8.

[18] See the discussion throughout Martin Meyerson and Edward C. Banfield, *Politics, Planning and the Public Interest* (New York, 1955).

the electorate for programs that might not otherwise meet with council approval. Such community leadership is more a product of the individual executive's view of his role in office and of his personality and style than it is of formal institutional arrangements. There is evidence to indicate that, even in cities where the mayor is not directly elected by the people but is the recipient of the highest number of votes for a council seat or is elected by the council, the people expect the man who holds the office of mayor to exercise policy leadership. In fact one leading scholar, after conducting careful empirical research in three communities, concluded that "it is impossible to conclude whether the manner by which the mayor was selected affected his role as a policy leader." [19]

Much of the comment about the ability of the "weak" mayor to act as a policy leader is as appropriate to the mayor in the council-manager form as it is to the executive in the mayor-council structure. In terms of institutional powers, the mayor in the manager city has perhaps the fewest of any executive. However, experience with this form of government has indicated that the mayor does in fact exercise policy leadership and that this frequently brings him into conflict with the city manager.[20]

Although it has not been empirically documented, it should be noted that the leadership patterns discussed above can be reversed. An institutionally "strong" mayor conceivably might not exercise much leadership or influence over the decision-making process. In spite of the extensive powers of his office, such a mayor could well be dominated by his party or by various groups and factions within the community. He might continue to lay heavy stress upon the representative nature and professionalism of the executive office and to almost slavishly react to the pressures placed upon him by the community and the council. Under such circumstances the strength of the office would remain largely potential and unrealized.

STRUCTURAL STRENGTHS AND WEAKNESSES IN THE OFFICE OF MAYOR. Although the preceding discussion serves as a warning against placing too much stress on the structure of the office of mayor, this structure is still an important variable to be considered in understanding the decision-making process at the municipal level. Tables 7–2, 7–3, and 7–4 indicate some of the more important dimensions of these structural strengths. Several assumptions are necessary in order to interpret these tables. With respect to Table 7–2, the usual assumption is that the directly elected mayor with a vote on the council is in the strongest position vis-a-vis the council.

---

[19] Charles R. Adrian, "A Study of Three Communities," *Public Administration Review* 18 (1958): 211.

[20] Gladys M. Kammerer, Charles D. Farris, John M. DeGrove, and Alfred B. Clubok, *The Urban Political Community* (Boston, 1963), pp. 197–198.

TABLE 7–2: **Method of Selection and Voting Powers of Mayors in Cities over 5,000**

		PERCENT OF REPORTING CITIES			PERCENT OF DIRECTLY ELECTED MAYORS VOTING	
Form of Government	*Number of Cities Reporting*	*Directly Elected*	*Selected by Council*	*Highest No. Votes in Council Election*	*On All Issues*	*In Case of Tie*
Mayor-Council	1,558	95.6	3.9	0.5	13.5	64.7
Commission	234	76.1	23.0	0.9	94.5	3.7
Council-Manager	1,230	51.1	47.8	1.1	48.6	47.5
All cities over 5,000	3,022	76.0	23.3	0.7	29.7	55.2

SOURCE: International City Managers' Association, *Municipal Yearbook, 1967* (Chicago, 1967), p. 104. Reprinted by permission of the International City Management Association.

Empirical studies cast grave doubts upon this assumption. With respect to mayor-council government, it is obvious that nearly all mayors, whether strong or weak, are directly elected. In the commission and council-manager forms, the studies by Kammerer et al. and Adrian cited earlier indicate that the mayor has a constituency of importance in the community regardless of his method of selection. The assumption that the possession of a vote on all issues facing the council gives added bargaining power to the mayor remains to be tested.

Table 7–3 indicates the degree to which the chief executive possesses a veto power. The standard assumption in all of the literature dealing with the executive branch of government in this country is that the veto power is an important tool of executive leadership. Note that only in mayor-council cities does the executive have extensive veto powers, and then only in slightly over one-third of the cities using the form. The municipal executive is obviously nowhere near as fortunate as his state and national counterparts when it comes to the veto power. This cannot presently be listed as an important source of strength for the large majority of mayors in this country.

We have also assumed that a long term of office adds to the powers of the executive. One of the traditional efforts to limit executive strength has been that of reducing his term of office to a minimal one or two years. Table 7–4 shows the status of the office terms for mayors. There is obviously a preference for two- rather than four-year terms. This preference reflects the further assumption that frequent elections serve to reinforce the responsibility of public officials and to guarantee their responsiveness to the desires of the public. While there is little evidence that the four-

TABLE 7–3: Veto Power of Mayors in Cities over 5,000

Form of Government	Total Number of Cities [1]	Number of Cities Reporting	PERCENT OF REPORTING CITIES		
			Veto All Measures	Veto Selected Items	No Veto
Mayor-Council	1,489	1,299	33.6	33.8	32.6
Commission	178	152	4.6	3.9	01.4
Council-Manager	629	605	10.0	18.5	71.4
All cities over 5,000	2,296	2,056	24.6	27.0	48.3

SOURCE: International City Managers' Association, *Municipal Yearbook, 1967* (Chicago, 1967), p. 105. Reprinted by permission of the International City Management Association.

[1] Table limited to cities in which the mayor is directly elected by the people.

year term has in any way diminished the responsibility of mayors, the tendency has been for cities to proceed slowly in granting longer terms. In most cases the mayor's term coincides with that of the council (or commission), and he does not seem to suffer by comparison with that body.

THE MAYOR AS A LEADER. In the final analysis, whether the executive draws his strength from institutional or noninstitutional sources, the current literature of municipal government expects him to be a policy leader. The process of developing policy has tended to be a highly individualized one in which each mayor used his own particular method of arriving at the policies that he would recommend to the council and to the community. Those few who were versed in the traditional literature of public administration had a key word that they frequently used to describe the ideal policy development process—POSDCORB. This stands for Planning, Organizing, Staffing, Directing, Communicating, Reporting, and Budgeting. In discussing this concept, a talented practitioner of the art, Mayor Henry Maier of Milwaukee says, "It labels the kinds of activities he carries out and the problem areas he encounters. But it fails to account adequately for and describe the mayor's actual involvement, the requirements of his institutional leadership, and the procedural concerns of his operation." [21]

Mayor Maier finds the leadership role of the executive to be much more complex, and he sees it divided into several parts:

[21] Henry W. Maier, *Challenge to the Cities: An Approach to a Theory of Urban Leadership* (New York, 1966), p. 32.

TABLE 7–4: **Term of Office of Mayor in Cities over 5,000**

		PERCENT OF REPORTING CITIES					
Form of Government	Number of Cities Reporting	One Year	Two Years	Three Years	Four Years	Five Years	Six Years
Mayor-Council	1,490	2.7	53.6	1.1	42.4	0.0	[1]
Commission	224	4.0	18.8	6.3	67.4	3.1	[1]
Council-Manager	1,190	20.6	53.3	2.4	23.5	[1]	[1]
All cities over 5,000	2,904	10.1	50.8	2.1	36.6	[1]	[1]

SOURCE: International City Managers' Association, *Municipal Yearbook, 1967* (Chicago, 1967), p. 105. Reprinted by permission of the International City Management Association.

[1] Less than 0.5 percent.

He [the mayor] faces multiple pressures and problems as complex as our society. His life is complicated by the fact that he must be one part institutional leader, one part political leader, one part educator, one part scapegoat, and some other part for whatever purpose his community wishes to use him. Of his various roles, however, that of institutional leader stands out as basic and crucial.[22]

To describe this institutional leadership role, Mayor Maier uses what he calls his "D-STEPP Formula." This formula states that Decision-making is accomplished through the sequential use of Strategy, Tactics, Enrollment, Power, and Philosophy:

1. Strategy is the mayor's total planning perspective, the overall design of his objectives.
2. Tactics is [sic] his procedures to implement the strategy.
3. Enrollment is both his specific and his broad efforts to enlist people in support of his objectives.
4. Power is his capability to effect results.
5. Philosophy is his system of leadership as exercised through his understanding of the demands of institutional leadership and the ways of people.[23]

While even Mr. Maier would not claim that this is a fully satisfactory theoretical framework within which to examine and ultimately understand the executive role in decision-making, it remains a challenging and helpful first step toward developing such a theory.

---

[22] Maier, *Challenge to the Cities*, p. 29.
[23] Maier, *Challenge to the Cities*, p. 33.

One of the major difficulties of looking at the D-STEPP formula as a description of purely institutional leadership is that it implies the use of other kinds of leadership as well. Enrollment and Power turn out to be crucial to the making of the ultimate decision and to its eventual implementation. As described by Maier, these two processes most surely would imply employing the roles of political leader and educator which he so carefully distinguished from institutional leadership earlier. The engineering of consent which he identifies as a central problem of the mayor [24] is the essence of political leadership. Maier himself best states the argument when he says:

> Whatever a mayor's choices or decisions may be, the desired results of his public leadership can be vetoed by others—by the Common Council. . . , by department heads, by the channels of communication, or by the combined opposition of groups—unless he has carefully reckoned with the human element.[25]

THE MANAGER AS A LEADER. Once the artificial distinction between policy and administration had been removed, it was inevitable that the manager should be recognized as a policy leader. However, some attempt is usually made to offer elaborate rationalizations for managerial leadership as if it were somehow sinful:

> Managers, in following the Childs concept of their policy-initiation role, have tended in recent years to rationalize this kind of involvement on the following grounds: (1) managers know the problems of the community better than anyone else; (2) the council commonly fails to fulfill the policy-making task ascribed to it under the plan; (3) the leadership of a single individual is necessary to continuing political leadership, and since the plan removes the mayor from this position, the manager is the only one who can fill the gap; and (4) the increasing complexity of community problems inevitably pushes political leadership into the hands of the "expert" and out of the hands of the legislative body.[26]

These rationalizations do not have equal value when it comes to justifying managerial policy leadership. The claim that the manager knows more about the community's problems than anyone else can easily be questioned, especially if he is an outsider and a professional who is brought in to do the job and whose tenure in office will only average five years. On the other hand, there is no question that the council does not and perhaps cannot initiate policy in the manner for which reformers had hoped. The fourth justification for managerial leadership is one of the most important

---

[24] Maier, *Challenge to the Cities*, p. 182.
[25] Maier, *Challenge to the Cities*, p. 190.
[26] Kammerer, et al., *City Managers in Politics*, pp. 8–9.

reasons for council inactivity. The government of our cities is not immune to the general trend in our highly technological society for the expert to dominate the decision-making process. Finally, the need for continuity and focus in policy leadership is certainly recognized by most observers. However, it is precisely because the plan *in practice* does not remove the mayor from this position of leadership that conflict often occurs. The manager must be sure that a leadership gap exists before he tries to fill it.

While the literature on managerial leadership makes increasing use of the word "political" to describe the manager's activities, practitioners of the art are still somewhat shy about accepting the word with all of its sordid connotations of compromise. For example, the standard guide to city managers on the subject states that "managers can possess political sense without being involved in partisan political questions." [27] Here the word "political" is used to describe pursuits carried out in the public interest, and "partisan political" is reserved to describe those questions over which groups express some differences of opinion. This largely artificial distinction implies a series of normative judgments about the "public interest" that are open to serious question. It is precisely this assumption—that there is a public interest that is separable from the various individual and group interests in the community—that disturbs the most outspoken critics of the council-manager form of government. Managerial leadership is more acceptable when it is oriented toward politics in the more traditional sense rather than in the specialized sense noted above. When faced with the practical demands of maintaining a position within a community, managers frequently discard the theoretical niceties of their position in favor of an effort to be aware of community attitudes as reflected by organized groups.[28]

Managerial leadership styles vary considerably with the situation in which the manager finds himself. Obviously, not all councils are impotent when it comes to initiating policy. If an extragovernmental power structure exists, the council may reflect the policy desires of that structure and be totally unreceptive to leadership efforts on the part of the manager. We have already seen that the mayor can take an active leadership role and that the manager must avoid too frequent clashes with him. Karl Bosworth has suggested that these considerations force the development of three identifiable styles of policy leadership.[29] The manager may be an administrator, a policy researcher, or a community leader. The administrator effects changes in policy primarily through budget preparation and the

---

[27] Clarence E. Ridley, *The Role of the City Manager in Policy Formulation* (Chicago, 1958), p. 3.

[28] Ridley, *Role of the City Manager*, p. 13.

[29] Karl A. Bosworth, "The Manager *Is* a Politician," *Public Administration Review* 18 (1958): 216–222.

setting of management goals and priorities. The policy researcher initiates policy studies, provides suggestions for alternative policies, provides information, and attends to public relations. The community leader openly takes the initiative in policy formation and attempts to mobilize support in the community for his programs. While most city managers would probably fall into the policy researcher category, a significant number of managers do fall into the other categories when the characteristics of their communities demand it. Maintaining community satisfaction with his style of leadership is the important factor.[30]

An awareness of the demands of groups within the community is frequently not enough to support managerial leadership if the community is socially and economically heterogeneous and if the cleavages between the various groups are particularly sharp. Most managers feel that they must avoid leadership in these situations, where conflict politics are the usual pattern.[31] This leadership failure in heterogeneous communities is the single most important reason why council-manager government has not successfully penetrated many of our major cities. Nearly all such cities are heterogeneous and are characterized by conflict politics. The existing empirical studies indicate that managerial leadership is difficult; in smaller communities characterized by conflict or competitive politics, managers have markedly short tenures in office.[32] Managerial leadership is most effective in homogeneous communities characterized by consensus politics. It is even more helpful if the city is middle or upper class in social and economic orientation so that the values of the community—economical, efficient, business-like government—are likely to coincide with those of the manager.

If one assumes that the public will not be satisfied with its municipal executive until the three criteria of representativeness, neutral competence, and leadership are all present, it becomes somewhat easier to evaluate the effect of particular governmental structures on the performance of the executive. No structure appears to offer hope of satisfactory performance in every community. But both the mayor-council form and the council-manager form can be modified so as to be satisfactory in most communities. The mayor-council structure places particular emphasis on representation and leadership, especially in the heterogeneous community. The use of the strong mayor, according to current theory, tends to increase the visibility of the executive and thereby to increase the representativeness and responsiveness of the office. Deficiencies of professionalization and neutral competence can be met by adding a chief administrative officer or other management expert to strengthen the mayor's office. Council-

---

[30] Bosworth, "The Manager *Is* a Politician," p. 220.
[31] Ridley, *Role of the City Manager*, p. 21.
[32] Kammerer, et al., *City Managers in Politics*, p. 16.

manager government probably does an adequate job of satisfying all three criteria in the homogeneous community. In a heterogeneous community, the ideal-type structure can be modified by adding a directly elected mayor to perform the leadership function and to concern himself with questions of representation. In terms of the executive, it is not so much what kind of a structure a city has for its government but whether that structure as it is employed adequately reflects the political realities of the community which determines success or failure.

The City Council

It is frequently assumed that the roles played by city councils under the different structures of municipal government do not vary as much as those played by the executive. The obvious exception to this statement is commission government in which the council members fulfill both legislative and executive functions, but this form, so little used today that it is disappearing, can be safely put aside for purposes of this discussion. Students of city government have often ascribed to the municipal legislature a secondary albeit important role. In reporting the results of his study of several communities, one observer wrote:

> The picture of the council, in summary, was one of a largely passive body granting or withholding its approval in the name of the community when presented with proposals from a leadership outside itself.[33]

Negative, simplistic statements such as this can generally be traced to a serious lack of study of legislative behavior in municipal government as well as to the assumption that policy initiative was far more important to the decision-making process than the more passive role that the legislature appeared to be playing. Studies of legislative behavior at the national and state levels have revealed that many important roles are played by legislators in the exercise of their functions, and the daily newspapers give plentiful testimony that even a passive legislative body that does not initiate policy can be important as a roadblock in the decision-making process.

The few empirical studies of city councils which have been conducted have been particularly valuable because they have caused many political scientists to question the "conventional wisdom" that had so long been the basis for much of the literature of municipal government. One such pioneering study was conducted by J. Leiper Freeman.[34] Freeman identi-

---

[33] Adrian, "A Study of Three Communities," p. 212.

[34] J. Leiper Freeman, "A Case Study of the Legislative Process in Municipal Government," *Legislative Behavior*, ed. John C. Wahlke and Heinz Eulau (Glencoe, 1959), pp. 228–237.

fied three basic types of decisions made by a council: (1) "those . . . which are beyond controversy and are taken in an atmosphere of consensus attributable either to overwhelming agreement or indifference;" (2) those "taken in conformity with the pattern of majority vs. minority organization of the body;" and (3) "types of combinations of minority factions which on given issues can form a voting majority, even though the members of the particular voting alliance have not stood and would not stand together to organize the legislative body." [35] While the traditional literature of legislative behavior has revealed that most of the decisions are of the first or noncontroversial type, Freeman found in the city he studied that the second type was unusually prevalent, thereby giving added importance to the questions of councilmen's party affiliation.[36] He further noted that the nature of the issue on which the council was voting did not seem to be important in determining voting alignments on the council except in some cases that involved factional control. In those cases, he found constituency preferences as perceived by the councilmen to be more important than the legislators' personal values with respect to the issue.[37]

In recent years a monumental study has been undertaken by political scientists at Stanford University under the direction of Dr. Heinz Eulau. This study is designed to provide more information about the operation of city councils. Although the results of this study based on a sample of 89 cities in the San Francisco Bay Area are not yet complete, preliminary reports of the findings are quite helpful. For example, these reports demonstrate that city councilmen assume a variety of roles which reflect their perceptions of the office they hold.[38] These roles, in turn, appear to affect the manner in which the councilmen approach their tasks and the strategies they use. The combination of roles and styles adopted by the council materially affects its posture and importance within the governmental structure. A councilman who takes the view that he is merely performing a set of legally determined tasks is likely to rely heavily upon executive leadership and initiative or upon such devices as public hearings, and to take little active part in policy-making. If on the other hand he views himself as a community leader or as an arbiter of community conflict, he adopts far more active strategies that involve, among other things, attempting to develop support for a particular policy position both among other councilmen and in the community at large. While one can disagree

---

[35] Freeman, "A Case Study," p. 230.

[36] Freeman, "A Case Study," pp. 230 and 235.

[37] Freeman, "A Case Study," p. 235.

[38] Charles F. Levine, "Purposive Role Orientations of Non-Partisan City Councilmen" (Paper delivered at the American Political Science Association Annual Meeting, in Chicago, September 5–9, 1967).

about the propriety of the various roles and strategies which have been identified, the decision-making process cannot be adequately understood without using some concept of legislative role and strategy.

Further interpretation of the Stanford data by Dr. Eulau and Dr. Eyestone has postulated that the concept of role does not exhaust the attitudes that a councilman brings with him to his job and that affect the decision-making process:

> It has been the burden of our argument that the systematic study of public policy cannot be content with correlating indicators of environmental challenges or indicators of resource capability to policy outcomes. Rather, it was our assumption that policy development is greatly influenced by the predilections, preferences, orientations and expectations of policy-makers—in short, by the political process itself.[39]

These attitudes constitute the "policy map" of the councilman and help him to determine the kinds of policy decisions which he will support. These "maps" not only help to shape policy; they also reflect in part earlier policy decisions since they are a product of the legislator's experience after joining the council as well as his prior experiences. The Eulau and Eyestone study focuses on the types of policy outcomes which result from these policy maps. It finds that these outcomes, measured in terms of expenditures for particular municipal functions, permit the classification of cities into three stages and two phases of a developmental sequence. Cities move from the Retarded stage through the Emergent phase to the Transitional stage, and from there through the Maturing phase to the final Advanced stage. The major criteria used in formulating these stages and phases are expenditures devoted to adapting the political system to its environment and those devoted to changing the environment of the system.[40] The major importance of the study lies in its attempts to relate the stages and phases of development to the policy maps of councilmen. The emphasis turned out to be on the coincidence of policy maps or upon the degree of consensus on the council. Development seemed closely related to how much council members agreed upon the importance of problems and problem areas and upon the desirability of single improvements or improvement areas. However, they also found that "the less developed a city's policy, the greater the proportion of councils reaching high agreement on the image of city future." [41]

---

[39] Heinz Eulau and Robert Eyestone, "Policy Maps of City Councils and Policy Outcomes: A Developmental Analysis," *American Political Science Review* 62 (1968): 143.

[40] Eulau and Eyestone, "Policy Maps," pp. 127–128.

[41] Eulau and Eyestone, "Policy Maps," pp. 136–142; quotation at p. 142.

Peter Lupsha's analysis of the nature of council leadership is a final contribution from the Stanford study.[42] Using a typology of council behavior patterns which resembles Freeman's, Lupsha describes the characteristics of council leaders as perceived by other councilmen in each situation. In discussing the council, he finds that:

> 1) Leadership in the more harmonious settings is based on many personal and external attributes that are connected with the leaders' image and prestige in the community at large. . . .
> 2) Leadership in the bipolar councils is basically majority faction leadership directed at getting the tasks done and the majority coalition formed and maintained rather than at providing prestige or giving socio-emotional support to the group. . . .
> 3) In the multipolar setting both the instrumental and socio-emotional aspects of leadership are needed and we find that more instrumental and integrative qualities tend to be attributed to leaders.[43]

Such data indicates that leadership patterns and councilmanic behavior are closely tied to the nature of their constituency and the manner in which they represent their constituency. Generally, the findings appear to support Freeman's earlier work.

The results of these preliminary studies of city councils seem to indicate that these bodies are far more complex than has been assumed to date. Until further studies explain more of its mysteries, the council's role in the municipal decision-making process will be extremely difficult to understand.

An Evaluation of Reform

As indicated earlier in this chapter, much of the literature dealing with the structures of municipal government has been oriented toward the reform of these institutions. The tendency has been to assume, because a certain set of policy outcomes did not appear to be "rational" or did not conform to the normative judgements of particular groups, that these outcomes could be altered by altering the structure of municipal government. While such an alteration might achieve the desired results, there was no guarantee that it would do so. Too many other sociopsychological variables affect the ultimate decisions made by the holders of public office. Of course, it is possible that some structural reforms might have the desired effects simply because they alter the ability of the community to

---

[42] Peter A. Lupsha, "Leadership, Expertise, and Decision-Making in Small Legislative Bodies" (Paper delivered at the American Political Science Association Annual Meeting, September 5–9, 1967).

[43] Lupsha, "Leadership," p. 28.

express its character in the decision-making process. As we have seen, the use of nonpartisan, at-large elections appears to have discouraged political participation on the part of lower income groups. This in turn may result in the election of a council which is quite homogeneous or unipolar simply because it reflects only the participation of middle and upper income groups. When such a council is combined with a manager who espouses economy and efficiency in government, the result may be policy outcomes that are acceptable to the reformist element but that do not adequately reflect the desires of a majority of the members of the community.

Given our present knowledge about the operation of municipal institutions and the behavior of municipal officeholders, it appears that much of the reform effort has been devoted to seeking change without really understanding what it is that we want changed or why it needs to be changed. Altering municipal institutions may possibly be the best course of action for a community that wants more satisfactory government. If, however, such alteration is to do any real good, it should be made only after careful study has revealed the source of the dissatisfaction.

Suggested Readings

Bollens, John C. *Appointed Executive Local Government.* Los Angeles, 1952.

Childs, Richard S. *Civic Victories.* New York, 1952.

————. *The First 50 Years of the Council-Manager Plan of Municipal Government.* New York, 1965.

East, John Porter. *Council-Manager Government: The Political Thought of Its Founder, Richard S. Childs.* Chapel Hill, 1965.

Kammerer, Gladys M.; Farris, Charles D.; DeGrove, John M.; and Clubok, Alfred B. *City Managers in Politics: An Analysis of Manager Tenure and Termination.* Gainesville, Fla., 1962.

————. *The Urban Political Community.* Boston, 1963.

Maier, Henry W. *Challenge to the Cities: An Approach to a Theory of Urban Leadership.* New York, 1966.

Ridley, Clarence E. *The Role of the City Manager in Policy Formulation.* Chicago, 1958.

Stewart, Frank M. *A Half Century of Municipal Reform.* Berkeley, 1950.

Woodruff, Clinton R. *City Government by Commission.* New York, 1911.

chapter 8
The Urban Judiciary

⟨[The local trial court is the judicial institution of the local political system. For many matters local in nature, it is the authoritative means whereby conflict is resolved or other branches of government are compelled to act in a particular way; it is the means to power for some, the key to profits or avoidance of burdens for others.[1]

Judicial Structure

Unlike the United States Constitution and state constitutions, the charters of American municipalities are strangely silent on the subject of judicial institutions. This silence has led many students to observe that there is no purely local judiciary and that the judicial function is performed entirely by state and federal courts. Such observations are accurate as far as they go. However, they are far too often an excuse for paying no attention whatsoever to the judicial process as it affects the urban political community. It is important to recognize that the function is performed and that some courts are more important than others in this performance.

Figure 8–1 outlines the structure of a "typical" state court system. The court structure of each state is, however, unique; the following description of the jurisdictions of the various courts is intended to be illustrative, not definitive. The courts which are of particular interest to the student of

---

[1] Kenneth M. Dolbeare, *Trial Courts in Urban Politics* (New York, 1967), p. 3.

Figure 8–1. **State Court Structure**

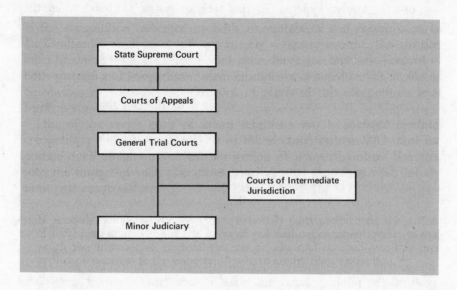

urban government are those at the trial level or those below the courts of appeals and the supreme courts in the state system.

JUSTICE AND MAGISTRATE'S COURTS. The lowest and most localized courts in the system are those presided over by justices of the peace or magistrates. These courts can hear minor criminal matters involving relatively light penalties, for example up to $500 fine and six months in jail. The cases might involve local ordinances, breach of the peace, or traffic law violations. Justices of the peace and magistrates are also frequently permitted to conduct preliminary hearings to determine whether there is enough evidence to continue the detention of an arrested person and to turn his case over to the grand jury or the prosecutor's office for further disposition. The lower courts can also hear civil suits involving small amounts of money. In all of these proceedings these courts are not courts of record—they do not keep a full transcript of proceedings but merely record the nature of the case, the names of the participants, and the final disposition made of the case.

Magistrates and justices of the peace are usually elected by the voters in their particular jurisdiction, which tends to give the voters a proprietary feeling about these courts even though they are technically part of the state system. The citizens often consider their judicial officers as community representatives and expect them to dispense a type of justice which reflects the standards and values of the community. Before the interstate highway system allowed motorists to bypass small towns, many out-of-state tourists experienced this type of justice firsthand when they were victimized by differences in the enforcement of traffic laws. Small towns would establish speed traps along major traffic arteries to pull in unsuspecting visitors. The local J.P. would then assess the maximum fine. Pleas of not guilty were futile. Local residents were not arrested, even though they might have violated the same law. The tendency toward such localized justice has been accentuated by the fact that many magistrates and justices of the peace have not been lawyers. Men without any legal training can hardly be expected to appreciate the subtle nuances of due process of law. To make matters even worse, many of these men occupied "fee offices" in which their level of compensation was determined by the number of cases heard and the amount of fines levied.

The big cities have a minor judiciary that corresponds to the justice of the peace. Unfortunately, it shares many of the characteristics of those courts. The major difference has been that the lowest courts in the large cities have tended to be specialized rather than courts of a more general jurisdiction. Traffic courts, police courts, and small claims courts often perform the minor judicial functions in such cities. In most cases these courts are also presided over by elected officials who have little if any formal legal training. It is, however, less common to find these judges in "fee offices;" most of them are compensated according to salary scales.

The total picture of justice at this level has unfortunately been bleak. Although the cases heard, whether criminal or civil, have been minor, they have served to encourage a cynical attitude on the part of many people toward the judicial process at local levels.

COURTS OF INTERMEDIATE JURISDICTION. In some areas, additional courts of limited jurisdiction have been established. These courts, often called simply "municipal courts," have been given jurisdiction slightly broader than that of the minor judiciary. That is to say, they can hear criminal cases involving slightly higher penalties, and civil cases involving slightly greater amounts of money. Most of these courts are courts of record; they maintain complete records of the proceedings brought before them. Most of the judges at this level are also elected, but it is less likely that the office will be filled by a nonlawyer.

GENERAL TRIAL COURTS. The most important courts in our judicial system are the general trial courts. These courts possess unlimited original jurisdiction in all matters both criminal and civil. It is in the general trial court that most felonies are tried and most civil matters disposed of. In the more sparsely settled areas a single general court will handle all cases. As the population increases this court is frequently broken up into divisions. In some areas of only moderate population density the additional judges serve as associate judges of the court and preside over cases dealing with the full range of the court's jurisdiction. In areas of very high population density it is more common to find a high degree of specialization in the divisions of the general trial courts. Criminal, Juvenile, Domestic Relations, Probate, and Equity represent only a few of the divisions which might be created to handle specialized problems.

Courts at this level also exercise appellate jurisdiction over the courts of the minor judiciary and courts of intermediate jurisdiction. However, this appellate jurisdiction is unlike that exercised at higher levels in the state system. Because of the limitations of the minor judiciary, cases brought to a court of general jurisdiction on appeal are considered *de novo* proceedings. This means that the case is tried over again from the beginning rather than simply reviewing the trial of the lower court. This is largely due to the fact that the lower courts are not courts of record and, therefore, there is very little for the general trial court to review on appeal.

Most general trial courts are found either at the county level or in a judicial district that may include several counties. They are not easily recognized by name since the terminology used to identify them varies widely from state to state. They may be called Superior Courts, Circuit Courts, Common Pleas Courts, District Courts, and so forth, depending upon the tradition of the particular state.

Structural and Procedural Problems

JURISDICTIONAL CONFUSION. In the large cities, where specialized municipal courts and specialized general trial courts are frequently used, there has all too often been considerable confusion in the minds of laymen and lawyers alike as to which court had jurisdiction over which cases.[2] Some of this confusion can be traced to the number of courts involved at the several levels within large cities. Another contributing factor is the tendency toward overlapping jurisdictions which result in more than one court being empowered to hear a single case. This second factor is particularly significant when it permits experienced attorneys to select the court they wish to take their cases to on the basis of the attitudes of particular judges, rather than being forced to accept a more neutral jurisdictional determination made by the legislature. Such tactics might well result in an advantage for the wealthy who can afford to hire the most experienced counsel and a disadvantage for the poor and the middle class who must frequently make do with less talented attorneys.

---

[2] Jewell Cass Phillips, *Municipal Government and Administration in America* (New York, 1960), p. 341.

DELAY. Crowded court calendars are known to be a particular problem in urban areas. Such crowding can be traced to at least two factors. In the first place, some states have not established enough courts to handle the rapidly increasing urban population. The most casual observer of the legal process can see that the number of cases brought to court are in part a function of the number of people within the court's area of jurisdiction. In most rapidly growing urban areas, however, the increase in the number of courts has not been proportional to the increase in population. To make matters worse, there is evidence to indicate that both civil and criminal actions increase at a more rapid rate than population in the large cities. The end result must be an ever-expanding backlog of cases if remedial action is not taken.

In the second place, some urban courts have resisted any move toward the specialization of their jurisdictions.

Failure to specialize has become especially burdensome in metropolitan areas, where the volume of cases could usually be high enough to justify establishing specialized tribunals. Litigants must often take their problems to courts whose judges may not understand the technical problems involved. A high volume of certain kinds of cases may lead to a delay in all cases.[3]

The long delay often experienced in bringing cases to trial is considered a problem primarily because of the almost universal acceptance of the aphorism, "Justice delayed is justice denied." Our Anglo-American legal heritage holds that every man is entitled to a speedy trial. While this value is more frequently expressed with respect to criminal cases than to civil cases, it does serve to alarm us about the crowded calendars of both types of courts. Dissatisfaction with the speed with which the courts operate clearly translates itself in many cases into a more generalized dissatisfaction with the courts as an instrument of conflict resolution in the community.

MASS PRODUCTION. The tendency to dispense assembly-line justice is, at least in part, a result of the crowding of calendars mentioned above. One of the easiest ways to clear a court calendar is to run all of the cases through at breakneck speed. One student of the judicial process has noted:

The most significant fault in our present system of criminal justice is that in those areas where it comes in contact with the average citizen . . . its performance is poorest. Mass-production techniques in traffic courts and misdemeanor arraignment courts are apt to create disrespect for law and the judi-

---

[3] Herbert Jacob, *Justice in America* (Boston, 1965), p. 143.

cial process. Scant regard for human dignity and the worth of the individual can be evidenced where judges face daily calendars in the hundreds.[4]

This mass production manifests itself in an assortment of ways. There are mass arraignments and bail settings, the necessity for group counsel, the universal passing of maximum sentences without consideration of the previous record of individual defendants, and the inclusion in mass proceedings of large numbers of defendants against whom there was insufficient evidence to gain a conviction.[5] The results can be serious. In commenting on the urban disorders of 1967, the National Advisory Commission on Civil Disorders said:

> We have found that the apparatus of justice in some areas has itself become a focus for distrust and hostility. Too often the courts have operated to aggravate rather than relieve the tensions that ignite and fire disorders.[6]

If the attitudes displayed toward the urban trial courts by the respondents to the Advisory Commission's survey become more widespread, the entire system of law and order in our cities could break down. Such a breakdown could result in a totally ungovernable urban society that would make the sporadic outbreaks of past long, hot summers look minor.

Judicial Reform

The major effort in judicial reform has been aimed at the trial courts, the municipal courts, and the inferior courts—those courts which we have already identified as being the urban judiciary. This reform movement has had four major objectives: [7] (1) the removal of judges from politics; (2) a coordinated system of state courts under a chief justice; (3) a unified court system; and (4) more rational judicial districts. While statewide judicial reform efforts have not been successful in every state, they have had some major effects where they have been implemented.

As we shall see later, judges cannot be removed from politics as that word is used by most political scientists. What has really happened as a result of this objective is that much attention has been devoted to the method of selecting judges and to the criteria that are used for this selection. A great many questions have been raised. Should judges be elected

---

[4] Edward L. Barrett, Jr., "Criminal Justice: The Problem of Mass Production," in *The Courts, The Public, and the Law Explosion,* ed. Harry W. Jones (Englewood Cliffs, N.J., 1965), p. 115.

[5] *The Report of the National Advisory Commission on Civil Disorders* (New York, 1968), pp. 340–354.

[6] *The Report of the National Advisory Commission,* p. 337.

[7] Charles Adrian, *State and Local Governments,* 2d ed. (New York, 1967), p. 397.

or appointed? If elected, should it be a partisan or nonpartisan election? What role should the bar associations as spokesmen for the legal profession play in the selection of judges?

These questions have been answered in a number of ways. For the most part, courts have been immune to reforms. Most judges are still elected on partisan ballots. In cases where reforms have been instituted, they have followed the traditional pattern by moving to nonpartisan elections in an effort to remove the influence of political parties, and thereby to remove the politics from the judicial process. The state of Illinois chose to combine reforms in an unusual system in which circuit court (general trial court) judges are first elected on a partisan ballot. They subsequently run unopposed on a nonpartisan ballot to obtain public approval of their conduct in office. The lower judiciary in Illinois (outside of Cook County) consists entirely of magistrates appointed by the circuit judges. The number of magistrates is determined by the population of the judicial circuit.

Many reform movements have favored appointment as the best method of selecting judges. This is believed to allow bar associations to bring professional criteria to bear on the selection process. The preceding discussion indicates that such suggestions have not been particularly popular. It is difficult to convince the electorate that they are not qualified to select any public official. In addition, serious students of the judicial and political processes have expressed some concern that such a scheme would permit the bar associations to capture the judiciary for their own purposes.[8] While public purposes and those of the bar associations may often coincide, there is no guarantee that they will always do so.

One of the biggest accomplishments in the area of judicial selection has been the tendency toward the elimination of nonlawyers from judicial office. In many states in which no other judicial reform has been possible, requirements have been changed in such a way as to eliminate nonlawyer justices of the peace and magistrates and to replace them with men with the proper legal credentials. While it is possible to argue that graduation from law school and admission to the bar are not necessarily related to an ability to perform in minor judicial offices, the public appears to accept the word of the bar associations that such a background is necessary. This particular reform has the advantage of being one of the few sponsored by bar associations that is attractive to their membership. Lawyers appear slow to back judicial reform unless it is aimed at nonlawyers.[9]

The coordination of the court system under the state chief justice is a reform that follows the administrative principle of centralization of control. While organization charts such as Figure 8–1 seem to indicate a

---

[8] Jacob, *Justice in America*, p. 205.
[9] Jacob, *Justice in America*, p. 50.

hierarchical relationship in state court systems, such appearances can be deceiving. These charts really indicate only the flow of cases on appeal in most states. The higher courts have little administrative control over the trial courts. The centralization of the system under the chief justice is an attempt to provide such control and to standardize rules and procedures throughout the state. Such reforms also give a central office the ability to deal with such problems as crowded court calendars by shifting judges from one district to another or from one court to another in an effort to reduce backlogs. The most notable example of such a reformed judiciary is that of New Jersey, which has successfully used these procedures since the adoption of its new constitution in 1947.

The unification of the court system implies the integration of the courts as well as their centralization under the state supreme court. This integration is accomplished by eliminating overlapping jurisdictions and consolidating the courts that perform similar functions within the system. The end result is a more specialized and less complex judiciary at the trial court level. The use of this principle is evident in many of the early efforts at municipal court reform which antedate the more generalized court reform movement. These early reforms were attempted in Chicago in 1906 and Philadelphia in 1913 with notable success. However, both of these municipal court systems are less than fully unified and integrated.[10]

The final objective, that of more rational judicial districts, is less important in urban areas than elsewhere in the state system. The concentration of population in relatively small areas which is characteristic of urbanization makes it relatively easy to justify the existence of the present judicial districts in urban areas. Many states have responded to this increase in population by increasing the number of judges sitting within the trial court districts, rather than by increasing the number of districts. This response fits in particularly well with the other objectives of centralization and unification. The major objection to the progress made in this area has already been noted. This is the tendency to lag behind population growth when establishing new courts within a judicial district.

These objectives of court reform are not ends in themselves. They are aimed at resolving some of the particular problems which plague our local courts. The problems that receive the greatest emphasis in these reform efforts are delay and mass-produced justice. While initial reports from reformed judicial systems, such as that in New Jersey, indicated that reform had made judicial calendars in the trial courts more manageable, the long-run results are not as startling as expected. One assessment states that "there is not acceptable evidence that any remedy so far devised has

---

[10] Phillips, *Municipal Government*, pp. 336–340.

been efficacious to any substantial extent." [11] Lack of success in reducing the load on judicial calendars has made some scholars reexamine the assumptions upon which the identification of delay as a particular problem in our trial courts are based. They have concluded that the end to be sought in judicial reform is quality, not speed.[12] These conclusions inevitably lead to greater concern with mass-produced justice as a perversion of our legal system than with sheer speed in processing cases. We have surely not yet found a structural reform for our judicial system that will enable us to deal with the extraordinary demands now placed upon our courts. In a time of mass demonstrations which all too often become riots, it is extremely difficult to find a system of justice which meets the standard criteria that we have established. Is it possible to treat hundreds or even thousands of demonstrators or rioters individually and still meet the guarantees of speedy justice established by the Constitution of the United States? The answer to this question must be Yes. The question that plagues us is, How?

All too often proponents of judicial reform have assumed that failure in effecting the adoption of reforms or failure of reforms once adopted is traceable to public ignorance and apathy or to the evil machinations of sinister "political" forces. But perhaps these failures can be traced to a more fundamental problem within the reform movement itself. Professor Herbert Jacob has identified such a problem: "What is especially striking about most reform proposals is that they are founded on impressions of how the judicial system operates rather than on factual analysis." [13] Recent research in political science has focused primarily upon the operation of the appellate courts within our judicial system and has excluded the vital questions surrounding the operation of the trial courts which are so important to the understanding of the urban political process. It is often misleading to depend upon "common knowledge"—even that of the experts in the legal profession—as a basis for structural reform. The expert fifteenth century navigators all knew that the earth was flat. As the techniques of empirical research are extended to the urban trial courts we will have a better foundation upon which to build a series of structural reforms—if, in fact, such reforms should prove necessary and desirable in the light of this research. Until we have the results of the research, facile explanations of the impact of existing judicial reform movements should be avoided. Judicial reform movements have obviously not all been successful in achieving the ends desired by their proponents. We are not yet able to state why this is so with any degree of certainty.

---

[11] Maurice Rosenberg, "Court Congestion: Status, Causes, and Proposed Remedies," in Jones, *The Courts, The Public*, p. 55.

[12] Rosenberg, "Court Congestion," p. 57.

[13] Jacob, *Justice in America*, p. 206.

The Courts and Urban Politics

For many years, political scientists have been branded as heretics by fellow scholars and by the community at large for suggesting—even insisting—that the courts are political institutions. Dr. Jacob states the argument for modern political science succinctly:

> Every day, courts in America make "political" decisions. They settle conflicts that otherwise would have to be settled by legislative or executive action. Not only do courts mediate disputes, but they also formulate policy in the same manner. It makes little difference to those affected whether desegregation is the consequence of a legislative act, an executive order, or a court decision. It is a governmental policy that must be obeyed at the risk of imprisonment.[14]

Conflict resolution and policy formulation are both inherently political acts. However, the political activity of the courts does not stop here. The courts' decisions are alleged to have some impact on the policy formulations of other governmental agencies.[15] Much research is currently being devoted to the study of the impact of court decisions, especially those of the United States Supreme Court, on policy. Unfortunately, most of the research to date has been confined to the study of noncompliance with court decisions and has been limited to well-publicized national issues.[16] Very little has been done to note the degree to which other agencies comply with court decisions or to study the more routine decisions of the trial courts with respect to the operation of urban governments.

THE JUDGE AS A POLITICAL ACTOR. Since the predominant means of selecting judges is through partisan election, it is appropriate to look for a moment at the effect of party on the judge as a decision-maker. In examining the judiciary of New York City, Sayre and Kaufman have noted that "the dominance of the party hierarchies over the selection of elected judges is virtually uncontested by the only respectable nongovernmental groups in the community that consistently pay any attention to this phase of politics." [17] Other studies of judicial behavior have tended to confirm

---

[14] Jacob, *Justice in America*, pp. 3–4.

[15] Dolbeare, *Trial Courts*, p. 15.

[16] See for example David Manwaring, Donald Reich, and Stephen Wasby, *The Supreme Court As Policy-Maker: Three Studies on the Impact of Judicial Decisions* (Carbondale, Ill., 1968); Gordon Patric, "The Impact of a Court Decision: Aftermath of the McCollum Case," *Journal of Public Law* 6 (1957): 455; Frank Sorauf, "*Zorach* v. *Clauson:* The Impact of a Supreme Court Decision," *American Political Science Review* 53 (1959): 777; and Stephen Wasby, "Public Law, Politics, and the Local Courts: Obscene Literature in Portland," *Journal of Public Law* 14 (1965): 105–130.

[17] Wallace S. Sayre and Herbert Kaufman, *Governing New York City* (New York, 1965), p. 551.

this finding and to go on to indicate that "judges who identify with a particular political party are likely to reflect the ideological leanings of that party." [18]

One current study of the urban judiciary, however, casts some doubt on such overly simplified explanations of judicial behavior. Kenneth Dolbeare found the parties to be every bit as important in judicial selection as Sayre and Kaufman had suggested, but that the consequences of this involvement might not be as great as had previously been presumed.[19] In the first place, he found that judges tended to avoid partisan contacts once on the bench since such contacts might be incompatible with the image of the judiciary. In the second place, there appeared to be very little effort on the part of the political parties to determine the political and ideological orthodoxy of their nominees for judicial position. As long as the nominee had a satisfactory record of party support, no further questions were asked. Given the wide range of ideological positions within the two major parties, this appears to be quite practical. Even within the narrow confines of local party activity not all Democrats lean toward liberalism on all issues nor do all Republicans lean toward a more conservative ideological position. Rather, Dolbeare found that "the direction which a judge takes as he settles into his judicial position and the level of energy which he invests in it are likely to be products of his previous life pattern and the degree of aspiration he still retains." [20] This suggests that if the judge retains some hope of attaining higher elective office he might well attempt to atune himself to the party in his decisions to the degree that they involve areas in which party positions are available and relevant.

Another limitation on purely partisan explanations of judicial behavior is the role played by judges and the courts as enforcers of norms of behavior. While many of these norms are contained in state law as applied by the courts, the way in which a particular judge chooses to apply these standards of behavior affects the standards themselves. In turn, the judge's choice is affected by the necessity of adapting these legal norms to the particular values of the community in which he is serving.[21] While most judges do not view themselves as performing a primarily representative function, there is some indication that many trial court judges are especially concerned with their role in the community. This concern frequently manifests itself as a restraining factor when judges are tempted to move toward a different interpretation of the norms. As Jacob points out:

A restraining factor that is particularly significant for trial judges occurs as a result of the judge's roots in his community and his place in American soci-

---

[18] Adrian, *State and Local Governments*, p. 397.
[19] Dolbeare, *Trial Courts*, pp. 64–67.
[20] Dolbeare, *Trial Courts*, p. 65.
[21] Jacob, *Justice in America*, pp. 23–24.

ety. Since most trial judges come from the community in which they hold court, and few outsiders are chosen, they often share the local norms. As members of the local Establishment, they often favor the status quo and are unwilling to change it.[22]

Partisan affiliations are only one of several factors which help to determine the way in which the judge views his role in the governmental process. Other factors, such as social position in the community and personality, may coincide with and reinforce party affiliation, or they may operate as cross-pressures that modify the ideological content of party affiliation. In any event, a great deal more than a judge's party preference must be known if one attempts to predict the attitude with which he will approach his role as a decision-maker. Such attempts may well be crucial to an understanding of the courts in the political process if, as Dolbeare claims, "the way in which the judge conceives of his judicial role is . . . the most significant single factor in the whole decisional process."[23]

IMPACT ON URBAN POLICIES. While trial courts do not appear to issue the type of broad, sweeping policy statements which we have come to expect from the appellate courts, their opinions in individual cases can and do have an impact on the public policies that are determined by urban governments. Table 8–1 indicates the subject matter of cases dealing with urban policies which came before the trial courts of an urban New York county during the period of Dr. Dolbeare's study. It is obvious from these data that zoning and land use is the major policy area in which the courts are involved. This does not serve, however, to diminish the importance of court decisions in other areas. Even though there are far fewer cases in the nonzoning areas, they may well be of greater substantive importance with respect to the political process. A single decision dealing with the scope of governmental powers or the nature of the electoral process may have far greater community-wide impact than 50 or even 100 decisions on zoning variances.

The nature of the courts' impact becomes much clearer once the breakdown in Table 8–2 is examined. This table provides a more detailed picture of the nature of the claims and of the courts' involvement. It also indicates the degree to which the courts serve to modify policy decisions by overruling urban governments in individual cases. Governmental policies received a high level of support (better than 66 percent) in only three substantive areas. In all other areas the support is rated as either moderate or low. This is particularly noteworthy in the area of taxation, in which the courts supported government's attempts to raise additional

---

[22] Jacob, *Justice in America*, p. 185.
[23] Dolbeare, *Trial Courts*, p. 69.

TABLE 8–1: Case Totals, by Year, by Court, by Form of Proceeding, and by Subject

Year	Total Cases	Subjects of Cases	Number
1948	7	Zoning and Land Use	
1949	7	Seeking permit after Board	
1950	14	denial	101
1951	12	Other	99
1952	6	Other Than Zoning	
1953	3	Nominations, elections	16
1954	10	Education	25
1955	12	Taxation	9
1956	24	Licensing, other regulations	30
1957	44	Government powers and procedures	34
1958	52	Work with, by, for government	19
1959	41	Labor relations	9
1960	54	Sunday Laws	6
1961	62	Miscellaneous other	40
1962	49		
1963	41		
Total	438	Total (substantive only)	388

Court	Total Cases	Form of Proceeding	Total Cases
Supreme, Special Term	401	Article 78	194
		Declaratory judgment	63
Supreme, Trial Term	12	Injunction	42
County	9	Damages, other relief in an action	44
City/Village	7	Statutory review or	
District	9	taxpayer's suit	38
		Other	9
Total	438		
		Total (substantive plus relevant other)	390

SOURCE: Kenneth M. Dolbeare, *Trial Courts in Urban Politics* (New York, 1967), p. 35. Reprinted by permission of John Wiley & Sons, Inc.

revenues in only one-third of the cases. The record is not much better in zoning and land use where those challenging the application of ordinances had a better than 50 percent chance of success. But policy impact does not occur only in cases that are lost by government. The support of urban governments by the courts fulfills the vital function of legitimating governmental decisions, thereby helping governments to gain public acceptance for their acts.[24]

Dolbeare arrived at a noteworthy series of conclusions relative to the use of the courts to affect urban policies.[25] He found that the rules of the courts can encourage the use of judicial processes to affect policy if these

[24] Dolbeare, *Trial Courts*, p. 113.
[25] Dolbeare, *Trial Courts*, p. 62.

TABLE 8–2: Summary of Court Impact in Major Substantive Areas, Indicating Major Elements Relevant to Outcome

Subject Area	Total Cases	Percent Support for Govt.	Nature of Claims Involved and Basis of Resolutions	Overall Character of Court Involvement in Area
NONZONING AREA				
Nominations and elections	16	75	Intraparty contests by insurgents, resolution controlled by Election Law.	Courts endorse technical determinations, appellate review immediately available.
Education	25	80	Challenges to school budgets, employee reinstatements, parental claims, decided by Education Law.	Courts irrelevant except as safety valves, but enforce parental rights.
Taxation	9	33	Claims for reductions in assessments or attacks on local nonproperty taxes. Decided on facts of valuations and authorizations.	Courts establish valuations at sharp variance with County and void local taxes. Major policy-making role.
Licensing, other regulations	30	43	Businesses oppose local regulations, challenge administrators of State regulatory authorities.	Courts support business freedom, scrutinize procedures of State agencies. Effect is to stress economic rights.
Government powers and procedures	34	62	"Constitutional" powers of County government, Democratic Party use; control by general laws of State.	Courts allocate power and define government structure, control incorporation and annexation. Primary area of court impact.
ZONING AND LAND USE AREA				
Article 78, for permit, business	63	44	Applicants allege prezoning rights, special privileges, arbitrariness of denial of business use. Decided on basis of factual support for findings.	Courts protect rights to use property when they have vested character. Constant tension between courts and government standards.
Artcle 78, for permit, residential	38	47	Applicants seek to build on substandard lot. Facts as to date of ownership control rights vs. zoning.	Courts enforce vested rights against government efforts to maintain standards.
Article 78, to annul grant of permit	25	68	Applicants attack extension of business use into residential area and grants to build on substandard lots. Factual support in record controlling.	Courts uphold governments more readily, grantee seen as having the vested rights.
Injunctions	18	50	Efforts by governments to enforce zoning standards in affirmative fashion.	Courts grant governments no special advantage and appear unreceptive to such efforts.
Declaratory judgments	46	54	Plaintiffs attack constitutionality of ordinance control over use of property. Due process of law standards control.	Courts void ordinance where it precludes all reasonable uses, restrain upzoning, insist on comprehensive rather than spot zoning.

SOURCE: Kenneth M. Dolbeare, *Trial Courts in Urban Politics* (New York, 1967), pp. 108–109. Reprinted by permission of John Wiley & Sons, Inc.

rules are drawn in such a way as to make the courts more available to the public. Simplified procedures that enable the citizen to challenge an act of his government quickly and easily obviously make the courts an attractive device. On the other hand, factors within the community may serve to encourage or discourage litigation. Some communities clearly place greater emphasis on the courts as a device for challenging governmental policies than do others. These community attitudes may be related to the availability and effectiveness of judicial remedies, but they may also be related to less pragmatic considerations. For example, does the community consider legal challenges unacceptable even though they might be quite effective? In Dolbeare's study, the trial courts proved to be essentially negative institutions. In addition to the propensity to overturn or veto policy that has already been mentioned, they also serve to delay the operation of policies which have been challenged until the case can work its way to the top of a crowded calendar. In some areas, the courts are the only channel available for challenging the operation of government. If a city chooses to interpret its charter so as to perform additional services or to regulate additional activities, the courts are the only effective vehicles for questioning this interpretation. In other areas—that is, areas in which other channels are available—the courts are likely to be used as a last resort when political forces in the legislative and administrative arenas are unfavorable.

WHO USES THE COURTS? According to our democratic tradition, the courts are open to any citizen who wishes to use them. In fact, however, there are significant groups of people who either cannot or do not use the judicial process to affect policy decisions in the urban arena. The operation of the courts outlined in the preceding paragraphs encouraged certain categories of people to use the courts more than others:

> The availability of the court structure for purposes of delay and alternative-vetoing means that those who seek to defend the status quo will be encouraged to use the courts. At the same time minority elements seeking political power were able to employ the court structure to increase their chances within the political system.[26]

Thus any group or individual interested primarily in change or in possession of sufficient access to political decision-makers in other arenas is not likely to resort to the courts. For example, Dolbeare found that banks, business associations, educational groups, major law firms, and veterans groups were not using the courts in the county he studied although all

---

[26] Dolbeare, *Trial Courts*, p. 58.

of these groups had significant interests at stake in local political decisions.[27]

Participation in court political activity also appears to be highly individualized. As Table 8–3 shows, the vast majority of cases are initiated by
individuals or businesses rather than by groups or governmental bodies.
While no one would deny the importance of interest groups in initiating
litigation in areas that attract attention by virtue of the broad policy
statements issued at the appellate level, such groups do not appear to be
significant in most urban trial court proceedings with policy impact.

TABLE 8–3: **Character of Complainants or Plaintiffs, All Cases, 1948–1963**

Complainant or Plaintiff	ZONING AND LAND USE		ALL OTHERS	
	Number	*Percent*	*Number*	*Percent*
Individuals [1]	81	43	106	61
Businesses [1]	77	41	48	27
Groups [1]	8	4	3	1.5
Towns/Cities	11	6	2	1
Villages	10	6	1	0.5
School Districts	0	0	1	0.5
County	0	0	1	0.5
Totals	187 [3]	100	175 [2]	93 [2]

SOURCE: Kenneth M. Dolbeare, *Trial Courts in Urban Politics* (New York, 1967), p. 38.
Reprinted by permission of John Wiley & Sons, Inc.

NOTES: [1] These distinctions are not wholly satisfactory. A suit may be initiated by an
individual on behalf of a group, or for a business purpose, in both of which cases the
clarity of this categorization would be undermined. Every effort has been made to meet
the first possibility by classifying under "groups" those cases where from the opinion or
from newspaper accounts there appeared to be some form of organized associational support for the complainant, and the second by classifying under "businesses" those instances where the complainant was an entrepreneur.
[2] Totals and percents do not add because thirteen criminal prosecutions (Sabbath Law
and other prosecutions otherwise meeting the public policy criteria of the study) have
been excluded. These are treated separately in the text.
[3] Thirteen cases in this area involved unclassifiable or miscellaneous complainants or
plaintiffs, such as decedents' estates and trustees in bankruptcy. They have been eliminated throughout the analysis of use of courts, although not from the analysis of effects.

Many individuals who might like to use the courts more frequently are
unable to do so. Unfortunately, access to the courts and success once before a tribunal have all too often been a function of an individual's economic position. In the first place, the cost of hiring an attorney has proven
to be too great for many people. In recent years great progress has been
made in this country in overcoming this barrier. Those who are unable to
hire a lawyer must receive one at public expense in criminal proceedings.

[27] Dolbeare, *Trial Courts*, p. 44.

In more and more jurisdictions, the poor are able to receive free legal advice in civil proceedings as well. Most attorneys will accept a civil suit for damages or some monetary award on a contingency fee basis. That is to say, they will take the case for a percentage of the award received by their client. However, many of the policy-related actions discussed earlier in this chapter do not result in a monetary award. In these cases, free legal assistance may be available through Legal Aid or a Legal Services Bureau sponsored either through private subscriptions and the local bar association or through government grants under the Economic Opportunity Act. This type of legal assistance is generally limited to those whose income falls below the poverty level as currently defined by government agencies.

And yet many people still have less than perfectly free access to the courts because of economic barriers. There are those whose income is above the poverty level who are unable to hire an attorney to represent them in a case protesting a zoning action that may cost them their livelihood or a tax assessment that would be an unfair burden for them. For these working-class citizens there appears to be little help in the offing.

Another problem in using the courts as a political instrument is the inability of every individual to go to court with the same chance of success. The stature, quality, and tactics of the attorney who represents an

TABLE 8–4: **Results in Cases Involving Certain Types of Counsel, by Subject Areas**

	ZONING		NONZONING	
	Total No. of Cases	Private Success Ratio, Percent	Total No. of Cases	Private Success Ratio, Percent
Political law firms	24	90	7	71
Specialists	36	64	15	33
Over-all average in all cases	200	49	188	33

SOURCE: Kenneth M. Dolbeare, *Trial Courts in Urban Politics* (New York, 1967), p. 74. Reprinted by permission of John Wiley & Sons, Inc.

NOTES: (a) "Specialists" are those who are represented by at least eight cases in closely related fields. Six such specialists are involved, none of them intimately connected with party politics.

(b) "Political law firms" are firms at least one of whose members holds or has held a major elective or party office on the Town level or above. Five such firms are involved; their key members are (1) Congressman, Town Leader, National Party Chairman, (2) County District Attorney, (3) County Chairman, (4) County Executive and County Leader, and (5) Speaker of the State Assembly and County Leader, respectively. All were Republicans.

(c) The proportions shown in the success ratio column exclude, for the political law firms, cases where the judge was of the opposite party; thus the percentages are of slightly smaller total numbers of cases than the totals shown.

individual seriously affects the outcome of the case.[28] For example, Table 8–4 indicates the advantage inherent in selecting a political law firm or a specialist to represent you in a case before an urban trial court. Only in the case of specialists in nonzoning cases did attorneys in these two categories fail to achieve a far better than average record of success. The implications of this are clear when one recognizes that the ability to hire legal talent depends on economic position. Because of the greater demand for their services and because of their greater reputation for success, the best attorneys demand a great deal of money for their services.

Top legal talent is not generally within the reach of the ordinary citizen, especially in the large cities where specialization and prestige law firms are more common. While there are some firms that undoubtedly will take cases from the poor and middle-class citizenry and charge them a lower rate, they are the exception rather than the rule. The fact remains that the more money the individual has, the more likely he is able to successfully use the courts as agents to affect public policy. The only way that such difficulties can be overcome is through using interest groups as sponsors of litigation. The problem with this solution lies in the highly individualized nature of many of the cases arising in the urban trial courts, and in the tendency for the courts to avoid the sort of sweeping policy decisions which might reach all the members of a particular group.

Summary

The trial courts provide a vehicle through which a variety of different political functions can be performed in the urban community. The courts act as enforcers of community norms and the "rules of the game" and as devices through which minority views can be promoted. They allocate power and control procedures for other units of local government according to constitutional provisions, state laws, and local charters. They serve as protectors of property rights. They act as a safety valve for protest and provide a cooling off period for those who are unable to accept a particular policy decision. And finally, the courts place the stamp of legitimacy upon governmental acts by ruling them to be in accordance with general societal norms.[29]

These functions are not all performed in every community. The degree to which the courts are employed for any of these functions is dependent upon the degree to which particular communities view the courts as a normal political channel. In some places court action is the exception; in others it is the rule. This in turn is dependent in many cases upon the

---

[28] Dolbeare, *Trial Courts*, p. 71.
[29] Dolbeare, *Trial Courts*, pp. 112–113.

degree to which the relevant political actors—those who are interested in affecting policy decisions—can find satisfaction through institutions and devices outside of the court system. Although even the directly elected judge does not view his role as primarily a representative one, community attitudes and values have an impact on judicial behavior and help him to determine the role he will play in the political process.

The two major difficulties attendant on the operation of the courts in urban politics are the tendency toward conservatism on the part of the courts and the inequality of access to the full benefits of the judicial system. To the extent that the vast majority of court decisions dealing with urban policy issues favor the maintenance of the status quo, the system places extraordinary barriers in the way of those who seek social change. There is at present no way that we can state with any degree of certainty whether this conservatism of the courts is in response to the desires of a majority of the people. However, as long as the court system is more accessible to those with above-average incomes than it is to those with below-average incomes, it does not satisfy the criteria of many people as a fully responsible and responsive democratic institution. Since there appear to be few if any effective short-run remedies for these difficulties, the working-class urbanite who is seeking change might be expected to seek action from the other branches of government and to hope that the defenders of the status quo will not block or overturn these changes through the courts.

Suggested Readings

Blair, George S. *American Local Government*. New York, 1964. See especially Chapter 15.

Dolbeare, Kenneth M. *Trial Courts in Urban Politics*. New York, 1967.

Jacob, Herbert. *Justice in America*. Boston, 1965.

Jones, Harry W., ed. *The Courts, The Public, and the Law Explosion*. Englewood Cliffs, N.J., 1965.

Sayre, Wallace S., and Kaufman, Herbert. *Governing New York City*. New York, 1965. See especially Chapter 14.

chapter 9
Administrative Organization and Personnel Management

《[In spite of the myth that the legislator decides what should be done and the administrator does it, the administrator picks up the bits and pieces of legislative ideas and attempts to fit them into a coherent program.[1]

The Nature of Administration

The very fact that a book on urban government devotes a separate chapter to the subject will indicate to many that the "myth" of the separation of policy (or politics) and administration is being perpetuated. In order to dispel such notions, it is necessary to reiterate the point made in Chapter 7 that such a separation is not only impossible but perhaps undesirable as well. Furthermore, the inseparability of politics and administration does not prevent real distinctions between executive and legislative behavior. Although both types of behavior are highly political and policy oriented, the institutionally defined and individually perceived roles are frequently quite different. This alone would justify a chapter dealing with those who see themselves as performing primarily administrative roles within the urban executive establishment.

Definitions offered for public administration—of which urban administration is but a subcategory—are never quite precise enough to satisfy the perceptive student who would like to know just what it is he is study-

---
[1] William J. Gore, "Decision-Making Research: Some Prospects and Limitations," in *Concepts and Issues in Administrative Behavior*, ed. Sidney Mailick and Edward H. VanNess (Englewood Cliffs, N.J., 1962), p. 51.

ing. One of the leading textbooks in the field demonstrates the problem clearly when it states that "public administration may be defined as the coordination of individual and group efforts to carry out public policy." [2] However, the authors of the text realize that this definition is far too narrow and excludes the more political aspect of administration which is the shaping of public policy before and while it is carried out.[3] The difficulty inherent in including the political dimension in any definition of public administration is that we are forced, as the preceding paragraph attempted to demonstrate, to a purely institutional rather than a functional definition. What we appear to be saying is that administrators administer while judges and legislators do not. This, of course, is no definition at all. This definitional problem has led many of us in political science to claim public or governmental administration as an inseparable part of the discipline, rather than to allow it to drift free by itself.

Unfortunately, scholars have fared little better in their attempts to distinguish between public and private administration. The sample leading textbook is not very satisfying when it tells us that the major difference is that "in effect, the public environment fosters a more legalistic, self-protective attitude on the part of administrators, including procedures that insure greater impartiality and accountability but less adaptability." [4] There is little doubt that the average city manager is supervised in the conduct of his office by his city council somewhat more closely than is the average corporation president by his board of directors, but a great many studies have shown that legalism and lack of adaptability are characteristics that may be found in the private bureaucracy as well as the public. As a result of the inability to distinguish clearly between the two types of administration, a literature common to both business and public administration has been developed. This literature serves as the basis for much of the newer knowledge of administrative organization and behavior. The work of sociologists and psychologists serves as a foundation for much of this new literature, thereby strengthening the interdisciplinary status of the study of administrations and further weakening the hold of the political scientists on the study of the problems and processes peculiar to public administration.

Organizations and Theory

There are at least two reasons for a student of urban politics to be interested in theories of administrative organization and behavior. In the first

---

[2] John M. Pfiffner and Robert Presthus, *Public Administration*, 5th ed. (New York, 1967), p. 7.

[3] Pfiffner and Presthus, *Public Administration*, p. 5.

[4] Pfiffner and Presthus, *Public Administration*, p. 7.

place, reliable theoretical formulations improve our understanding of how decisions are made by urban governments and ultimately permit us to pass judgment if we wish on the process by which decisions are made as well as on the content of the decisions. From a civic action point of view this understanding also provides a greater ability to alter the decisions themselves. In the second place, a useful and highly predictive theory would enable the administrative practitioner to better understand the ways in which personnel can be used in order to achieve the desired results once policy decisions have been made. This second or instrumental use of administrative theory has a Machiavellian tone to it that often offends those who fear totalitarian manipulation. The only consolation that can be offered them is that understanding and use of the administrative process is a far cry from control of the process. However, such assurances must be as alarming to those who focus on democratic control of the administrative process and on responsible government as they may be comforting to those who fear the shadow of *The Prince*.

TRADITIONAL ADMINISTRATIVE THEORY. In spite of the fact that research findings for the last thirty years have tended to discredit its assumptions, traditional administrative theory continues to have an inordinate influence over the practices and attitudes of administrators, especially those in our cities. This theory generally holds that maximum efficiency is achieved when a series of basic organizational principles are followed. These principles in turn are expected to materially affect the conduct of administration. In the first place, organizations are to be hierarchical with a great deal of emphasis placed upon unity of command. This requires a pyramidal type of organization with a single administrator at the top who can hold his subordinates responsible for the exercise of delegated authority. The same principle is applied in each subordinate office until the base of the pyramid is reached in the working-level employees who have no subordinates. Policy decisions are transmitted down the pyramid to the appropriate action agency, and the results are reported back up the chain.

The second principle is that of specialization of work tasks. The theory holds that, in a complex society, greatest efficiency is achieved when workers and agencies are so organized that each performs the task for which they are best suited and trained. The idea of division of labor which is implied here essentially holds that well-trained experts working together can achieve results that no single man with general knowledge can hope to obtain. Chapter 1 has already demonstrated that this principle is particularly suited to the general developments that characterize urban society, and it would be highly unusual if urban governments did not reflect the same tendencies as the rest of society.

The third principle is that of limited span of control. Traditional theorists assumed that there were definite limits to the number of personnel that a single supervisor could direct. Once those limits were exceeded, it would no longer be possible for him to effectively monitor the degree to which subordinates implemented basic policy, and the result would be a loss of efficiency. After some initial experimentation, a rule of thumb was developed which indicated that the effective span of control was between three and seven subordinates, with the actual number dependent upon the task being performed and the talent of the supervisor.

Finally, traditional theorists attempted to develop further guidelines for the organization of the various administrative agencies in the hierarchy. Who would be responsible for performing what duties within the organization? The answer lay in four basic methods of grouping workers: purpose, process, clientele, and area. Purpose organization dictated that the workers be grouped according to the function performed. For example, those workers who were concerned with the provision of water service to the citizens would be grouped together as a Department of Water. The department would include office workers, truck drivers, ditch diggers, engineers—all those necessary to providing the service. On the other hand, process organization grouped workers according to their particular specialization or type of work. When carried to its logical extreme, it would have all typists in a central secretarial pool, all drivers in a motor pool, all engineers in an Engineering Department, and so forth. Clientele organization depended primarily on the common characteristics of the group being served. For example, a single agency could be established to deal with the problems of the poor providing them with economic assistance, health services, and education, all from a single office. Finally, areal organization would simply divide the city into zones, and all of the pertinent services would be provided by all of the necessary specialists to all of the relevant clients in each zone through a single office.

It is easy to see that each of these forms of organization has its advantages in responding to modern urban problems. Purpose organization emphasizes the performance of services and functions. Process organization emphasizes specialization of work functions. In clientele organization, interrelated purposes and processes can be combined to meet the particular needs of special groups in the population. Areal organization brings the performance of functions closer to the people and facilitates access to the administrative process. However, an examination of the actual organization of urban governments reveals that these organizational forms are not mutually exclusive. For example, the Fire Department is obviously a purpose organization, but the nature of the function performed permits and even requires that the department be areally organized as well. The performance of the function depends upon the ability of the citizen to have immediate access to the service when he needs it. Another example is furnished by the attempts to impose areal on purpose organization in the public schools of large cities such as New York, in the hope that the proximity of decentralized school administration will give the public a greater opportunity to control the administrative decision-making process.

Close examination of traditional administrative theory has revealed that its principles are inadequate to the task of effectively understanding the administrative process. This is because so many of the principles contain contradictions that practically guarantee that anyone who attempts to follow them will be working at cross purposes with himself. In the first place, as Herbert Simon has pointed out, purpose, process, clientele, and areal organization each involve a type of specialization. In fact, any group effort must to some degree be specialized, and the specialization or lack thereof may have absolutely nothing to do with the degree of efficiency displayed by the organization.[5] Simon further claims that no organization is truly single-purpose. Therefore, clientele organization and areal organization are but further specifications of multifunctional organization.[6] What is involved then is a set of factors which are considered in establishing an organizational structure, rather than principles that can be obeyed or violated.

In the second place, unity of command and specialization as principles create conflicts.[7] Although the idea of unity of command demands a single channel of communication, specialization inevitably creates alternative channels between specialists with other, higher ranking specialists who provide professional guidance for the day-to-day conduct of operations. This guidance can conflict with the policy guidance received through command channels. For example, the school nurse receives guidance with respect to the conduct of her responsibilities to school children from other medical professionals in the field of public health, such as the local public health officer. This advice can easily conflict with the policy guidance promulgated by the superintendent of schools. All such conflicts must be resolved in a way that results in the compromise if not the outright violation of principles. "What evidence there is of actual administrative practice would seem to indicate that the need for specialization is to a very large degree given priority over the need for unity of command."[8] Such a priority is not necessarily evil and may, in fact, be the only practical choice available, but it does raise interesting questions about the degree of responsibility and control possible in the execution of public policy as well as in its formulation.

---

[5] Herbert A. Simon, *Administrative Behavior*, 2d ed. (New York, 1957), pp. 21–22.
[6] Simon, *Administrative Behavior*, pp. 30–32.
[7] Simon, *Administrative Behavior*, p. 23.
[8] Simon, *Administrative Behavior*, p. 25.

While the principle of span of control no doubt represents a statement of the obvious fact that there are human limits to one man's ability to control others, it should also be noted that the number of subordinates involved is only one variable that helps to determine these limits. Quite clearly, the simpler the work tasks being performed by the subordinates, the more of them one man can supervise. Arbitrary numbers such as the three-seven rule contribute little to effective organization. The United States Army has discovered through sad experience in recent years that slavish devotion to purely numerical concepts of span of control limited its ability to respond as an organization to the changing environment in which it was forced to perform its functions. Unfortunately, the same discovery has all too frequently eluded urban administrators. Then too, the attachment to the principle of a relatively narrow span of control has increased the altitude of the hierarchical pyramid, thereby serving to slow the decision-making and policy-implementing processes by increasing the number of levels which must consider an action before it can be taken.[9]

Traditional administrative theory is not without value, however. It does provide us with "relevant insights into the nature of organization." [10] Even though administrative systems do not operate with the crispness and clarity that the "principles" demand, traditional theory continues to be reflected in expectations that administrators have with respect to administrative efficiency. The traditional, hierarchical system remains, then, as an ideal for many professional administrators, perhaps because it creates the illusion of a rational, manageable system. Let us emphasize once again that many of the variables considered in traditional administrative theory are real and important factors in every urban administrative system. Some degree of specialization is indeed necessary and even inevitable in our complex modern society. A certain amount of hierarchy is necessary to avoid chaos, and the limits of individual capacity to control have already been admitted. The important thing about these factors is that they do not necessarily fit into a neat, integrated theoretical system in the traditional sense. The "principles" are frequently contradictory and must be balanced against one another in viewing the operation of administrative organizations.[11] Traditional theory obviously does not consider all of the variables important to understanding administration. In this type of theory, the major emphasis has been placed on technical skills and the relationship of these skills to the legal structure of authority, and this ignores the important factors of interpersonal relations within orga-

---

[9] Simon, *Administrative Behavior,* p. 26.

[10] William G. Scott, "Organization Theory: An Overview and an An Appraisal," in *Managerial Behavior and Organizational Demands,* ed. Robert T. Golembiewski and Frank Gibson (Chicago, 1967), p. 16.

[11] Simon, *Administrative Behavior,* p. 36.

nizations and the values, norms, and ideologies of society and the community.[12]

DECISION-MAKING THEORY. One of the more interesting theoretical emphases to develop out of criticism of traditional administrative theory was Herbert Simon's focus on the decision-making process.

> The task of "deciding" pervades the entire administrative organization quite as much as does the task of "doing"—indeed, it is integrally tied up with the latter. A general theory of administration must include principles of organization that will insure correct decision-making, just as it must include principles that will insure effective action.[13]

This emphasis was quite different from that which was current in the 1940s when Simon began his work. Obviously the decision-making approach places a great deal of stress on the policy-making or political aspects of the role of the administrator. While traditional theory dealt primarily with execution of policy, decision-making focused primarily on the process by which policies were formulated.

One of the major contributions of Simon's work was the recognition that the administrative process was a good deal more complex than the traditionalists had believed. Professor Simon saw the process primarily as a problem in social psychology.

> It is a task of setting up an operative staff and superimposing on that staff a supervisory staff capable of influencing the operative group toward a pattern of coordinated and effective behavior.[14]

The changes in language here are particularly significant. Rather than speaking about commanding, directing, or even leading, the decision-making approach speaks of influencing administrative employees toward certain goals. This strongly implies that all of the employees participate in the decision-making process to some degree, and that the channels established by administrative organization are two-way rather than one-way pipelines.

There has been a great deal of criticism directed against the decision-making approach on the grounds that it places too much emphasis on the rationality of the administrative process.[15] However, this criticism is not

---

[12] Charles Press and Alan Arian, "Empathy and Ideology: Aspects of Administrative Innovation," in *Empathy and Ideology*, ed. Charles Press and Alan Arian (Chicago, 1966), pp. 3–4.

[13] Simon, *Administrative Behavior*, p. 1.

[14] Simon, *Administrative Behavior*, pp. 2–3.

[15] Pfiffner and Presthus, *Public Administration*, pp. 109–110.

necessarily valid. Students of the process have usually defined rationality in administrative behavior as an attempt to achieve predetermined goals or to maximize certain values through the decision-making process. The archetype of the rational decision-maker is the legendary economic man who attempts to maximize profits. The study of the decision-making process has revealed that:

> There is every evidence that in complex policy situations, so-called decision-makers do not strive to optimize some value nor is the notion of optimization a useful way of ordering and analyzing their behavior regardless of their intentions.[16]

This fact does not deter those who wish to focus on decision making, since assumptions of rational behavior on the part of administrators are not necessary, even though they might make the study of the administrative process a great deal simpler. The end result is a complex approach to the study of administration:

> Decision-making is not a dramatic, determinative act shaping destiny through setting goals, molding values, and building alliances. Rather, the most crucial kind of decision-making is a catalytic agent by which a number of decision-makers seek to muddle through tangled values, inconsistent goals, and mutually neutralizing techniques toward a response that will to some extent insure the continuity of an organization.[17]

THE SMALL GROUP AND ADMINISTRATION. The questions raised by Simon and his successors ultimately led to what some have called a neoclassical theory of administration. This approach directed scholars' attention to six major factors in the administrative process:

1. The impact of specialization on individual motivation.
2. Problems in the delegation of authority and responsibility.
3. Human disruption of structural neatness.
4. The human determinants of span of control.
5. Informal organizations as agents of social control.
6. The interaction of formal and informal organization.[18]

Concentration on these factors brought many students to make small group theory play an integral part in their understanding of the administrative process. The small group with which such theorists are con-

---

[16] Raymond A. Bauer, "The Study of Policy Formation: An Introduction," in *The Study of Policy Formation*, ed. Raymond A. Bauer and Kenneth J. Gergen (New York, 1968), p. 2.

[17] Gore, "Decision-Making Research," pp. 54–55.

[18] Scott, "Organization Theory," pp. 16–20.

cerned "is composed of the interrelations of a limited number of people
. . . who have developed shared ways of perceiving their environment and
of behaving within it." [19]

A number of properties of small groups have particular relevance to
discussions of the administrative process.[20] In the first place, the small
group has its own structure. There are roles to be played within the group
that can be traced primarily to the fulfillment of group needs. These
roles are given a status or rank that orders them according to prestige or
importance to the group. Each group also has its own leadership which
may in part be determined by the status held by individuals within the
group, but which may also be widely distributed rather than concentrated in just a few members. Groups may also be characterized according
to the degree of cohesiveness which they display with the more cohesive
groups having frequent, intense communication between the members, a
stronger influence over the conduct of members, and greater solidarity in
the face of an outside challenge. Finally, a matter of prime concern to
students of public administration is the degree to which these structural
properties coincide with those of the formal, administrative organization.
Are the roles observed in the small group comparable to those in the
administrative structure? Do those who have roles with status in the small
group have roles with status in the formal hierarchy? Do formal supervisors hold meaningful leadership positions within the small group as
well? Does small group cohesiveness carry over to a cohesive formal organization? All of these are questions of great significance in understanding
administrative behavior. The greater the structural integration of the
small group with the formal organization, the greater the degree to which
group members can and will contribute to the satisfaction of organizational tasks and goals.

Structural properties are not the only relevant small group characteristics, however. It is also necessary to observe the style or method of
operation of the group in order to understand the ways in which it might
affect administration. In the first place, roles are performed in different
ways in different groups. In some groups, the atmosphere is informal and
highly permissive, while in others it is much more highly regularized and
directive. Group norms of behavior are also of great significance and are
closely linked to the performance of roles. A key factor in administrative
analysis is style integration, or the degree to which the goals, norms, and
behavior patterns of the group coincide with those of the formal organization. A work group that has a highly permissive atmosphere and that

---

[19] Robert T. Golembiewski, *Behavior and Organization: O and M and the Small
Group* (Chicago, 1962), p. 89.

[20] This discussion draws heavily from Golembiewski, *Behavior and Organization*, pp.
100–159.

places great value on friendly, personal contact between the members would find it difficult if not impossible to fulfill the expectations of a formal organization which was extremely hierarchical, impersonal, and directive in its approach to the performance of work tasks. The absence of an adequate degree of style integration can lead to a refusal to accept the goals and methods of the formal organization and to feelings of alienation and frustration on the part of administrative employees. On the other hand, a high degree of style integration creates a feeling in the small group that it is participating in the decision-making processes of the formal organization, with the probable result that shared program goals are achieved more quickly and completely.

Small group research has revealed that the needs, drives, and characteristics of the individual members are important factors in determining group and organizational style. There are some people who have a psychological need for control by the group and the organization. These people will not only fail to achieve organizationally desired goals in a permissive atmosphere, they will also be unhappy and frustrated by the freedom that such an atmosphere provides. It has been suggested that this need for control is to some degree a function of intelligence, and that brighter people perform better in a more permissive group atmosphere. In addition to this response to the presence or absence of control, group members also respond to the task or work assignments themselves. While part of this response is affected by the role structure, status assignments, and norms of the group, part of it is also a highly individualized reaction to different kinds of work tasks. For example, some people find a job that calls for the repetitive performance of a single task so boring as to be unacceptable. There are others who find such repetition reassuring. These attitudes and reactions may also be a function of intelligence, but such a determination would depend heavily upon the definition and measures of intelligence used. The important point for administrators is that the employees' responses to their job assignments are vital factors in the achievement of organizational goals.

Some students of administration have criticized the small group approach on the grounds that it has a tendency to be manipulative.[21] These critics see much of the attention which has been given to the small group as an attempt on the part of top management to learn how to more effectively "use" their employees. Two responses might be appropriate to such criticisms. First, there is clearly no necessary connection between any approach to the study of administration and a desire on the part of the student to use whatever results he obtains in a manipulative manner. Any theoretical approach is likely to be used to achieve better results, if the

---

[21] Scott, "Organization Theory," p. 22.

student is a practicing administrator. Second, many would suggest that it is particularly appropriate in a democracy for practitioners of public administration to be manipulative in the application of administrative theory. After all, if those who are responsible to the public do not attempt to control the decision-making process to some degree, it probably makes little sense to talk about representative democracy at all. There are great differences between using the available knowledge about small groups to help to control the behavior of public employees, and treating these employees as if they were automatons.

MODERN ORGANIZATIONAL THEORY. None of the theoretical approaches discussed so far has been totally satisfactory in enabling scholars to understand the administrative process. Each has tended to focus on a particular variable or set of variables, and to exclude from consideration other factors that appear to be important. Modern organizational theory differs from these earlier approaches in that it consciously sees the organization "as a system of mutually dependent variables." [22] This suggests three important questions that modern organization theorists are attempting to answer: (1) what are the parts of the system and how are they interdependent?, (2) what processes link these parts together?, and (3) what goals are sought by administrative systems? [23] The answers to these questions are as yet incomplete. However, we do have some bare outlines that are helpful in understanding the process of public administration.

In the first place, the basic unit in any human system is man himself. The motives, attitudes, and behavior of the individuals who are part of any administrative system are vitally important to understanding the way in which that system operates. Secondly, modern theory continues to draw heavily from the observations of the traditionalists with respect to the importance of formal organization. A third factor—informal organization—can be traced to the contributions of the small group theorists. Finally, the physical setting or environment in which the administrative system operates is a significant factor. These factors are closely interrelated. The behavior of the individual is affected by the physical environment as well as by his formal and informal organizational setting. On the other hand, individuals can and do seriously affect organizations, and in some cases even the physical environment of the administrative process. The earlier discussion of the small group has already emphasized the importance of the interrelationships between formal and informal organization and the degree to which the status and role concepts of the two types of organization are integrated. The picture finally obtained is one of

---

[22] Scott, "Organization Theory," p. 22.
[23] Scott, "Organization Theory," pp. 22–23.

a series of highly complex interrelationships between the parts of any administrative system. Realizing the complexity of such systems, we should be extremely cautious about the statements we make concerning public administration as a process and administrative organizations.[24]

The processes by which these parts are linked together are vital to any understanding of administrative systems. Formal and informal communications channels serve as major ties between the component parts of the system. The parts of the system are also linked by balancing or equilibrating mechanisms that serve to provide the means by which the system is held together. Finally, the decisions to produce or to participate in the system at all constitute a basic linking process through which the individual or the group is initially brought into the system and through which they remain in the system.[25]

The last question asked by modern administrative theory focuses on the goals of the administrative system. The emphasis is on the goals of the entire system, not just on the clearly articulated programmatic goals of the formal organization. The more complex goals of the system which focus on growth, stability, and interaction within the system are vitally important.[26] Not all of these systemic goals will be compatible with one another, and the identification of conflicting and complementary goals can reveal a great deal about the operation of an administrative system.

SUPPORT OR EXCHANGE THEORY. Most of the approaches to the study of administration which have been discussed up to this point have focused primarily on factors and characteristics within the administrative system itself. Administrative behavior cannot be discussed intelligently without considering the degree to which outside influences affect administrative decisions. One of the ways in which these influences are most usefully considered is through the medium of support or exchange theory. This approach "concerns itself with bargaining between organizations and relevant external groups." [27] An external group may be considered relevant if it makes an attempt to influence the decisions of administrators. It may be a clientele group that is closely linked to a particular agency by virtue of a continuing interest in agency activities. However, a great many relevant groups have a much more generalized interest in administrative activities and may only occasionally be involved in contact with a particular agency. No matter what type of group may be involved, exchange theorists focus on the policy concessions that are made by administrative

---

[24] Portions of this discussion depend heavily upon Scott, "Organization Theory," pp. 23–24.

[25] Scott, "Organization Theory," pp. 25–27.

[26] Scott, "Organization Theory," p. 28.

[27] Robert Presthus, *Behavioral Approaches to Public Administration* (University, Ala., 1965), p. 75.

agencies in order to gain the support of the group in the agencies' dealings with popular representatives and the public at large. It is in activity of this sort that the political nature of the administrative process probably asserts itself most clearly.

SUMMARY. The purpose of this oversimplified discussion of the theory of organizations is to emphasize the complexity of the administrative process as an area of urban politics. Far too little attention has been devoted to the public administrative process in our cities. Although reform groups have been attempting to introduce modern business methods into urban government for the past fifty years, there appears to be a significant time lag between business and government in the study of administrative behavior. The result is a conception of public administration in our cities that is idealistic at best and hopelessly inaccurate at worst. We must use concepts of urban administration which have empirical reality—concepts that describe decision-making as it really is.[28]

Raymond Bauer has summarized this empirical emphasis in a particularly appropriate manner:

> When we focus on those strategic moves that direct an organization's critical resources toward perceived opportunities in a changing environment, we are at once concerned with the (1) intellectual activities of perception, analysis, and choice which often are subsumed under the rubric "decision making"; (2) social process of implementing policies formulated by means of organizational structure, systems of measurement and allocation, and systems for reward and punishment; and finally (3) the dynamic process of revising policy as changes in organizational resources and the environment change the context of the original policy problem.[29]

The Administration of Public Employees

One of the logical results of recognizing that communication within an administrative organization flows both ways and that small work-group attitudes can affect both policy and performance is an increasing emphasis on public personnel administration. The personnel programs established by the agencies of urban government obviously affect not only the competency of the public employee but also his work attitudes.

THE PROBLEM OF IMAGE. Most Americans are skeptical about their public servants. Public employment is usually ranked well down the list of jobs ranked according to social status. This tendency has at least two serious effects on government. In the first place, the prophecy may well be self-

---

[28] Simon, *Administrative Behavior*, p. 37.
[29] Bauer, "Study of Policy Formation," p. 2.

fulfilling. If public employment is generally held in low esteem, it will obviously not attract the most talented individuals. The most able members of society want employment that offers status and recognition commensurate with their abilities, and that reflects this social position in the compensation received. Secondly, the poor image of public service has an impact on the performance of public employees on the job. Diligence, initiative, and enthusiasm among our civil servants are difficult to maintain if low esteem is expressed by the general public in their day-to-day contacts with government employees and by the mass media in their treatment of these employees. We end up in a circular situation in which the poor image of public employment results in hiring new employees with modest talents and few expectations of social or monetary rewards for hard work. The public then accepts the performance of these employees as proof that the original evaluation was correct.

Another factor that has contributed to the poor image of public employment has been the persistence of Jacksonian democracy at all levels of government. The first important Jacksonian assumption has been that most government jobs are not very demanding and, therefore, that almost anyone could hold a government job and perform satisfactorily. The second assumption has been that responsible administration is best obtained through the control of the various jobs by the political parties. This led in turn to the spoils system, in which the party that controlled the appointment power "cleaned house" upon election and replaced the old public employees with people fully loyal to the party in power. In the Jacksonian scheme, these two assumptions were closely related. Since governmental employment was not very demanding anyway, it did not make any difference that party loyalty and administrative talent did not necessarily go together.

When the reformers of the late nineteenth and early twentieth centuries began their effort to dismantle the spoils system, it was because they had come to reject the second of these two assumptions. The graft and corruption that appeared to be endemic at all levels of government in the late 1800s was particularly noticeable in the cities. In most of these cities, the political party served as a vehicle of convenience for this graft and corruption, rather than as a device for insuring responsible government. The reformers hoped that the abolition of the spoils system, and in some cases of the parties themselves, at the local level would put a stop to the graft and corruption. In Chapter 5 we saw that this was an unrealistic hope. It was a good deal later in the history of the urban reform movement that the first assumption was seriously questioned. The complexity of modern urban problems made it quite impossible to maintain that anyone could perform the tasks of urban administration. At this point the more perceptive reform leaders attacked the spoils system because it failed to provide the experts and specialists who were so badly needed in our cities and towns. However, to the extent that either argument has been persuasive, the assault on amateur government has gained far less acceptance by the general public than has the attack on the political party as a vehicle for graft and corruption. Many communities have adopted nonpartisanship as a basic administrative reform without attempting to get at the heart of the spoils system and its wholesale replacement of amateur public employees with each change in the group in power.

CIVIL SERVICE REFORM. The more prevalent approach to the insulation of the administrative process from the ravages of the spoils system was the establishment of a civil service. There are two main characteristics of civil service systems. First, the plan initiates a guarantee of job tenure in order to insure that public employees are not dismissed from their positions capriciously. Under the system, a protected employee may only be dismissed after his incompetence or malfeasance in office has been established before an impartial bipartisan or nonpartisan commission that administers the system. Second, it is not unusual to find that overt, partisan political activity on the part of protected employees has been prohibited as a price of the job protection which they have received.

One of the difficult problems in any civil service system is deciding which employees will be covered. If all administrative employees are included, the process of divorcing administration from the electoral process is so complete as to make responsible government impossible. If too few positions are covered, the spoils system remains in effect to some degree. Most governments that use a civil service system attempt a compromise by including or classifying those positions deemed to be of a more routine, administrative nature and excluding those thought to be essentially policy-making positions. Such decisions are obviously a matter of degree. The general tendency has been to exclude department, agency, or bureau heads and sometimes their immediate assistants from civil service classification, and to include all lower positions. This obviously extends protection to many employees who are closely involved in the policy-making process. The result may be that some of the decision-making in the administration is too well insulated from the political process in its electoral form to satisfy those who are particularly concerned about maintaining responsive and responsible democratic government. However, there does not appear to be an answer to this dilemma short of a return to a spoils system. This solution is probably unacceptable to most reformers.

Another major shortcoming of simple civil service reforms is that they failed to alter the image of public service materially.[30] Although classified

---

[30] Pfiffner and Presthus, *Public Administration*, p. 257.

employees were fairly well insulated from the alleged corruption of political parties, there was nothing in the system to guarantee that the employees were particularly qualified to perform their duties. As a matter of fact, there has always been a strong tendency in this country to be somewhat suspicious of those whose jobs are protected by tenure. Many critics of the system feel that this protection tends to eliminate the most important sanction that can be applied to those who fail to perform their duties adequately—dismissal. Although civil service employees can be fired, such action is a long and involved process that supervisory personnel do not undertake lightly. Suspicious outside observers feel that this means that employees do just enough to get by and that they have inadequate motivation to be creative and diligent. While a certain amount of this criticism is undoubtedly accurate, it does overlook the fact that fear of dismissal is only one of many motivational factors which must be considered in a complex work situation.

Those who manage public personnel systems are as aware as anyone and perhaps more aware than most of the failure to adequately consider the need for qualified administrative employees. This has led them to expand their concept of civil service to include a wide variety of programs designed to obtain more qualified employees and to adequately reward those employees who improve their qualifications and skills on the job. While much of the active recruiting of personnel from colleges and universities for professional positions in public management is still confined to national and state governments, most of our major cities have developed such programs. Recruiting of this type is designed to attract those with better general educational background and preparation to public service. In addition to attracting more applicants, personnel agencies are seeking to develop means of selecting only the best of those who do apply. Examinations, interviews, and an evaluation of training and experience provide a basis for ranking applicants both in terms of their achievement and of their aptitude so that the appointing officers may have the best candidates from which to select.[31]

Once an employee has passed the probationary period and has received the full protection of civil service laws, most competent supervisors continue to try to motivate the worker to perform his work to the best of his ability. To the extent that promotions were a matter determined primarily by seniority or time on the job under old civil service systems, the criticisms suggested earlier were justified. However, in modern public service there has been a movement toward what can be called a merit system, in which promotions and pay increments are awarded according to the supervisor's assessment of present skills and future aptitude as displayed on the

---

[31] Pfiffner and Presthus, *Public Administration*, pp. 284–286.

job. A system of this type depends upon efficiency or performance reports prepared by the immediate supervisor and upon competitive examinations to provide the basis for determining eligibility for promotion. Employee reaction to the merit system is less than enthusiastic in most instances. The use of efficiency reports and performance ratings has always upset those being evaluated because of the extreme subjectivity of the evaluation. In the first place, most employees are afraid to trust the judgment of one man in determining their fitness for advancement, a determination that obviously has great impact on their entire future. They fear that they will be discriminated against by a supervisor who simply does not like them, regardless of their level of performance on the job. Employees show a strong tendency to explain any low rating in these terms; it is a good deal easier than admitting poor performance. Partly in recognition of these factors and partly in the fear that low ratings of employees will reflect adversely upon their own performance as supervisors, rating officers have tended to inflate the ratings they give.[32] The response to this inflation of ratings has been to seek new rating formats with different adjectival descriptions of the employee. The assumption is that the problem can somehow be avoided by changing the words and numbers that are used. So far this has not proved to be the case.

The competitive examination for promotion has been a somewhat more useful tool in determining job potential. However, it is not without its difficulties. It is not always easy to develop an examination that is relevant to the job skills to be utilized. As any honest educator can testify, the examination process is at best uncertain. Oral examinations or interviews and evaluations of prior training and experience are, of course, highly subjective. The written examination has only recently become available to the smaller urban governments, since they have not in most cases had enough money or expertise to construct examinations. Even now, the exams available to them are frequently limited to standardized initial tests from the various national professional groups. Only the largest cities have anything resembling a complete set of competitive examinations.

We have already discussed the existence of roles and status in the work group and their relationship to the roles in the formal organization. Modern administrators have recognized that the coincidence between formal and informal roles and status hierarchies is largely dependent upon the job classification process in the formal organization.[33] Employee satisfaction and performance are likely to be a good deal higher if the formal organization accords recognition and status to the same people as does the informal organization. Most governmental organizations depend upon

---

[32] Pfiffner and Presthus, *Public Administration*, p. 292.
[33] Pfiffner and Presthus, *Public Administration*, p. 295.

verbal descriptions of the jobs to be performed and a highly subjective ranking of the jobs based upon those descriptions. In some cases the incumbent describes his own job, while in others the description is prepared by a supervisor or a management consultant. In neither case is there any guarantee of job descriptions that will satisfy both the incumbent and the "objective" appraisals of supervisory personnel.

Perhaps even more important than the classification process itself is the overt indication of the status awarded to particular positions by the formal organization. The indication that receives the greatest amount of attention is the system of pay scales. The major principle accepted here, both by employees and supervisors, is that of equal pay for equal work. Nothing is more destructive of employee morale than the suspicion that A is working harder at a more demanding task than B but is receiving lower pay. The satisfactory implementation of this principle is quite obviously dependent upon the achievement of some semblance of agreement between administrators and employees upon standards of work as well as classification of positions. Since such agreement is rare, the principle is not usually applied satisfactorily for all concerned, and it remains one of the major problems in modern personnel administration.

A major assumption of current public personnel systems in our urban areas is that there will be a sufficient number of qualified applicants to choose from in filling the lower level positions, and that there will be sufficient competition between qualified employees for vacancies at the higher levels within the system. As the administration and operation of our cities becomes an increasingly complex operation involving a greater and greater degree of competency and specialized knowledge on the part of governmental employees, it becomes increasingly difficult to find adequately prepared applicants for jobs. The greater demands of major administrative positions and the general lack of adequate in-service training programs make it difficult for the promotional process to continue to fill the upper positions in the hierarchy with personnel whose qualifications meet the demands of their jobs. This problem has become so acute that it has been described as "a truly crisis condition." [34]

UNIONS AND PUBLIC EMPLOYEES. One of the developments which has most disturbed public administrators in recent years is the increase in the unionization of public employees. Table 9–1 illustrates both the extent and variety of public employee organization in our cities. It is clear that the national unions have an edge in the organizing activities even in the

[34] Edgar L. Sherbenou, "Personnel Administration: Major Issues in 1968," in *Municipal Yearbook, 1968*, International City Managers' Association (Washington, 1968), p. 179 ff.

TABLE 9–1: National and Local Union and Association Membership

Population Group	No. of Cities Reporting	NATIONAL UNIONS		LOCAL UNIONS		ASSOCIATIONS	
		Number	Percent	Number	Percent	Number	Percent
Over 500,000	23	21	91	8	35	7	30
250,000 to 500,000	25	17	68	6	24	8	32
100,000 to 250,000	78	49	63	3	4	25	32
50,000 to 100,000	154	69	45	9	6	62	40
25,000 to 50,000	289	85	29	6	2	64	22
10,000 to 25,000	578	105	18	7	1	50	9
All cities over 10,000	1,147	346	30	39	3	216	19

SOURCE: International City Managers' Association, *Municipal Yearbook, 1966* (Chicago, 1966), p. 178. Reprinted by permission of the International City Management Association.

smallest communities. For the most part, the national union referred to is the American Federation of State, County, and Municipal Employees, which had locals in 247 of the 1,147 cities reported in Table 9–1.[35] Although this union does make an attempt to organize municipal employees as a broad category, in many instances some employees will choose to be represented by local unions or other associations even though there is a national union operating in their city. This is particularly true of the police and firemen who frequently have their own associations with a highly professional orientation.

Many reasons have been suggested for this increase in union activity on the part of public employees.[36] The successes achieved by other activist groups in labor-management relations and elsewhere have encouraged confrontation in public employment. The employers have in many instances been inconsiderate of employee feelings and attitudes when adopting personnel policies. In many cases, the social distance between management and employees is not nearly so great in public service as it is in the private sphere. This encourages boldness and militancy on the part of the employees. Like their counterparts in the business community, public managers feel that many areas of decision-making are wholly within the prerogatives of management, and they are unwilling to discuss these issues in the absence of the sort of pressure that unions can apply. Finally, extraordinary pressures frequently must be applied if the employees are to get beyond the managers in the executive branch of government to the legislative bodies that can make the most important decisions. All of these

[35] International City Managers' Association, *Municipal Yearbook, 1966*, ed. Orin F. Nolting and David S. Arnold (Chicago, 1966), p. 178.

[36] Rollin B. Posey, "The New Militancy of Public Employees," *Public Administration Review* 28 (1968): 111–117.

factors have contributed to a new attitude of militancy on the part of public employees, especially those employed by urban governments.

There are important differences between these public unions and associations and their counterparts in the private sphere.[37] There is no provision for a union shop or required union membership. Pressures from union members within the work group can be quite effective on occasion, however. The strike is not officially recognized as a weapon and may even be specifically outlawed. The fact that civil service systems have frequently provided tenure for public employees has decreased the emphasis on job security that usually characterizes union operations. Governmental unions also suffer from frequently being unable to gain recognition as the official bargaining agents for employees, since much of the legislation dealing with the rights of labor does not apply to public employees. Finally, the rivalry between professional associations and local and national unions for recognition as bargaining agents as well as for members' loyalty seriously weakens the power of the unions.

One handicap of the movement to unionize public employees which is frequently cited as particularly important is the need for a recognition of the right to organize and for the provision of a series of bargaining procedures similar to those found in the Wagner Act and the Taft-Hartley Act.[38] In recognition of this need, state legislatures have been active in recent years in providing the statutory basis for union activity. In 1967 alone, eighteen states passed new legislation and many more were considering action.[39] Some form of collective bargaining has been authorized specifically in twenty-seven states. Although the number and classes of public employees covered under these statutes varies widely from state to state, municipal employees are covered in twenty of the twenty-seven states. Four of the remaining states provide coverage for such highly important urban employees as firemen and teachers.[40] "Recognition of unions for collective bargaining without specific state statutory authorization also occurs in some cities in sixteen states and in the District of Columbia." [41]

The procedures established by a few of these statutes reflect a desire of some states to provide real assistance to local governments and their employees. The Wisconsin statute is an excellent example of such an at-

---

[37] Alice H. Cook, "Adaptations of Union Structure for Municipal Collective Bargaining," *1966 Annual Spring Proceedings of the Industrial Relations Research Association*, pp. 81–90.

[38] Jean T. McKelvey, "The Role of State Agencies in Public Employee Labor Relations," *Industrial and Labor Relations Review* 20 (1967): 179–197.

[39] Richard S. Rubin, "A Summary of State Collective Bargaining Law in Public Employment," *Public Employee Relations Reports*, no. 3 (1968), New York State School of Industrial and Labor Relations, Cornell University, p. i.

[40] Rubin, "Summary," pp. i–iii.

[41] Posey, "New Militancy of Public Employees," p. 112.

tempt.[42] The act provides for a Wisconsin Employment Relations Board which conducts elections to determine employee desires with respect to representation, limits unfair labor practices by both employers and employees, and acts as a fact finder in impasses between parties in the bargaining process. The major purpose of the board is to encourage the collective bargaining process and to avoid the unpleasantness of arbitration or work stoppages. Although the law provides for relatively free access to the services of the board, the high charges assessed for these services effectively prevent frivolous claims of unfair practices and frequent representational elections.

No issue of public personnel policy has been more hotly debated in recent years than the strike. It is safe to say that in most jurisdictions strikes by public employees are considered illegal, either by virtue of court interpretation or by virtue of specific legislative prohibitions.

> If strikes are thought to be harmful in the private sector of the economy where they are perfectly legal, this is doubly true of the public sector. Not only are strikes illegal, but they are also seen as constituting a far greater interruption of essential services.[43]

The opponents of the strike strongly emphasize the vital nature of the services provided by governments, the lack of alternative products or services which could satisfy the same public needs, and the nonprofit and sovereign nature of governments, to suggest but a few arguments against the strike. On the other hand, unions and professional associations often minimize the differences between public and private employment and stress the necessity of maintaining the threat of the strike if collective bargaining is to be taken seriously.

> In summary, when the theoretical arguments for and against anti-strike laws are reduced to simplest form, they seem to boil down to this: one side says, "Strikes against the public cannot be tolerated!" and the other side says, "Why not?" [44]

From the point of view of the organized public employee, several considerations appear to support the strike as a weapon. In the first place, these employees generally receive lower wages and fringe benefits than

---

[42] James Belasco, "Public Employee Dispute Settlement: The Wisconsin Experiment," *Government Labor Relations in Transition*, Personnel Report no. 662, Public Personnel Association, 1966, pp. 9–21.

[43] Andrew W. J. Thomson, "Strikes and Strike Penalties in Public Employment," *Public Employee Relations Reports*, no. 2 (1967), New York State School of Industrial and Labor Relations, Cornell University, p. 1.

[44] Gordon T. Nesvig, "The New Dimensions of the Strike Question," *Public Administration Review* 28 (1968): 131.

their counterparts in the private sector. In services like sanitation and street repair that employ large numbers of unskilled workers, the over-supply of unskilled labor in the market would serve to keep wages low were it not for vigorous union activity and the possibility of strong sanc-tions such as the strike. In the second place, it is not nearly as easy for many public employees to seek alternative employment elsewhere if wages and working conditions are unsatisfactory. Some essential public services like education and law enforcement require specialized personnel whose skills, once developed, are not easily used in the private sector. There is a limited demand for private school teachers and private policemen, and their wages and working conditions tend to reflect the dominant public practices. Finally, in the public sector the ultimate employer is also the consumer—the public. The natural desire to keep taxes as low as possible frequently results in pressures that encourage the public's managerial representatives to be even more conservative in responding to employee demands than are their private counterparts.

However, the governments' claim to special status is also justifiable. There is little doubt that, although some private industries are vital and their production must be maintained if the economy is to survive, the services performed in the public sector are often vital in a more immediate sense. Surely no one would wish to claim that we can go without the protection offered by our police departments for as long as we can go without steel production. Stockpiles and the ability to substitute one product for another make an industrial strike of several weeks bearable. However, the absence of police or fire protection for twenty-four hours could be disastrous in a major city, and would not be without some serious social costs even in a small town.

Many states have responded to the challenge of the strike by enacting stringent antistrike laws for public employees, even in cases in which collective bargaining has been recognized. The New York law, the Taylor Act, has received a great deal of attention as one of the most recent at-tempts to deal with the problem. The Taylor Act requires the employer to seek an injunction against public employees who are striking and pro-vides for contempt penalties of up to $10,000 or one week's dues, whichever is less, for unions, and up to $250 or thirty days in jail for individuals for each day on which the injunction is defied.[45] While other states have pro-vided less stringent penalties or no penalty at all for violating their antistrike laws, the major intent of the legislation is the same—to stop strikes. From a practical point of view such legislation must be considered a less than satisfactory response to the problem. In the year that followed the passage of the Taylor Act, New York City suffered serious strikes by sanitation

---

[45] Thomson, "Strikes and Strike Penalties," pp. 15–16.

workers and school teachers, to name but two striking groups. The antistrike law did not prove effective in discouraging the strikers, even after injunctions had been obtained.

> The fact is that public employees have never completely deterred from striking, and that strikes have become more frequent in recent years. What is more, they are likely to continue to strike, despite any abstract rights or potential penalties, so long as gains can be made which outweigh any losses suffered.[46]

The importance of the unionization of public employees to urban governments can hardly be overrated. While wages, hours, and working conditions certainly are the subject of much of the collective bargaining effort, even a cursory survey of recent strikes by public employees in our cities will reveal that other factors are involved as well. Mixed in with the basic economic issues are questions of basic program philosophy and policy— questions that public employees feel to be vital to their interests. For example, police officers in many of our cities have been faced with challenges from other groups in the community that have demanded that the governing body provide for a civilian review board to review the conduct of police operations in cases of citizen dissatisfaction. The response to these challenges has frequently been vigorous lobbying against the proposal by police associations. In New York City, the Patrolmen's Benevolent Association successfully sponsored a referendum to abolish the board established by Mayor John Lindsay as a fulfillment of a campaign promise. In some cases, there have been mass "illnesses" that greatly reduced the effectiveness of the police department. Such "illnesses" are often used to avoid the unpleasant picture of policemen conducting an illegal strike.

The police are not the only public employees who use the collective bargaining process to affect basic policy. School teachers have also kept a close eye on the policy implications of collective bargaining. When in 1968 New York City attempted to decentralize its huge school system in order to increase citizen access to and participation in educational affairs, the American Federation of Teachers, which represented a large number of the teachers in the system, reacted strongly. The ostensible issue over which the teachers eventually went on strike was the protection of jobs and the maintenance of normal dismissal procedures in the new neighborhood districts. However, beneath the surface of this traditional union issue were basic questions about who was going to control the policy of the New York schools. The teachers strongly suspected that the decentralized system would give the advantage to parents and other local citizens, and

---

[46] Thomson, "Strikes and Strike Penalties," p. 4.

that the professional educator would seriously lose ground in the policy-making process.

One must conclude that, in our cities, "it is impossible to separate collective bargaining from politics." [47] In some cases this merely means that the administrators trade economic benefits for more overtly political ones. In these cases:

> The collective bargaining relationship is a swapping of political power assets. The Mayor grants salary and benefits to the employee organization in return for their support in a variety of political activities. The trading of votes and support for salaries and benefits is the heart of the negotiation process.[48]

In other cases, the relationship is more subtle and raises more serious questions. Felix Nigro sees a new phase of administrative policy-making evolving in which there is a "codetermination of policy by management and organized employees." [49] Policy-making of this kind has its advantages for those who would emphasize conflict-free labor-management relations and the smooth operation of the administrative process as primary goals in urban government. It does, however, introduce a particularly powerful element into the process over which the general public has even less control than it has over top level professional administrators. This does not suggest that public employees are likely to control urban government through the use of unions and collective bargaining. There will always be forces in the political process that prevent such absolute control. But it seems quite clear that, even if the democratic processes operate with complete efficiency, the public's influence over public policy will be appreciably reduced by the organization of militant public employees.

Suggested Readings

Bauer, Raymond A., and Gergen, Kenneth J., eds. *The Study of Policy Formation.* New York, 1968.

Golembiewski, Robert T. *Behavior and Organization: O and M and the Small Group.* Chicago, 1962.

——. *Organizing Men and Power.* Chicago, 1967.

——, and Gibson, Frank, eds. *Managerial Behavior and Organizational Demands.* Chicago, 1967.

Mailick, Sidney, and VanNess, Edward H., eds. *Concepts and Issues in Administrative Behavior.* Englewood Cliffs, N.J., 1962.

---

[47] James Belasco, "Collective Bargaining in City X," *Government Labor Relations in Transition,* Personnel Report no. 662, Public Personnel Association, 1966, p. 50.

[48] Belasco, "Collective Bargaining," p. 50.

[49] Felix A. Nigro, "The Implications For Public Administration," *Public Administration Review* 28 (1968): 142.

Nigro, Felix A., ed. "A Symposium: Collective Negotiations in the Public Service." *Public Administration Review* 28 (1968): 111–147.

Pfiffner, John M., and Presthus, Robert. *Public Administration*. 5th ed. New York, 1967.

Press, Charles, and Arian, Alan, eds. *Empathy and Ideology*. Chicago, 1966.

Presthus, Robert. *Behavioral Approaches to Public Administration*. University, Ala., 1965.

Simon, Herbert A. *Administrative Behavior*. 2d ed. New York, 1957.

Warner, Kenneth O., ed. *Collective Bargaining in the Public Service: Theory and Practice*. Chicago, 1967.

———, ed. *Developments in Public Employee Relations*. Chicago, 1965.

———, and Hennessy, Mary L. *Public Management at the Bargaining Table*. Chicago, 1967.

chapter 10
Financing
Urban Government

⟨[Financial difficulties have compounded themselves as governments have lagged in making needed major adjustments, tinkering instead with traditional arrangements. At the heart of these difficulties is a two-pronged anomaly—municipal costs are increasing while the base for the property tax, the long-time chief means of city government support, is shrinking.[1]

This statement represents the standard argument for financial reform in the urban community. This chapter will show that there is good reason to challenge at least a portion of the statement. The central fact remains, however, that raising revenue adequate to the service demands of the modern city is a major problem. No matter how much money is raised, there always seem to be services that are either not performed at all or that are performed inadequately, primarily for financial reasons. Only the rare and extremely wealthy community can claim to have no financial difficulties.

One of the major problems which arises in any discussion of expenditures and revenue is selecting standards by which to judge these variables. Is this community spending a lot of money on a particular function? Are property taxes high in this taxing jurisdiction? These and similar questions cannot be answered without setting explicit standards of comparison to other communities. In making such comparisons it is necessary

---

[1] Ruth L. Mace, *Municipal Cost-Revenue Research in the United States* (Chapel Hill, 1961), p. 1.

to adjust the public financial data according to the value of the dollar, population size, and the condition of the economy. Such data can be expressed as a percent of the Gross National Product on a per capita basis and in constant dollars.[2] Tax rates are comparable only if the base on which they are levied is the same. The absence of fully comparable data on revenues and expenditures makes broad statements extremely hazardous, but it does not prevent much narrower statements comparing the revenue and expenditure patterns within a single city over a fairly short time span or to talk about national trends over short time spans in which the impact of inflation is not likely to be so great. However, even in these cases the factors mentioned above should always be kept in mind in order to give additional perspective to the analysis.

One other analytic problem must be raised before further discussing urban finance. Chapters 1 and 4 emphasized that modern urban government is broader than municipal government. To give a fully accurate picture, then, any description of urban finance should include the relevant data from urban counties and special purpose districts that make up the rest of the fabric of urban government. However, the financial data reported for these governmental units is included with other nonurban counties and districts or is reported as part of metropolitan area figures. The data for all counties and districts include too much, and the data for metropolitan areas fails to include nonmetropolitan but nevertheless urban governmental units. For illustrative purposes, this chapter will focus primarily on the admittedly incomplete data for municipalities on the assumption that the trends illustrated and the problems raised are generally representative of urban finance.

Expenditure Patterns

One clear fact emerges from even the most casual study of municipal expenditures. Our cities are spending more and more money with every passing year in order to provide the services demanded of them. Table 10–1 shows the pattern that these increases have taken over a fifteen-year period. If one projects this pattern onto urban government in general, the annual rate of increase is roughly 10 percent—a figure that can be adjusted down to 6 to 7 percent when adjusted for population growth, and to 3 to 3½ percent when adjusted further for inflation.[3] In some places, per capita expenditures have been increasing more rapidly than the Gross National

---

[2] Frederick C. Mosher and Orville F. Poland, *The Costs of American Governments* (New York, 1964), pp. 9–14.

[3] Allen D. Manvel, "Changing Patterns of Local Public Expenditure," in *Public Expenditure Decisions in the Urban Community,* ed. Howard G. Schaller (Baltimore, 1963), p. 36.

TABLE 10–1: Data Reflecting Trends Between 1952 and 1962 in General Expenditure of Municipal Governments, by Function

Item	PERCENT DISTRIBUTION			AMOUNT OF INCREASE (MILLIONS OF DOLLARS)			PERCENT OF TOTAL INCREASE		AVERAGE ANNUAL PERCENTAGE INCREASE		
	1962	1957	1952	1957 to 1962	1952 to 1957	1952 to 1962	1957 to 1962	1952 to 1962	1957 to 1962	1952 to 1957	1952 to 1962
Total	100.0	100.0	100.0	3,783	3,389	7,172	100.0	100.0	6.8	9.0	7.9
Education	14.5	15.2	15.1	477	520	998	12.6	13.9	5.7	9.2	7.4
Highways	12.6	13.7	13.6	374	468	841	9.9	11.7	5.1	9.0	7.1
Public welfare	5.3	5.1	6.9	214	58	272	5.7	3.8	7.4	2.6	4.9
Health and hospitals	6.6	7.3	7.6	186	222	408	4.9	5.7	4.9	7.9	6.4
Police protection	10.9	10.7	10.9	434	356	790	11.5	11.0	7.3	8.7	8.0
Fire protection	7.3	7.3	8.0	278	205	484	7.3	6.7	6.8	7.1	7.0
Sanitation	11.1	11.9	11.6	345	428	774	9.1	10.8	5.4	9.7	7.5
Parks and recreation	4.8	4.7	4.4	182	182	363	4.8	5.1	6.8	10.7	8.7
Housing and urban renewal	4.8	2.5	2.3	395	99	494	10.4	6.9	21.0	10.8	15.8
Libraries	1.6	1.5	1.6	67	45	111	1.8	1.5	7.9	7.7	7.8
Financial administration and general control	4.8	5.3	5.8	138	145	282	3.6	3.9	4.9	6.9	5.9
General public buildings	1.5	1.6	1.4	49	68	117	1.3	1.6	5.6	12.0	8.7
Interest on general debt	3.8	3.2	3.2	203	107	310	5.4	4.3	10.7	8.9	9.8
Other and unallocable	10.4	9.9	7.5	442	485	927	11.7	12.9	7.9	15.2	11.5

SOURCE: *Finances of Municipalities and Township Governments*, vol. IV, no. 3, U.S. Census of Governments 1962 (Washington, 1962), p. 2.

Product, which is considered to be the best measure of the general growth of the economy.[4] This is all the more impressive when the data are compared with the growth of comparable domestic expenditures by the national government, which have been increasing at a much slower rate.

Figure 10–1 illustrates the current breakdown of municipal expenditures by function. The expenditures for utilities and insurance trusts have been separated from general governmental expenditures in order to give a clearer picture of the division between the business and governmental functions. The necessity for excluding special purpose districts from the presentation somewhat distorts the picture. Since most municipalities no longer operate their own school systems, having abandoned this function to independent school districts, the $2 billion figure for education clearly does not represent the importance of this function as a drain on urban resources. Were it possible to give accurate totals based upon a clear definition of the urban area, education would be the function upon which most money is spent by far. In addition, if county and state expenditures in urban areas are counted, the highway function would represent a greater drain than police and fire protection by a significant amount.

Why should expenditures be increasing so rapidly at this level of government? The answer may be found in several places. Of course, some of the growth may be traced to inefficiency and waste, but there is little evidence to indicate that these factors are not at worst constant and at best diminishing in our cities. Another answer may be found in the desire for expansion on the part of program administrators within urban governmental programs. We are all aware that such bureaucratic empire builders exist and exert an upward pressure on expenditure levels. However, too many people stop the analysis at this point, before discovering the most significant causes of rising expenditures.

The greatest encouragement for expanded public services and, therefore, for rising public expenditures is provided by the private rather than the public sector of our economy.[5] The tremendous increase in urban population has placed great pressures on existing governmental services and facilities and has required a healthy expansion of expenditures just to stay even with demands. If, as was suggested earlier, per capita expenditures are also increasing, it is obvious that population increases cannot account for all expenditure increases. The forces of urbanization have required the addition of new services as well as the continuation of the old. Technological change has brought massive demands for public services that are not directly related to serving the needs of the citizenry. Industry places great

---

[4] Dick Netzer, "Financing Urban Government," in *The Metropolitan Enigma*, ed. James Q. Wilson (Washington, 1967), p. 59.

[5] This discussion draws heavily on William J. Baumol, "Urban Services: Interactions of Public and Private Decisions," in Schaller, *Public Expenditure Decisions*, pp. 1–18.

Figure 10--1: **Expenditure of Municipal Governments, by Function: 1962**

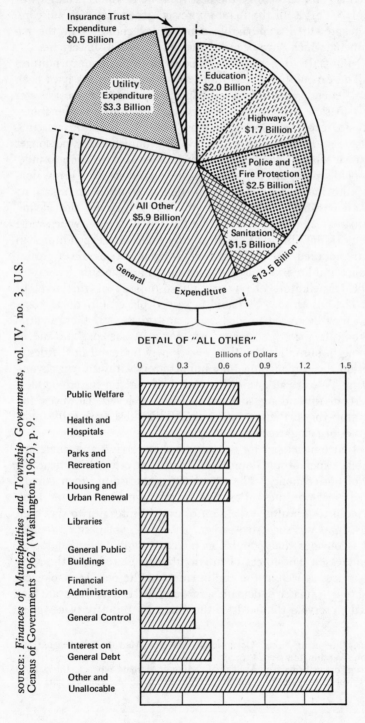

TOTAL EXPENDITURE $17.3 BILLION

Insurance Trust Expenditure $0.5 Billion

Utility Expenditure $3.3 Billion

Education $2.0 Billion

Highways $1.7 Billion

Police and Fire Protection $2.5 Billion

All Other $5.9 Billion

Sanitation $1.5 Billion

$13.5 Billion

General Expenditure

DETAIL OF "ALL OTHER"

Billions of Dollars

0   0.3   0.6   0.9   1.2   1.5

Public Welfare

Health and Hospitals

Parks and Recreation

Housing and Urban Renewal

Libraries

General Public Buildings

Financial Administration

General Control

Interest on General Debt

Other and Unallocable

SOURCE: *Finances of Municipalities and Township Governments*, vol. IV, no. 3, U.S. Census of Governments 1962 (Washington, 1962), p. 9.

demands upon the public utilities for such services as power, water, and sewage disposal that require the construction of additional public facilities. Industry and technology have also created a demand for such new public services as air and water pollution control, so that their by-products will not render the urban environment uninhabitable. The expanding physical scale of the city which has been made possible by developments in transportation technology has placed additional demands for streets and highways on urban governments as well as demands for additional public transportation facilities to carry the population from suburban residences to places of work in other parts of the urban area. The simple passage of time also creates the need for greater expenditures. Any automobile owner can testify that as his vehicle gets older it requires a greater outlay of funds just to keep it in minimal running condition. The city is not much different from that automobile. The physical deterioration of the central cities has demanded that more money be spent just to keep them minimally habitable; massive sums must be expended if they are to be returned to ideal conditions. Finally, the citizen in urban society is no longer satisfied with the mere maintenance of old governmental service levels. The growing national productivity and wealth has resulted in rising public service expectations. As the general view of the good life has become increasingly opulent, the view of governmental services has changed. Yesterday's frills have become today's necessities. These factors have led to the continuing increase in urban expenditures in real terms. A certain unreal growth has been experienced in this sector of the economy as in all others, a growth that is traceable to inflationary pressures and the resulting rising prices. Governments, like their constituents, must pay more for everything these days.

Our discussion of expenditure patterns thus far has been centered on the broad, general picture presented by aggregate figures. However, some important differences between communities with respect to expenditure patterns must be noted. In the first place, if one compares the expenditure levels of several communities—adjusting for population, inflation, and the other variables noted earlier—it is necessary to make sure that one is not comparing apples and oranges. That is to say, one must determine whether the respective states have assigned the same or comparable functions to the relevant municipalities.[6] These differences in the assignment of functions in part explain the great state-to-state variations in local expenditure levels. "In 1962 direct local government expenditures ranged from 39.4 percent of total state-local expenditures in Vermont . . . to . . . 77.8 percent in New York . . . ."[7] While these differences can be traced to a

[6] Alan K. Campbell and Seymour Sacks, *Metropolitan America: Fiscal Patterns and Governmental Systems* (New York, 1967), pp. 46–47.

[7] Campbell and Sacks, *Metropolitan America*, p. 44.

variety of functions which are performed to a greater degree by municipalities in one state, by counties in another state, by special districts in a
third state, or even by the state itself, the assignment of the welfare
function appears to be the most important factor in explaining these
differences.[8]

Another source of differences in expenditure patterns is the location of
the city within metropolitan areas, that is, central city-suburban differences. The major change experienced between central cities and suburbs
is more one of allocation than of level of expenditure. Although per capita
expenditures may not be as different as we often think, the central cities
spend more on municipal services, while the suburbs spend more on education.[9] This is another point where the comparison of purely municipal
expenditures breaks down. Few suburban education expenditures are included in municipal totals, since education is almost always administered
by an independent district in the suburbs. This factor frequently contributes to a picture of urban expenditures which shows the costs of government to be much higher in the central cities than in the suburbs.
While such a picture is frequently accurate, it is almost as frequently
inaccurate.

Another source of variation in expenditure levels from community to
community are the differing social and economic characteristics of the
communities.[10] These expenditure levels vary with the socioeconomic
status of the community, the age of the residents, and the mobility of the
population. For example, those communities with low socioeconomic status spend more per capita on police, fire, general control, water, housing
and urban renewal, parks and recreation, and employee retirement than
communities with higher status. An older population can be expected to
spend more per capita for health and hospitals, employee retirement, and
parks and recreation. Finally, a more mobile population indicates greater
municipal expenditures for interest on debt and housing and urban renewal.

An interesting theory of local expenditure difference has been proposed
by Charles M. Tiebout.[11] This theory is based upon an economic model
that views the municipality as a producer of public goods and services in
competition with other such producers for residents who fulfill the role of
consumer-voter. These consumer-voters are described as selecting as a
place of residence that community whose package of services comes closest
to meeting their demands. As Tiebout himself points out, the theory is

[8] Campbell and Sacks, *Metropolitan America*, p. 45.

[9] Campbell and Sacks, *Metropolitan America*, p. 124.

[10] This discussion is drawn from Louis H. Masotti and Don R. Bowen, "Communities and Budgets: The Sociology of Municipal Expenditures," *Urban Affairs Quarterly*
1 (1965): 39–58.

[11] Charles M. Tiebout, "A Pure Theory of Local Expenditures," *Journal of Political
Economy* 64 (1956): 416–424.

based upon a series of assumptions that are often found to be unrealistic. It assumes, for example, that expenditure patterns are fixed for each community, that the population has both full knowledge of these patterns and full mobility to enable them to enjoy the services, that in every case there is a large number of communities from which to choose, and so forth. In spite of the fact that the theory falters upon these assumptions, it does provide a helpful insight into a process that surely does take place when expenditure levels are determined for the community as a whole and when decisions are made as to the level of expenditure appropriate to particular functions. Consumer-voter demands are obviously taken into consideration, and a conscious effort is made to develop an expenditure pattern that will serve either to maintain satisfaction among existing residents or to attract new residents and industries to the community. Most municipalities, especially those in metropolitan areas, are fully aware of the fact that they are competing with other municipalities. Even though the model functions imperfectly as some of its basic assumptions prove incorrect in a given case, there does appear to be evidence that it does function and that it helps us to understand one more factor that influences expenditure levels.

Sources of Revenue

One of the major questions facing urban governments today is where to get the money these increased expenditure pressures demand. It is a frequently deplored fact that urban governmental expenditures and demands that remain unsatisfied by expenditures are growing at a faster rate than the ability of these governments to raise revenue from local sources. Table 10–2 illustrates this slowness in growth in many of the most important local sources of revenue. A more detailed consideration of each of the important sources of local revenue should reveal some of the reasons for this problem. Figure 10–2 indicates the revenue currently being received from the various sources available to municipalities.

THE PROPERTY TAX. The property tax remains at the heart of urban finance after over two hundred years as the mainstay of local government in America. As Table 10–2 indicates, 40 percent of all municipal general revenue is raised through this source. But a series of problems has beset the property tax, and it is declining in importance as a local revenue source. A brief look at some of these problems will reveal the dilemma in which many of our cities find themselves in a world of increasing revenue demands.

In its ideal form, the property tax has two major characteristics—uni-

TABLE 10–2: Data Reflecting Trends Between 1952 and 1962 in General Revenue of Municipal Governments, by Source

Item	PERCENT DISTRIBUTION			AMOUNT OF INCREASE (MILLIONS OF DOLLARS)			PERCENT OF TOTAL INCREASE		AVERAGE ANNUAL PERCENTAGE INCREASE		
	1962	1957	1952	1957 to 1962	1952 to 1957	1952 to 1962	1957 to 1962	1952 to 1962	1957 to 1962	1952 to 1957	1952 to 1962
Total	100.0	100.0	100.0	3,841	2,934	6,776	100.0	100.0	7.1	7.9	7.5
Intergovernmental revenue	20.3	18.9	19.1	912	544	1,456	23.7	21.5	8.8	7.7	8.3
Taxes, total	60.5	63.6	65.9	2,032	1,725	3,757	52.9	55.4	6.0	7.1	6.7
Property taxes	44.3	46.3	49.5	1,515	1,153	2,668	39.4	39.4	6.2	6.5	6.4
General sales taxes	6.6	6.5	5.7	264	242	506	6.9	7.5	7.6	10.8	9.2
Selective sales taxes	3.3	3.6	3.8	105	93	198	2.7	2.9	5.7	6.8	6.2
Other taxes, including licenses	6.3	7.3	6.9	149	236	384	3.9	5.7	4.1	9.0	6.5
Charges and miscellaneous general revenue	19.2	17.5	15.1	897	665	1,536	23.4	23.1	9.2	11.2	10.1
Current charges	11.5	10.3	8.6	557	408	965	14.5	14.2	9.6	11.8	10.7
Other	7.7	7.2	6.5	340	256	596	8.9	8.8	8.6	10.2	9.4

SOURCE: *Finances of Municipalities and Township Governments*, vol. IV, no. 3, U.S.Census of Governments 1962 (Washington, 1962), p. 9.

Figure 10–2: Revenue of Municipal Governments, by Source: 1962

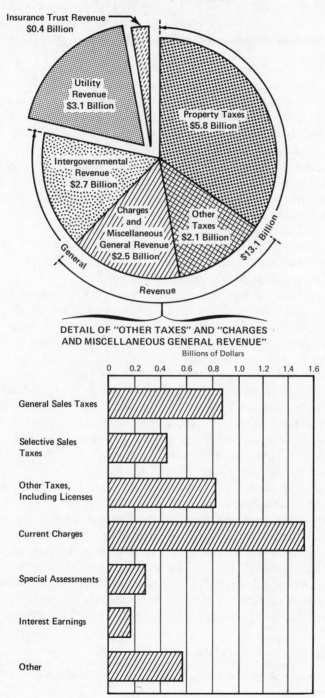

TOTAL REVENUE $16.8 BILLION

Insurance Trust Revenue
$0.4 Billion

Utility
Revenue
$3.1 Billion

Property Taxes
$5.8 Billion

Intergovernmental
Revenue
$2.7 Billion

Charges
and
Miscellaneous
General Revenue
$2.5 Billion

Other
Taxes
$2.1 Billion

$13.1 Billion

General

Revenue

DETAIL OF "OTHER TAXES" AND "CHARGES
AND MISCELLANEOUS GENERAL REVENUE"

Billions of Dollars

0   0.2   0.4   0.6   0.8   1.0   1.2   1.4   1.6

General Sales Taxes

Selective Sales
Taxes

Other Taxes,
Including Licenses

Current Charges

Special Assessments

Interest Earnings

Other

SOURCE: *Finances of Municipalities and Township Governments,* vol. IV, no. 3, U.S. Census of Governments 1962 (Washington, 1962), p. 9.

versality and uniformity.[12] That is to say, the tax is levied upon all forms of property, and it is levied at a constant rate. Unfortunately, neither of these two characteristics has been maintained or can be maintained in the real world. In the first place, universality becomes almost impossible to achieve as the kinds of property multiply. Real property—land and improvements—is the easiest to reach through taxation. Such assets are highly visible and relatively immobile, and tax officials have no difficulty in recognizing them. However, as our society has progressed from an agricultural to an industrial economy, less and less of our personal wealth is held in the form of real property. Instead, this wealth is held in the form of personal property. Tangible personal property such as home furnishings, appliances, automobiles, inventories, and machinery in factories is somewhat harder to locate than real estate because of its lower visibility and higher mobility. Efforts to locate such property are so time-consuming and often so unrewarding that some jurisdictions have resorted to assessing tangible personal property by formula, especially in the case of the individual citizen as differentiated from commercial and industrial activities. Our economy has developed to the point that even tangible personal property does not represent our true wealth in combination with real property. Much of our wealth is in the form of cash, stocks, and bonds, which is usually classified as intangible personal property. Although many schemes to tax intangibles through the property tax have been tried, none have succeeded, and most jurisdictions have abandoned even the pretense of universality and have concentrated on real and tangible personal property. Such a concentration obviously removes a significant portion of the wealth of the community from the reach of any urban government which is primarily dependent upon property taxes as a source of revenue. Frequently, such developments placed the property tax in violation of state constitutional requirements which had been drafted to reflect the ideal of a universal and comprehensive property tax.

Uniformity has fared little better as a principle of property taxation. Although most states began by requiring that all property be taxed at a uniform rate, many have now modified their original position by recognizing that greater productivity may be realized from the property tax if some cognizance is taken of the ability to pay criterion. The general position has been that industrial and commercial taxpayers have a greater ability to pay than individual citizens. This has meant that different rates have been applied to property in these categories than to purely residential property and the tangible personal property held by its owners. While

---

[12] Sumner Benson, "A History of the General Property Tax," in George C. S. Benson, Sumner Benson, Harold McClelland, and Procter Thomson, *The American Property Tax: Its History, Administration, and Economic Impact* (Claremont, Calif., 1965), pp. 34–44 and 52–59.

such strategems have been productive where used, many states continue to emphasize equity rather than ability to pay as the major criterion for taxation, and such states have maintained their constitutional or statutory requirements for uniform property tax rates.

The Advisory Commission on Intergovernmental Relations has devoted much of its time and effort to studying the property tax as a source of local revenue. Its conclusions are far from encouraging:

> By all odds, this $26 billion revenue producer stands out as the "sick giant" of our domestic revenue system—a fiscal pathology that can be traced to *individual* and *group* property taxpayer overburden situations.[13]

The individual burdens have been identified as overassessment of the individual's real and personal property and below average family incomes which render the family unable to pay the relatively high taxes on their home and its often meager contents. The entire community often suffers from the high costs of administering the tax in jurisdictions that suffer from poor management techniques, the lack of adequate property tax base which results from the division of metropolitan areas into residential, commercial, and industrial enclaves, and inadequate tax bases that result from high concentrations of poverty. These are all serious problems, but the inability of individuals and impoverished communities to raise any more money for urban government through the property tax is uppermost in the mind of many of our citizens today. Perhaps this is the place to lay to rest one of the great myths of American local finance—that those who do not own property do not pay real property taxes. Even though many of these poor people rent their homes, they pay the property tax that is levied upon that property. The only landlords who do not pass property taxes on to their renters in the form of higher rents are those few who still remain under rent control in New York City and the few wealthy humanitarians who can afford to be poor businessmen. That those who rent property are unable to participate in referenda on property tax increases in some jurisdictions remains one of the glaring injustices of our time.

Central to both individual and group burdens imposed by the property tax are the problems of assessment. The tax assessor is charged with the responsibility of determining the value of property for tax purposes. Under a properly administered tax system, the assessor does not determine the size of the individual tax bills. The assessed valuation of all property is divided by the amount of money which must be raised by the taxing jurisdiction in order to determine the tax rate. Within the legal limits estab-

---

[13] Advisory Commission on Intergovernmental Relations, *State and Local Taxes: Significant Features, 1968* (Washington, 1968), p. 7.

lished by state statutes and constitutions, the tax rate is really determined, then, by the amount of money that the particular government decides to spend. Unfortunately, however, most of our property tax systems are far from ideal. In the first place, different jurisdictions assess on different bases. Some assess at 100 percent of market value while others may assess at 25 percent. Within a single state such differences in assessment ratios may result in significant differences in tax bills under the same rate limitations. In order to remedy this situation, most states now provide for an equalization procedure that adjusts the assessed valuations of each assessing jurisdiction so that they are on as nearly equal a basis as possible. But this does not reach all of the assessment difficulties. Within many of our local governmental units various parcels of real property are assessed at different ratios to their market value. In some cases, this can be traced to a simple failure on the part of assessors to bring their assessments up to date with changes in the market value of real estate. The result is that newer property that has been assessed more recently bears a higher relative assessment than older property. This obviously undermines the uniformity of the tax. In other cases, serious underassessment of undeveloped land results from pressures by land developers and real estate interests to maintain the assessment at the levels dictated by agricultural uses in order to maximize their profit when the land is later sold for residential, commercial, or industrial use.

Many local governments have adopted the policy of assessing land at its highest and best use in order to remedy this second type of inequitable assessment. The old, single-family residence in the center of the city is assessed at a much higher value when zoning and other land use changes indicate that its site might be more profitably used for apartment houses or new commercial developments. Citrus groves in Southern California suburbs are assessed as potential residential subdivisions in recognition of the large profit which can be realized by selling the land for such purposes. When such practices are combined with frequent reassessments in order to keep pace with rapidly changing market situations, the property tax is indeed uniformly applied. However, it is not all that simple. Such policies can and do result in serious social costs. In the first place, they force land out of agricultural use in the areas surrounding our cities because the taxes make such use uneconomical. This frequently conflicts with the desires of our urban planners to discourage urban sprawl with the view toward making our urban centers more compact. Secondly, the assessment of deteriorating residential units at highest and best use results in taxes that the owners cannot bear, since many of them are poor and living on relatively fixed incomes. The elderly home-owner is forced to sell a home he has worked a lifetime to own and to move into quarters that are often substandard. The slum dweller is forced to pay higher rent when the landlord passes on the increased taxes, or is deprived of his home and forced to move into even more crowded and less desirable quarters.

An additional reform that has been suggested as a remedy for some of the side effects of more equitable assessment is the granting of tax credits for low income elderly persons.[14] Such credits would recognize the special status of these citizens and reduce the heavy burden of the property tax on them without continuing the injustices of present inadequate assessment practices.

Many experts place great emphasis on such assessment reforms as a means for increasing the productivity of the property tax. They point out that the real property in this country can be valued at $1 trillion, and yet it yields but $17 billion in taxes for a rate of 1.7 percent. If such reforms were combined with the removal of state tax limits, the separate taxing of land and improvements to encourage improvements, the removal of the personal property tax except on producer durables and cars, and the elimination of low-tax shelter jurisdictions, these experts claim that the property tax would not only be more productive but also a great force for social improvement.[15]

One of the reasons that it is so difficult to achieve reform of the property tax is that it is a focal point for the political interests of the community, most of which are not noted for their support of any measures which will result in higher taxes. The crucial political importance of the property tax has been emphasized by Dr. Charles Gilbert in his study of the Philadelphia suburbs:

> It [the property tax] limits the counties' fiscal and administrative capacities. Its fairness may be affected by political and governmental structure. The nature of the tax base may shape voters' attitudes toward local policy. Certain individuals and interests, moreover, are especially sensitive to property taxes and, in tracing out a power structure, the tax system is a logical place to begin since it conditions all governmental action.[16]

A second problem is that most municipal governments have no control over assessments and collections. These functions are usually performed at the county or township level. Any reform of the property tax must originate in the state legislature which exercises primary control over those agencies of government which administer the tax. Although many states have made great strides in requiring equalization of tax assessments between jurisdictions and in requiring minimal training of tax assessors, no

---

[14] Advisory Commission on Intergovernmental Relations, *State and Local Taxes*, p. 7.

[15] Fortune Magazine, "The Great Urban Tax Tangle," in *Metropolis in Crisis*, ed. Jeffrey K. Hadden, Louis H. Masotti, and Calvin J. Larson (Itasca, Ill., 1967), pp. 360–381.

[16] Charles E. Gilbert, *Governing the Suburbs* (Bloomington, Ind., 1967), p. 142.

state has managed to achieve a fully reformed property tax system for its local governments. Such reform is a necessary if not a sufficient condition for successful urban government. As a panel of tax experts recently said:

> None of us would dream of suggesting that local tax reform will cure all the ills of our cities. But most of us see a clear, close, and causal connection between what is wrong with our cities today and what is wrong with their tax systems.[17]

THE SALES TAX. In an effort to supplement the revenue resources of local governments, seventeen states have authorized the imposition of a local sales tax.[18] For the most part, these taxes are levied by munipicalities, although counties may impose them in some states, and school districts can use them in Louisiana. Table 10–2 shows the steadily increasing importance of the sales tax as a source of municipal revenue over the last fifteen years. Most states have followed the recommended practice of permitting the local government to levy the tax in addition to a state sales tax and retaining the collection and administration of the tax at the state level. Such practices guarantee uniformity of administration and collection and reduce the administrative costs to the local government while maximizing the revenue produced. The major difficulty with the sales tax is that it is severely regressive. That is, it creates a greater proportional burden for lower income groups than for the wealthy. This is true because lower income groups must spend a greater proportion of their income in order to survive. Such taxes have particularly unfortunate side effects when they are applied to groceries, medicines, and other necessities of life. It is disconcerting to many that in some cities and states one must pay a tax for the privilege of eating when hungry or for the privilege of getting well when ill. Middle- and high-income groups can pass off such taxes as minor irritations, but citizens who live at or below the subsistence level may find them unbearable burdens.

THE INCOME TAX. As property and sales taxes failed to produce adequate revenue, many cities began to look for other ways to reach the wealth within their limits. The income tax appeared attractive in some areas because of its high productivity at the national level. Eight states have currently authorized some or all of their municipalities and counties to levy an income tax. Table 10–3 gives a complete breakdown of the local units over 50,000 population that presently use income taxation. This tax is obviously highly important in some cities, since it provides over half of the local tax collections in several communities and over two-thirds in

---

[17] Fortune Magazine, "The Great Urban Tax Tangle," p. 361.
[18] Advisory Commission on Intergovernmental Relations, *State and Local Taxes*, p. 6.

two. Current research has allayed some of the fears about the regressivity of flat-rate income taxes such as those levied by local government. Some experts now believe that "a broad-based flat rate tax can pack both a heavy revenue punch and provide a substantial degree of progression when combined with personal exemptions." [19] This means that the burden of the tax may be lightened for low-income groups by exempting significant portions of their income from taxation.

TABLE 10–3: **Local Income Taxes, Rates and Collections**
(Dollar amounts in thousands)

State and Local Government	Rate January 1, 1968 (percent)	Total Tax Collections	INCOME TAX COLLECTIONS Amount	INCOME TAX COLLECTIONS As a Percent of Total Collections
MUNICIPAL TAX COLLECTIONS, 1965–1966 (CITIES WITH OVER 50,000 POPULATION IN 1960)				
Alabama:				
Gadsden	2.0	$ 4,004	$ 2,139	53.4
Kentucky:				
Berea	1.0	xxx	xxx	xxx
Bowling Green	1.0	xxx	xxx	xxx
Catlettsburg	1.0	xxx	xxx	xxx
Covington	1.75	2,831	792	28.0
Flemingsburg	0.5	xxx	xxx	xxx
Frankfort	1.0	xxx	xxx	xxx
Glasgow	1.0	xxx	xxx	xxx
Hopkinsville	1.0	xxx	xxx	xxx
Lexington	1.5	6,993	3,596	51.4
Louisville	1.25	26,882	13,912	51.8
Jefferson County [1]	1.75	xxx	xxx	xxx
Ludlow	1.0	xxx	xxx	xxx
Mayfield	0.67	xxx	xxx	xxx
Maysville	1.0	xxx	xxx	xxx
Middlesboro	1.0	xxx	xxx	xxx
Newport	2.0	xxx	xxx	xxx
Owensboro	1.0	xxx	xxx	xxx
Paducah	1.25	xxx	xxx	xxx
Pikeville	1.0	xxx	xxx	xxx
Princeton	1.0	xxx	xxx	xxx
Richmond	1.0	xxx	xxx	xxx
Maryland:	% of State Tax			
Baltimore City	50%	144,451	[2]	[2]
12 counties [3]	20%	xxx	xxx	xxx
1 county	25%	xxx	xxx	xxx
1 county	30%	xxx	xxx	xxx
3 counties	35%	xxx	xxx	xxx
1 county	45%	xxx	xxx	xxx
4 counties	50%	xxx	xxx	xxx

[19] Advisory Commission on Intergovernmental Relations, *State and Local Taxes*, p. 6.

TABLE 10–3 (*continued*)

State and Local Government	Rate January 1, 1968 (percent)	Total Tax Collections	Amount	As a Percent of Total Collections
			MUNICIPAL TAX COLLECTIONS, 1965–1966 (CITIES WITH OVER 50,000 POPULATION IN 1960)	
			INCOME TAX COLLECTIONS	
Michigan:				
Battle Creek	4	xxx	xxx	xxx
Detroit	4	$158,246	$45,176	28.5
Flint	4	16,465	2,292	13.9
Grand Rapids	4	8,312	2	2
Hamtramck	4	xxx	xxx	xxx
Highland Park	4	xxx	xxx	xxx
Lapeer	4	xxx	xxx	xxx
Pontiac	4	5,668	2	2
Saginaw	4	5,572	904	16.2
St. Johns [5]	4	xxx	xxx	xxx
Missouri:				
Kansas City	0.5	42,128	10,157	24.1
St. Louis	1.0	80,709	27,265	33.8
New York:				
New York City	0.4–2.0 [6]	2,302,939	2	2
Ohio:				
Akron	1.0	18,519	9,936	53.7
Canton	1.0	5,374	4,015	74.7
Cincinnati	1.0	44,061	17,313	39.3
Cleveland	0.5	54,300	2	2
Cleveland Heights	0.5	2,962	2	2
Columbus	1.0	22,247	15,720	70.7
Dayton	1.0	21,467	11,689	54.5
Euclid	0.5	3,762	2	2
Hamilton	1.0	2,723	1,441	52.9
Lakewood	0.5	2,866	2	2
Lima	1.0	1,779	1,125	63.2
Lorain	0.5	2,423	2	2
Parma	0.5	3,202	2	2
Springfield	1.0	3,669	2,480	67.6
Toledo	1.5	18,763	10,735	57.2
Warren	1.0	3,164	2,024	64.0
Youngstown	1.0	8,354	4,590	54.9
143 cities and villages (with less than 50,000 population)	0.25–1.0	xxx	xxx	xxx
Pennsylvania:				
Cities, 50,000 population and over—				
Abington Township	1.0 [7]	11,969	2	2
Allentown	1.0 [7]	5,140	1,170	22.8
Altoona	1.0 [8]	2,320	494	21.3
Bethlehem	1.0 [7]	3,810	979	25.7
Chester	1.0 [9]	2,229	2	2
Erie	1.0 [7]	6,679	1,162	17.4

TABLE 10–3 (*continued*)

State and Local Government	Rate January 1, 1968 (*percent*)	MUNICIPAL TAX COLLECTIONS, 1965–1966 (CITIES WITH OVER 50,000 POPULATION IN 1960)		
		Total Tax Collections	INCOME TAX COLLECTIONS	
			Amount	As a Percent of Total Collections
Pennsylvania:				
Harrisburg	1.0 [7]	$ 3,884	[2]	[2]
Johnstown	1.0 [8]	2,211	$ 403	18.2
Lancaster	0.5 [10]	2,117	528	24.9
Penn Hill Township	1.0 [8]	1,533	608	39.7
Philadelphia	2.0 [9]	217,919	90,867	41.7
Pittsburgh	1.0 [8]	50,130	10,273	20.5
Scranton	0.5 [11]	4,555	690	15.1
Wilkes Barre	1.0 [7]	2,426	[2]	[2]
York	1.0 [7]	1,971	162	8.2
Approximately 3,000 other local jurisdictions (including over 1,000 school districts)	0.25–1.0	xxx	xxx	xxx

SOURCE: Advisory Commission on Intergovernmental Relations, *State and Local Taxes: Significant Features, 1968* (Washington, 1968), pp. 45 and 46.

NOTE: Excludes Washington, D.C., which has a graduated net income tax that is more closely akin to a State tax than to the municipal income taxes.

"xxx" Signifies cities under 50,000 population.

[1] A taxpayer subject to the 1.25 percent tax imposed by the City of Louisville may credit this tax against the 1.75 percent levied by Jefferson County.

[2] Tax went into effect after reporting period.

[3] Excludes Montgomery County, which levied a tax at the rate of 20 percent for calendar year 1967. As of January 1, 1968, the County Council had not set a rate for 1968.

[4] Under the Michigan "Uniform City Income Tax Act," the prescribed rates are 1.0 percent for residents and 0.5 percent for nonresidents. A resident is allowed credit for taxes paid to another city as a nonresident.

[5] St. Johns adopted the uniform income tax ordinance on November 7, 1967. Petitions for referendum have been filed and an election will be held on February 20, 1968.

[6] New York City residents' rate ranges from 0.4 percent on taxable income of less than $1,000 to 2.0 percent on taxable income in excess of $30,000. An earnings tax of 0.25 percent of wages or ⅜ of 1 percent on net earnings from self-employment, not to exceed that which would be due if taxpayer were a resident, is levied against nonresidents.

[7] The school district rate is the same as the municipal rate.

[8] The school district rate is 0.5 percent.

[9] There is no school district income tax.

[10] The school district rate is 1.0 percent.

[11] Combined city and school district rate may not exceed 2.0 percent.

There are several serious problems with the local income tax. The cost of administration and collection is particularly high in most places where the states do not collect the local tax as part of a state income tax. In addition to this, the efficient collection of the tax through employers at the point where wages and salaries are earned includes many nonresidents among the taxpayers. While this is justified by municipal authorities as a means of making suburbanites contribute for the central city services that they enjoy, the suburbs rarely take the same view, and the practice adds to the already serious antagonism between components of metropolitan systems. Finally, local income taxes tend to be levied upon wages and salaries to the exclusion of such other important sources of income as interest and dividends.[20] While income taxes have added appreciably to the revenue produced locally by urban governments in some areas, they do not appear to be adequate long-run solutions to the revenue problems of the cities.

OTHER TAXES AND LICENSES. Most cities can also add to their revenue through the imposition of a variety of minor taxes and license fees upon activities that take place within the city. Many cities have adopted a wheel tax upon automobiles that are driven within the city by residents or by commuters who work in the city. Others impose taxes on cigarettes and amusements, to name but two examples. Licenses are required for the sale of alcoholic beverages, the operation of places of entertainment, the operation of taxicabs, and so forth, both as a matter of regulation of these activities and as a source of income. In most communities, however, these minor taxes and licenses do not provide a significant portion of the revenues raised.

USER FEES AND CHARGES. One particularly popular form of raising revenue is the imposition of charges and fees for services rendered. These are based upon the amount of service rendered. Those who do not enjoy the service are not required to pay for it. The publicly owned utilities are financed in this way in order to provide adequate water, sewer, and transportation facilities. Other improvements such as streets, sidewalks, and street lighting are frequently financed through the use of special assessments against the property owners in the affected area. This type of financing appeals to the sense of fairness of many of our citizens. The problem lies in the inability of many citizens to pay the fees, charges, or assessments even though they need the services. In some cases, such as public transportation, those who need the service most are unable to pay charges that are

---

[20] Advisory Commission on Intergovernmental Relations, *State and Local Taxes*, p. 6.

high enough to support the service, thereby requiring subsidies out of general tax revenues if the service is to be continued.

INTERGOVERNMENTAL REVENUE. More and more revenue is produced for our urban areas from sources outside of local governmental jurisdictions. This revenue arrives in the form of grants-in-aid from state and federal governments. In the form of shared taxes, the states return to local governments a certain portion of some taxes collected within the local jurisdiction. The outstanding example of the latter type of tax is the motor fuel tax of many states, in which a percentage of the state tax is returned to local governments for the maintenance and improvement of local streets and highways. These grants and shared taxes have been the major state response to the inability of the property tax to adequately support local governmental activity.[21]

Both state and federal governments have tended to emphasize categorical grant programs that are directed at particular aspects of particular functions. These functional categories are determined by state and national authorities to be areas of national significance in which local inability or unwillingness to act is most serious. This fact, plus the matching requirements that demand the allocation of a certain amount of local funds to each grant program, has led many defenders of local government to claim that the higher levels of government are taking over local functions and making the crucial decisions with respect to resource allocation. While a certain amount of this charge is true, "grants-in-aid do not inevitably produce shifts in policy control in direct proportion which the amount of the grant bears to the total cost of the function." [22]

The facts seem to indicate that grants and shared taxes will continue to increase in importance as a source of local revenue, particularly in urban areas. Even if the productivity of the property tax continues to expand by virtue of an expanding economy and comprehensive tax reforms, it is not likely to be able to raise the vast amounts of money which appear to be needed over a relatively short period of time if our cities are to catch up on their public spending. The federal government and the states possess a superior revenue-producing capability by virtue of their access both potential and realized to the progressive income tax. The grant-in-aid enables them to share this capability with local government. In addition, the grant-in-aid enables the state and national governments to equalize the ability of local governments to meet the pressing demands of urban society by passing on greater sums of money to those jurisdictions with a tax base inadequate to support necessary services.

---

[21] Rowland Egger, "Nature Over Art: No More Local Finance," *American Political Science Review* 47 (1953): 474.

[22] Egger, "Nature Over Art," p. 473.

Many observers see room for improvement in the present grant structure. The replacement of categorical grants by block grants might well enable each city to decide which functions and services are most in need of help, and when. Such block grants would also encourage the standardization of grant requirements so that one simple set of rules would apply to the expenditure of grant funds, thereby simplifying the life of many city officials and lowering administrative costs. Such reforms might easily be achieved by making the income tax a shared tax and returning a percentage of its revenues to the urban government from which it was collected. This would, of course, involve making the assumption that local officials are honest and competent enough to spend this money in the best interests of their constituents. While such an assumption might appear shocking, no evidence leads us to believe that local officials are any less honest or competent than the federal or state officials who are presently dominating much of the policy-making.

URBAN DEBT. As Figure 10–3 shows, the amount of money which our urban governments have borrowed in order to finance their activities has increased significantly in the last five years. Most of this debt is long-term debt directed toward the purchase of capital goods, such as buildings and equipment, which have a life of at least as long as the term of the bond. However, there are some local governments who also engage in some relatively short-term borrowing for more current expenses, and this debt is secured primarily by anticipated taxes that have been levied but not yet collected.

Because of a series of unfortunate experiences with state and local debt in the nineteenth century, most states now place serious limitations on the borrowing power of local governments. In the first place, a debt limit is placed upon the jurisdiction, and this limit is usually expressed as a percentage of the assessed valuation of property in the jurisdiction. Many local governments are also limited as to the interest they may pay on bonds they have issued. And finally, many states require local referenda to approve the sale of bonds.

Most of these state limitations are directed at the type of bond referred to as general obligation or full faith and credit. These bonds are secured by an obligation against the entire community and all of its assets. They are retired primarily through the revenues raised by local property and other taxes. In fact, it is not unusual for the referendum that approves the bond issue to state the increase in the property tax rate that will be required to retire the bonds. There are other types of indebtedness which are largely free from the restrictions imposed by the states. Revenue bonds are frequently used when the asset for which the money is to be used will itself produce sufficient revenue to retire the debt. For example, any

Figure 10–3: Long-term Debt of Municipal Governments,
by Type and by Purpose of Issue: 1957 and 1962

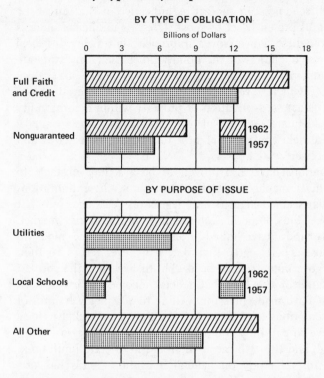

BY TYPE OF OBLIGATION

Billions of Dollars

SOURCE: *Finances of Municipalities and Township Governments*, vol. IV, no. 3, U.S. Census of Governments 1962 (Washington, 1962), p. 10.

urban service that is supported by user fees and charges is amenable to the use of revenue bonds for capital financing. Because more and more urban governments have reached the rather low legal limits for general obligation bonds, and because more and more services in our cities are being provided on a revenue-producing basis, the revenue bond is increasing in importance. In some areas, elaborate schemes have been developed in order to enable governments that have exhausted their legal borrowing powers to make capital expenditures for assets that are not generally revenue-producing. These schemes are usually centered upon some form of lease-purchase agreement. A special purpose district that can borrow the money through revenue bonds or a private group that is willing to put up the money on a contractual basis provides the necessary capital. The government then leases the asset for what would normally be the life of the bond and for a rent that includes both debt retirement and generous interest. At the end of the lease, the government or group that holds the asset turns it over to the government that has been leasing it.

The fact that such schemes can succeed is indicative of the unrealistic nature of the debt limits presently set by most states. As municipal officials like to point out, the best control over imprudent borrowing by local governments is the free operation of the bond market itself. Investors are not likely to buy municipal and other local bonds if they are not reasonably assured that they will receive their money and their interest at the time agreed upon. The assessed valuation of property within a community is obviously not an adequate measure of a government's ability to make such assurances. State debt limits are at best too low in most states and at worst totally unnecessary.

Interest rate limitations have also proven to be a serious obstacle to effective urban financial management. In many cases, these limitations were set at a level that seemed high to state legislators years ago, but that is now too low to meet the competing interest rates in the money market. Attempts to curb inflation have raised interest costs to new highs in recent years, and most experts agree that they will never return to their earlier levels. Local governments have been able to live with the interest limitations only because of the fact that federal income tax exemptions on this bond interest have made investors willing to accept lower rates of interest. If these exemptions are eliminated, as they may well be, local governments will have to pay fully competitive rates of interest to borrow the money they need, and this will mean the removal of state limitations.

The requirement for referenda on general obligation bonds has provided urban governments with a serious obstacle to capital improvements. There is a strong tendency in America to vote No on bond issues. Part of this tendency can be traced to a natural desire to keep taxes low. Since property tax burdens are often unreasonably heavy, it is difficult to convince voters that they ought to agree to making them heavier. Another problem lies in the frequently presented argument that it is wrong to burden future generations with expenditures that are made in this generation. There are many who oppose all public borrowing on this basis. The shortcomings of such an argument should be evident. If money is carefully reserved for thirty years out of general tax revenues in order to build a new school building, the people who paid for the building would get no immediate use or benefit from it. If, however, the money is borrowed now, and the coming generations are taxed to repay it over a thirty-year period, then those people whose children are occupying the school and enjoying its benefits will be paying for it. This argument is rarely presented with any effectiveness in the campaigns surrounding bond referenda.

The rapid growth in borrowing by our urban governments cannot continue unless some of the problems suggested in earlier sections on taxation and intergovernmental payments are solved. The bonding power of any government is ultimately dependent upon its ability to repay the money borrowed. There are many services that cannot be turned into revenue producers in order to enjoy the benefits of revenue bond financing. It is reasonable to anticipate a slowdown in the growth of both general obligation and revenue bond financing until our cities and urban areas are assured of additional income and until some of the more unreasonable restrictions have been removed by state governments.

The Budgetary Process

The decisions as to how much money a particular city needs to raise and how the available funds are to be expended lie at the very heart of the urban political process. Few people really enjoy paying taxes, and taxpayers' groups and real estate interests use the voters' understandable antipathy to maintain constant pressure on city councils and other local governing boards. On the other hand, there are obvious countervailing pressures. As the discussion earlier in this chapter indicated, the demands of the citizenry for municipal and other urban services have reached unprecedented heights and show signs of continuing to increase. These contradictory trends frequently engender great pressure in the political process and result in bitter conflict. In most municipalities today the pressures are relieved and the conflicts are resolved—at least in part—through the process of adopting a budget.

Chapter 7 indicated that the assignment of the responsibility for preparing the budget to the chief executive constituted part of the general strengthening of executive institutions which has taken place in this century. However, such an assignment is far from being complete since many cities still have their budgets prepared by the legislative body, a legislative committee, or by the executive in conjunction with a legislative committee. For example, in New York City the major budgetary influence is exercised by the Board of Estimate on which the mayor has only one vote.[23] In most cases, however, it is accurate to attribute to the mayor or manager the formal policy initiative that goes with the preparation of the budget. Of course, in the larger cities the chief executive benefits from the assistance of a budget director or a finance director who supervises the collection of data and the actual formulation of the budget within the guidelines established by the chief executive.

The budget itself is an imposing looking document in even the smallest of communities. The opening pages are usually devoted to the executive's

---

[23] Wallace S. Sayre and Herbert Kaufman, *Governing New York City* (New York, 1965), p. 628.

budget message. This message is designed to present an overall picture of the policies and programs recommended for the community for the coming year. It provides the justification for the expenditures and taxes contained in the budget and attempts to make both palatable to the council and attentive community groups. The second section of the document contains a summary of the general financial picture of the city for the coming year and indicates expenditures and revenues according to major categories. The next section is a detailed breakdown of anticipated revenues for the coming year and a comparison of those figures with revenues in the previous fiscal year and collections to date in the current year.

The actual detailing of planned expenditures can be presented in several ways. Until a few years ago, it was common to present them by "line item." This form placed each item of expense into a separate category without any real reference to the way in which it was used. So much money was allocated for secretarial salaries, office supplies, equipment maintenance, etc., with no clear indication of how these expenditures related to the level of service which the taxpayer was experiencing. To make matters worse, the prevailing practice with line item budgets was to prohibit the transferal of funds from one item to another after the adoption of the budget, even though a department head found that he could more productively use the money for maintenance than for office supplies. Current budgetary doctrine has called for the replacement of line item budgeting with performance budgeting. In the latter form, expenditures are listed according to the function or service performed. In this way it is possible for administrators, councilmen, and the attentive public to evaluate expenditures of public funds according to their assessment of the value of the service performed. The shift in manner of presentation also has been frequently accompanied by a greater latitude in transferring funds within program categories in order to maintain the maximum possible service output according to administrative standards.

In most budgets, the capital budget is presented as a separate section. The revenues and expenditures presented earlier were those devoted to current operations. The capital budget details anticipated purchase and construction of long-term assets and the anticipated revenues to be used for such acquisitions. This budget may cover only the coming fiscal year, but, as we shall see in Chapter 11, it may also be a long-term document that programs such capital expenditures into the future. The major determinant of the time period which such a budget covers is whether or not the budgetary process is closely linked with the planning process. In all too many communities it is not.

DRAWING UP THE BUDGET. Because of the realization of the increased importance of the budget as a policy instrument, much more attention has been devoted in recent years to the manner in which the document is prepared. Since most city councils—in practice if not by law—must content themselves with reducing budgetary items or, in rare instances, deleting them, the decision as to what will be included in the budget as it is presented to the council and what the expenditure levels recommended will be is clearly of crucial importance.

One of the most important decisions is whether the budgetary process should be incremental or zero-based.[24] In the incremental approach, each department operates under the assumption that it will receive at least as much in the coming fiscal year as it has received in the current fiscal year. The basic decision to be reached is how much more each department will need. The assumption of the zero-based approach is quite different. Under this alternative, each department must begin from scratch and justify its entire operation to the budget officer and ultimately to the council. Each of these methods has its advantages. Only the zero-based budget can effectively inspire a full and complete evaluation of the operations of the city each year. Nothing is taken for granted; everything must be fully justified. For those who desire economy and efficiency in government no other approach will suffice. However, it cannot be assumed that incremental budgeting continues to exist only at the urging of the champions of governmental waste and inefficiency. In the first place, it is far less time-consuming to develop a justification for a modest expansion of existing programs than it is to completely reexamine the programs themselves. In the second place, budgeting by increments tends to minimize the amount of conflict inherent in the budgetary process. If the general pattern is followed and nobody loses while everybody gains a little, there is less chance that the budget will be challenged when it is presented to the council. This something-for-everybody approach emphasizes compromise between the various interest groups within the city as well as between the departments and agencies of the government itself.

PPBS. These initials, innocent as they may appear, have been at the heart of a great controversy over the budgetary process and probably represent the wave of the future in budgeting. They stand for Planning, Programming, Budgeting Systems. The concept grew out of the operations research and systems analysis techniques that were developed in military policy-making research during and after World War II. It became established as a budgetary decision-making process in the early 1960s when it began to be used in the Department of Defense and soon spread to the rest of the federal government. After its adoption at the national level, it was only a matter of time until it would be considered as useful for local

---

[24] Leonard E. Goodall, *The American Metropolis* (Columbus, Ohio, 1968), p. 157.

governments as well. While local experiments with PPBS are still few and far between, the general assumption of most financial planners is that it will be adopted by most major cities within the next decade or two.

What is PPBS, and how is it important to the decision-making process? Selma Mushkin and her associates at George Washington University have offered perhaps the most succinct definition of the term:

> PPBS is primarily a planning system which leads to program decisions which are then used as guidance for preparation of the detailed budgets. . . . Its essence is the development and presentation of relevant information as to the full implications—the costs and benefits—of the major alternative courses of action.[25]

Such a planning system contributes to the decision-making process, at least in theory, by introducing greater rationality and providing "a sensitive and powerful methodology which identifies the interrelationships among municipal goals and objectives and the resources required to attain them." [26]

Figure 10–4 presents the theoretical PPBS decision-making process schematically.[27] The Objective Set constitutes the broad, desired behavior patterns for the community, such as economic growth, adequate housing, and public safety. Derivative Objectives identify the more specific policy variables, such as the actual rate of desired growth or the crime rate that will serve as the focus of governmental attention. The Political Function determines the selection of both objective sets and derivative objectives and hopefully contributes to their compatibility. It is at this point that the criteria for judging the efficacy of the decision-making mechanism are developed.[28] The resources available are identified and evaluated in the Research, Development, and Test Function, and these resources are related to specific program areas such as industrial development and juvenile delinquency, through the System Feasibility Function, to determine resource capabilities in each area. Resource capabilities in the various program areas are fed back to the policy-makers so that the priorities established for various objectives can be reevaluated. Specific programs are selected and implemented and finally evaluated according to earlier developed criteria and standards of program performance. Judgments as to Program Impact are then returned to policy-makers by way of the Control

---

[25] Selma J. Mushkin, et al., "What is PPBS?" *Planning Programming Budgeting for City, State, County Objectives*, vol. 1 (Washington, 1967), pp. 7 and 1.

[26] Don H. Overly, "Decision-Making in City Government," *Urban Affairs Quarterly* 3 (1967): 43.

[27] This entire discussion draws heavily on Overly, "Decision-Making in City Government," pp. 49–51.

[28] See Yehezkel Dror, *Public Policymaking Reexamined* (San Francisco, 1968), p. 25, for the distinction between "criteria" and "standards."

Function in order that objectives, priorities, and selection of programs may be reexamined. The preparation of the budget document itself fits into the process immediately upon the selection of specific programs, and the rest of the PPBS process provides the rationale for the policies reflected in the budget.

Much of the consideration of alternative allocations and the evaluation of program performance is based upon the much publicized technique of cost-benefit analysis. The technique is not particularly complicated in principle. In fact, many of us use a form of cost-benefit analysis to assist us in day-to-day decision-making. The costs of each particular program are determined by totaling the value of the resources assigned to that program. Then the benefits, either real or anticipated, of the program are identified and quantified. That program whose benefits exceed its costs by the greatest margin is identified as most valuable. In practice, however, life is not quite that simple. Figure 10–4 and the earlier discussion vastly oversimplify the process and assign a far too narrow role to the political function. Since there is no single utility scale for costs and benefits, the major question that returns time and time again is, "Whose criteria and standards will prevail?" The unpleasant fact of cost-benefit analysis is that conflicts over the values assigned to various costs and benefits are frequently resolved in the time-honored manner of politicians—logrolling.[29] While such activity may be perfectly rational from the point of view of the political scientist, it is most assuredly not what PPBS advocates like Overly had in mind when they described it as "a rational decision-making process."[30]

Financial Administration

One of the major difficulties in municipal finance is the lack of unity and coherence in financial administration. Throughout this chapter it has been demonstrated that there are few areas of finance over which the municipality, or any other governmental unit for that matter, has complete control. The office of Finance Director is almost always a good deal less imposing that the title would indicate. His major duties are to monitor the expenditure of resources once collected for the administration, to assist in budget preparation, and to collect those few minor local taxes and fees that are totally within municipal authority. Major resources remain under the administrative control of higher governmental authority,

---

[29] Aaron Wildavsky, "The Political Economy of Efficiency: Cost Benefit Analysis, Systems Analysis and Program Budgeting," *Public Administration Review* 26 (1966): 292–310. Contrast this view with that in Roland N. McKean, "Costs and Benefits from Different Viewpoints," in Schaller, *Public Expenditure Decisions*, p. 159.

[30] Overly, "Decision-Making in City Government," p. 43.

Figure 10–4

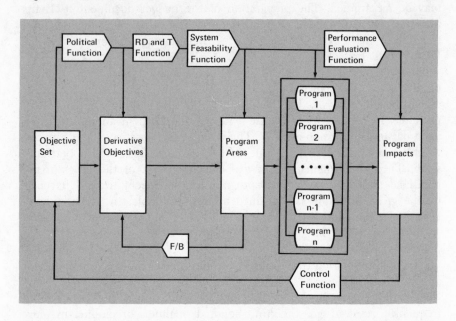

SOURCE: Don H. Overly, "Decision-Making in City Government," *Urban Affairs Quarterly* 3 (1967), 52. Reprinted by permission of the Publisher, Sage Publications, Inc.

especially the state. Property assessments are determined and taxes collected by county or township officers. The piggy-backing of sales tax collections in many states leaves the administration of that productive revenue source to the state. The major administrative decisions with respect to the collection and distribution of intergovernmental revenues and shared taxes clearly rest at the state or higher level.

All of this should not be interpreted as an argument for "returning" the administration of urban finance to the municipality. In the first place, many of these administrative functions never were performed by the cities. Secondly, it is frequently far more efficient and effective for higher governmental jurisdictions to administer taxes. While it may be politically necessary and desirable to retain the decision as to the magnitude of local expenditures and, therefore, the size of the total local tax bill at the local level, there appears to be no generally acceptable reason for administering taxation at the local level. Most of the reforms so far suggested for the local revenue system have involved increasing state administrative control over local taxation while decreasing the states' control over the basic policy decision as to the amount of taxation. That our present local taxes frequently fail to conform to any of the criteria for acceptable taxation in this country—ability to pay, benefits received, or equity—is in most cases traceable to maladministration of these taxes or inability to administer them at a local level.

Little progress has been made in realizing the reforms suggested above. Until such progress is made it may make little sense to talk about municipal finance administration as if it were a discrete function that could be performed in a single office in city hall. It is interesting to note in this regard that recent discussions in the Finance Administration portion of the *Municipal Yearbook* have contained little if any information on administration.[31]

Suggested Readings

Advisory Commission on Intergovernmental Relations. *Measures of State and Local Fiscal Capacity and Tax Effort*. Washington, 1962.

——. *State-Local Taxation and Industrial Location*. Washington, 1967.

——. *State and Local Taxes: Significant Features, 1968*. Washington, 1968.

——. *The Role of the States in Strengthening the Property Tax*. 2 vols. Washington, 1963.

Benson, George C. S.; Benson, Summer; McClelland, Harold; and Thomson, Procter. *The American Property Tax: Its History, Administration, and Economic Impact*. Claremont, Calif., 1965.

Campbell, Alan K., and Sacks, Seymour. *Metropolitan America: Fiscal Patterns and Governmental Systems*. New York, 1967.

Gilbert, Charles E. *Governing the Suburbs*. Bloomington, Ind., 1967.

Mace, Ruth L. *Municipal Cost-Revenue Research in the United States*. Chapel Hill, 1961.

Maxwell, James A. *Financing State and Local Governments*. Washington, 1965.

Mosher, Frederick C., and Poland, Orville F. *The Costs of American Governments*. New York, 1964.

Mushkin, Selma J., et al. *Planning Programming Budgeting for City, State, County Objectives*. 7 vols. Washington, 1967.

Schaller, Howard G., ed. *Public Expenditure Decisions in the Urban Community*. Baltimore, 1963.

---

[31] See for example J. Richard Aronson, "Trends in Municipal Finance," *Municipal Yearbook, 1967*, ed. Orin F. Nolting and David S. Arnold (Chicago, 1967), pp. 197–203.

Part Three
The Functions of
Urban Government

Only through examining in detail some of the most important operations of urban governments can the importance of the general questions raised in Part Two be fully appreciated. Most of the current criticism directed toward urban governments is centered upon the manner in which they perform or fail to perform functions that many consider to be vital to the survival of urban man. The functional areas that serve as the subjects for these six chapters were not selected at random. They are the subjects which are most frequently identified as problem areas in our cities. In addition, they include thirteen of the fifteen categories listed by the Advisory Commission on Inter-governmental Relations in its publication *Performance of Urban Functions: Local and Areawide* as comprising 85 percent of total local governmental expenditures. In each instance there has been a conscious attempt to focus on the political problems inherent in the performance of the particular functions under discussion. The fact that some of the same problems will appear again and again in each service context serves to further underline their importance to the study of contemporary urban life.

chapter **11**
Planning
and Land Use
Controls

❡[City planning may be regarded as a means for systematically anticipating and achieving adjustment in the physical environment of a city consistent with social and economic trends and sound principles of civic design.[1]

The Urban Planning Effort

For many people in the United States the word planning triggers a violent reaction. These people identify the planning effort with the controls imposed by totalitarian systems in order to achieve their purposes and goals. This fear of planning has been heightened by the tendency of socialist governments to focus their activities upon a plan. As a result, many people connect governmental planning with socialist systems and oppose the former simply because they oppose the latter. This is unfortunate because there are all kinds of planning, some of which involve more control over individual behavior by government than others. As Alan Altshuler has pointed out:

> Planning is, in the final analysis, simply the effort to infuse activity with consistency and conscious purpose. All men and organizations plan in this sense, of course, but some plan more systematically and effectively than others.[2]

---

[1] F. Stuart Chapin, Jr., *Urban Land Use Planning*, 2d ed. (Urbana, Ill., 1965), p. vi.
[2] Alan A. Altshuler, *The City Planning Process: A Political Analysis* (Ithaca, N.Y., 1965), p. 409.

Planning becomes necessary when evidence shows that tomorrow will bring developments that are inconsistent with the aspirations of an organization. The planning process consists of developing alternative responses to these developments, considering the costs and benefits of each alternative, selecting the appropriate alternative, and developing the necessary policies to implement the course of action selected.[3] The goals or purposes of the organization may be altered so as to be more consistent with changes considered to be inevitable in the physical or social environment. Changes designed to minimize the impact of environmental changes on the goals and purposes of the organization may be made in the organization. Or the environment itself may be altered to prevent changes from taking place or to mitigate the impact of such changes on the organization.

The need for planning has been recognized in urban governments more clearly than at any other level, particularly in the United States. While state and national planning efforts are still viewed with considerable suspicion, some type of local planning effort has been largely accepted. This is particularly true of city or municipal planning where planning has progressed even further than in urban counties and special districts, which can be said to be just beginning in earnest. Those engaged in the planning process have translated the more general kinds of definitions of planning suggested above into particular functions that can be performed with a greater or lesser degree of success by governmental agencies.[4] In the first place, planners must conduct research and gather information in order to accurately predict the environmental changes to which planning must respond. They must also participate in the process of general goal formation for the community in conjunction with public and voluntary organizations and elected and appointed officials. Once these processes are completed, the planners can then turn to the job of drafting specific plans which reflect both future environmental developments and the goals of the community. When the plans are approved, planning agencies begin to coordinate the efforts of various government departments and agencies in carrying out policies that are in consonance with the plans, and to assist and advise executive and legislative policy-makers. Our discussion of these planning functions will demonstrate that the process is far more complex than this preliminary statement suggests.

AMERICAN PLANNING: A BRIEF HISTORY. Although much of the emphasis on planning can be seen as a contemporary phenomenon, American planning

---

[3] Britton Harris, "The New Technology and Urban Planning," *Urban Affairs Quarterly* 3 (1967): 23–24.

[4] This list of functions is derived from Henry Fagin, "Planning Organization and Activities Within the Framework of Urban Government," in *Planning and the Urban Community*, ed. Harvey S. Perloff (Pittsburgh, 1961), pp. 107–110.

is rooted in the early colonial and immediate postnational periods. The layout of street patterns which constituted most of the planning done in this early period was a far cry from the more ambitious comprehensive plans of today, but it was a beginning. Some rudimentary planning must have been conducted in every urban settlement, but these plans were informal and were soon lost. The enduring plans of early American history were those mapped out for some of our major cities. William Penn's Philadelphia plan in 1682, L'Enfant's design for Washington, D.C. in 1791, the Detroit plan of 1807, and the Manhattan plan in 1811 all represent layouts of street patterns which have had a lasting effect upon the development of those cities.[5]

This important early emphasis on planning suffered a serious setback as national development began in earnest in the late eighteenth and early nineteenth centuries. The colonial planning tradition was halted by four forces: "an anti-urban political theory, economic competition among cities, the decline of municipal government, and the rise of land speculation."[6] These factors combined to stimulate a wild period of urban growth and to weaken the mechanisms of control over that growth. By the end of the nineteenth century, the consequences of the halt in planning effort were obvious to every observer of our major cities. Urban reformers were horrified by slums and urban blight and dedicated themselves to the support of programs which would in some way or another restore the city to a habitable state. The real rebirth of planning was dependent upon the civic support for such activities generated by the City Beautiful Movement at the turn of the century.[7] While the major focus of this movement was upon aesthetic considerations, it may well have provided the justification for a much broader approach to planning.

It is possible to claim that modern planning began with the twentieth century. In fact, Harvey Perloff has selected the period 1900–1933 as the first phase of urban planning in the United States.[8] At first, the effort was feeble and somewhat disorganized. This lack of inventiveness and vigor is shown by the fact that one of the earliest symbolic efforts in the rebirth of planning was the exhuming of L'Enfant's plan for Washington, D.C. in 1902.[9] However, once started, the planning movement quickly gathered headway. Two events of 1909 are indicative of the rapid tendency to ex-

---

[5] Robert A. Walker, *The Planning Function in Urban Government*, 2d ed. (Chicago, 1950), p. 4.

[6] James G. Coke, "Antecedents of Local Planning," in *Principles and Practice of Urban Planning*, ed. William I. Goodman and Eric C. Freund (Washington, 1968), p. 14.

[7] Walker, *The Planning Function*, p. 15.

[8] Harvey S. Perloff, "Metropolitan Politics and Organization for Planning," in Perloff, *Planning and the Urban Community*, p. 78.

[9] Walker, *The Planning Function*, p. 5.

pand beyond purely aesthetic considerations. The first national city planning conference held in that year placed its heaviest emphasis on economic rather than aesthetic considerations in justifying and promoting the planning movement.[10] In addition, the Chicago Plan was completed; this represented the first major effort at large-scale city planning in the United States. Although this plan was an immediate outgrowth of the City Beautiful Movement, it was not wholly concerned with aesthetic considerations. "Despite a predominant architectural emphasis, the Chicago Plan expressed an appreciation of the objectives of planning which put it well in the vanguard of the trend toward comprehensiveness." [11]

Although interest in planning spread rapidly in the next decade, most cities were primarily concerned with the physical layout of the community. This concern was broader than the initial emphasis on aesthetics and architecture, but it fell far short of comprehensive planning. The 1920s were productive years for American city planning in spite of their shortcomings:

> The major changes in local planning during the twenties were (1) the addition of engineers and lawyers to the ranks of the planning profession, (2) the beginnings of state and metropolitan planning, and (3) the rapid rise and immense popularity of zoning.[12]

Not until the economic tragedy of the Great Depression of the thirties did social problems become so acute that they were bound to have a significant impact on the planning process. In the depths of the Depression we entered into what Perloff has identified as the second phase of planning.[13] This phase, which lasted well into the 1960s, was characterized by a focus on urban development and redevelopment and by a broadening of the scope of the planning effort to include the metropolis and the urban region. Planners also began to display a significant amount of concern over the impact of planning on government operations and over the necessity for coordinating planning activities, particularly with the executive branch of government.

The period immediately following World War II was particularly significant in the history of American urban planning. There was a burst of planning activity, much of which is traceable to the surge of urban growth following the war. The prewar emphasis on physical and land-use planning guaranteed that these principles were well enough established that uncontrolled development was no longer considered acceptable. By now

---

[10] Walker, *The Planning Function*, pp. 10–11.
[11] Walker, *The Planning Function*, p. 19.
[12] Coke, "Antecedents of Local Planning," p. 19.
[13] Perloff, "Metropolitan Politics," p. 79.

the special interests that dealt with community development in the physical sense were firmly convinced that the maintenance of property values and economic advantage was tied closely to the planning movement. Some minimal effort at planning was therefore evident throughout the vast areas of postwar urban growth. The federal government gave additional impetus to this expansion of the planning effort by providing seed money for the support of urban planning in Section 701 of the Housing Act of 1954. With this kind of encouragement even the smaller and poorer communities could hope to plan, since the high initial costs were defrayed by the national government. In addition, federal grants-in-aid for urban renewal required a workable program of community improvement which, in turn, had at its center a comprehensive community plan. A significant amount of the money available to local governments from national sources was thereby tied to the successful completion of at least some minimal planning effort. As time went on, metropolitan and regional planning were also linked to federal grant programs through further requirements that many of the projects supported by federal funds be coordinated with a regional planning body before those funds would be granted.

Planning has thus been accepted as appropriate governmental activity in all of our major urban centers as well as in many of the smaller urban settlements. From the depths of unrestrained development in the mid-nineteenth century, through the rather tentative efforts of middle- and upper-class citizens' groups, we have progressed to the frantic flurry of governmentally sponsored planning activity which characterizes the urban scene today. The fact that planning is a largely accepted activity for our local governments and that there is a lot of it does not tell the whole story. It is still necessary to know more about how the process works and where it is taking us before we can understand its full impact on modern urban governments.

CURRENT CONCEPTS AND TRENDS. Urban planning today, at the beginning of what might be called its third phase of development, has taken on new directions and techniques. In examining the literature of modern planning, it is possible to identify several major areas of concern.[14] In the first place, most city planners are still concerned with problems of aesthetics and design. Even though they long ago decided that aesthetics do not constitute the whole of planning, it is clear that for most planners there is no planning without some consideration of the aesthetic impact on the urban environment. Secondly, the modern planner appears to be concerned with the impact of the community power structure and of citizen

---

[14] William I. Goodman and Eric C. Freund, "Introduction," in Goodman and Freund, *Urban Planning*, pp. 2–4.

participation in general on the planning process. The problems that have been unearthed in this area will be discussed in detail later in this chapter. Thirdly, the current planning effort seems to be particularly conscious of the relationship that exists between environmental factors and social welfare.

Finally, urban planners appear to have taken full advantage of the progress made in the social sciences in introducing quantitative methods to social research. The research effort in urban planning has always been heavily quantitative. Much of the relevant material for describing our environment lends itself best to quantitative statement, such as population, land values, and tax rates. Computer technology and electronic data processing has enabled planners to manipulate and display a wider range of data in a much shorter period of time than was ever before possible. Planners are thus able to handle more environmental variables and to gather more data with accuracy. However, the sheer ability to gather more data in quantitative form and to manipulate it more easily is in itself of only small value. The major question that remains is what to do with the data after you have it.

The earlier discussion in this chapter indicated that a good part of the planning process is dependent upon the ability of planners to make predictive statements about the future development of the urban environment and the impact of social policy on that environment. If planners are to predict, they must have some crude, preliminary conception of the way in which the variables for which they have data interrelate. This conception has usually been a rather vague set of unstated assumptions and hypotheses about the urban social, economic, and political system that has been carried around in the back of the planner's mind. There has been no guarantee that planners, policy-makers, and the attentive public were operating on the basis of the same assumptions. The results were frequently confusing to all parties, if not disastrous. Contemporary planners are moving in the direction of correcting this particular shortcoming by formulating more explicit theoretical statements about the operation of the urban system.

Frequently, planners have sought to add particular rigor to their theoretical statements by making them in the form of mathematical models which attempt to simulate the operation of the planning universe. In such a model it is necessary to state assumptions explicitly and to formulate hypotheses that can be empirically verified. If these models are to be useful in urban planning, they must fulfill certain minimum requirements: [15]

---

[15] Melville C. Branch, "Simulation, Mathematical Models, and Comprehensive City Planning," *Urban Affairs Quarterly* 1 (1966): 21 and 22.

1. They must include all relevant variables and data.
2. They must be simplified or generalized distillations of the system for which planning is being conducted.
3. They must have basic conceptual structures that hold the models together.
4. The decision-makers must be able to understand the model or models used.
5. The information and analysis provided should clarify rather than confuse the conceptions of the planning universe.
6. The models must relate both directly observable, empirical components of the system *and* abstractions.
7. They must incorporate past and present data while having some predictive ability with respect to the future.
8. The validity of the models must be tested against the real world and modified or discarded as appropriate.

Although the introduction of models and simulations has introduced greater clarity and precision into the urban planning process, these models have not been a cure-all for the planner. At least two serious problems limit their utility.[16] The models remain imperfect predictive devices because they fail to reflect the full dynamics of the city. This failure can largely be traced to their inability to handle variables that are either non-quantifiable or are quantified only with great difficulty and subsequent loss of precision. In the second place, there are great dangers inherent in depending too heavily upon models that have not been verified by testing their validity in the real world; there has been an unfortunate amount of model-building with far too little empirical verification.

LAND USE PLANNING. The greatest part of the urban planning effort is devoted to land use planning. This type of planning "is basically concerned with the location, intensity, and amount of land development required for the various space-using functions of city life—industry, wholesaling, business, housing, recreation, education, and the religious and cultural activities of the people." [17] Land use planning follows the same general sequence of activity that has already been described. Objectives are identified, existing conditions surveyed, future needs anticipated, and plan alternatives and policy implications considered.[18] However, a brief examination of the leading textbook in the field will show that the planning process is infinitely more complex than this.

---

[16] Branch, "Simulation," pp. 27 and 28.
[17] Chapin, *Urban Land Use Planning*, p. 1.
[18] Chapin, *Urban Land Use Planning*, pp. 359–369.

One of the first steps in land use planning is the analysis of the urban economy: [19]

What is termed *the urban economy* is regarded here as a system of production, distribution, and consumption embracing the sum total productive activity within an urban center and that part of its hinterland which is dependent to a marked degree on facilities and services available in the city.[20]

Like most planning tasks, the study of the urban economy obviously increases in complexity with the size of the planning unit involved. It may not be too difficult to describe present production, distribution, and consumption patterns in the small, single-industry town or even in medium-sized cities, but the task becomes a good deal more demanding if the planning unit is the New York metropolitan area. The more complex the system, the greater the opportunity for error in analysis.

The second set of variables which must be part of the preliminary study in land use planning is that which deals with population.[21] The planner must determine the size, composition, and distribution of the population of the planning unit. These tasks appear deceptively simple. In most urban areas, population size is determined with some exactness only in the decennial census conducted by the national government. In between censuses, planners are dependent upon estimates to help them find out just how many people live in the area. Similar techniques must be used if the planners are to be able to forecast population growth with any degree of accuracy. The extent and rate of population growth or decline are two of the most important variables for intelligent land use planning. In addition to gathering this data for the area as a whole, planners must also concern themselves with subareas or neighborhoods, since the overall population changes are not likely to be equally distributed throughout the planning area. They must also gather data on the distribution of the population according to age, income, household size, sex, race, national origin, education, and any other variable that might be of some importance to land use patterns. This whole set of data must be obtained for both daytime and nighttime populations, since the two groups differ significantly in almost every community.

A somewhat newer and more radical type of study for land use planners is the study of urban activity systems.[22]

---

[19] See Chapin, *Urban Land Use Planning*, Chapters 3 and 4.
[20] Chapin, *Urban Land Use Planning*, p. 108.
[21] See Chapin, *Urban Land Use Planning*, Chapter 5.
[22] See Chapin, *Urban Land Use Planning*, Chapter 6.

"Activity systems" is defined here as behavior patterns of individuals, families, institutions, and firms which occur in spatial patterns that have meaning in planning for land use.[23]

Obviously, some of the interaction patterns which are studied under this heading have already been detailed in the study of the urban economy. The economic system is just one of many activity systems whose interactive patterns have a significant impact on land use. Other such patterns may serve to define subcommunities within the planning area. Under ideal circumstances, this type of study would reveal not only present activity patterns but also those patterns that would be likely to fulfill the needs and desires of individuals, families, institutions, and firms in the future. With this information in hand, planners would be able to allocate land uses according to empirically derived social patterns, rather than merely according to abstract principles of design or architecture. Unfortunately, studies of this type are so new to the planning effort that full scale survey and analysis techniques have not yet been developed.

Finally, but certainly not of least importance, land use planning must obviously involve detailed studies of the land itself.[24] These studies concentrate on the physical attributes of the land and its improvements. The planning area must be mapped carefully to show not only the natural topographic features of the urban environment but also the important man-made features such as streets, railroads, and dams, that could affect the way in which the land is used. During this stage of planning a classification system must be developed that will identify the different types of land use, and the system must then be applied to the existing plots of land in the area. In most instances, the system is based upon some variation of the standard classification of land into residential, commercial, industrial, and public uses. Once existing uses are mapped, it is relatively easy to study the vacant land in the area and to determine what portion of it can be used. Planners quite frequently apply some standards of structural and environmental quality to the improvements on the land in use in order to identify areas in which the improvements fail to meet contemporary views of an adequate and decent environment. These standards are usually of the sort developed by housing and health officials and will be discussed in greater detail in the next chapter. It is also appropriate at this point for the planners to study land values and their changes over time in order to get a clear picture of the market for land and of the effect that certain uses can have on land values. Related economic studies focus on the cost-revenue picture with respect to certain land uses, that is, the cost in

---

[23] Chapin, *Urban Land Use Planning*, p. 224.
[24] Chapin, *Urban Land Use Planning*, Chapter 7.

governmental services compared to the public revenue generated by each potential use of a parcel of land.

Once all of this data is gathered, the real planning can begin. The planners put it all together to form a land use plan that reflects the goals and objectives that have been agreed upon earlier. This plan divides the planning area into districts, each of which is designated a particular type of permitted land use. Furthermore, these districts and land uses also carry with them certain other judgments with respect to structural quality and condition, population density, and so forth. Sites for public uses are indicated showing the streets, parks, buildings, and public utilities that are necessary to support the other designated uses. The end product not only specifies uses for presently vacant land; it also suggests changes in existing patterns of land use which might be desirable in the future.

SOCIAL WELFARE PLANNING. In recent years some planning circles have been haunted by the feeling that the type of physical planning represented by the land use plan is inadequate to the task of providing a basis for man's mastery of his total urban environment. Most modern planners have assumed that there was a basic link between physical and social problems in our urban society, but until recently they have tended to assume further that the physical environment determined the social environment. Now, there is a strong tendency to view the relationship between the two as reciprocal.[25] While the land use plan obviously has a significant impact on such welfare-related governmental functions as housing, education, health, and recreation, the more subtle impact of planning on the restriction or provision of economic and social opportunity, the attainment of financial security, and the enhancement of psychological security is frequently missed.[26] One of the reasons for this appears to be that planners lack a systematic way of approaching the study of the connection between physical and social factors. "There is a great demand for social planning, but little consensus at this time as to what it involves from a technical point of view."[27] The study of urban activity patterns that has begun as part of physical land use planning may provide, if carried to its logical conclusion, a systematic source of information concerning the relationship between physical and social phenomena. Unless this information can be obtained regularly and systematically, the social results of physical planning are likely to continue to be unanticipated and antithetical to the planning effort. The social costs of such a disjointed effort may be high. "It is obvious, at any rate, that some planning activities

---

[25] William I. Goodman, Eric C. Freund, and Paul Davidoff, "Social Welfare Planning," in Goodman and Freund, *Urban Planning*, pp. 295–296.

[26] Goodman, Freund, and Davidoff, "Social Welfare Planning," pp. 303–306.

[27] Goodman, Freund, and Davidoff, "Social Welfare Planning," p. 300.

undertaken with the intention of helping the underprivileged were actually more painful than the conditions the planners were trying to alleviate." [28]

COMPREHENSIVE PLANNING. The word comprehensive has become insepably linked to the planning process over the last fifty years. The professional literature is full of discussions of "comprehensive plans." The federal government requires evidence of comprehensive planning as a condition of receiving grants-in-aid under many of its programs. Even a cursory examination of planning literature or of plans themselves would reveal that the word comprehensive means many things to many people, and that what serves as a comprehensive plan for one planner is piecemeal planning for another.

In its most frequently-used sense "comprehensive" plans are nothing more than particularly thorough physical plans for the community. "A comprehensive plan is an official public document adopted by a local government as a policy guide to decisions about the physical development of the community." [29] These plans include material on private land use, community facilities, and circulation patterns within the planning area. Although the scope of this type of planning has been broadened to include social, economic, administrative, and fiscal matters, these other factors are considered mainly in terms of their impact on the three physical elements mentioned earlier.[30] But this emphasis falls a good deal short of true comprehensiveness.

A significant number of planners take a broader view of the comprehensive plan. Alan Altshuler has found that:

> Those who consider themselves comprehensive planners typically claim that their most important functions are (1) to create a master plan to guide the deliberations of specialist planners, (2) to evaluate the proposals of specialist planners in the light of the master plan, and (3) to coordinate the planning of specialist agencies so as to ensure that their proposals reinforce each other to further the public interest.[31]

This view of planning focuses on the major social purpose of integrating larger wholes and linking physical planning with all other public and private planning in a more or less reciprocal manner.[32] The major emphasis in this type of comprehensive planning is to mold all public and private

---

[28] Goodman, Freund, and Davidoff, "Social Welfare Planning," p. 308.

[29] Alan Black, "The Comprehensive Plan," in Goodman and Freund, *Urban Planning*, p. 349.

[30] Black, "The Comprehensive Plan," pp. 350 and 358.

[31] Altshuler, *City Planning Process*, p. 279.

[32] Melvin M. Webber, "Comprehensive Planning and Social Responsibility," in *Urban Planning and Social Policy*, ed. Bernard J. Frieden and Robert Morris (New York, 1968), p. 14.

behavior within the community so that it is rational in the sense that it is consistent with the broadly supported goals set forth in the master plan.

There are at least two major difficulties with planning of this type. In the first place, the more comprehensive the planning effort really is, the more restrictive of individual and group behavior it tends to be. This restrictiveness serves to stimulate significant opposition to planning within the community.[33] This opposition is not always conservative, middle- and upper-class opposition. In many important instances the objections to the comprehensiveness of planning come from minority racial and ethnic groups who find their life styles disturbed by the essentially middle-class values espoused by the planners in drawing up the master plan.[34] In the second place, the complexity of our urban social system has resulted in a series of programs centered on key social problems that cannot easily be resolved into consistent, rational patterns. Each of these programs tends to serve as its own center of planning. "This proliferation of planning centers has been decried and has met with harsh criticism on the grounds that it destroys the essential unity of comprehensive community planning."[35] This criticism depends largely either upon the assumption that unified comprehensive planning reflects a community that is ideally unified, or upon the assumption that planning must enforce unity even where the community is not unified with respect to its long-range goals. Neither of these assumptions is acceptable to many people, and they serve as a basis for much of the political conflict over the planning process.

POLITICS, PARTICIPATION, AND PLANNING. For many years the planning movement was self-consciously apolitical in its approach to urban problems. Planners viewed themselves essentially as professionals and technicians whose task consisted primarily of applying their skills to the problems at hand. Plans were largely developed according to the planners' understanding of what the goals of the community were or should be. The frequent result was that the plans were rejected out-of-hand by city councils and other governing bodies or were accepted but allowed to gather dust on the shelf with no attempt at implementation. This lack of success soon led planners to place a greater emphasis on results and to be more pragmatic.[36] The task then became one of selling the plan to the governing body and to those portions of the general public which were

---

[33] Altshuler, *City Planning Process*, pp. 312–314.
[34] Webber, "Comprehensive Planning," pp. 18 and 19.
[35] Robert Morris and Martin Rein, "Emerging Patterns in Community Planning," in Frieden and Morris, *Urban Planning and Social Policy*, p. 31.
[36] Frederick Gutheim, "The Politics of the Metropolis," in Perloff, *Planning and the Urban Community*, p. 85.

attentive and likely to exert influence over the ultimate making of policy decisions. Planners were thus fully involved in the political process.

This type of political involvement was not sufficient in many instances. The planning process was still largely based upon the assumption that the long-range goals of the planners themselves were those that were or ought to be shared by the community. The result has been planning that is peculiarly suited to a particular type of community.

> The traditional methods are particularly useful in planning for the isolated, middle-sized city, or the well-to-do suburb where there is a steady growth rate, plenty of room for expansion, adequate development resources, and widespread agreement concerning goals.[37]

> Most planners throughout the country seemed to assume that all cities sought more or less the same goals, and that these were relatively well-known to their colleagues . . . . In practice, of course, those planners who were anxious to succeed politically tempered their recommendations to avoid clashing with the better known preferences of powerful politicians and interest group leaders. In doing so, they often barred themselves from proposing any significant changes in the *status quo*.[38]

Planning of this kind can be significantly elitist and antidemocratic in its orientation, and it can be particularly poor planning from a professional point of view. While many communities are as socially and economically homogeneous as those described above, they probably do not constitute a majority of our urban settlements and most certainly do not include the largest of our cities, which still remain predominantly heterogeneous settlements. In heterogeneous urban areas, the best course of action is beyond the capability of either planners or elected officials to identify and even "the better is seldom self-evident; for the city's many publics rarely hold mutually compatible objectives."[39] What frequently happens is that the objectives of particular publics are selected for elevation to community goals through public policy. There are seldom any well-articulated criteria for the selection of these publics, although the earlier chapter on the structure of community power suggests that wealth and social position may be important in some communities. In others, it may simply be a case of the planner reverting to the older pattern of setting his own objectives, which happen to coincide with those of a particular public. However these goals are set, there is little evidence of broad-scale community participation.

The impact of this type of objective selection on the quality of planning

---

[37] Franklyn H. Beal, "Defining Development Objectives," in Goodman and Freund, *Urban Planning*, p. 329.

[38] Altshuler, *City Planning Process*, p. 190.

[39] Webber, "Comprehensive Planning," p. 16.

is no less important. When planners focus on objectives that are supported by only a portion of the general public, they automatically narrow the range of the planning effort. The need for a professional planning staff is diminished, since a blue-ribbon planning commission could do almost as good a job of maintaining the status quo. Even in those cities where change is accepted and professional planning skills are used, planners usually find themselves engaged in a much narrower and more routine type of activity than they had hoped for when they joined the profession. If the quality of our planning effort is to be judged by the professional standards and criteria established by the schools of planning and design, then it obviously falls short, largely for political reasons.

For political scientists and many contemporary urban political activists, the crucial question centers on the degree of public participation in the formation of planning policy. There are essentially two ways in which this question can be approached, direct participation and participation through representation. Chapters 5 and 6 have already covered these subjects in some detail, but their direct application to planning may not yet be obvious. The role of representative bodies, particularly city councils, in the development of community goals has been largely unfulfilled. Planning officials, in an effort to remove some of the policy-making burden from their shoulders, have encouraged legislative bodies to adopt some sort of basic statement or policies plan that will serve to focus the attention of the general public and of other government officials on the direction in which government and the community are moving.[40] This effort has been largely unsuccessful.[41] The failure of councils to adopt policy plans is certainly attributable in great part to the fact that "the majority of people in a typical American community pay little attention to what their local planning agencies are doing—until they are affected personally." [42] This makes it virtually impossible for a city councilman to establish long-range goals for the community while reflecting the desires of his constituents. Few if any of his constituents have any desires with respect to long-range community goals. Thus the councilman who would participate in the development of a statement of goals or a policy plan must do so with few cues as to the political consequences of his action. His must be a community leadership role. The legislative role analyses conducted in city councils that were discussed in an earlier chapter clearly reveal that few councilmen desire such a leadership role. Broad policy statements run the risk of antagonizing constituents and of arousing interest groups; it is much safer for the elected official to leave the planning entirely up to the

---

[40] Beal, "Defining Development Objectives," pp. 331–338.

[41] Altshuler, *City Planning Process*, p. 5.

[42] Wilford G. Winholtz, "Planning and the Public," in Goodman and Freund, *Urban Planning*, p. 564.

"experts" and to react to whatever constituent and interest group criticism occurs after the fact.[43]

The second option is, of course, broad-based citizen participation in the formation of policy goals. Such participation could be achieved through community-wide public hearings or through the operation of neighborhood advisory groups. The major difficulty here is that this method of democratic control of the planning process requires even more of the individual citizen in the way of interest and formulation of long-range goals than does dependence upon the process of representation. Many, however, would be satisfied with something less than full participation by individual citizens in the formation of community goals. Perhaps interest groups and neighborhood action groups could serve as focal points for public interest and as spokesmen for the citizen. There is little doubt that this could be the case, but there is also little or no evidence to indicate that such efforts have been successful. The groups that have participated most in the planning process have been the relatively few groups that have broad civic interest, and even in these groups there is some indication that the leaders are not particularly representative of the followers.[44] In areas where neighborhood units have been formed for planning and participation, they have not generally been used effectively.[45]

> We are left facing a particularly difficult problem: Thus, while increasing urbanization and technical complexity are working toward making true citizen-involvement in government more difficult to achieve, many other factors are reaffirming the need for increasing participation of the public in planning.[46]

Comprehensive planning may be nearly impossible in a setting that is at once democratic and heterogeneous.

> The comprehensive planner must assume that his community's various collective goals can somehow be measured at least roughly as to importance and welded into a single hierarchy of community objectives . . . .
> It is fair to assume, however, that only when government moves at a snail's pace and deals with issues of rather direct and immediate impact can a significant proportion of the great multitude of interests express themselves. Therefore, comprehensive democratic planning is virtually impossible.[47]

The urban planning effort is in the position of being able to abandon neither the effort toward comprehensiveness nor a commitment to participation. This is true at the most practical level because the federal government

---

[43] Altshuler, *City Planning Process*, pp. 316–317.
[44] Altshuler, *City Planning Process*, p. 309.
[45] Winholtz, "Planning and the Public," pp. 567–570.
[46] Winholtz, "Planning and the Public," p. 567.
[47] Altshuler, *City Planning Process*, pp. 301–302 and 311.

requires both comprehensive planning and participation as preconditions for receiving grants under many of its programs for the cities. Were Washington to take its requirements very seriously, it would be virtually impossible for any socially and economically heterogeneous city to qualify for federal aid. Even if this were not the case, it would be difficult for planners and decision-makers to abandon either comprehensiveness or participation. Each of them is a logically defensible adjunct of the planning effort.

The end result of this dilemma is an urban planning process that is less than fully satisfactory no matter what set of criteria one employs. Urban planners are more conscious than ever of the problems of living in a pluralistic society and appear to be less and less involved in formulating goals *for* the community and more and more involved in crying plaintively to citizens and decision-makers, "Think ahead!" The planning goals that are formulated appear to be largely focused upon the short-run response to problems that have attained crisis dimensions. When the situation gets bad enough in a particular program area, the affected group or groups responds vigorously enough to warrant some action from the governing body. The fact that many of the current crises have occurred in social welfare program areas and that both political activists and governmental agencies have placed a greater emphasis on participation has had the effect of introducing new groups to the politics of planning. While it would surely be premature to suggest that the poor enjoy full-scale participation in the process of planning social welfare programs, this process is certainly no longer the exclusive domain of middle-class liberal reformers.

The emphasis on pluralism and conflict that this discussion implies is unsettling to many. Some object to any view of urban life which sees conflict as the normal state of affairs. There is no doubt that living in a society characterized by consensus is more comfortable, but if that consensus is artificially imposed by one group in society, whether it be planners or a socioeconomic elite, the cost in terms of loss of freedom may be too great. This dynamic tension between planning and freedom bothers liberals and conservatives alike.[48] A second and perhaps more serious objection to this view of urban planning is that it essentially denies man's ability to manage his environment. It may even cast grave doubts upon man's ability to satisfactorily react to his environment. This is particularly frustrating, since urban man has at his disposal more resources and greater technological skills than he has ever before commanded. This frustration makes many men of good will impatient with pluralism and participation. Democracy, even in its crudest, most imperfect forms, appears to be a

---

[48] For an excellent discussion see Allison Dunham, "Property, City Planning, and Liberty," *Law and Land*, ed. Charles M. Haar (Cambridge, Mass., 1964), pp. 28–43.

serious impediment to rational attempts to achieve the good life for urban man. For those who adopt a more relative view of the good life for our cities, however, the frustration and slowness of the case-by-case, emergency-oriented approach to planning vindicates itself by virtue of its preservation of human freedoms. For these people there is little doubt that the individual must yield in the face of clearly expressed majority will in the adoption of planning goals. But in the absence of such a clear expression, there appears to be little justification for the imposition of comprehensive community planning with its concommitant loss of freedom.

PLANNING ORGANIZATION. The organization of the planning effort is closely linked to the debate over the relationship between politics and planning. No single organizational chart can adequately describe the way in which planners fit into structure of urban governments. In the first place, if planning is viewed in the most traditional way as a primarily municipal activity, the planners may be tied to an independent planning commission, to the legislative body, to the chief executive, or to any combination of the three. Secondly, the planning function in urban areas may be seen in a more modern intergovernmental context, which increases the organizational complexity of planning tremendously. The organization of the planning effort has gone through a number of evolutionary stages, some of which have already been briefly suggested. The planning process began with informal meetings of community leaders concerning community development, progressed through regular citizens' committee meetings and the formalization of the planning effort by granting the citizens' group governmental status as a planning commission, until it reached the point at which the planning commission engaged full-time technical personnel for planning purposes. In the years following this, a more centralized executive in many cities has tended to downgrade the role of the planning commission and to encourage the development of departments of urban development to integrate planning with all other governmental activity.[49] Communities vary widely with respect to their positions along this evolutionary continuum. Most of our largest cities have long since passed into the centralized executive stage, while many of the small towns have only recently established a planning commission.

Figure 11-1 illustrates the planning structure under an independent commission. The independence of the commission stems from the fact that the mayor and/or the council can appoint its members, but removal is possible only under rare circumstances and other sanctions are largely unavailable. This independence was designed to take planning out of

---

[49] James H. Pickford, "The Local Planning Agency: Organization and Structure," in Goodman and Freund, *Urban Planning*, p. 525.

Figure 11–1: Independent Planning Commission

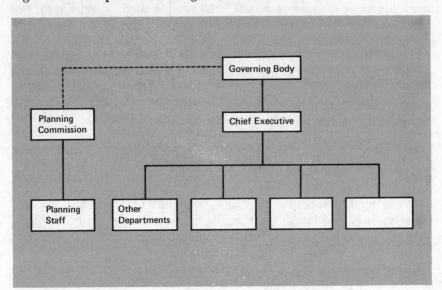

SOURCE: James H. Pickford, "The Local Planning Agency: Organization and Structure," *Principles and Practice of Urban Planning,* ed. William I. Goodman and Eric C. Freund (Washington, 1968), p. 528. Reprinted by permission of the International City Management Association.

politics—an obviously unattainable goal even if it were desirable. While the planning commission is supposed to serve as a link between the general citizen of the community and the planning effort, it obviously has not done so in a very systematic manner. These commissions appear to be selected more with an eye toward coopting possible opposition leadership than with any clear representational goals in mind. In fact, some observers stress the need for a small, intelligent, compatible commission in order to better perform the planning function.[50] This recommendation is the antithesis of popular representation in most communities.

Doubts about the ability of planning commissions to perform a representational role might well lead to greater focus on the other possible roles of the commission—promotional, advisory, and coordinative.[51] The last two roles can be disposed of rather quickly. It is clear from Figure 11–1 that there are no formal channels through which either advice or coordination can be attempted, where the planning commission is truly

[50] Branch, "Simulation," pp. 32–33.
[51] Pickford, "Local Planning Agency," p. 527.

independent and runs the entire effort. This, of course, does not mean that the commission cannot advise and coordinate the efforts of operational agencies within government, but there is little empirical evidence that such informal communication occurs frequently enough to materially affect the operation of urban governments. On the other hand, the commission seems to be particularly well-suited for the promotional role. If, in fact, commission members are selected with a view toward coopting the leadership of any opposition to the planning effort, then the commission is obviously an ideal public relations channel for planners. In this respect the commission becomes a vitally important political body. By working with a citizens' commission, the planner can exercise the option of building his own constituency and seeking support from outside City Hall if he so desires.[52]

The shortcomings of the planning commission as the director of the entire planning effort led to a greater emphasis on planning as part of the normal functioning of the executive office. In the book that for years was considered the definitive work on planning organization, Robert Walker insisted that it was impossible to develop a continuous and consistent planning operation unless planning was considered a staff function attached to the chief executive.[53] Figure 11–2 illustrates this type of planning structure, which recognizes three of the four roles mentioned earlier as important to planning. The planning staff is in the chain of command and is responsible to an elected executive or to a city manager, who is in turn responsible to an elected council. Thus there is some provision for control over planning decisions by men who are elected representatives of the people. Because the planning agency is linked closely to the chief executive in a staff relationship, the channels for advising policy-makers are clearly established. Finally, the planning commission remains in use so that it may continue its efforts to perform the promotional role. The coordinative role still is not performed with any degree of success unless informal channels of communication are established, since the formal structure does not anticipate regular contact with operating agencies within municipal government let alone outside the formal governmental structure of the municipality.

The more modern organizational structure illustrated by Figure 11–3 retains the representational, promotional, and advisory advantages of the executive-staff organization, but also makes provision for the coordination of the wide range of planning activities which are conducted in modern urban areas. Especially in larger cities, there are many types of planning which are conducted by nearly every agency in urban government. As long

---

[52] Altshuler, *City Planning Process*, p. 390.
[53] Walker, *The Planning Function*, pp. 330–335.

Figure 11–2: **Planning As Staff Function**

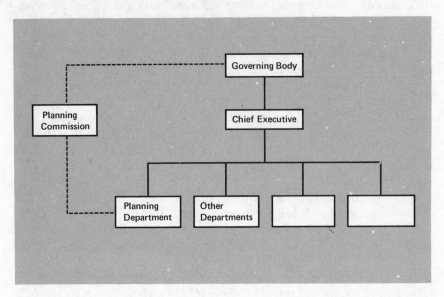

SOURCE: James H. Pickford, "The Local Planning Agency: Organization and Structure," *Principles and Practice of Urban Planning*, eds. William I. Goodman and Eric C. Freund (Washington, 1968), p. 529. Reprinted by permission of the International City Management Association.

as decision makers continue to give at least lip service to the idea of comprehensive planning, some attempt must be made to coordinate these efforts. Staff and management planning, comprehensive physical planning, general social and economic planning, functional or program planning, and project planning are all interrelated.[54]

Most of the discussion up to this point has centered upon the organization of the planning effort within the city. The contemporary urban environment with its multiplicity of agencies and governments has rendered "city planning" almost obsolete as a descriptive term. The focus is clearly upon regional or area-wide planning. Regional planning groups are involved to a degree in performing each of the roles of the local planning agency. Their representational role is extremely indirect since, at best, their governing body is made up of elected officials from each of the constituent governments and, at worst, that body is a super planning commission made up of citizen appointees. The advising that such groups do must be approached with great delicacy, since the constituent governments are

---

[54] Perloff, "Metropolitan Politics," pp. 80–81.

Figure 11–3: Integrated Planning Structure

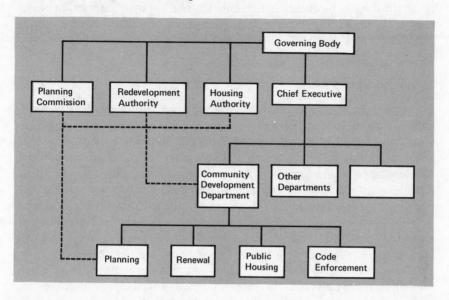

SOURCE: James H. Pickford, "The Local Planning Agency: Organization and Structure," *Principles and Practice of Urban Planning*, eds. William I. Goodman and Eric C. Freund (Washington, 1968), p. 530. Reprinted by permission of the International City Management Association.

jealous of their decision-making prerogatives. Formal channels for advice are being opened with greater frequency as these regional planning agencies develop professional staffs whose expertise is particularly useful to local planners.

Regional planning groups have been able to perform most effectively in the role of coordinator. Much of this effectiveness can be traced to the requirement in many federal grant programs that particular program plans be approved by a regional planning body before federal funds will be approved. Such requirements force the governments of our urbanized areas to communicate and to discuss at least their short-range plans. The exchange of information is invaluable, even if the constituent governments do not always see eye to eye with respect to their development goals. Finally, these regional planning groups can contribute to the performance of the promotional role by engaging in effective public relations efforts.

A point that has been made in earlier chapters should be recalled here. The structure of an organization does not tell the whole story. To presume that the roles of representation, promotion, advice, and coordination will be adequately performed because the structure of the planning organization takes some cognizance of them is to presume too much. All that this structure does is to encourage certain kinds of human interaction which may lead, under the best possible conditions, to the desired types of behavior.

Implementing Plans

One of the major deficiencies in depending upon an independent planning commission to conduct planning is the gap between the planning effort and action based on the completed plan. No matter how good or acceptable a plan may be, it is a waste of time unless the appropriate executive and legislative bodies formulate and execute policies based upon the plan. A wide variety of devices are used singly or in combination to translate plans into policy, especially in the area of physical planning. The discussion that follows will briefly explain the operation of some of the more commonly used of these devices. However, one warning is particularly appropriate here. The use of these implementation devices does not depend on the existence of a plan.[55] In fact, in many communities the implementation device precedes the plan. The confusion that results makes the policy-making process particularly difficult to understand.

ZONING. Perhaps the most common implementation device that has received extensive public attention is the zoning ordinance. Robert M. Leary's excellent definition of zoning indicates its close tie with land use planning:

> Zoning is essentially a means of insuring that the land uses of a community are properly situated in relation to one another, providing adequate space for each type of development. It allows the control of development density in each area so that property can be adequately serviced by such governmental facilities as the street, school, recreation, and utilities systems. This directs new growth into appropriate areas and protects existing property by requiring that development afford adequate light, air, and privacy for persons living and working within the municipality.[56]

From a purely legal point of view, zoning is a dynamic concept. While the practice is well-established in Anglo-American law, the basic justification for it has shifted slightly over the years. The early acceptance of zoning was "to a certain extent an outgrowth of the ancient common law of nuisances, which rests upon the principle that no person should be per-

---

[55] Lachlan F. Blair, "Programming Community Development," in Goodman and Freund, *Urban Planning,* p. 379.

[56] Robert M. Leary, "Zoning," in Goodman and Freund, *Urban Planning,* p. 403.

mitted so to use his property as to cause injury to others." [57] This type of justification for zoning ordinances served as the basis for their widespread acceptance on primarily economic grounds. Many good citizens and civic leaders have been convinced of the wisdom of zoning, primarily because of its alleged ability to protect property values. However, beginning with the basic statement of the United States Supreme Court on zoning, a slow and subtle shift in attitudes developed.[58] Zoning was justified on the basis of its broad impact on community life rather than on specific dangers to particular individuals and property.

> The general principles of law with respect to zoning regulations are that they must be reasonable and not arbitrary or discriminatory and that they must have a substantial relation to the health, safety, morals, comfort, convenience, and welfare of the community.[59]

The broadness of this language clearly indicated a major trend away from the narrow acceptance of zoning as a regulation of nuisances toward a more general view that recognizes not only the value of planning but also the interaction between physical environment and major social problems.

The standard zoning ordinance divides the community into areas in which all property conforms to certain standards of basic land use, bulk, area, and population density. Traditionally, these ordinances have assumed a hierarchy of land uses ranging from heavy industry at the low end to single-family residences at the high end. The zones were intended to be homogeneous, with the exception that higher uses would be permitted. For example, the existence of commercial uses in an industrial zone did not constitute a violation or a nonconforming use. Zoning of this type is largely based upon the assumption that something inherent in the "lower" uses of property adversely affects those higher uses in the same area and that the owners of higher use property should not involuntarily be subjected to this adverse effect. This assumption is closely related to nuisance regulation and the economic justification of zoning. As more and more planning has been conducted, the idea that some uses are inherently higher than others and that different land uses are socially and economically incompatible has been challenged. The result is that more progressive communities have provided for a special exception to their zoning ordinances in order to permit planned unit developments in which land uses are mixed without serious economic damage.[60] In fact, such developments

---

[57] Walker, *The Planning Function*, p. 20.

[58] For the Court's position see *Village of Euclid* v. *Ambler Realty Company*, 272 U.S. 365 (1926).

[59] Walker, *The Planning Function*, p. 81.

[60] David W. Craig, "Regulation and Purchase: Two Governmental Ways to Attain Planned Land Use," in Haar, *Law and Land*, p. 191.

frequently add to the value of surrounding property while creating a more self-contained neighborhood that contributes to social closeness while cutting down on traffic problems. The planned development also serves to break up the dull repetitive nature of the homogeneously zoned community.

Zoning ordinances are enforced largely through the use of building permits and use permits. The building permit is required for the construction of new buildings and for the modification of existing structures. At the time of application, code enforcement officers can check to see if the structure itself is in compliance with the zoning ordinance. The use permit covers new uses for existing structures and provides enforcement officers with a method of controlling the use to which buildings are put. Such a permit is required whenever a structure changes from one use to another and whenever a new occupant wishes to continue a use that does not comply with the zoning ordinance.

The planned development is not the only type of special exception granted in the administration of zoning ordinances. There are many unique land uses that would alter the general, homogeneous pattern provided by the ordinance. Such uses as cemeteries, schools, hospitals, and churches do not fit easily into the categories of standard zoning. Special provision must be made for those uses in the ordinance, or they may be forced to locate in areas that are inconvenient to the public, if they can locate at all. For instance, it would be difficult indeed to establish a cemetery if the strict requirements of the zoning ordinance required a minimum fifty-foot frontage on every parcel of property sold—a mighty big cemetery lot. However, these special exceptions are not granted automatically by the ordinance. Some manner of control over the location of exceptional uses is usually established by requiring the prospective user to seek an official granting of an exception from a Board of Zoning Appeals or from the Planning Commission. The major practical difficulty in the administration of these exceptions is that the local review board has a tendency to grant them without adequate consideration of their impact on the community as a whole.[61]

A particular property owner may also under certain circumstances be granted relief from the specific requirements of the zoning ordinance as it applies to his property. Such relief is called a *variance* and is usually granted or denied in the first instance by the Board of Zoning Appeals. In reviewing the actions of local boards, the courts have developed a particularly rigid set of guidelines for the granting of variances. These guidelines are designed to guarantee that the ordinance is enforced uni-

[61] Lawrence A. Sullivan, "Flexibility and the Rule of Law in American Zoning Administration," in Haar, *Law and Land,* p. 141.

formly so as to provide the "equal protection of the laws" guaranteed by the Fourteenth Amendment, while at the same time it is not enforced in such a manner as to constitute a "taking" of property without "due process of law." Briefly summarized, the guidelines are as follows: [62]

1. The applicant must be able to show that he is unable to make any reasonable use of his property under the ordinance.
2. The hardship must be unique to the property of the applicant.
3. The hardship must come from the application of the zoning ordinance.
4. The hardship must be suffered specifically by the property in question.
5. The hardship must not result from the applicant's own actions.
6. The variance must be in harmony with the general purpose and intent of the ordinance.
7. In most states, variances as to the basic use of the land cannot be granted.
8. The variance must preserve public safety and welfare.

If these guidelines were followed closely, few variances would be granted. However, local boards tend to give the loosest possible interpretation to the law—when they know what it is—and to grant considerably more variances than the equitable enforcement of a regulatory ordinance would allow. In fact, these boards may be fairly good representatives of the general climate of opinion toward zoning enforcement in the community, even though there is frequently no attempt to make these appointive bodies broadly representative.[63] Even if most citizens generally support planning and zoning in principle, they are quite unprepared to accept the impact of such activity in terms of the economic hardship suffered by the individual property owner.

Present practice in granting and denying variances leaves much to be desired. While some of the greatest injustices can be traced to poorly written zoning ordinances, a good part of the problem is administrative. Local boards of appeal have too great a tendency to ignore the rule of law in granting variances, thereby undermining the planning and zoning process. That they may be reflecting public opinion is no excuse, since they are quasi-judicial bodies and without the authority to amend ordinances and change the law no matter how worthy their motives. On the other hand, the rule of law as promulgated by the courts lacks the flexibility necessary to respond to very real changes in the urban environment. What is needed is a system that provides for a balance between flexibility and the rule of law.[64]

---

[62] Leary, "Zoning," p. 439.
[63] Sullivan, "Flexibility," p. 135.
[64] Sullivan, "Flexibility," pp. 139–140.

A final problem in using zoning ordinances to implement plans is that of nonconforming uses. Whenever any established community adopts a zoning ordinance there are always a significant number of structures and uses which do not conform simply because they were instituted prior to the passage of the ordinance. In many cities these uses continue for years and years until they die out of their own accord, since there is no systematic attempt by zoning enforcement authorities to eliminate them. While immediate elimination of nonconforming uses would undoubtedly be harsh and unfair to the owners of the affected property, in most cities there is no reason to believe that such uses cannot be terminated in a large number of cases after a reasonable grace period.

A general survey of decisions involving nonconforming use removal provisions indicates that such requirements will be upheld with respect to open-land uses and with respect to the removal of nonconforming uses in buildings which are themselves conforming and hence adaptable to permitted uses. The trend also indicates that the required removal of nonconforming billboards after a few years will also be approved. As respects substantial buildings, however, it is likely that the required elimination of such structures by zoning will prove to be either not constitutional or not feasible.[65]

SUBDIVISION CONTROL. The control of the subdivision of land within the planning area is an implementation device closely related to zoning.

Subdivision regulations are locally-adopted laws governing the process of converting raw land into building sites. They normally accomplish this through plat approval procedures, under which a developer is not permitted to make improvements or to divide and sell his land until the planning commission has approved a plat (map) of the proposed design of his subdivision.[66]

Such developments must generally comply with the provisions of the zoning ordinance insofar as possible, but there are different requirements that must be met in addition to those involving basic land use, bulk, density, and so forth. Many of these additional requirements involve improvements to the land that are of particular interest to the city, such as streets, sidewalks, curbs and gutters, storm and sanitary sewers, and street lights. In addition, the city may require the reservation or dedication of land in the subdivision for such public purposes as schools and parks. If the land is to be dedicated, it is given outright to the appropriate governmental unit. Reserved land is set aside for governmental purchase at some later date. The expense of the required improvements and dedicated land is borne proportionately by those who purchase property in the

---

[65] Craig, "Regulation and Purchase," p. 207.
[66] Philip P. Green, Jr., "Land Subdivision," in Goodman and Freund, *Urban Planning*, p. 445.

subdivision. This procedure relieves urban governments from the necessity of making these improvements out of funds provided by the general taxpayers.

EMINENT DOMAIN. One of the most important ways in which urban governments can affect their physical environment and their social environment as well is through the acquiring of title to land. In many instances, the mere regulation of the use of property is not sufficient to achieve the goals outlined by the planning process. Government may then purchase the land through the process of eminent domain. Eminent domain is a legal action through which government requires the property owner to sell his land at a fair market price. The fairness of the price and the purpose for which the land is to be used may be questioned in court if the owner objects to the conditions of the sale. The traditional court interpretation was that land could be taken in eminent domain proceedings only for public *use*.

> In recent years, particularly in its application to planned land-use control, eminent domain goals have been broadened from "public use" to a wider concept of "public purpose," thus minimizing the importance of the public's mere title in the taken property and emphasizing the purpose, possibly negative, for which the title has been taken.[67]

This broader interpretation has led to the use of eminent domain to acquire title to land for resale and redevelopment under urban renewal programs, and to the gradual approval of "excess condemnation" of land which can be used to provide additional, badly-needed open space in a crowded urban environment.

CODE ENFORCEMENT. Another important implementation device for the planning effort is the enforcement of health, housing, building, and fire codes to better control the condition of buildings. Housing and building codes will be discussed in greater detail in the next chapter. It is sufficient to note here that the code enforcement process is designed to insure the construction of safe and durable structures and their adequate maintenance over the years to guarantee their aesthetic suitability and their fitness for human habitation.

Summary

The planning process is man's attempt to rationally manage his environment and to adapt his institutions and programs to that portion of the

---

[67] Craig, "Regulation and Purchase," pp. 182–183.

environment which is beyond his immediate control. As such, it is crucial to the development of all urban policy. Without some successful planning the environment will triumph, and our cities will become largely unlivable. But there appears to be no foolproof mechanism for devising the goals toward which planning should move our cities. Urban policies are plagued by major and minor inconsistencies that reveal government to be working at cross purposes with itself and with private enterprise. The major implementation devices are used unevenly and with results that are far from ideal, even when rudimentary planning goals have been adopted. One of the major challenges of our urban future is to devise and use a political process that will enable us to formulate satisfactory goals and to develop policies that will lead to the rational realization of these goals. Until this challenge is met, we will continue to "muddle through" while adopting a strategy of minimal goals and minimal programmatic progress toward their realization.

Suggested Readings

Altshuler, Alan A. *The City Planning Process: A Political Analysis*. Ithaca, N.Y., 1965.

Chapin, F. Stuart, Jr. *Urban Land Use Planning*. 2d ed. Urbana, Ill., 1965.

Frieden, Bernard J., and Morris, Robert, eds. *Urban Planning and Social Policy*. New York, 1968.

Gans, Herbert. *People and Plans*. New York, 1968.

Goodman, William I., and Freund, Eric C., eds. *Principles and Practice of Urban Planning*. Washington, 1968.

Haar, Charles M., ed. *Law and Land*. Cambridge, Mass., 1964.

Perloff, Harvey S., ed. *Planning and the Urban Community*. Pittsburgh, 1961.

Walker, Robert A. *The Planning Function in Urban Government*. 2d ed. Chicago, 1950.

chapter **12**
Renewal, Redevelopment, and Housing

([Too many people think of the slum dweller as the creator of the slum. Too few realize that he is, by economic selection, not the creator but the inheritor of the slum.

The process of economic selection forced him to restrict his search for a place to live to those locations that he could afford. Thus, the old and deteriorating sections of the city which offer facilities at a price he can pay determines his home. Couple this fact with the migration of the more affluent to the suburbs, and you have started the establishment of a segregated community with the poor in the cities and the affluent living in the suburbs.[1]

Slums and Urban Housing

This statement by a leading expert in the field of housing is typical of the concerns expressed about the living environment in our cities. Especially when speaking of our largest cities, modern social commentators tend to focus on the necessity for solving the problems of slums and blight in order to create a satisfactory urban condition. This concern might indicate that students of urban problems have developed definitions of *slum* or *blight* that could be used to identify the areas and structures of primary

---

[1] Don Hummel, "Housing as One Element of Ghetto Conditions," in *Urban America: Crisis and Opportunity*, ed. Jim Chard and Jon York (Belmont, Calif., 1969), p. 114.

concern. And yet we are once again lacking a generally accepted definition of either of the two terms:

> The criteria for what is a slum—as a social *fact*—are subjective and relative: for one brand of mystic this world is a slum (relative to the next) and for another there *is* no slum, because the proper objects of desire are as available in one area as another.[2]

Somewhere between these two extremes lie most current efforts to arrive at a useful operational definition of slum. These efforts focus primarily upon the physical condition of structures and upon the presence or absence of certain amenities which many have come to regard as essential to a healthy and reasonably comfortable human existence. Those who evaluate our housing note whether the structure is "sound," "deteriorating," or "dilapidated," and whether it possesses adequate plumbing, heating, ventilation, and light. In spite of efforts to use categories with universal meaning in the evaluation of structures, the subjective element remains strong, and there is little guarantee of consistency from one city to another or even from one census tract to another.[3] While the presence or absence of heat, running water, and flush toilets can be determined more objectively, housing experts are plagued by the fact that the extent to which amenities are used to judge the adequacy of housing is closely tied to the culture of the society. In America, where affluence and technological progress have combined to provide a general standard of living notable for the degree of creature comforts which it provides, housing that was and is entirely adequate according to the standards of the last generation is viewed by many today as seriously deficient.

The standards used in judging housing are not wholly culture-bound, however. The American Public Health Association has developed criteria that serve as guidelines for many communities in the identification of substandard housing areas which can be designated as slums. The Association obviously finds a connection between the condition of housing and the state of public health. But our standards of public health have risen to the degree that a house constructed fifty years ago and maintained in mint condition today could fall far short of providing the facilities that the A.P.H.A. deems adequate.

Even assuming that we can arrive at satisfactory definitions of slum and blight, and that we can identify those areas in which housing is truly

---

[2] John R. Seeley, "The Slum: Its Nature, Use, and Users," in *Urban Renewal: People, Politics, and Planning*, ed. Jewel Bellush and Murray Hausknecht (Garden City, N.Y., 1967), p. 105.

[3] For an illustration of the process and its problems see U.S. Bureau of the Census, *1960 Censuses of Population and Housing: Procedural History* (Washington, 1966), pp. 232–236.

inadequate, at least two problems remain in the application of these concepts in an urban setting. In the first place, we must make some judgment as to the extent of the problem of urban slums. Most people operate on the assumption that slums are an urban problem. The opening statement of this chapter clearly reflects the wide concern that our major central cities will decay into a mass of substandard housing. There is some reason to doubt this gloomy picture. The proportion of the total housing supply in the United States that is substandard has decreased steadily from 49 percent in 1940 to 37 percent in 1950 to 19 percent in 1960. Of the substandard housing which did exist in 1960, 82 percent was located outside the central cities and mostly in rural areas, while 89 percent of the housing in central cities was listed as standard by the Census Bureau.[4] These figures do not indicate that there is no urban housing problem. The absolute number of substandard dwelling units remains shockingly high in a country as affluent as this. Furthermore, the fact that substandard dwellings in the city are concentrated rather than dispersed as they are in rural areas at least makes them a more visible, aesthetic problem, and perhaps a greater social problem as well.

The second difficulty in applying the concept of the slum is that most of us tend to consider it an unmitigated evil. This overlooks the fact that the slum performs some vital social functions. For members of the American middle class, the slums have often provided a location for activities that are officially viewed with disfavor, but are privately sanctioned, encouraged, and even supported financially.[5] Surely if gambling, prostitution, and the array of other vices frequently housed in the slums had to depend wholly upon the residents of the area for their support they would soon fade from the scene. On the other hand, the acceptance of a house of ill repute into a "respectable," middle-class neighborhood would create embarrassing problems.

A second function performed is that of providing an acceptable residential area for a significant number of urban residents.[6] Although having a place to live that they can afford is important, the most salient aspects of the slum to its residents appear to be something quite different. "The common core lies in a widespread feeling of belonging someplace, of being 'at home' in a region that extends out from but well beyond the dwelling unit."[7] Some would carry this argument too far, however, and

---

[4] Martin Anderson, "Consequences of Urban Renewal," in Chard and York, *Urban America*, p. 123.

[5] Seeley, "The Slum," p. 109.

[6] For a more detailed discussion of this point, see Herbert J. Gans, *The Urban Villagers* (New York, 1962), and Marc Fried and Peggy Gleicher, "Some Sources of Residential Satisfaction in an Urban Slum," in Bellush and Hausknecht, *Urban Renewal*, pp. 120–136.

[7] Fried and Gleicher, "Sources of Residential Satisfaction," p. 123.

claim that this feeling of residential satisfaction and this sense of belonging are adequate reasons for refusing to recognize the housing problems in
our cities. This, of course, entirely misses the point. The satisfaction that
the slums provide derives from the neighborhood and patterned social
relationships to be found there rather than from a particular, substandard
dwelling unit. As the discussion of public housing and urban renewal later
in this chapter will clearly indicate, it has been in the disruption of these
social patterns, not in the provision of adequate housing, that governments have disrupted the functional aspects of slum life.

The one question that remains unanswered is, "Why is government
so concerned about housing problems?" The question may seem simple
or even foolish, but the way in which it is answered can have a great deal
to do with the kind of housing programs which are developed and the
kinds of political support which can be brought to bear. There are at least
two basic arguments that can be raised in behalf of social programs such
as those dealing with the problem of housing.[8] Social reformers have
traditionally emphasized the social-cost argument. This involves the claim
that the poverty, misery, and squalor that have been traditionally held to
characterize life in the slums breed crime, violence, and social dissatisfaction. Since few good citizens are willing to accept these threats to their
comfort and safety, the results should be obvious.

> Arguments of social cost, therefore, have often served to persuade and mobi-
> lize the indifferent; they generate the belief that slum clearance and slum
> relief serve the interests of the middle and upper classes as well as of the
> poor.[9]

The well-being of the entire community is closely linked to the clearance
of slums and the subsequent provision of adequate housing for the poor.

Although this argument has much to recommend it from the point of
view of logic, and although the social statistics do appear to show that the
slums contribute a disproportionate share of our social ills, there is a
tendency to push the social-cost concept of slum clearance too far. Empirical research has not yet been able to establish a causal link between inadequate housing and these other social problems. The fact that they
frequently occur together is not sufficient evidence upon which to base
the contention that substandard housing causes crime. Under these circumstances, it is possible to raze the slums and to replace them with housing that meets contemporary standards without seriously affecting such
social indicators as the crime rate. This information no doubt proves

---

[8] This discussion draws heavily from Lawrence M. Friedman, *Government and Slum
Housing* (Chicago, 1968), pp. 1–18.

[9] Friedman, *Government and Slum Housing*, p. 6.

discouraging to the middle- and upper-class reformers whose support for housing programs has been based primarily on the contention that they will provide immediate and significant benefits to the community as a whole. While the benefits may well be forthcoming, they are not nearly so immediate and widespread as the earliest housing reformers would have had us believe.

There is obviously another level on which support might be rallied for programs dealing with urban housing problems. It can be argued that the benefits which accrue to the individual, poor slum resident by virtue of housing programs are an adequate justification for the existence of these programs. If our urban poor are warmer, healthier, and in any way happier by virtue of the new housing which we are able to provide for them, then the program can be justified from a welfare point of view. For those who accept this argument, it is only necessary to establish individual need. The elaborate calculations of social cost are not relevant. While it is possible to discern the religious basis for this argument in the Judeo-Christian tradition (and in other traditions as well), the position was not widely accepted in this country until experience with housing programs led us to recognize the inherent weaknesses of the pure social-cost approach.

In the best of all possible worlds, our housing programs would benefit the individual and society equally, and it would no longer be necessary to attempt to distinguish between the social-cost and welfare approaches to such problems. In our present urban environment, neither justification appears to be adequate by itself. The frustrations of the social-cost argument are matched by those inherent in the welfare approach. "Too great solicitude for the welfare of the current poor could conceivably lead to neglect of ultimate causes and solutions." [10] Slums might well be considered symptoms of a more persistent and illusive disease. And, to carry the metaphor further, treatment of symptoms alone frequently insures only that the patient dies without too much pain.

PRIVATE HOUSING. The assumption that housing ought to be constructed and, for the most part, owned by private individuals and corporations lies at the heart of America's attempts to solve her housing problems. Although the public sector has become increasingly involved in regulating, stimulating, and even owning and managing housing units, the major thrust of the housing effort remains private.

In its simplest form, the private approach to housing problems can be called a "trickle down" theory. The theory is based upon the assumption that the economy is healthy and expanding. It further assumes free and

---

[10] Friedman, *Government and Slum Housing,* p. 13.

easy social mobility on the part of the population. Given these conditions, all that is necessary to eliminate substandard housing is to build adequate housing elsewhere. This housing could easily be middle- and upper-income units in the suburbs. The theory simply holds that the upwardly mobile members of urban society who occupy this new housing will vacate units of adequate housing in their old neighborhoods and that these vacant units will then be available to upwardly mobile members of the working class. The process, if continued long enough, will ultimately move everyone into standard housing and leave the slums vacant and ready for demolition. The theory is ideal from the point of view of private enterprise, since it allows concentration of construction efforts in those areas that will bring the highest profits.

There are, however, some problems with the "trickle down" theory. Adequate housing just has not been trickling. The reasons for the failure of this totally private and unregulated approach to housing lie in the assumptions upon which it is based. Unfortunately, the national economy has not been uniformly healthy and expanding. Periods of inflation and depression have slowed the economic progress of large segments of society. The fruits of the expansion which has occurred have not been uniformly distributed, as seen in the inability of the social system to match the unemployed to the jobs available in a period of nearly full employment. The end result is that large numbers of slum residents still do not possess adequate resources to take advantage of whatever standard housing might trickle in their direction.

The second problem with the theory lies in the obvious absence of perfect social mobility. It has traditionally been next to impossible for large numbers of our slum residents to find housing in an acceptable neighborhood even after they have enough money to rent or buy standard housing. Such imperfect social mobility can largely be traced to the patterns of discrimination which have developed in this country, patterns that appear in most cases to reflect little more than differences in skin color and thus work primarily against our black population, although other racial minorities suffer as well. Attempts to break the pattern of discrimination through federal, state, and local open housing laws have met with limited success, but the absence of true social mobility still renders the "trickle down" approach to housing unworkable.

There have been other, more direct attempts by the private sector to come to grips with substandard housing. The earliest of these were probably based on the rather naive assumption that ignorance and poor management on the part of residents were the major contributory factors to slum conditions. Private groups with a philanthropic bent built housing units which they then offered to slum residents on a rental basis and with the expectation that they would realize a handsome profit. By the end of the nineteenth century, most people realized that the poor usually lived in the slums because they could not afford to rent standard housing. This realization led to the development of projects based on more modest expectations of profit. The profits were so modest, however, that they did not serve to attract enough capital into the area, and the number of dwelling units constructed under such programs was small. To make matters worse, the projects that did realize a modest profit and were, therefore, successful from the point of view of private enterprise were those that catered primarily to white-collar and upper working-class tenants. The poor remained in the slums, and the slums continued to spread. Most reformers were prepared at this point to admit that unsubsidized housing for the poor was a practical impossibility.[11]

Government subsidization of private housing development has become an accepted part of American life. In fact, it may not be too farfetched to claim that government subsidies have been one of the most important factors in shaping the form and style of urban development. The earliest of these subsidies were the granting of tax exemptions and the power of eminent domain to limited dividend private housing corporations in New York City in the 1920s.[12] These governmental supports for private efforts soon proved inadequate to the task of bridging the gap between what the poor could afford to pay for housing and the private sector's assessment of the cost of standard housing. The subsidies that have been utilized most heavily in more recent years have been clearly aimed at encouraging the construction of middle-class housing. To the extent that government was at all concerned about the housing problems of the poor, this concern seemed to manifest itself in a vague and rather tentative subscription to the "trickle down" theory.

The major programs of subsidy for middle-class housing have been those of the Federal Housing Administration and the Veterans' Administration. While the mechanics of the two programs differ, they are both essentially devices for insuring home loans. Under both programs, the federal government guarantees the repayment of privately obtained mortgages in return for a commitment to low down payments (or none in the case of some VA loans) and interest rates that are lower than those demanded in the current money market. There is a strong tendency to criticize these programs because they largely ignore the plight of the poor and because they contribute to the process of suburbanization and urban sprawl. On the other hand, they have also extended the home and property ownership to a greater proportion of the population and, by doing so, they have contributed to the satisfaction of vast numbers of average

---

[11] Friedman, *Government and Slum Housing*, pp. 73–87.
[12] Friedman, *Government and Slum Housing*, p. 88.

people and have enabled these people to better withstand the challenges of modern urban living.

The fact that many programs involving governmental subsidies have ignored the poor has led to the development of some new programs in recent years. FHA insurance of loans has been extended to cover persons whose incomes were too low to qualify under the initial program by Section 221 (d) (3) of the Housing Act of 1964. But this program falls a good deal short of providing direct housing assistance to the poor. It is designed primarily to fill the gap between public housing and the private market. This is an important gap to fill; 221 (d) (3) undoubtedly can make a significant contribution to the relief of substandard housing conditions, but it does not enable the private sector to get at the basic problem of providing housing for the poor.

The program of federal rent supplements represents a much more radical (and perhaps imaginative) attempt to subsidize the housing of the poor by the private sector of the economy. The program is designed to provide the difference between 25 percent of the family income and the cost of adequate housing in the private market. To date, however, the program has been beset by problems. In the first place, many critics have felt that the upper income limits for families who might qualify for such assistance are too high and that the housing into which families might move under such a program might be more luxurious than standard. Because of the doubts which have surrounded the program, Congress has displayed some reluctance to appropriate the full amount of money which was recommended by administrative officials, and the program in its present form is woefully inadequate to the task of housing the poor. In the third place, few nonprofit groups have stepped forward to sponsor local programs that would take advantage of the funds available, and such action is crucial since the program is not designed to guarantee profits for the private sector. Finally, the rent supplement idea is based upon the assumption that slum housing problems can best be solved by scattering slum residents throughout the city so that the total environment as well as particular housing conditions will be changed.

> The program implicitly assumes that the poor are distinguished from others *only* by a lack of money; that their values, aspirations, and styles of life are not meaningfully different from others; that once the lack of money has been compensated for they will merge relatively easily into their new surroundings.[13]

Such assumptions are largely unwarranted oversimplifications. The impact of a program based upon them might well be as alarming and unaccept-

---

[13] Jewel Bellush and Murray Hausknecht, "Public Housing: The Contexts of Failure," in Bellush and Hausknecht, *Urban Renewal*, p. 457.

able to the poor as it is to the middle class and the wealthy. The rent supplement program can succeed only if it is part of a much broader program to minimize the differences in culture and social class in our urban population. Even a broader program raises serious questions as to which culture and set of values should be adopted as the standard and which eliminated as below standard.

PUBLIC HOUSING. By the late 1920s it was clear to most observers that private efforts to provide adequate housing for our urban population had not been wholly successful. When the depression of the thirties struck, the number of individuals who were unable to afford standard housing increased sharply. Some of these people were former members of the middle and working classes who were left unemployed by the depression. Others were migrants from rural areas who had come to the city in the hope of finding relief from poverty. "Housing was available and rentals were low. Yet since construction had virtually ceased, the quantity and quality of the housing relative to the population had declined." [14] The depression was the era of the slum. It was not possible in most cases for the slum dweller to work his way into standard housing by exercising the old-fashioned virtues of sweat and thrift. In this context, further governmental action appeared acceptable to all but the most conservative Americans.

Since the 1930s were characterized by a scarcity of resources at the state and local level, the first responses to the increased housing problem naturally came from the national government. Initially, Washington responded by authorizing the Public Works Administration to build public housing units. The P.W.A. represented an immediately available governmental device that was appropriate to the task of constructing housing and that could provide badly needed employment for the local labor force. However, among the more serious problems that beset this initial effort was the inability of a national government agency to use the power of eminent domain to clear out existing slum units. As a result, the P.W.A. was forced to build its units on vacant land in the immediate vicinity of the slum neighborhood. Since such land was at a premium, few dwelling units were constructed under this program. [15]

P.W.A.'s failure to provide housing for the poor was not the end but the beginning of the public housing program. The thirties was a particularly inventive period in our governmental history, and it did not take long for our national, state, and local governments to find the formula that could eliminate some of the more glaring deficiencies of the P.W.A.

[14] Friedman, *Government and Slum Housing*, p. 100.
[15] Friedman, *Government and Slum Housing*, p. 99–103.

program. The solution was embodied in the Housing Act of 1937. The establishment of a local housing authority under state-enabling legislation was central to the new concept of public housing. Through the use of such an authority, government could exercise greater control over the placement of housing units at the local level and could use the power of eminent domain to acquire existing slum property for public housing sites. The act provided for national government participation through several types of financial assistance which were to form the basic subsidization for the housing. The local authority could receive loans for land acquisition and development and for the maintenance of the units once they were constructed. Such loans were obviously made in anticipation of the revenues which would be produced by renting the units and did not constitute a real subsidy except to the degree that they gave the local authority relief from the prevailing rate of interest. Two other provisions in the act provided more in the way of a direct subsidy. The local authority had its choice of asking either for an annual contribution from the federal government to make up the difference between rents and costs or for a capital grant to cover major construction costs. In either case, public housing advocates hoped that the subsidy would solve the age-old problem of the gap between the cost of adequate housing and the rent that a poor family can afford to pay.

The public housing program created by the Housing Act of 1937 is still alive today. Although it has experienced some modification over the years, it retains its essential characteristics. Most observers are willing to admit that the program has not been totally successful. There are still vast numbers of people living in substandard housing, and the public housing units that have been built have been much criticized.

One of the central difficulties with the present public housing program is that it is not designed to provide housing for all the poor or all the slum dwellers. The program has traditionally been aimed at the "deserving poor." Minimum rents have always guaranteed that the residents of public housing have some income and that, in most cases, this income is regular. The program focused upon the housing needs of those who were willing and able to work but who were temporarily suffering from the kind of economic reversal that characterizes periods of economic depression. Public housing has been considered as a way station for the upwardly mobile poor. Residents were expected to continue to improve their lot and to move on to privately supported standard housing as soon as the expanding economy rewarded their industry and diligence with a higher income.

The idea of the "deserving poor" has been further implemented under our public housing laws by the establishment of social standards which bar families that do not subscribe to middle-class values. Criminal convictions, arrest records, use of narcotics, alcoholism, children born out of wedlock, all can and have been used to disqualify the poor who might make use of public housing. Applicants who display these characteristics are turned down; residents who deviate from established norms are evicted. It is interesting to speculate as to the impact of the imposition of such rigid standards of morality to middle- and upper-class residential areas. Social statistics from some of our suburbs concerning arrests, narcotics, and alcoholism indicate that there would be many more involuntary slum dwellers if these standards were applied to the general population as zealously as they are applied to the poor under our public housing programs.

Other related applications of the concept of the "deserving poor" are evident in the day-to-day administration of public housing. Tenants are subject to eviction for deviation from behavioral norms less fundamental than those just mentioned. Like most administrators, the managers of public housing prefer normal, well-adjusted tenants to those who cause problems, and "roughly, normalcy means adherence to the middle-class way of life or to as close an approximation as possible." [16] On the other hand, such standards of behavior are often linked to educational programs within the housing project that are designed to resocialize the poor and to prepare them not only to live in standard housing but also to move out into the middle-class environment. Such programs reinforce the view of public housing as a way station for the upwardly mobile. Most citizens are members of the middle class and see nothing inherently evil in such attempts at resocialization. At least these attempts appear to recognize that the problems of the poor are not solely dependent upon the immediate physical environment. These values are relative, however, and it is difficult to find any justification for adopting one set as a standard rather than another.

The realization that many of the poor who inhabit our slums are less than deserving in terms of their ability and desire to be upwardly mobile has had a significant impact upon the acceptability of public housing programs among members of the middle- and upper-classes. The allocation of governmental resources to help those who are "down on their luck" in a period of depression is one thing, but to offer such assistance to the apparent incorrigibles in a period of prosperity and nearly full employment is something quite different. As a result, many of the supporters of public housing have deserted it. The desertions have probably been in favor of a "let them eat cake" position rather than in favor of alternative proposals which would house the poor regardless of their employment status or their personal value systems.

It would be unfair to paint such a bleak picture of the attitude of public

---

[16] Friedman, *Government and Slum Housing*, pp. 138–139.

housing officials toward the poor without noting the attempts that have been made to make admission and retention standards for public housing more realistic. Although the provision of the Housing Act of 1949 which permitted local authorities to admit tenants who were receiving welfare payments has been repealed, many authorities continue to admit such tenants if other criteria can be met.[17] The Housing Act of 1954 provided a new emphasis on public housing for the aged and for those displaced by urban renewal programs. In neither case were these new classes of tenants necessarily the type of upwardly mobile workers that public housing supporters had originally envisaged. Finally, many local housing authorities have adopted a less rigid view of the moral standards necessary for a tenant to maintain his eligibility. For example, the governing board of the Jackson County Housing Authority in Illinois voted in May, 1969 to permit women who bear children out of wedlock to continue as tenants. Although such signs of enlightenment probably do not signal a total abandonment of the concept of the "deserving poor," they do represent a step in the right direction if government housing programs are to prove useful in providing safe and decent places to live for the nation's poor.

The physical aspects of public housing have contributed a great deal to the generally poor public image which it has enjoyed. The obvious shortage of land which the market would allow to be used for public housing forced housing authorities to adopt plans calling for intensive use of the available land. This meant that most public housing was in high-rise buildings located relatively close to the old slum area. While many people in this country find living in a high-rise apartment in the center of a large city wholly acceptable, other tenants consider this style of life less than fully satisfactory. This is particularly true of families with a large number of children. It may also be true that the continuation of high-density living conditions contributes to the maintenance of old life styles and helps to justify the charge that public housing is nothing but a high-rise slum.

The political and economic advantages of this high rise construction should not be underestimated, however. Intensive land-use enables government to provide housing for some of the urban poor without removing much potentially productive land from the tax rolls. This is, of course, a vital consideration for most cities that find themselves searching desperately for new sources of income. In the second place, the concentration of public housing units helps to minimize the political problems that arise when government attempts to break down some of the social and economic segregation which characterizes American society. Middle-class

---

[17] Friedman, *Government and Slum Housing*, p. 109.

support for public housing tends to diminish rapidly when such housing is planned for middle-class neighborhoods.[18]

We can understand, then, why efforts to establish low-rise, scattered-site public housing have been less than fully successful. Although social planners and housing experts appear to be sold on both ideas, the forces of opposition are too strong. In many instances, opponents do not need to resort to overt action to defeat plans for scattered-site housing. The market for urban land performs the function admirably by maintaining such high prices on land in middle-class neighborhoods that housing authorities cannot afford to buy there in spite of their government subsidies. In cases in which direct action is necessary, the combination of the opponents of social and economic integration with the opponents of public housing in general is an extremely potent force. The problem becomes even more complex when many of the organized poor oppose scattered-site housing because social and economic integration and the loss of the safety provided by familiar surroundings are phenomena that are particularly threatening to them.

The physical condition of many public housing units has also been a significant point of contention between tenants and housing reformers on one hand and public housing management on the other. There can be little doubt that the life styles of the tenants and the high density of population in public housing are major factors in the deterioration of many projects. There are other factors that contribute much to the process, however. In its commendable desire to guard the taxpayers' money, Congress has placed limits on the cost per dwelling unit in the construction of federally subsidized housing. The results of these cost limitations are a minimal standard of construction and buildings that are largely either incapable of withstanding the wear and tear of daily use by poor families or that have the spartan utility of a prison. In the second place, maintenance subsidies have not risen as rapidly as maintenance costs. Since it would obviously be counterproductive to pass these increased costs on to tenants in the form of higher rent, the necessary maintenance remains unperformed, and the buildings deteriorate to near-slum conditions. Urban society is then presented with the embarrassing picture of poor tenants conducting a rent strike against their slum lord, the government. There are certainly resources in the United States adequate to the task of constructing and maintaining durable, safe, decent public housing. The present political status of public housing raises serious doubts as to whether our governments will choose to allocate these resources for such purposes.

---

[18] For some interesting examples see Martin Myerson and Edward C. Banfield, *Politics, Planning, and the Public Interest* (Glencoe, 1955).

Public housing is in the doldrums. Its critics appear to far outnumber its supporters. Even though most tenants express satisfaction with public housing, those among the poor who do not like it either have great difficulty getting in and staying in under the rules or have left of their own volition.[19] The number and intensity of tenant organization efforts and the new spirit of militancy among many of the poor might well signal the end of the general satisfaction expressed by tenants.

Americans have obviously not accepted the idea of public housing as the solution to the problems of providing safe, clean, adequate housing for the population. The Housing Act of 1949 authorized the construction of 810,000 units of public housing, but by 1968 we had managed to construct only a little over 500,000 units.[20] Even though it can be argued that the present ills of public housing ought to be cured, that its problems ought to be solved, and that only government can focus the massive resources on the housing problem that present slum conditions demand, it is unlikely that such action will be taken in the near future.

Urban Renewal

THE NATURE OF THE PROGRAM. One of the most important programs to focus on physically changing the urban environment has been the urban renewal effort that has grown out of the Housing Act of 1949 and its subsequent amendments. As originally passed, this program directed national and local government attention to the twin goals of removing existing substandard dwelling units or slums and of providing safe, decent housing for urban residents. In spite of the emphasis placed by Congress on housing in passing the bill and including provisions to expand public housing programs, the major emphasis in this program has been upon the removal of slums and blight. Let us recall that the standards by which areas are designated as slums or blighted are highly subjective. This has frequently been the case with respect to the urban renewal program. All too often the existence of blight is determined by demand for alternative uses of the land rather than by the condition of existing structures.

The essence of the urban renewal effort lies in its combination of the efforts of private enterprise, local government, and national government. Local government is represented by the Local Public Authority, commonly called the LPA. "LPA's may be subagencies of a city government, they may be combined with existing housing authorities, or they may be

---

[19] Alvin Schorr, "Slums and Social Security," in Bellush and Hausknecht, *Urban Renewal*, p. 418.
[20] Alvin L. Schorr, "Housing the Poor," in *Power, Poverty, and Urban Policy*, ed. Warner Bloomberg, Jr. and Henry J. Schmandt (Beverly Hills, 1968), p. 131.

separate legal entities." [21] In any event, the LPA selects a certain area or site and declares it to be blighted. Then, using the power of eminent domain, it buys the land and clears it for reuse. It is at this point that private enterprise enters the picture officially. The program assumes that the cleared land will be attractive to private developers who can foresee a profitable use for it in standard housing, commercial activity, or industry. In order to make the land even more attractive, the LPA may price the land below its market value. The federal government enters the picture by underwriting two-thirds of the net program cost, which is the difference between what the LPA paid for the land plus clearance costs and what the agency received for the land when it was sold to private developers.

There are a few conditions under which the urban renewal program has operated from the start. Initially, the uses to which land cleared under the program could be put had to be "predominantly residential." There was no requirement, however, that the residential units constructed had to meet any specific criteria as to the income level for which they were designed. Apparently, the "trickle down" theory of housing was assumed to be operative here. The slum residents who were displaced by urban renewal were supposed to be able to find shelter either in public housing or in the areas of standard housing vacated by those who moved into the expensive new buildings in the renewed area. The problems of this approach are now obvious. To make matters worse for those interested in low-income housing, subsequent legislation watered down the "substantially" residential requirement even further. This served to encourage more nonresidential development, particularly of the commercial variety.

The very nature of the program under the Housing Act of 1949 encouraged local officials to concentrate their efforts upon eradicating spots of blight on the urban landscape without paying much attention to the renewal of the urban environment as a whole. The Housing Act of 1954 introduced new federal requirements that were designed to gain a broader perspective of the renewal process and to stimulate more practical renewal programs that would achieve greater community support. The key to these requirements is the Workable Program for Community Improvement. Each community wishing to participate in the renewal program must develop a workable program that meets federal standards and must maintain that program at a satisfactory level throughout the period of its participation. The workable program consists of seven basic parts:

1. An adequate set of codes covering housing, building, health, fire, etc., and a program that will guarantee code enforcement.

---

[21] Scott Greer, *Urban Renewal and American Cities* (New York, 1965), p. 11.

2. A complete and comprehensive land-use and capital development plan.
3. A detailed neighborhood-by-neighborhood analysis of blight and potentially blighted areas.
4. Evidence that the administrative structure of the LPA and other local government units is adequate to the task of running the renewal program.
5. A program that provides for the relocation of people who are displaced either residentially or commercially by urban renewal.
6. Evidence of participation in the planning and decision-making process by the citizens of the community.
7. Evidence that the LPA possesses adequate financial resources to meet its portion of program costs.

The redefinition of the program and the addition of the workable program requirements has turned attention away from the simple redevelopment of neighborhoods toward the renewal of the entire city and toward rehabilitation and preventive maintenance in housing rather than the wholesale destruction of neighborhoods.

Before entering into a discussion of some of the more specific problem areas in urban renewal, one single fundamental objection to the whole program as it is presently constituted should be noted. Dr. Martin Anderson, one of the most articulate critics of the program, has questioned the entire legal basis of urban renewal in claiming that the power of eminent domain is available to governments only for land that is to be put to a public use, not for land that is to be put to private use for private profit although consonant with some public purpose.[22] Although state courts have for years been moving from the strict doctrine of public use to the more flexible doctrine of public purpose when interpreting the powers of eminent domain, and although the Supreme Court has upheld this movement,[23] there are many who with Anderson would question the taking of a citizen's land against his will so that it might be used profitably by another citizen. While these legal critics are not numerous, they find great support within potential renewal areas, and the fires are fanned by some of the more unusual interpretations of public purpose which have received judicial approval. Many of us viewed with some sympathy the plight of the man evicted from his home, albeit with adequate compensation, to make way for a museum dedicated to the motion picture industry and designed to promote tourism in the Los Angeles area.

---

[22] See Martin Anderson, *The Federal Bulldozer* (Cambridge, Mass., 1964), and "The Sophistry that Made Urban Renewal Possible," in Bellush and Hausknecht, *Urban Renewal*, pp. 52–66:
[23] *Berman v. Parker*, 348 U.S. 26 (1954).

REHABILITATION. The serious failures of urban renewal between 1949 and 1954 especially with respect to providing additional standard housing for the poor led, among other things, to an increasing emphasis upon the rehabilitation of existing dwelling units and to a concomitant reduction in the wholesale destruction of buildings in the name of slum clearance. This aspect of the renewal program has received particular emphasis since 1961, and received special attention in the Housing Act of 1964.[24] The arguments for rehabilitation as an approach to the problems of housing and the slums are particularly persuasive. It is clear that old buildings are not always slums. While the evidence for this proposition is not always compelling in the United States, a quick glance at the buildings of the older urban centers abroad should be enough to convince us that age alone does not make a slum. Many older buildings are the result of higher construction standards and more durable materials than those currently in use. It is often cheaper to modify and repair existing structures than it is to build entirely new structures. This fact might well result in the availability of standard housing at relatively low rents. In addition, rehabilitation clearly involves moving fewer people than does demolition, since it is necessary only to move enough people to reduce the population density per dwelling unit to acceptable proportions. This has the added advantage of permitting large numbers of people to remain in their old neighborhood if they so desire. The final two arguments for rehabilitation are that it obviously takes less time than demolition and reconstruction, and that the property involved has a proven rental value and market that might make it attractive as an investment.[25]

The rehabilitation effort also has its share of problems, however. There is still no direct evidence that the program is any more able to provide safe and decent housing for the urban poor than was the older bulldozer approach. The major problem remains money. The fact is that even though rehabilitation is often less expensive than new construction, it still increases the rent of the dwelling unit. The unpleasant fact remains that the poor are by definition incapable of paying the rent for standard dwelling units. Current programs simply do not provide enough money to do the job. For example, the Housing and Urban Redevelopment Act of 1965 provides grants of up to $1,500 to low-income householders for the rehabilitation of their property. Such programs have a much greater impact in a shantytown environment than they do on big city tenements,[26] where $1,500 will not go far toward meeting the serious problems of structural decay. In the absence of massive subsidies which would enable

---

[24] Charles Abrams, *The City is the Frontier* (New York, 1965), pp. 86–87 and 185.
[25] Abrams, *The City is the Frontier*, pp. 184–185.
[26] Friedman, *Government and Slum Housing*, p. 179.

the poor to live in rehabilitated housing without increasing their rent payments significantly, rehabilitation is either window dressing or a program that largely benefits only the relatively well-to-do. In the first instance, the exterior trim and gingerbread of the slums is reworked to establish a facade of standard housing which is more pleasing to the eye of the nonresident. The conditions within the buildings are likely to remain deplorable. In the second case, old neighborhoods like the Society Hill section of Philadelphia are completely renovated, and the remodeled buildings become townhouses for the wealthy. In neither case has rehabilitation made much of a contribution toward housing the poor or toward the real elimination of slums.

CODE ENFORCEMENT. One of the most straightforward and seriously oversimplified approaches to substandard housing and slums has been to pass laws that prohibit substandard conditions. This approach is obviously closely linked to rehabilitation, since it legally identifies many of the defects which are to be remedied through the repair and remodeling of dwelling units. Although most urban code enforcement programs have grown out of the Workable Program for Community Improvement and federal grants-in-aid that are available under urban renewal programs, the idea can be traced back to the early restrictive approach to slum housing that was manifest in tenement house laws in the nineteenth century. "The basic idea of restrictive housing legislation is much the same now as it was in 1867." [27]

The problem of code enforcement is compounded by the proliferation of municipal codes dealing with dwelling units. However:

> We can analytically reserve the term housing code for ordinances and statutes which set up standards for minimum facilities and equipment which are required in each dwelling unit for "maintenance of the dwelling unit and of facilities and equipment" and for "conditions of occupancy of the dwelling unit." . . . The provisions of the codes are arrived at through a process part political, part idealistic, and part economic.[28]

The subject matter of housing codes overlaps that of building, plumbing, electrical, and fire codes to some degree, but this represents a problem only when the codes are inconsistent in the demands they place upon the maintenance of the best housing conditions that our society knows how to produce. This best of all possible worlds is tempered by the political realities of what property owners will accept from their elected representatives and by the economic realities of what can be accomplished with the resources available.

---

[27] Friedman, *Government and Slum Housing*, p. 27.
[28] Friedman, *Government and Slum Housing*, pp. 52–53 and 54.

There are two serious drawbacks to the attempt to provide safe, decent housing through code enforcement. The first of these is the breakdown of the enforcement effort itself. In spite of the availability of code enforcement grants from the federal government under the Housing Act of 1964, most of our cities do not have enough enforcement personnel to regularly inspect all of the dwelling units within their jurisdictions. The end result is a program of selective enforcement. Code enforcement officers inspect areas of the city in which they suspect that violations might exist and that the enforcement effort might do some good. This leads them generally to avoid both the best and worst areas in their cities.[29] Of course, these officials also supplement their regular inspections with complaint investigations which are largely initiated by tenants who are unhappy with the maintenance services performed by their landlords. Neither system of enforcement provides wholly satisfactory coverage.

The second drawback centers around an assumption basic to the code enforcement effort. This assumption goes back to the original tenement laws from which present housing codes were drawn:

Since reform laws imposed costs on landlords without reimbursing them in any way, and since no one expected or wanted rents to rise, it was morally necessary to believe that rents were exorbitant and that costs could be absorbed without giving up a fair return. It was convenient, therefore, to assume that landlords were a class of evil men, overcharging ignorant tenants and callous to the point of criminality.[30]

There is good reason to question the universal validity of this assumption. The best available study of the slum landlord indicates that a significant proportion of the properties may be owner-occupied or at least owned by residents of the slum area, that many slum properties are the only property owned by the landlord, and that the market for slum real estate is so weak as to make exorbitant profits highly improbable.[31] To the extent that these findings are generally applicable, and there is every reason to believe that they are, it is obvious that a program of vigorous code enforcement can result in higher rents that obviously work a hardship on the poor tenants. This is clearly not the purpose of the program.

RELOCATION. One of the most troublesome questions with respect to the urban renewal program is, What happens to people who are compelled to move because of renewal activities? Every renewal effort involves some displacement, since even rehabilitation and code enforcement are designed

---

[29] Greer, *Urban Renewal and American Cities*, p. 44.
[30] Friedman, *Government and Slum Housing*, p. 40.
[31] George Sternlieb, *The Tenement Landlord* (New Brunswick, N.J., 1966).

to reduce the density of the population in slum areas. Where do these people go? Early in the program this question usually went unanswered. It was somehow assumed that the displaced would find another home, that their new home would not be a slum, and that the rent on their new quarters would not be significantly higher than that on their old homes.

Unfortunately, this has not been the case. Logically, the program could not operate in this manner. If standard housing facilities were readily available at a price that the poorest slum dweller could afford, then, by definition, no housing problem would exist.[32] Careful studies of individual projects have revealed the magnitude of the problem:

> Although the results of forced relocation appear to vary widely from project to project, on the whole relocation has made a disappointingly small contribution to the attainment of "a decent home in a suitable environment for every American family." . . . Not only have the gains been limited, but they have been accompanied by widespread increases in housing costs, often incurred irrespective of an improvement in housing or the ability or desire to absorb these costs.[33]

Part of this problem can be traced to the inescapable fact that the urban renewal program has resulted in a net loss in housing.

> The national program has, over-all, cleared property which is 85 per cent residential; redevelopment plans indicate new uses will be only 50 per cent residential. [Furthermore,] the national program has resulted in the destruction of four dwelling units for each unit built.[34]

To make matters worse, the new dwelling units are almost invariably higher priced than those they have replaced and are therefore unavailable for relocation purposes. The only course of action open to those who have been displaced is to find housing elsewhere, either in an existing slum, or by creating a new slum by doubling up with friends and relatives in marginal housing. It is obvious then that:

> Given the realities of the low-income housing market and the impact of public programs, it is likely that, for many families, relocation may mean no more than keeping one step ahead of the bulldozer.[35]

In recognition of the severity of the problem, the federal government added the relocation plan requirement to the Workable Program for

[32] Abrams, *The City is the Frontier*, p. 135.
[33] Chester W. Hartman, "The Housing of Relocated Families," in Bellush and Hausknecht, *Urban Renewal*, p. 330.
[34] Greer, *Urban Renewal and American Cities*, p. 56.
[35] Hartman, "The Housing of Relocated Families," p. 342.

Community Improvement and subsequently demanded full-scale reports from the LPA on the extent to which displaced families had been satisfactorily relocated. The result of this program has been a set of statistics which appear to have satisfied most LPAs and many of the officials in the Urban Renewal Administration of the Department of Housing and Urban Development. However, many students of urban housing problems find the reports of the LPAs unacceptable.[36] The wide variation between standards and criteria used for declaring an area to be blighted for renewal purposes and those that are used in selecting relocation housing are frequently obvious. Large numbers of individuals are simply "lost" in the relocation process. There is a strong temptation to ignore the space requirements of families which have to be relocated. Even the former head of the URA and former Secretary of HUD, Robert Weaver, has recognized that the glowing statistics reported in the past by LPAs have not taken the cost of relocation housing into consideration.[37] The fact that fully adequate relocation facilities do not exist in most communities would be enough, if recognized, to bring urban renewal efforts to a grinding halt. Since our cities largely feel that urban renewal is a source of badly needed funds, they cannot afford to recognize the problem:

> It is these discrepancies between law and fact that have made the renewal administration the perplexed executors of a statutory absurdity and turned them into jugglers of statistics.[38]

Two groups are hit particularly hard by problems of relocation. In the area that is most directly relevant to the housing problem, it is the low-income black citizen who suffers most directly. Patterns of social and economic discrimination have rendered this group least able to withstand the move to a new environment and least able to afford higher rents. In many of our urban centers, the urban renewal effort became identified as "Negro Removal" and was bitterly resented as an attempt by the white man to "get rid" of his racial problems. Observers often noted these facts but suggested that the absence of political power among low-income, aged, and minority groups would preclude any major program changes.[39] However, successful political organization of these groups in recent years may well prove to be the impetus for an adequate relocation program.

Another hard-hit group has been the small businessmen.[40] While

---

[36] James L. Short, "Relocation: A Myth or Reality?" *Urban Affairs Quarterly* 3 (1967): 62–74.

[37] Robert C. Weaver, *The Urban Complex* (Garden City, N.Y., 1966), p. 111.

[38] Abrams, *The City is the Frontier*, p. 136.

[39] See for example Weaver, *The Urban Complex*, p. 51.

[40] Basil Zimmer, "The Small Businessman and Relocation," in *Urban Renewal: The Record and the Controversy*, ed. James Q. Wilson (Cambridge, Mass., 1966), pp. 380–403.

physical relocation of many of small businesses has been possible, most
of them have had to relocate so as to lose their traditional clientele and
goodwill. While most of the businesses that are driven out of operation
by urban renewal are strictly marginal operations, the impact on the pro-
prietor is no less severe than if they were booming operations. In addition,
many of the residents of the area lose the convenience of neighborhood
stores, a convenience that is of major significance in the absence of adequate urban transportation systems.

PARTICIPATION AND POLITICS. Several types of participation materially affect the way in which an urban renewal program develops and may even
help to determine if such a program develops. One factor that is stressed
again and again in the studies of renewal programs which have been found
successful—meaning that some physical accomplishment has been achieved
—is leadership.

> Renewal stands or falls on the ability of some entrepreneur . . . to elicit the
> necessary support and to neutralize the existent opposition. Those individuals
> and groups at the federal and local level whose participation is essential to
> the launching of a project must be persuaded to cooperate. Those whose
> interests are affected adversely by a project must be bypassed, accommodated,
> or persuaded to weaken their opposition.[41]

Such leadership is particularly well-suited to elected executives who
possess the political assets and attributes that are indispensable to success.
Mayor Richard Lee of New Haven, Connecticut, is an outstanding
example of an elected executive who has successfully performed such an
entrepreneurial role. In council-manager cities, however, the mayor is
likely to play a less important role, and the manager will be the most
committed of the active leaders in urban renewal. Although the leadership
role is less dynamic here than in mayor-council cities, council-manager
cities seem to have a slight edge when it comes to renewal achievements.[42]
(Much of this statement depends upon how one measures achievements.
Achievement differences could also be traced to factors other than governmental structure and executive leadership styles.)

In many cities, the fact that the LPA is not directly connected to the
city government encourages the renewal agency managers to attempt to
perform the entrepreneurial function themselves.[43] The number of instances in which these managers will have sufficient political assets and

---

[41] Harold Kaplan, Urban Renewal Politics (New York, 1963), p. 4.
[42] George S. Duggar, "The Relation of Local Government Structure to Urban Renewal," in Bellush and Hausknecht, Urban Renewal, p. 200.
[43] Jewel Bellush and Murray Hausknecht, "Entrepreneurs and Urban Renewal: The
New Men of Power," in Bellush and Hausknecht, Urban Renewal, pp. 213–214.

talents to perform the function fully and successfully is limited. The Workable Program for Community Improvement requires close coordination with municipal authorities and other agencies, and the LPA is ultimately dependent upon sanctions that can only be imposed by general governmental authority to gain adherence to its decisions. Even under the circumstances of closest coordination with the city government, the LPA lacks some of the formal authority necessary to get the job done.[44]

Participation by citizens in the urban renewal process can occur on several different levels. The most frequently observed type of participation is that which is encouraged by the Workable Program through the Citizens' Advisory Committee. The members of such groups are frequently the "civic leaders" who represent the various middle- and upper-class groups that have the resources necessary for participation.[45] These groups have a strong tendency to support the recommendations of professional staff members in the LPA. This tendency may be traced to at least two factors. First, urban renewal programs are frequently justified in terms of the public welfare or the public good, concepts inherently attractive to the middle and upper classes.[46] Second, the use of the Citizens' Advisory Committee may not constitute meaningful participation at all but may just be an attempt by the professional staff to co-opt civic leaders in order to prevent their active opposition to renewal efforts.[47]

The second type of participation, that which includes consultation with the residents of the affected area, has not been particularly widespread until recent years. The renewal officials have been relatively content with this state of affairs since it relieves them from a great deal of pressure. As one official put it:

> By and large, people don't understand what we're after—or even what we're talking about. This is fortunate, for if they did, we'd all have to run for cover.[48]

As James Q. Wilson has pointed out, it is extremely difficult to organize the residents of the areas to be affected by renewal unless they perceive a very real threat and unless there is adequate leadership.[49] Recent events have tended to stimulate the organization of the poor, minority group

---

[44] Duggar, "Local Government Structure," p. 183.
[45] For the middle-class character of group participation, see Jewel Bellush and Murray Hausknecht, "Planning, Participation, and Urban Renewal," in Bellush and Hausknecht, *Urban Renewal*, pp. 278–286.
[46] James Q. Wilson, "Planning and Politics: Citizen Participation in Urban Renewal," in Bellush and Hausknecht, *Urban Renewal*, p. 292.
[47] Greer, *Urban Renewal of American Cities*, p. 41.
[48] David A. Wallace, quoted in Greer, *Urban Renewal of American Cities*, p. 37.
[49] Wilson, "Planning and Politics," p. 294.

members who are likely to be residents of renewal areas. They are capable
of organizing at least to the point at which they can exercise a degree of
veto power over decisions made by the LPA, even if they cannot yet
develop positive housing and renewal policy. This leads inescapably to
Wilson's conclusion: "The higher the level of indigenous organization in
a lower-class neighborhood, the poorer the prospects for renewal in that
area." [50]

The key to many of the problems raised by participation in the renewal
process is conflict and the attitude displayed by public officials toward it.
Participation becomes a stumbling block when community conflict becomes so intense that "innovation in public programs is thus an accident
thrown up by the forces of nature." [51] Those who are primarily interested
in program performance and progress—namely the professional administrators in the LPA and those who are performing the entrepreneurial
function—deliberately attempt to develop a strategy of conflict avoidance.
In some cases, this involves a rather loose organization and an uncoordinated approach:

> A centralized structure that requires clear-cut, consistent choice can bring to
> the surface all the latent conflicts contained in a renewal program. A more
> diffuse structure may make it easier to avoid conflicts or to resolve them
> through the give-and-take of informal negotiations. A certain lack of coordi-
> nation, then, may be one price of significant renewal achievement.[52]

A complete, open-ended pluralism of the sort suggested by wide-scale
participation in the decision-making process is not highly compatible with
program performance. Once the problems of urban renewal are brought
into the open, it is clear that neither the ends nor the means of the program are the subject of widespread popular approval, especially in the
areas that are to be most drastically affected, the slums. Although the
differences over ends and means are sharpened by economic and class
differences within society, they exist within social and economic groups
as well. Current experiments in neighborhood organization and participation indicate that slum residents disagree seriously among themselves as
to the kinds of solutions which they would find appropriate to their
housing problems.

RENEWAL REAPPRAISED. The pages of the professional literature on urban
problems have been filled with the debate over the successes and failures

---

[50] Wilson, "Planning and Politics," p. 296.
[51] Scott Greer and David W. Minar, "The Political Side of Urban Development and
Redevelopment," in Bellush and Hausknecht, *Urban Renewal*, pp. 165–166.
[52] Kaplan, *Urban Renewal Politics*, p. 92.

of urban renewal. Urban renewal officials have stoutly maintained that the program has been a resounding success. One of them has said:

> Hundreds of communities of all sizes have shown that renewal is a necessary and desirable means of eliminating blight, aiding those people afflicted by it, and rebuilding the physical, economic, and social vitality of urban areas on a scale consistent with the demands of a growing urban Nation. The record fully justifies the judgment of Congress in creating the Federal program which provides the aid that these and other cities must have if they are to continue their efforts. The program has done much to revitalize our urban areas and is increasingly emphasizing the human aspects of renewal. While much remains to be accomplished, I am confident of the outcome if we maintain the present momentum and aims of the program.[53]

Such claims appear exaggerated when one considers the impact of the program on housing. Urban renewal does not seem to have made an adequate dent in the housing problem. There is a very real question as to whether there has been a net loss in slums and blighted areas traceable to urban renewal. To be sure, some defenders of the program have pointed out that urban renewal was not aimed solely at solving our urban housing problems.[54] However, we should be able to reassure ourselves that we are at least not making such problems worse through urban renewal, and that we are not doing violence to valuable neighborhood social and psychological relationships that may add greatly to the stability and productivity of urban society.

The greatest achievements of urban renewal may have been in the emphasis that the program was able to put upon the planning process and upon improvements in urban design. Cities that have participated in the program are engaged in the planning process and are more self-consciously aware of the implication of their program decisions than they might otherwise be. In addition—and this point is debatable—the buildings that have been constructed as part of urban renewal frequently represent a significant aesthetic improvement over their predecessors.

With all its shortcomings, urban renewal will probably remain one of the major programs for dealing with urban problems.[55] It generates large sums of money for small towns and suburbs as well as for major metropolitan centers. In many instances, building and commercial interests representing both labor and capital have found it profitable. Such characteristics render the program almost invulnerable to assault in Congress.

---

[53] William L. Slayton, "The Operation and Achievements of the Urban Renewal Program," in Wilson, *Urban Renewal: The Record*, p. 229.

[54] Robert P. Groberg, "Urban Renewal Realistically Reappraised," in Bellush and Hausknecht, *Urban Renewal*, pp. 67–73.

[55] Friedman, *Government and Slum Housing*, pp. 170–172.

This is especially true since the opponents of renewal are likely to be both poor and black, thereby lacking the necessary assets to eliminate the program altogether.

Some Housing Objectives

The task of providing safe and decent housing for every American is not as hopeless as might appear from the foregoing discussion. Progress is possible, if new and inventive approaches are tried. The following program that has been suggested by Charles Abrams is full of such approaches: [56]

1. Home ownership for low-income families through government subsidies for interest on mortgages geared to ability to pay.
2. Insurance against unemployment and illness to prevent default on mortgages in times of financial crisis.
3. A public housing program that would hold onto tenants by increasing rents along with income and that could broaden ownership through sale of units to nonprofit groups.
4. A rent subsidy program that would provide a market for new and rehabilitated dwellings with special attention to the housing needs of the single, widows, large families, migrant workers, etc.
5. A slum clearance program based upon the removal of unoccupied, delapidated dwellings that are surplus to the housing needs of the community.
6. Antidiscrimination and integration programs designed to guarantee freedom of movement to all members of society.
7. Preservation and improvement of existing housing.
8. Stimulation of the building industry to produce more units and to utilize the economies of modern technology.
9. The development of new towns and epicentric cities to create a greater dispersal of population.

Any or all of these programs, if vigorously pursued, could lead to a closer approximation of our present urban housing goals.

Suggested Readings

Abrams, Charles. *The City is the Frontier.* New York, 1965.

Anderson, Martin. *The Federal Bulldozer.* Cambridge, Mass., 1964.

Bellush, Jewel, and Hausknecht, Murray, eds. *Urban Renewal: People, Politics, and Planning.* Garden City, N.Y., 1967.

---

[56] Abrams, *The City is the Frontier,* pp. 258–283.

Bloomberg, Warner, Jr., and Schmandt, Henry J., eds. *Power, Poverty, and Urban Policy*. Beverly Hills, 1968.

Frieden, Bernard J. *The Future of Old Neighborhoods*. Cambridge, Mass., 1964.

Friedman, Lawrence M. *Government and Slum Housing*. Chicago, 1968.

Gans, Herbert J. *The Urban Villagers*. New York, 1962.

Greer, Scott. *Urban Renewal and American Cities*. New York, 1965.

Kaplan, Harold. *Urban Renewal Politics*. New York, 1963.

Sternlieb, George. *The Tenement Landlord*. New Brunswick, N.J., 1966.

Weaver, Robert C. *The Urban Complex*. Garden City, N.Y., 1966.

Wilson, James Q., ed. *Urban Renewal: The Record and the Controversy*. Cambridge, Mass., 1966.

chapter **13**
Public Safety

([In a highly urbanized setting, with its clash of racial and alien interests,
devious political methods, baffling labor problems and the like, popular
government and law enforcement often seem to work at cross-purposes.
The results are common knowledge. Whatever the causes for this collision
of democratic processes and high standards of criminal justice administration, there can be no doubt of its grave potentialities.[1]

The Police

The police power of the states of the United States authorizes these governments to provide for "public health, welfare, and safety." This chapter
will deal with the last of these three basic governmental functions as it is
performed by urban governments as agents of the state. Anyone who has
read a newspaper or given more than a passing glance to the television
screen in the past few years knows that the most controversial and perhaps
the most important aspect of the public safety function is that which
is performed by the police. Of all the questions of public policy which
face our urban governments, none strike as close to the heart of the
democratic process as those dealing with the operation of our police
departments. To a great extent the policies of the police can determine
whether we continue to walk free or whether we are confined, whether

---

[1] Bruce Smith, *Police Systems in the United States*, 2d rev. ed. (New York, 1960),
p. 104.

332

we live in security or in fear (either of the lawless or of the police themselves), and even whether we live or die.

Police departments are largely a product of urbanization. The sheriffs
and constables in early American rural counties and towns bore little
resemblance to police departments, largely because of their inability to
perform law enforcement functions. As our cities grew larger, some form
of protective device was necessary in order to preserve life and property
in a relatively densely settled environment. Boston, Philadelphia, and
New York established night watches before 1800 for the purpose of
performing crude and preliminary police functions, and in the early
nineteenth century these cities found it necessary to expand their watches
to include the daytime hours as well. These watches served their purpose
well until the depression of the 1830s and increasing population concentrations fed the fires of social discontent and disorder and demanded
broader police service. In response to this pressure, New York City established the first real police department in 1844. Other cities followed the
New York example rather quickly. The interesting aspect of the history
of the American police departments is that urban society has traditionally
considered them a necessary evil rather than an unmitigated social good.
Much of this attitude can be traced to the rather low caliber of early
policemen and to the graft, corruption, and spoils politics that characterized nineteenth century police work and that was only partially relieved
by the advent of civil service at the turn of the century.[2]

While most of us today visualize the large urban police department
when we think of police work at all, this is a somewhat misleading view.
As Bruce Smith indicates, most of our police departments are quite
different:

> There are about forty thousand separate and distinct public police agencies
> in the United States. The vast majority consist of one, two, or three men,
> who are employed on a part-time basis. Many of them are compensated solely
> by fees, are selected without regard to physical or mental qualifications, are
> wholly untrained and largely unsupervised, are ill-equipped and undisciplined.[3]

Thus while most of our policemen are located in large, metropolitan
centers, most of our police departments are in the small towns and
suburbs. Such vast disparities make it extremely difficult to generalize
about the competency or general performance levels of police departments. The generalizations that will be offered in this chapter deal primarily with the nature of the police function and its relation to other

---

[2] Raymond E. Clift, *A Guide to Modern Police Thinking*, 2d ed. (Cincinnati, 1965),
pp. 11–13.
[3] Smith, *Police Systems*, pp. 22–23.

social processes. In addition, there will be some discussion of the particular problems of the larger, more heterogeneous cities which have been the subject of current controversy. These current problems are not wholly irrelevant to small towns and suburbs. They may be beyond their current experience, but the whole nation must ultimately feel the burden of the often violent confrontations which have plagued our large and medium-sized cities.

THE PROBLEM OF SOCIAL CONTROL. One of the keys to understanding the nature of the present public policy conflict over the police is a firm grasp of what the police do and what they can reasonably be expected to do. The reference here is to the general social function of the police department and not to specific day-to-day functions, a subject that will be discussed later in this chapter. The discussion of social functions is, of course, properly within the realm of the sociologist, but the politics of public safety cannot be studied without an appreciation of the social context in which they occur.

First and foremost, the police are an agency of social control.[4] They are engaged in the process of attempting to guarantee that the behavior of individuals and groups in a particular society and community conforms to the norms of that community. However, the police are not *the* agency of social control. They are simply one among many. The family, the church, the school, peer groups—all act as socialization agents and, therefore, as agents of social control. The police are probably the agency of last resort when it comes to controlling abnormal behavior in the community. Criminal behavior in particular is an indication that the primary agencies of social control have not succeeded in their job, rather than an indication of low efficiency on the part of the police. "The level of control, be it high or low, is determined by the kinds of social relationship that exist among the individuals who make up society, and their effectiveness in getting people to follow prescribed patterns of behavior."[5] Chapter 1 anticipated some of the more serious social problems in the area of law enforcement when it pointed to the tendency of urbanization to weaken the primary group as an agent of social control and to replace such groups with the less effective agency of formal control—in this case, the police.

Social control and the relative importance of the police as an agent also vary with the kind of community involved.[6] In the stable, small, homogeneous community, there is a high degree of social integration or sharing

---

[4] A most illuminating discussion of this point can be found in Michael Banton, *The Policeman in the Community* (New York, 1964), pp. 1–8. This study is particularly valuable as a comparative study of policemen in Great Britain and the United States.

[5] Banton, *The Policeman in the Community*, p. 1.

[6] Banton, *The Policeman in the Community*, pp. 3–8.

and acceptance of the norms of behavior. Under these circumstances, the police are required to play a less active role in society. They serve more as police officers who remind individuals and groups of community norms than as law enforcement officers engaged in the process of apprehending criminals. To the degree that the community is larger, less stable, and more heterogeneous, there is a greater tendency to disagree as to appro-priate norms of behavior and to maintain subcommunities with widely varying norms. It then becomes necessary for the police as formal agents of social control to impose norms on the population, and these norms are often wholly unacceptable to many groups in the community. When this is the case, the task of the police becomes impossible.

This, then, is what the police cannot do. They cannot stop crime all by themselves. They cannot correct all of the social ills of the community. In fact, professional policemen frequently complain that the public ex-pects too much of them and too little of itself when it comes to maintain-ing acceptable patterns of behavior in the community.[7] Of course, the problem is made more difficult by the fact that the police generally con-sider themselves to be primarily law enforcement agencies and to judge their own successes and failures in terms of increases and decreases in crime rates and of the number of cases "cleared" by arrest. The fact is that an increase in the crime rate does not necessarily mean that the police are doing a bad job any more than a decrease in the crime rate means that they are doing a good job. Such simple criteria for judging the police are misleading because they are at once not demanding enough and too demanding. They do not demand enough of the policeman as a peace officer who must deal with the social intricacies of everyday interpersonal relationships without resort to arrest. They demand too much when they expect the police to significantly reduce the number of social deviants in a community.

THE CRIME PROBLEM. The extent of the failure of agencies of social con-trol or the extent of the crime problem is the subject of a much current debate. The prevalent position is that crime, especially crimes of violence against persons, is increasing in this country at an alarming rate.[8] Pro-ponents of this view further point to the fact that crime statistics reveal that a disproportionate amount of this crime occurs in cities and espe-cially in major urban centers. In fact, some criminologists are concerned that, because a vast number of crimes go unreported, the situation is really a good deal worse than the statistics indicate. The data reported

---

[7] See for example International City Managers' Association, "Police Chiefs Speak Out," *Public Management* 50 (1968): 284–290.

[8] For a concise formulation of this position see Smith, *Police Systems*, pp. 25–41.

Figure 13–1: Crime and Population, 1960–1966,
With Percent Change over 1960

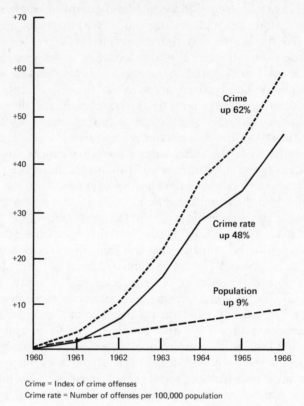

Crime = Index of crime offenses
Crime rate = Number of offenses per 100,000 population

SOURCE: *Crime in the United States, Uniform Crime Reports—*1966 (Washington, 1966), p. 2.

in Figure 13–1 are indicative of the reasons for concern with crime statistics. They indicate that crime is increasing at more than six times the rate of population increase in recent years. With such figures available, it is no wonder that politicians and average citizens are raising a hue and cry about the safety of our city streets. To make matters worse, crime statistics seem to indicate that the increase in violations of the law is greater for juveniles than for the general population and that, although our major central cities are still the major high-crime areas, the suburbs appear to be catching up.[9] If this is not enough to alarm any reader as

---

[9] Edward Eldefonso, Alan Coffey, and Richard C. Grace, *Principles of Law Enforcement* (New York, 1968), pp. 25 and 26.

to the nature of American urban society, the realization that 30 percent of the population is annually either arrested or summoned and charged by the police for a violation of the law and that nearly every citizen at one time in his life will fall into this category should at least lend some credence to the charge that we are a lawless society.[10]

Efforts to link increases in crime statistics with other social factors have produced additional evidence for the earlier contention that social control is a general problem that is not limited to police activity. Eldefonso, Coffey, and Grace have listed the following social conditions as particularly relevant to the crime rate: [11]

1. The density and size of the community population and the metropolitan area
2. The age, sex, and race distribution of the population
3. The economic status and mores of the population
4. The stability of the population
5. Climate, including seasonal weather
6. Educational, recreational, and religious characteristics
7. The effective strength of the police force
8. Standards governing appointments to the police force
9. Policies of the prosecutors and the courts
10. The attitude of the public toward law enforcement
11. The administrative and investigative efficiency of the police.

Only three of these factors are directly related to the operation of the police force. The rest are more general community conditions that might lend support to the contention that the rising crime rate is adequate evidence that ours is indeed a "sick society."

Some people do draw some consolation from the activity of law enforcement agencies in response to the increase in crime even though this activity may be only providing short-range symptomatic relief. As Figure 13–2 indicates, the vast majority of crimes against persons are cleared by our police departments through arrest. The police at least appear to be responding well to the challenge of catching some criminals, even if they cannot prevent these crimes. The record of arrests in cases involving property is obviously not nearly so good. The problem with these figures is that they do not reflect the final picture of law enforcement activity. The conviction rates for the two classes of crime are almost completely reversed. These rates vary between 45 and 65 percent for those accused of crimes against persons, and between 75 and 80 percent for those ac-

---

[10] Smith, *Police Systems*, p. 41.
[11] Eldefonso, Coffey, and Grace, *Principles of Law Enforcement*, pp. 19–20.

Figure 13–2: Crimes Cleared by Arrest, 1966

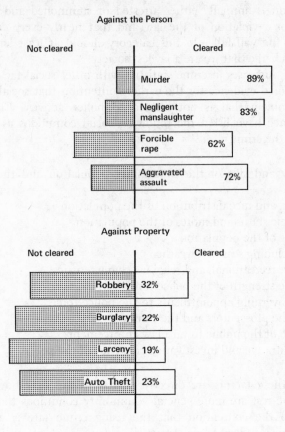

SOURCE: *Crime in the United States, Uniform Crime Reports*—1966 (Washington, 1966), p. 28.

cused of crimes against property, with a wide variation from state to state.[12] Obviously it is more difficult to obtain a conviction once arrest has taken place in crimes against persons.

Some criminologists take issue with the emphasis that has been placed on the increase in crime statistics in recent years. They are quick to point out that 86 percent of the reported crimes in this country are directed at property rather than at persons. Thus, the idea of a violent and dangerous urban environment may be grossly exaggerated. The picture painted by these experts is not pleasant, but it is certainly a good deal less alarming:

---

[12] Smith, *Police Systems*, p. 39.

Five times as many people are killed by automobiles as by murder, but murder seems to elicit more public concern. Yet, seven out of eight murders are committed by friends or relatives, not by strangers, and homicide rates have been falling since 1924. The statistics on rape include attempts, yet there have been very little increases in rape statistics in recent years. Even though auto thefts indicate an amount of stolen property in excess of $360,000,000, three out of four auto thefts are cases of joy-riding by juveniles, with the vehicle returned to the owners within three or four hours.[13]

Another factor that frequently is ignored when reporting crimes against property is the effect of inflation on the value of stolen property.[14] What might have been dismissed as petty theft twenty years ago achieves major proportions today because the value of the same stolen item has increased significantly without any commensurate change in the laws defining the seriousness of crimes.

A final objection to the conclusions generally reached by the interpreters of crime statistics concerns the apparent concentration of crime in our major urban centers. William Chambliss suggests that the higher crime rate for our major cities may be due in part to the fact that there is a greater concentration of police in these areas.[15] The increased number of police in heavily urbanized areas and the generally greater density of population simply render crime more visible and thus inflate crime statistics compared to suburban and rural areas. While this greater visibility does not explain all of the differences in crime rates between central cities and suburbs, it may well explain part of it. Later on in this discussion of law enforcement we will see that differences in visibility really do make a difference in the reporting of crimes within the city itself, and that the concentration of police in certain areas contributes to this visibility. However, the argument becomes circular when the police and others concerned about crime point out that more police are hired in our major cities because the crime rate is higher.

THE DEMAND FOR LAW AND ORDER. The general acceptance of the seriousness of the crime problem in our cities has led to an increasing concern with the need for law and order in our society. In spite of the fact that modern statistics on crime are more impressive than they have ever been, this is not a new concern for city dwellers.

Thus the current rhetoric of concern about crime and violence draws on established motifs of both older and newer vintage: an indignant sense of pervasive insecurity; a mounting current of crime and violence as a result of

[13] A. C. Germann, Frank D. Day, and Robert R. J. Gallati, *Introduction to Law Enforcement*, rev. ed. (Springfield, Ill., 1966), p. 253.
[14] William J. Chambliss, ed., *Crime and the Legal Process* (New York, 1969), p. 99.
[15] Chambliss, *Crime and the Legal Process*, p. 99.

both unaccustomed prosperity and prolonged poverty; the bad example of the self-indulgent wealthy; the violent proclivities of immigrants and other newcomers; and the ironic contrast between the greatness of the metropolis and the continued spread of crime.[16]

These motifs are older in the sense that many of them have been at the heart of complaints about urban violence for centuries; newer in the sense that many of them have been accentuated by the increased process of urbanization in recent years. Regardless of their age or source, they have resulted in a generalized demand for a decrease in crime and violence. To make the problem more serious, the public's standards of order have risen in industrial societies, and there has been an "increasing intolerance of criminality, violence, and riotous protest." [17]

Violent upheavals in Los Angeles, Detroit, Newark, and Chicago to name but a few representative cities and the assassination of three leading political figures in five years have led to a consideration of violence as a political act as well as simple criminal behavior. Political violence can be described as those "acts of disruption, destruction, injury whose purpose, choice of targets or victims, surrounding circumstances, implementation, and/or effects have political significance, that is, tend to modify the behavior of others in a bargaining situation that has consequences for the social system." [18] The greatest amount of work on violence in general and political violence in particular has been done under the auspices of the National Commission on the Causes and Prevention of Violence which issued its preliminary report and a series of background papers in 1969. The one conclusion which appears again and again in this literature is that violence is ubiquitous.[19] It is not simply "as American as cherry pie," to quote H. Rap Brown. It is part of the human experience irrespective of national boundaries.

There are a variety of explanations offered for the persistence of violence. Some have chosen to focus upon such individual variables as deprivation and frustrated expectations, while others have directed their attention to group conflicts or conditions within the social system itself.[20] In still other studies the major focus has been upon the cultural acceptance of violence as the appropriate method for settling disputes. All of

---

[16] Allan Silver, "The Demand for Order in Civil Society," in *The Police: Six Sociological Essays*, ed. David J. Bordua (New York, 1967), p. 3.

[17] Silver, "The Demand for Order," p. 20.

[18] H. L. Nieburg, *Political Violence: The Behavioral Process* (New York, 1969), p. 13.

[19] See Nieburg, *Political Violence*, throughout and Hugh D. Graham and Ted R. Gurr, eds., *Violence in America: Historical and Comparative Perspectives*, 2 vols. (Washington, 1969).

[20] Don R. Bowen and Louis H. Masotti, "Civil Violence: A Theoretical Overview," in *Riots and Rebellion: Civil Violence in the Urban Community*, eds. Louis H. Masotti and Don R. Bowen (Beverly Hills, 1968), p. 27.

these factors are relevant to a degree, but H. L. Nieburg is quite persuasive when he suggests that ultimately violence is the result of conflict and efforts to encourage social change. Nieburg's thesis is that every conflict proceeds toward violence in the absence of change and of mutually acceptable resolution of demands.[21]

No matter which of the current scholarly views of the causes of political violence prevails, there are certain implications for advocates of law and order and for policemen in the performance of their duty which stand out. No matter what the cause of political violence, it appears that attempts to quell such outbursts by force can be successful only in the short run. Ted Gurr's interesting comparative study of violence in 114 nations brings this point home sharply:

Large military and police forces alone appear to have no consistent deterrent effect on turmoil . . . and in some as yet undetermined circumstances turmoil tends to increase as the coercive forces increase in size.[22]

Such findings lead inescapably to the conclusion that social change of some sort is necessary to re-establish order in the face of political violence. Most observers believe that some sort of significant reallocation of resources and decision-making influence if not outright power lies at the heart of such a social change in most places where violence is particularly frequent and serious in its consequences.

For anyone who takes the time to survey the current professional literature the demand for law and order can be a perplexing phenomenon. In the first place, it is clear to even the casual observer that those who call for the establishment of law and order do not intend that all laws should be vigorously enforced or that all forms of disorder should be suppressed. The process is to be a selective one in which only the socially undesirable and most serious forms of lawlessness and disorder are curbed. Frequently, the law and order movement is focused on disruptive minorities and those who are most vocal in seeking social change. It is important to recognize here that law and order advocates may not be motivated in as pure a manner as they would have us believe.

A second problem lies in our basic inability to agree upon what law and order are. One current expert, Professor Jerome Skolnick, chooses to distinguish between the maintenance of order as a type of social control and the operation of the legal system.[23] However, most students of the problem agree that both law enforcement and the maintenance of order are

---

[21] Nieburg, *Political Violence*, throughout.

[22] Ted R. Gurr, "Urban Disorder: Perspectives from the Comparative Study of Civil Strife," in Masotti and Bowen, *Riots and Rebellion*, p. 59.

[23] Jerome H. Skolnick, *Justice Without Trial: Law Enforcement in Democratic Society* (New York, 1966), p. 1.

part of the process of social control, and that this distinction may not be helpful. However, most also agree that there is an important distinction between order maintenance as an exercise in keeping the peace, and law enforcement as a process of arresting or summoning those who violate the law. It is this distinction that may cause some of the difficulty which surrounds the realization of law and order today.

> [The] tension between the operational consequences of ideas of order, efficiency, and initiative, on the one hand, and legality, on the other, constitutes the principal problems of police as a democratic legal organization.[24]

The fears implied in this statement center on the possibility that in order to keep the peace the police will give insufficient attention to legal processes and due process of law. This view is largely supported by analysts of police behavior who have assessed the methods used by the police to maintain order:

> Traditionally, police hope to be feared by prospective law violators. They view social workers as having a quite different value system, with a permissive attitude that is inconsistent with efforts at control.[25]

In spite of the apparent justification for some of these fears, many urban experts continue to emphasize peace keeping or the maintenance of order as a prime function of the police. For example, James Q. Wilson holds out little hope for substantial improvement in the process of law enforcement on the part of the police and recommends that these agencies turn more of their attention toward maintaining order.[26] Wilson does not underestimate the difficulty of such a task, especially in those communities that are sufficiently heterogeneous as to lack a common normative framework that would serve as a guide to the kind of order which the police must maintain. A word of caution is necessary here. This emphasis on the maintenance of some kind of order rather than on law enforcement does not imply that the police should entirely give up their efforts to arrest those who commit serious violations of the law. This would obviously be disastrous. However, it does place a greater emphasis on the exercise of police discretion in acting in their official capacity. We will spend more time on this problem later in this chapter.

THE POLICE FUNCTION. Any standard list of police functions would include the preservation of the public peace, the protection of life and property,

---

[24] Skolnick, *Justice Without Trial*, p. 6.

[25] Herman Goldstein, "Police Response to Urban Crisis," *Public Administration Review* 28 (1968): 419.

[26] James Q. Wilson, "Dilemmas of Police Administration," *Public Administration Review* 27 (1968): 407–417.

the prevention of crime, the enforcement of laws, the arresting of offenders, and the recovering of property.[27] The most important aspect of the police function, however, is the fact that it is not restricted to these straightforward activities. It also includes other activities that are a good deal less glamorous. These include the protection of public safety through the regulation of traffic and parking, the guarding of public morals through censorship—at least in the initial stages—of books, movies, and plays, the licensing of a variety of activities which take place within the city, such as places of entertainment, inspections for code enforcement purposes, the emergency relief of citizens in distress and danger, and a variety of other social welfare responsibilities. While few police departments have been broadened to include all of these functions, most departments perform a good many such duties in the course of a day. The general contention of the police is that these minor regulatory duties interfere with their law enforcement activities and irritate generally law-abiding citizens, thereby weakening their support of police activities in general.[28] As a matter of fact, these other duties are more prevalent in the larger departments of our major cities where some contend that they serve to some degree to offset the advantages of large-scale operations.[29] Thus, while the police and scholars are engaged in the great debate over law and order and crime in the streets, the average policemen may be more directly concerned with issuing parking tickets, licensing a belly dancer to perform in a nightclub, or deciding whether the gatefold picture in the latest issue of the magazine for swingers makes the publication too salacious for the local newsstand.

POLICE ORGANIZATION. The actual organization of police departments follows certain general patterns, although there are of course important differences between large and small departments. In the first place, the force is commonly divided into shifts in order to provide functions on an around-the-clock basis. In breaking down the personnel available on each shift, police administrators usually follow the kinds of guidelines suggested in Chapter 9 with respect to span of control and chain of command. While there is some evidence that newer concepts of administrative organization are beginning to reach this level of operation, police departments for the most part adopt a military organization that tends to rigidly follow the older "principle." Since the police must perform many functions, specialization is introduced into their organizations as soon as they become large enough to support such a division of labor. The major categories of specialization are patrol, traffic, criminal investigation, com-

[27] Clift, *Modern Police Thinking*, p. 18.
[28] Smith, *Police Systems*, pp. 16–17.
[29] Smith, *Police Systems*, p. 113.

munications and records control, property management, personnel management, crime prevention (especially juvenile work), and morals regulation or vice squads.[30] One has only to look at the operation of small and necessarily unspecialized police departments to appreciate the value of specialization, especially in the areas like criminal investigation that require a degree of expertise not ordinarily possessed by the average policeman. However, this is an expensive mode of organization; many communities find it a luxury they cannot afford. In addition, many students of police organization have pointed out that specialization creates rivalries between officers which lower the overall efficiency of police operations. This rivalry has been noted particularly in the relationships between uniformed officers assigned to patrol duty and plainclothes officers engaged in criminal investigation work.

By far the greatest number of police functions are performed by the officers assigned to patrol duty. Most police work is of a reactive nature and, therefore, highly dependent upon communications and patrols.[31] This means that most of the time police officers are concerned with dealing with calls and complaints from citizens and that their organization must reflect this emphasis by placing policemen within relatively easy reach of the citizen. The organization and operations necessary for this work differ from the organization and operations necessary for traffic control or morals regulation, in which the officers must largely identify violators on their own without benefits of complaint. The biggest difficulty from an organizational point of view with respect to patrol work has been the controversy over motorized versus foot patrols. There are those who feel that the automobile and the motorized patrol have isolated the policeman from the community and reduced necessary communications between officers and citizens. These critics urge a return to foot patrol to increase communication. But there are also those who point out that motorized patrols have enabled the police to maintain contact with greater numbers of people with a limited number of officers, and especially to respond quickly to those citizens who need an officer.[32] This debate is not easily resolved in favor of either position. However, whichever group is correct, such organizational changes are not likely to reach the heart of either the basic peace keeping or the law enforcement functions of the police.

The most glamorous division of police work for officer and civilian alike is criminal investigation. Unfortunately, television, the movies, and novelists have presented something less than a fully accurate view of this aspect of police work. The arrest of criminals appears to depend to a much

---

[30] Smith, *Police Systems*, pp. 219–220.
[31] Albert J. Reiss, Jr. and David J. Bordua, "Environment and Organization: A Perspective on the Police," in Bordua, *The Police*, p. 40.
[32] For example see Clift, *Modern Police Thinking*, p. 33.

greater extent on knowledge of violators and potential violators gained through an intelligence network in the community (stool pigeons) than it does on detective work of the Sherlock Holmes variety. Since criminal investigation activities are usually more centralized geographically than patrol activities, especially in larger cities, it is increasingly difficult for the police to maintain the kind of necessary intelligence network to perform this function.[33] This fact may prove alarming to many Americans. The intelligence network and the informer tend to raise images more frequently associated with a totalitarian state than with a democracy, and Americans have always considered law enforcement activities of this type somehow unsportsmanlike. However, in spite of the progress made in the scientific detection of criminals, the public would be generally unsatisfied with the arrest and conviction rate that would result from such a gentlemanly pursuit of criminal investigation.

Perhaps the greatest organizational problem facing the police is that of direction and supervision of day-to-day operations. In spite of its paramilitary organization and highly developed rules and procedures, the police department of the average city has difficulty in controlling the behavior of its policemen. In the first place, many departmental rules and regulations are unrealistic. The officer in the field soon discovers that it is impossible to obey them all, and, what is more, that no one really expects him to. Field supervision of the activities of the individual officer is a difficult task, given the wide dispersal of police units at any given moment. In the second place, many of the crucial policy decisions which might be transmitted to the officer and which might alter his basic relationship with the public simply have not been made. In most cases, this failure can be traced to the absence of general rules which can serve as guidelines in the complex human interrelationships that face the officer every day. Finally, unlike its military model, the police department draws its commanders and administrators exclusively from the ranks. While firsthand experience with police problems is undoubtedly of great value to police unit commanders, it does not substitute for other qualities of leadership which the uniformed armed services have found valuable. The result of this leadership selection process may well be an organization that is inordinately oriented toward the status quo.

POLICE QUALIFICATIONS AND TRAINING. To some degree, the image suffered by the police officer of today is a product of the background and qualifications of the officer of the nineteenth century, when officers were generally "the shiftless, the incompetent, and the ignorant."[34] Recognizing the

---

[33] Reiss and Bordua, "Environment and Organization," p. 43.
[34] Smith, *Police Systems*, pp. 105–106.

importance of police work and of its demanding nature, police departments throughout the twentieth century have raised their qualifications
for officers. At least they have tried to raise them. The following requirements are generally used by major police departments.[35] The applicant
must have full citizenship status, which means that he must be a citizen
of the United States and of the state and the community for whose police
force he is applying. The community citizenship requirement is an unfortunate irrelevancy that is rapidly being removed in many areas. A prospective officer must meet health and physical standards that are higher
than the average for the population in general. He must be relatively
young—over 21, but usually under 30. While applicants must be of high
character, only the largest police departments make any real attempt to
investigate their prospective officers, and even these checks are frequently
inadequate. And finally, the applicants must meet the mental qualifications set by the department. While these latter qualifications are frequently stated in terms of formal educational requirements, such as high
school graduation, education per se is not an adequate measure of mental
capacity. Most experts are not yet quite sure what they are looking for.
The presumption is that a college graduate with no psychological quirks
or abnormalities who has a photographic memory and an almost uncanny
skill at getting along with even the most obnoxious of his fellow human
beings would somehow fill the bill. Most departments would consider
themselves lucky if they could develop instruments that could tell them
when and if they found this paragon.

Some departments are more particular than others about the characteristics of the personnel that they accept into police work. For the most
part, such fussiness is a function of size; major metropolitan departments
exhibit the greatest care in selecting their officers. While there are some
exceptions among the small but wealthy suburbs that can afford to exercise greater selectivity, the small town police department is less generally
demanding of its applicants.

But, one may ask, are these new policemen merely issued a uniform, a
badge, and a gun, and turned loose on the city streets? Unfortunately, the
answer to this question has all too often been Yes. Although August Voll-
mer developed the first in-service training school in this country in Berkeley, California, in 1908, and New York City established the first full
police academy for training recruits a year later,[36] the training of policemen has gathered momentum only since 1930. Police academies are operated by major cities, states, and the FBI, and training programs from
nondegree programs to the Ph.D. have been developed in junior colleges,
colleges, and universities. In recognition of the complexities of police

---

[35] Smith, *Police Systems*, pp. 128–131.
[36] Allen Z. Gammage, *Police Training in the United States* (Springfield, Ill., 1963),
pp. 6 and 7.

TABLE 13–1: Agencies Participating in Formal Police Recruit Training Programs

Classification	No. of Reporting Cities	F.B.I. No.	F.B.I. Percent	STATE POLICE No.	STATE POLICE Percent	LOCAL UNIVERSITY No.	LOCAL UNIVERSITY Percent	TRAINING OFFICER FROM OWN DEPARTMENT No.	TRAINING OFFICER FROM OWN DEPARTMENT Percent	U.S. ARMY No.	U.S. ARMY Percent	NEIGHBORING POLICE DEPARTMENT No.	NEIGHBORING POLICE DEPARTMENT Percent	OTHER No.	OTHER Percent
Population Group															
Over 500,000	22	4	18	1	5	3	14	22	100	2	9	1	5	3	14
250,000 to 500,000	25	7	28	2	8	5	20	24	96	3	12	2	8	6	24
100,000 to 250,000	85	17	20	16	19	15	18	72	85	7	8	7	8	17	20
50,000 to 100,000	176	40	23	25	14	36	20	105	60	4	2	36	20	52	30
25,000 to 50,000	285	61	21	73	26	82	29	126	44	3	1	70	25	87	31
10,000 to 25,000	581	163	28	210	36	164	28	154	27	10	2	180	31	166	29
Geographic Region															
Northeast	316	77	24	155	49	24	8	87	28	2	1	94	30	104	33
North Central	394	85	22	79	20	135	34	164	42	5	1	94	24	108	27
South	217	79	36	64	29	62	29	131	60	17	8	50	23	44	20
West	247	51	21	29	12	84	34	121	49	5	2	58	23	75	30
City Type															
Central	217	55	25	32	15	46	21	179	82	13	6	20	9	43	20
Suburban	615	116	19	168	27	173	28	175	28	10	2	201	33	197	32
Independent	342	121	35	127	37	86	25	149	44	6	2	75	22	91	27
All cities over 10,000	1,174	292	25	327	28	305	26	503	43	29	2	296	25	331	28

SOURCE: J. Robert Havlick, "Recruit Training: Police Chiefs' Dilemma," *Public Management* 50 (1968): p. 301. Reprinted by permission of the International City Management Association.

TABLE 13–2: Number of Hours of Training for Selected Topics
During Formal Recruit Training Program
(742 cities reporting)

Topic	Low	Lower Quartile	Median	Upper Quartile	High
History of law enforcement	0	1	2	4	80
Role of police in modern society	0	1	2	6	80
Need for discretion in law enforcement	0	1	2	4	80
Use and care of equipment	0	2	3	8	80
Criminal law of the state	0	8	16	27	90
Ordinances and bylaws of the city	0	1	5	10	80
Techniques of investigation	0	6	12	25	96
First aid	0	10	12	18	80
Art of self-defense	0	4	8	16	80
Crowd control	0	3	6	11	80
Juvenile procedures	0	3	5	8	50
Traffic signals with arm and hand	0	1	2	4	40
Sociology and race relations	0	1	4	8	55
Police-community relations	0	2	4	8	65
Courts and the police officer	0	3	4	9	72
Patrol techniques	0	4	8	16	99
Report writing	0	4	6	11	60
Traffic enforcement	0	4	8	16	80
Traffic investigation	0	4	8	16	72

SOURCE: J. Robert Havlick, "Recruit Training: Police Chiefs' Dilemma," *Public Management* 50 (1968): 302. Reprinted by permission of the International City Management Association.

service and under the encouragement of the International Association of Chiefs of Police, the states, beginning with California, New York, New Jersey, and Oregon, have started to require minimum training for all police officers.[37] In spite of this emphasis on training, a recent study by the International City Managers' Association revealed that 18 percent of the municipalities over 10,000 responding to the survey had no training program for their police officers.[38]

The curriculum of the various training programs changes from state to state and from community to community depending upon the nature of the organization doing the training. Table 13–1 indicates the variety of agencies conducting police training, and Table 13–2 shows the number of hours devoted to particular curricular items. The fact that appears most alarming to some analysts of this data is that so little effort is devoted to training in community relations and human relations, in spite of the emphasis which has been placed on problems in these areas in recent years.[39]

---

[37] Gammage, *Police Training*, p. 38.
[38] J. Robert Havlick, "Recruit Training: Police Chiefs' Dilemma," *Public Management* 50 (1968): 300.
[39] Havlick, "Recruit Training," p. 302.

Careful studies of individual programs and their impact on the officer have revealed other problems in police training. An analysis of the New York City program revealed that the training failed to reduce the recruits' uncertainties and questions about police work, that the program emphasized the development of controllable rather than autonomous personnel, and that the program emphasized ideal practices rather than customary or practical procedures.[40] The problem is compounded by the tendency of recruits to be retrained by veterans during the probationary period in procedures that vary greatly from academy doctrine.[41] Part of this may be traced to impractical instruction in the academy; part of it reflects the unwillingness of older officers to accept new doctrine. On the whole we have some important evidence to suggest that police training is not as efficacious as it should be.

POLICE SALARIES. The inability of our cities to attract a better quality of individual to police work is often traced to the low pay given to policemen. There is no doubt that, if we wish to raise educational criteria for police officers from the high school level to junior college or to a college degree, we will have to offer pay scales that are comparable to that level of education. While some observers have adopted a relaxed view of this problem, observing that there is an upward trend in police pay scales and that police have done pretty well compared to other government employees,[42] such observations tend to overlook the fact that we are demanding more of our police than ever before. If they are to be met, these increased demands must be accompanied by increased compensation. Other government employees do not have the grave responsibilities of the policeman.

POLICE MORALE AND ATTITUDES. The low morale of policemen is one of the problems that continues to impede the development of a police department which is wholly satisfactory to both the police and civilian members of urban society. Much of this problem can be directly attributed to the low esteem in which police officers are held by the general public. In a fascinating study of the Chicago Police Department conducted after the reorganization of that agency in the early sixties by Orlando Wilson, James Q. Wilson found that contacts with the public tended to be antagonistic and that the police perceived themselves to be the victims of inconsistent demands placed upon them by society.[43] In spite of the fact

[40] John H. McNamara, "Uncertainties in Police Work: The Relevance of Police Recruits' Background and Training," in Bordua, *The Police*, pp. 163–252.

[41] See Arthur Niederhoffer, *Behind the Shield* (Garden City, N.Y., 1967).

[42] Smith, *Police Systems*, pp. 109–112.

[43] James Q. Wilson, "Police Morale, Reform, and Citizen Respect: The Chicago Case," in Bordua, *The Police*, pp. 137–162.

that broad reforms had generally made the police department more professional and less venal and corrupt, the public still viewed policemen with disdain. Recognizing their own improvement, the police are frustrated when the public refuses to give them credit for the progress they have made. This frustration leads to an alienation from society and a tendency to draw within themselves. Speaking of the conflict between professionalism in the police department and low citizen respect, Wilson says: "To live with such conflict requires either a strong conviction as to the rightness of what one is doing, willingness to attach a low value to popular opinion, or both." [44] Wilson found that the Chicago police developed their own internal substitutes for the respect denied them by the community. The police practiced almost complete social isolation from the rest of the community, and they deliberately attempted to foster morale through the use of internal propaganda.

To make matters worse, the police perceive themselves as existing in a violent and threatening environment, and they see certain kinds of people as potential assailants.[45] As the courts and middle- and upper-class liberals join the attack on the police, and as more and more "respectable" people become involved in demonstrations that are occasionally on the borderline of illegal behavior, it is no longer possible for the policeman to distinguish between the "good guys" and the "bad guys." He therefore tends to perceive the entire society as threatening.[46] Both Wilson and Jerome Skolnick have found that this process tends to move policemen as a group to the right politically. According to Skolnick, the predictability that results from conservatism and support of the system tends to lessen the fear of danger and to make the officer's environment more manageable.[47] Wilson sees the process as leading even farther toward outright political extremism among the police. In support of these observations, many have noted the increasing tendency of policemen to affiliate with the John Birch Society and the Minutemen, organizations usually classed as extremist. This is not intended to be a tirade against the evils of conservatism and reaction among the police. These tendencies are understandable in the environment that the policeman perceives, and those of us who are not policemen bear greater responsibility for them than do the police themselves.

CIVIL ACCOUNTABILITY. The public, acting through its public officials, has very little control over the behavior of the policeman on the street. Every municipal governmental structure provides for some method of control.

---

[44] Wilson, "Police Morale," p. 155.
[45] Skolnick, *Justice Without Trial*, p. 45.
[46] Wilson, "Police Morale," p. 158.
[47] Skolnick, *Justice Without Trial*, p. 54.

The police may be responsible to a mayor, a city manager, a commissioner of public safety, or an independent board or commission. But theoretical responsibility and actual control are two different things. For years, American police departments have fought for a professionalization of law enforcement and peace-keeping efforts which would free these activities from "political control." "Political control" or any decision-making by civilians in police matters were viewed as inherently dangerous. This view was based largely on the presumption that such control would be used as a methods of obtaining preferential treatment for some groups in society and as a device that would destroy fair and impartial police work. There is adequate basis in history for such a presumption. Surely the experience of the nineteenth and early twentieth centuries with the control of the police by corrupt political machines and by essentially lawless elements in society would prevent us from dismissing the concern of professional policemen out of hand.

The dangers to impartial law enforcement and peace keeping are not reserved to those instances in which corrupt machines and gangsters attempt to control the police. Many ordinarily law-abiding citizens are convinced that the system ought to be responsive not only to the will of the majority but also to individual desires and needs.

> Hence various means are found for assuring that police administrators, and our prosecutors, magistrates, and judges as well, shall be quickly responsive to both political and personal influences.[48]

The reform and professionalism that has characterized our police departments, especially in our largest cities, has served to some degree, then, to insulate the police from what might be called democratic control. Executive officers find it difficult to demand the kind of responses which they find appropriate to modern urban problems. Mayor Lindsay of New York City has experienced particular difficulties in this respect. He was unable to maintain a civilian review board to oversee police practices, and the restraint that he demanded during racial demonstrations in the city met with vigorous criticism from the police. This criticism came from the rank and file officers through the Patrolmen's Benevolent Association, and not from departmental administrators who may well have agreed to the mayor's emphasis on restraint.[49]

Small towns can have problems even more severe than those of the big cities. For example, the city manager of Carbondale, Illinois brought in a former instructor in police science with extensive practical experience

---

[48] Smith, *Police Systems*, p. 5.
[49] Herman Goldstein, "Who's in Charge Here?" *Public Management* 50 (1968): 304–307.

as an air policeman in the Air Force to act as Director of Public Safety and to professionalize a small-town police department. The new director, acting for the manager and thus for the city council and the people—or so the assumption would have it—vigorously began his job. In a very short period of time, the director was at odds with the Chief of Police and the entire department. After a particularly unpleasant confrontation between the director and the chief, the chief resigned (or at least threatened to), and the entire police force submitted resignations as well. To make matters worse, the police enlisted the support of other city employees, and the entire group submitted resignations. Ultimately the city manager and the city council decided to fire the director of public safety for doing the job for which the manager had hired him. They really had no choice. Obviously, it is senseless to talk about control, democratic or otherwise, under conditions such as these.

Problems of control do not always resolve themselves into neat little questions of police-civilian relations. However, in its simplest form the problem is usually stated as one in community relations. Understanding, control and respect, and authority relationships provide a basis for a police system that satisfies basic democratic criteria:

> For the relationships between the policeman and the non-criminal subject to serve both parties' ends, they must understand each other. They must both be members of a community, sharing values and modes of communication.[50]

Community relations programs may well increase the degree of communication present between police agencies and civilian groups, but most commentators point out that the heterogeneity of American urban society makes broad-scale agreement on values improbable.

The problem of control becomes more complex when we realize that we are not necessarily dealing with a simple police-civilian controversy. It is quite possible that police supervisory personnel will accept policy direction from mayors, managers, and councils, but that they will be unable to obtain the kind of obedience necessary from the rank and file to implement that policy. The earlier discussion of organization pointed out that the emphasis on quasi-military organization, subordination, and chain-of-command may not always produce the desired results. Even though there is what amounts almost to an obsession with obedience in police organizations,[51] the sanctions available to police administrators are not always sufficient to achieve the desired results. The violence that appears to have characterized police behavior during the Chicago demonstrations in 1968 is a case in point. The Walker Report emphasizes the

---

[50] Banton, *The Policeman in the Community*, p. 168.
[51] Reiss and Bordua, "Environment and Organization," p. 52.

inability of commanders to control the behavior of their subordinates under conditions of stress.[52]

There is still another possibility worth considering, although it is even more alarming. The police behavior that is so often criticized by civil rights advocates and denounced as "brutality" by social critics may actually reflect the way in which a majority of Americans want their police to act. This is particularly true of the methods used to deal with demonstrators:

> Generally, the police of the nation have responded to the protest movements of the 1960's in precisely the way in which the political process has wanted— or directed—them to respond. The operating posture of the police generally reflects the posture of the political system itself.[53]

While many take positions of this type in identifying the police as symbols of a decadent, racist society, urban society's ills are probably not so easily categorized. In spite of the alienation of the police from society in general, there is one course of action upon which the police and some sort of urban majority can agree—the maintenance of the existing system and the status quo. If a heterogeneous society leads to the absence of generally accepted values and norms, including operational definitions of minority rights, then it is safest to change nothing. The behavior of black militants, student activists, draft protesters, and marchers for the poor represents the threat of change, and change is disturbing to the policeman and the average citizen alike. Thus the problem is as much one of getting the majority to accept a social system that is open to the dangers of change as it is one of getting the police to submit to the control of democratic institutions.

POLICE DISCRETION. One of the great dogmas of modern police training has been that the officer must be impartial in performing his duties. For example, a leading textbook used in training policemen states:

> He [the officer] may not be selective in his enforcement duties either as to persons or as to laws. *All* laws must be enforced in behalf of *all* people.[54]

However, not even the writers of textbooks are able to long maintain this fiction in the face of the overwhelming facts. In almost every case they finally recognize that:

> . . . it is the individual agent of law enforcement who usually determines how far popular attitudes shall control, to what degree official instructions

---

[52] Daniel Walker, et al., *Rights in Conflict* (New York, 1968).

[53] Gordon E. Misner, "The Response of Police Agencies," *Annals of the American Academy of Political and Social Science* 382 (1969): 119.

[54] Germann, Day, and Gallati, *Introduction to Law Enforcement*, p. 205.

shall be carried into effect, and what the net social result shall be . . . . The policeman's art, then, consists in applying and enforcing a multitude of laws and ordinances in such degree or proportion and in such manner that the greatest degree of protection will be secured. The degree of enforcement and method of application will vary with each neighborhood and community. There are no set rules, nor even general guides to the policy to be applied.[55]

This is, of course, the position to which most of the preceding argument in this chapter has been pointing.

Herman Goldstein has pointed out why this discretion is necessary in the face of the lip service given to full enforcement by most police administrators.[56] In the first place, our laws are necessarily general and ambiguous. They cannot anticipate every specific behavior pattern and every specific environment. Therefore, the policeman must judge whether a specific behavior in a specific environment falls under the prohibition of the law. Secondly, as an earlier portion of this chapter indicated, no community really desires full enforcement of the law. For many of us, the law is something designed for the other guy. In the third place, the limits on manpower and other resources dictate that the police must establish priorities and concentrate their efforts on the more serious crimes. Fourthly, the police have found that differential enforcement helps them to gain information from petty offenders which might lead to other arrests. In his study, Jerome Skolnick found that officers frequently avoided arresting informants whose criminal behavior lay outside of their field of specialization or that they reduced the charges when arrest appeared unavoidable.[57] For example, detectives on the burglary squad did not arrest informants for using dope if they could avoid it. This process appears to be particularly valuable in dealing with crimes in which there is no complainant and in which the police must develop their own leads. Finally, and cynics will find this hard to believe, the police often fail to arrest or arrest on reduced charges out of pure humanitarianism. In most jurisdictions, for example, a man who exceeds the speed limit while rushing his wife to the hospital to deliver a baby need not fear receiving a traffic citation.

The question that immediately suggests itself is, what criteria are used in the exercise of discretion, and who establishes them? By now it should be relatively clear that the officer himself frequently establishes his criteria often in conjunction with his fellow policemen. But a variety of criteria may be used, and some of them are established by higher authorities. The most obvious case is that of overtly acknowledged selective enforcement. Upon occasion crime statistics, accident reports, and records of police calls

---

[55] Smith, *Police Systems*, pp. 18 and 19.

[56] Herman Goldstein, "Police Discretion: The Ideal Versus the Real," *Public Administration Review* 23 (1963): 140–148.

[57] Skolnick, *Justice Without Trial*, pp. 112–138.

suggest that particular problems are of special importance to the community and that these problems would benefit from a special enforcement effort.[58] For example, studies of traffic accidents on limited access highways have shown that vehicles traveling below the minimum speed limit are a frequent cause of accidents. Therefore, some jurisdictions have instructed traffic officers to be particularly watchful for such offenders, and the motorist who travels at 30 m.p.h. is more likely to receive a citation than one who travels 5 m.p.h. over the speed limit. Similarly, a rash of liquor store holdups is likely to result in greater protection and attention for liquor stores in the affected area than might be given to service stations.

However, the criteria most frequently used by officers are much more difficult to justify than those just mentioned. Nonenforcement is all too frequently a function of the social position of the violator of law.[59] There is no doubt that the well-dressed, well-educated member of the middle or upper class is less likely to be arrested than his lower-class counterpart, and less likely to receive rough treatment should arrest become necessary. However, part of this is due to the visibility factor as much as it is to the application of discretionary criteria by policemen. The fact is that the poor live most of their life in the open and on the streets. Therefore, it is relatively easy for a patrolling officer to see them when they violate the law. The more affluent members of society may violate the law as frequently but they do so in automobiles, in single-family residences, and in private clubs. Unless there is a specific complaint issued about the behavior of the affluent, it is unlikely that the police will discover their lawlessness. Policemen are generally quite willing to accept the enforcement pattern that this differential visibility produces, even though they may recognize its inherent injustice. Ultimately, some policemen and the public in general arrive at the conclusion that the poor are inherently more criminal than the rich, and that blacks are more criminal than whites, even though there are alternative explanations for arrest patterns.

One of the most frequently cited criteria used by officers as a basis for the exercise of discretion is the attitude of the suspect or the alleged violator of the law. Policemen generally wish to be seen as symbols of the authority of society and desire to be treated with respect. Many of us have seen motorists virtually talk policemen into issuing traffic citations by using abusive language and threatening the officer with political reprisals. Black teen-age gang members have noted that they can frequently escape police harassment by adopting a respectful if not subservient posture free of all traces of irony. In addition, veteran officers pride themselves on their ability to sense whether or not a suspect is deserving of

---

[58] Chambliss, *Crime and the Legal Process*, p. 85.
[59] Carl Werthman and Irving Piliavin, "Gang Members and the Police," in Bordua, *The Police*, pp. 56–98.

arrest by virtue of the responses which the subject gives to basic questions. If the subject appears nervous or evasive, he is more likely to be arrested than if he can answer directly and with confidence. Finally, there are physical manifestations of attitudes which arouse police suspicions and are likely to lead to questioning and possible arrest. Black gang members (and others as well) have found that "walking cool"—a characteristic gait adopted for social purposes within the subculture of poor blacks—can be viewed by policemen as a challenge to their authority.[60]

In some instances, simple physical differences are used as a basis for differential treatment. In many communities, the mere presence of a Negro in an area and at a time normally reserved for whites is cause for special police attention. Such distinctions are not purely racial. There are communities in which people wearing working clothes or driving old automobiles after a certain hour in the evening are selected for special scrutiny. Moreover, in these days of social protest, brightly colored clothing, beards, and long hair on males are likely to encourage additional police activity. It is difficult to condemn such criteria out of hand. The police are trained that the best way to prevent crime and to succeed in arresting criminals is to be alert for the unusual. The technique is effective, although the assumptions on which it is based are frequently open to question.

Herman Goldstein suggests that the real problem in police discretion is to force the public and other governmental decision-makers to recognize the impossibility of full enforcement and to establish at least some rough guidelines for the police.[61] It would also help to realistically appraise many of our present laws with respect to their enforceability. Such actions would help considerably to reduce the number of confrontations between the police and citizens who object to the manner in which discretion is being exercised.

MINORITY RELATIONS. All of the problems of the police are focused most clearly when the police must deal with minority groups. While most current attention is devoted to police relations with the black community, there are problems in other neighborhoods as well, particularly in those settled by citizens of a Latin American background. There are two different levels at which this problem can be considered. The first concerns the relationships that exist between groups of officers on the police force. A study of the Philadelphia Police Department conducted more than fifteen years ago revealed that relations between Negro and white policemen were far from ideal, but that they were better than many would

---

[60] Werthman and Piliavin, "Gang Members and the Police," pp. 56–98.
[61] Goldstein, "Police Discretion," pp. 146–148.

have predicted.[62] The study concluded that, in 1953, race relations were probably better within this police department than they were in other employment areas. Although a majority of white policemen still objected to working with black partners, many voiced no such objections, and greater familiarity and contact with black officers led to greater acceptance of their ability and desirability as a partner. The major problem perceived by Negro officers was the relative slowness of promotions. This has improved markedly in recent years. More and more urban police departments are reasonably well integrated, although the proportion of blacks is still lower than in the general population. Promotions are coming faster for Negro officers, and demands that such officers be granted access to the highest command positions are frequently met.

The second and perhaps the more important aspect of this problem is closely related to the first. What kinds of contacts occur between police officers and members of minority groups? The answer to this question is not as simple as many modern social commentators would have us believe. It is not enough to dismiss the police as a racist institution, filled with evil and prejudiced men:

> There are . . . structural and situational contingencies associated directly with the process of law enforcement itself that make it difficult for even the most enlightened and saintly of policemen to avoid being seen as pariahs by a large segment of the ethnic poor.[63]

Nor can the problem be traced solely to the presence of "un-American" elements who seek to subvert democratic processes by fanning the flames of racial hatred:

> Policemen can be fair-minded, minority people can be law-abiding and peaceful, and yet both can still be suspicious and critical of one another. Tension between police and minorities is not a function simply of malevolent personalities. It is a function of different social roles and positions.[64]

On one hand, the police sincerely believe from the evidence available to them that the ethnic poor—Negro, Mexican-American, Puerto Rican— are more likely to be criminals than are members of the white majority. Given the nature of police contact with the population, such beliefs are understandable. The statistics do indicate, for example, a disproportionate arrest rate for the black population. We have seen how increased police

---

[62] William M. Kephart, *Racial Factors and Urban Law Enforcement* (Philadelphia, 1957), especially pp. 158–168.

[63] Werthman and Piliavin, "Gang Members and the Police," p. 68.

[64] David H. Bayley and Harold Mendelsohn, *Minorities and the Police* (New York, 1969), p. 203.

patrols in poor neighborhoods and greater social visibility on the part of the poor may contribute much to this differential. The average policeman knows only that the difference exists and that it is important in terms of the physical threat in his work.

On the other hand, minorities are particularly sensitive with respect to the police and look carefully for every slight and hint of brutality. Students of police-minority contacts almost uniformly point out that the police are symbols of authority and, therefore, of society in general. The poor, and particularly the black poor, have come to expect less than equal treatment from society over the years. In addition, the police role is largely negative and repressive. Those who have experienced occasional if not frequent rewards from society might be expected to accept an additional restriction or two administered by the police. To one whose life is largely been based upon deprivation, the additional restrictions may be unbearable, and the police can easily become a symbol of all the restrictions and deprivations of society. Given this situation, there would appear to be only one long-range solution to the problems of police-minority relations.[65] Obviously, simple education of the police and of minorities is not enough, since education cannot wholly overcome the differences between the two groups. The same comment also holds for communication or discussion between the groups. As a matter of fact, the current emphasis on dialogue frequently leads to a great deal of talk with very little communication, a situation that merely adds to existing frustrations and tensions on both sides. Finally, sympathy, impartiality, and understanding on the part of the police will help, but they will not get at the root of the problem. The solution lies in the elimination of social and economic conditions which serve as a basis for the deprivation and inequality of minority groups. Once the have-nots become haves, they will at least perceive themselves to have no more problems than the next citizen with the police, in the absence of real prejudice and racial discrimination on the part of the police.

Up to now, the discussion has almost excluded the possibility that prejudice and discrimination are a real factor in the serious conflict between police and minorities. This is not wholly accurate. It would be absurd to maintain that there are no bigots on our police forces. However, the emphasis that should be placed on sheer bigotry is open to question. The number of instances of clear brutality, either physical or verbal, on the part of the police is limited. The argument here is that whether I view a particular act of the police as brutal is in many cases going to depend more heavily upon my social and economic position than it is upon the nature of the act itself. The absence of easily documentable cases of clear

[65] Bayley and Mendelsohn, *Minorities and the Police*, pp. 203–205.

brutality may demonstrate, as many modern social critics claim, only that the police are very clever at disguising their misdeeds. However, the contention that the absence of evidence proves the hypothesis is one that most logical men would find difficult to accept. Because of the authority and the instruments of force which have been given to policemen, it is essential that society constantly review the exercise of that authority to determine its acceptability. But the generalization current among extremist groups that all policemen are "fascist pigs" does not add much to our understanding of police-minority relations.

Fire Departments

While the police are certainly the most controversial members of the public safety team, the fire department has its share of political difficulties. One of the major factors in much of the urban violence of the past few summers has been the use of fire as a weapon of social protest. In responding to fire calls during times of tension, the fire department has become the target for missiles of various dimensions and descriptions, including bullets. This may be attributable to a great degree to the natural desire of the arsonists to achieve their desired ends by burning a portion of the city to the ground. But it also may be traced in part to the fact that the uniformed fireman is also a symbol of the social system and of authority, although to a lesser degree than the policeman.

Firemen as a group are as active as any public employees in maintaining pressure on higher administrators and city councils for wages and fringe benefits appropriate to the dangers and skills involved in their work. In fact, in many cases, the demands of firemen are keyed to those of policemen, since firemen tend to equate the two occupations in terms of both dangers and skills.

A major difference between firemen and policemen and the political environments in which they operate lies in the areas of political control, organizational effectiveness, and discretion. The public and their policy-making representatives are less ambiguous in their devotion to both the goals and means of extinguishing fires and fire prevention than they are in the case of law enforcement and keeping the peace. Because the major activity of the organization is focused in a single location or in a limited number of locations, the quasi-military organization of the department is more effective, and supervision and control represent fewer problems. The range of discretionary activity is much narrower, and the chance that the exercise of discretion will engender great public opposition is diminished. In general, there are fewer problems in the politics of the fire department— outside of the internal jockeying for power and influence within the organization—than in most other areas of urban governmental activity.

Civil Defense

One final aspect of the public safety effort is worthy of brief mention. The civil defense program is organized to provide protection and shelter from disasters of both a military and a natural variety, and to assist in the operation and rehabilitation of the community following such a disaster. This program is probably the least well-developed aspect of public safety in most communities. Although it is highly intergovernmental in nature, depending upon interlocal cooperation and state and national effort, the major thrust of the program depends upon local initiative. In a time when the allocation of scarce resources is a particularly difficult problem, civil defense frequently is the activity that takes a back seat. For example, it would be difficult if not impossible to find a community which has a fully developed civil defense program that includes a complete system of shelters for the population, adequate emergency rations, complete provisions for the continued operation of vital government services, and plans and priorities for the physical reclamation of the community. However, the availability of generous grants-in-aid from the national government has encouraged communities of all sizes to establish minimal civil defense plans in order to receive funds for badly needed equipment in other areas of public safety. Many cities have purchased badly needed communications equipment for the police and fire departments as well as new fire trucks, inhalators, and other equipment through the civil defense program.

This is a potentially explosive public policy area. The kinds of rigid controls which are frequently necessary during a disaster and its immediate aftermath are inherently distasteful to citizens in a democracy. In most instances, such efforts are characterized by a spirit of cooperation and a tolerance for inconvenience and regulation that would be unimaginable in normal times. But these are emergencies of short duration. Whether a community could stand the pressures of prolonged constraints and the atmosphere of fear which would follow a nuclear disaster is anybody's guess at this point. The experiments that have been conducted with groups under conditions of prolonged shelter living give us reason to believe that the problems of social control would be enormous. Present civil defense planning and our present knowledge of urban politics give us little reason to be hopeful.

Suggested Readings

Banton, Michael. *The Policeman in the Community*. New York, 1964.

Bayley, David H., and Mendelsohn, Harold. *Minorities and the Police*. New York, 1969.

Bordua, David J., ed. *The Police: Six Sociological Essays*. New York, 1967.

Campbell, James S.; Sahid, Joseph R.; and Stang, David P., eds. *Law and Order Reconsidered*. Washington, 1969.

Chambliss, William J., ed. *Crime and the Legal Process*. New York, 1969.

Clift, Raymond E. *A Guide to Modern Police Thinking*. 2d ed. Cincinnati, 1965.

Eldefonso, Edward; Coffey, Alan; and Grace, Richard C. *Principles of Law Enforcement*. New York, 1968.

Gammage, Allen Z. *Police Training in the United States*. Springfield, Ill., 1963.

Germann, A. C.; Day, Frank D.; and Gallati, Robert R. J. *Introduction to Law Enforcement*. Rev. ed. Springfield, Ill., 1966.

Graham, Hugh D., and Gurr, Ted R., eds. *Violence in America: Historical and Comparative Perspectives*. 2 vols. Washington, 1969.

Kephart, William M. *Racial Factors and Urban Law Enforcement*. Philadelphia, 1957.

Masotti, Louis H., and Bowen, Don R., eds. *Riots and Rebellion: Civil Violence in the Urban Community*. Beverly Hills, 1968.

Momboisse, Raymond M. *Community Relations and Riot Prevention*. Springfield, Ill., 1967.

Nieburg, H. L. *Political Violence: The Behavioral Process*. New York, 1969.

Niederhoffer, Arthur. *Behind the Shield*. Garden City, N.Y., 1967.

The Report of the National Advisory Commission on Civil Disorders. Washington, 1968. See especially Chapter 11.

Skolnick, Jerome H. *Justice Without Trial: Law Enforcement in Democratic Society*. New York, 1966.

————, ed. *The Politics of Protest*. Washington, 1969.

Smith, Bruce. *Police Systems in the United States*. 2d rev. ed. New York, 1960.

Walker, Daniel, et al. *Rights in Conflict*. New York, 1968.

chapter **14**
Health and Welfare

([The attiudes toward it and a lack of real understanding of public welfare as it functions on a day-to-day basis provide a realm of controversy probably not equaled in any other public venture. On any given day, the administrator of a welfare department, be it large or small, will receive an approximately equal number of completely opposite opinions. About one-half of his daily contacts will accuse him of wild and reckless spending, complete disregard for the tax dollar, and the direct subsidization of immorality. The other half will accuse him of being a miser with no regard for humanity and a desire to deny the necessities of life to the worthy poor.[1]

This chapter deals in a general way with those portions of the police power of the state which remain outside of the framework of public safety, that is, with public health and welfare. As the statement quoted above clearly indicates, neither of these two areas escapes the realm of politics. The public policies most appropriate to the constitutionally mandated function of the state to provide for the welfare and health of its citizens are currently much debated. As we shall see throughout this chapter, urban governments are frequently at the center of this debate, and the positions that they take with respect to health and welfare policy can and do have a generalized effect on the urban political environment. Although the policy areas are often closely interrelated both conceptually and programmatically, this chapter will to a great extent deal with them separately, because

---

[1] Reed K. Clegg, *The Administrator in Public Welfare* (Springfield, Ill., 1966), p. 3.

the institutions of local government charged with their administration are usually separate.

Urban Poverty and Welfare

The concept of welfare is linked to the concept of deprivation. Government concern with welfare is focused on somehow providing a portion of the population with something that they lack, something that can be considered to be a necessity for normal human existence. Those who are identified as in need of such assistance are usually defined as being poor. However, this does not deal adequately with the very real question, What is poverty? The answers to this question are varied, since poverty is obviously a relative state. Subsistence definitions of poverty tend to identify poor people as those who are economically unable to enjoy a certain standard of existence. On the other hand, many prefer to define poverty as a state of relative deprivation, thereby focusing on the difference in material resources between the haves and the have-nots in a society. In American policy "all definitions of poverty used in policy, in the practice of providing relief, or in measurement, are variations of the notion of 'subsistence poverty'." [2]

This emphasis can be justified in human terms. An imposing array of writers, including such clearly different men as James Madison and Karl Marx, have pointed to relative deprivation and the unequal distribution of wealth as an enduring source of conflict in a social system. As such, it is a phenomenon with which governments will have to deal if they are to continue as viable institutions. But it is possible to view poverty as a matter of priorities. The presence of a considerable number of citizens who exist at a level below what society defines as the subsistence level can be considered a more important problem in both humanitarian and political terms than the gap between the highest and lowest income groups. This is, most assuredly, a short-run view. But it is an approach to the problem of poverty which is particularly attractive in a society in which most citizens are convinced that the opportunity for social and economic mobility exists and in which the major emphasis is on becoming wealthy rather than upon eliminating the wealthy as a group. That there are grave practical difficulties with such a view of the economic system may not be relevant as long as the vast majority of the American people, including a significant number of the poor themselves, are willing to accept it as accurate.

---

[2] Oscar Ornati, "The Spacial Distribution of Urban Poverty," in *Power, Poverty, and Urban Policy*, ed. Warner Bloomberg, Jr. and Henry J. Schmandt (Beverly Hills, 1968), p. 50.

Even the definition of subsistence poverty presents problems that have often interfered seriously with the development of welfare policy. Many people would be willing to accept as a general statement Thomas Gladwin's pragmatic definition:

Being poor, at least in the United States, consists in a lack of sufficient money to function effectively in the economic system through which everyone is forced to seek the necessities of life.[3]

But this definition is inadequate as a basis for policy decisions. How much money is "sufficient"? What constitutes "functioning effectively"? These questions demand specific answers. Any workable definition must identify the potential beneficiaries of programs and must show clearly what conditions need to be corrected.[4] It is in formulating such a definition that we have experienced the greatest frustration in our welfare program.

Most of the effort has been devoted to establishing an income level or line below which individuals may be identified as poor. There have been a variety of figures used, and none have been generally accepted, but the figure most frequently used in recent years has been $3,000 for a family. This means that those families whose incomes fall below that figure may be considered poor in the sense that they do not have a sufficient amount of money to adequately provide the necessities of life—food, shelter, and clothing—according to contemporary standards of adequacy. In a book that has probably had a greater impact on welfare policy than anything else written in the last ten years, Michael Harrington used income figures of between $3,000 and $3,500 to estimate that between one-fifth and one-quarter of our population or forty to fifty million people are poor in this country.[5] In terms of government policy, this poverty level and this estimate of target population have served as the basis for much of the current attempt to deal with poverty.

For a number of reasons, these definitions of poverty should be accepted with some caution. They run the risk of either seriously overstating or seriously understating the problem. Because they essentially ignore such important factors as family size, the age of family members, and geographic location, they may overstate the problem.[6] Small households require less to live on than a family of four. Older people require less than younger. The cost of living is lower in some areas than in others. However, those who have attempted to adjust the figures by using a sliding

[3] Thomas Gladwin, *Poverty U.S.A.* (Boston, 1967), p. 48.
[4] Lawrence Haworth, "Deprivation and the Good City," in Bloomberg and Schmandt, *Power, Poverty, and Urban Policy*, p. 28.
[5] Michael Harrington, *The Other America: Poverty in the United States* (New York, 1962), p. 182.
[6] Ben B. Seligman, *Permanent Poverty* (Chicago, 1968), p. 24.

scale that takes these factors into account have not been able to come up with estimates that are significantly below Harrington's forty million poor. This may be traced in part to the tendency of the fixed poverty line to underestimate the number of the poor for the same reasons. Many of the poor have families a good deal larger than the national average. Medical and other expenses peculiar to old age may more than offset the alleged savings available to the aged. Finally, the soaring cost of living, especially in the cities, may well have rendered the $3,000 figure totally unrealistic even for the ideal-type family.

The other problem implied in such definitions is the decision as to what constitutes subsistence. Those who are unsympathetic to welfare programs in this country often point out that even the very poor in this country enjoy incomes far in excess of those received by even the average citizen in most other countries of the world. While this is quite true, it misses the point. In the first place, cost structures vary, and even the wealthy in other countries are able to live in luxury on a good deal less than their American counterparts. Secondly, questions of need and subsistence are culture bound and crosscultural comparisons are not particularly useful. Our culture and society, particularly because of its urban character, have created a whole set of needs which are peculiar to this country and which exist to some degree in other countries only to the extent to which they have shared our urbanization and technological development. As Harrington has succinctly pointed out:

> One of the consequences of our new technology is that we have created new needs. There are more people who live longer. Therefore they need more. In short, if there is technological advance without social advance, there is, almost automatically, human misery and impoverishment.[7]

There are, however, some real dangers in culturally bound definitions of subsistence. In this country, these dangers are most clearly reflected in some of the judgments as to the adequacy of diet. Competent medical authorities generally concede that the average American positively gorges himself. He not only eats more than he needs, but more than is good for him. Questions of dietary subsistence then should probably be answered relative to the kind of balanced diet which contributes to good health and longevity, rather than according to the dietary habits of the average middle-class American. To do otherwise would be to put governments in the strange position of subsidizing the destruction of the health of the poor.

One final objection to subsistence definitions of poverty as a basis for

---

[7] Harrington, *The Other America*, p. 178.

welfare programs must be recognized. Almost every observer of contemporary problems of poverty is quick to point out that there is more to being poor than simple lack of money. Poverty is a way of life, a series of expectations and attitudes, which shapes an individual's entire approach to life. Being poor seriously affects not only the self-image of the poor but also their view of society and its opportunity structure. Given this view of poverty, it is possible to provide money for subsistence without reducing poverty as a social problem. This suggests two things: (1) subsistence definitions of poverty may understate the problem because they do not include the culturally poor; and (2) welfare programs based on the concept of subsistence poverty can only be a first step toward dealing with poverty. However, while support at the subsistence level may not be a sufficient condition for the elimination of poverty, it most assuredly may be considered a necessary condition for doing so.

WHO ARE THE POOR? Given our admittedly limited subsistence definitions of poverty, we must go on to determine further descriptive categories that will better enable us to identify and understand poverty. Perhaps the most important additional fact about poverty in America is that it is an urban phenomenon. Accepting a 1965 figure of 32.5 million poor (probably an underestimate), we find that only 6 percent of these people were located on farms and that 17.2 million lived in Standard Metropolitan Statistical Areas, with 10.6 million in the central cities.[8] It is further possible to identify a flow of poverty from rural to urban areas. The marginal farmer and farm laborer make up the bulk of the rural poor, and it is these marginal poor who are most likely to migrate from the farms to the city where they will quite probably continue to be poor.[9] Finally, poverty, the programs that attempt to deal with it, and the consequences of program failure are all particularly visible in urban areas because of the increased density of population.

The poor as we have defined them also tend to be the old, the young, and the black.[10] The data show that 22 percent of the poor are Negro and that nearly one-half of all Negroes are poor. Furthermore, one-third of the poor families in this country are headed by persons over sixty-five, and one-half of our aged families are poor. Finally, one-quarter of the poor families are headed by a woman, and one-half of all such families are poor. This last category is particularly important with respect to the young, since the

---

[8] Daniel P. Moynihan, "Poverty in Cities," in *The Metropolitan Enigma*, ed. James Q. Wilson (Washington, 1967), p. 301.

[9] Warner Bloomberg, Jr. and Henry J. Schmandt, "The Issue is Very Much in Doubt," in Bloomberg and Schmandt, *Power, Poverty, and Urban Policy*, p. 16.

[10] Seligman, *Permanent Poverty*, pp. 22–23.

families with a female head of household are most frequently those that qualify for assistance under the program of Aid to Families with Dependent Children.

Why are these people poor in this most affluent of all societies? Why don't they just go out and get a job like anyone else? There are many reasons for poverty, some of which will be discussed in greater detail in the context of specific welfare programs. It is sufficient here to suggest a few basic reasons for poverty. The disproportionate poverty of our black population can be traced directly to patterns of discrimination.[11] Negroes have been segregated socially and economically as well as physically from the rest of society. They have been the last to be hired and the first to be fired from the decent, remunerative jobs. They must pay high prices for inferior goods. Ghetto schools fail to adequately prepare their students for employment and for life in the city. All of these problems, combined with the decline in the need for unskilled labor that has accompanied urbanization, have left the black population either in poverty or slightly above the poverty line in the vast majority of cases.

The aged obviously present special problems as well.[12] Society generally considers those over sixty-five as too old to be productive, and only one-third of the aged are able to remain in the work force. Once out of the work force, the aged experience a sharp drop in income, sometimes up to 50 percent, which forces a sharp revision of their standard of living. Neither private pension plans nor OASDI (better known as Social Security) have been able to provide an adequate income for a large number of the population over sixty-five. To make matters worse, inflation and increased medical costs place abnormal financial burdens on the aged who are operating largely on the basis of fixed incomes. It is obviously not very difficult to become one of the aged poor in our affluent society.

Most people are surprised to learn that a massive number of our poor are children. For example, in September, 1968, 50.6 percent of those receiving public assistance payments in this country were children.[13] For the most part, these children are the products of the cycle of poverty. That is, they are the products of poor families and the recipients of poor educations. They are legally barred from the labor force for part of their childhood, and are educationally and culturally unqualified to enter the labor force after reaching the requisite age. As an illustration of this latter point, it should be noted that although young people under the age of twenty-five constitute but 20 percent of the eligible work force they make

---

[11] Seligman, *Permanent Poverty*, pp. 42–52.
[12] Seligman, *Permanent Poverty*, pp. 63–80.
[13] U.S. Department of Health, Education, and Welfare, *Welfare in Review* 7 (1969): 43.

up 40 percent of the unemployed.[14] It is clear, then, that poverty is a problem of the young.

TRADITIONAL WELFARE PROGRAMS. The first large-scale governmental responses to the problems of poverty in this country came as a result of the depression of the 1930s and the New Deal programs of the national government. Up to that time, the major state and local governmental response to poverty had taken the form of repressive poor laws and the kind of grim, indoor assistance which could be provided by the public's poor farms and orphanages. The massive unemployment and poverty generated by a major depression proved the traditional methods inadequate to the task of providing for the poor. In addition, the existence of poverty on a wide scale forced the national government to reexamine its assumptions and attitudes toward poverty:

> Through a variety of mechanisms it became clearly established in law and in custom that equality of opportunity was a right more to be respected even than private property.[15]

Although the change in attitudes and assumptions has been important, it is equally important to note that throughout the New Deal and subsequent governmental programs there remains a distinction between the deserving and the undeserving poor. The distinction is based largely on a work ethic which assumes that those who can work, but do not, deserve to starve. This assumption has been at the heart of all of our welfare programs, and was stated explicitly as a foundation of the reform program of family assistance proposed by President Nixon on August 8, 1969. The welfare system of the New Deal was designed primarily to provide relief for the temporarily unemployed and did not really come to grips with the problems of the more permanent, hard-core poverty:

> Thus a whole generation of very poor people, including large numbers of Negroes, grew to their maturity and on to a premature old age largely untouched by the forms of the New Deal and frequently ineligible for its benefits.[16]

Two basic types of welfare program exist in the United States today— categorical assistance and general assistance. Categorical assistance consists of those types of aid which grew out of the New Deal and the Social Security Act of 1935. These programs are characterized by the participation of the federal government in their funding and administration and

---

[14] Seligman, *Permanent Poverty*, p. 94.
[15] Gladwin, *Poverty U.S.A.*, p. 9.
[16] Gladwin, *Poverty U.S.A.*, p. 13.

TABLE 14–1: Amount of Public Assistance Payments in United States During September, 1968

Maintenance Assistance	Amount	Percent of Maintenance	Percent of Total Public Assistance
Old-Age Assistance	$138,091,000	28.7	16.8
Aid to the Blind	7,364,000	1.5	0.8
APTD	55,591,000	11.5	6.7
AFDC	239,942,000	49.9	29.2
General Assistance	37,340,000	7.7	4.5
Payments to Intermediate Care Facilities	1,626,000	0.3	0.2
Total	479,954,000		58.4

Medical Assistance	Amount	Percent of Medical Assistance	Percent of Total Public Assistance
Title XIX (Indigents)	$315,800,000	92.7	38.4
Titles I & XVI (Aged)	5,525,000	1.6	0.6
Vendor Payments Under OAA, AB, APTD	14,182,000	4.1	1.7
General Assistance	5,149,000	1.5	0.6
Total	340,656,000		41.5

| Total Public Assistance | $820,610,000 | | |

SOURCE: U.S. Department of Health, Education, and Welfare, *Welfare in Review*, 7 (1969): 42.

by an emphasis on certain types of poor people rather than on poverty itself. General assistance programs are those that are financed largely through state and local revenue and that at least in theory provide aid to all the poor, subject to eligibility requirements. As Tables 14–1 and 14–2 indicate, categorical assistance is by far the more important of the two types both in terms of the number of dollars spent and in terms of the number of persons reached. General assistance maintenance payments represent only 7.7 percent of the total, and the program handles only 9.7 percent of the maintenance case load. Perhaps the most startling fact revealed by the welfare data is the substantiation of the earlier claim that our traditional welfare programs do not reach many of the poor. As a matter of fact, categorical assistance and general assistance taken together do not even make a sizeable dent in the problem of poverty. If we adopt the fairly reasonable estimate of 40 million poor in this country, programs that reach only 8.6 million people obviously fall far short of the mark.

There are four basic types of categorical assistance. Originally, the New Deal programs provided assistance for programs of old-age assistance (OAA), aid to the blind (AB), and aid to dependent children (ADC). Subsequent amendments to the Social Security Act have added the new

TABLE 14–2: Number of Recipients of Public Assistance Maintenance
Payments in the United States During September, 1968

Programs	Recipients	Percent of Total
Federally Aided Programs		
OAA	2,023,000	23.5
AB	81,000	0.9
APTD	684,000	7.9
AFDC		
Total Recipients	5,801,000	67.5
Children	(4,351,000)	(50.6)
General Assistance	834,000	9.7
Total	8,589,000 *	

SOURCE: U.S. Department of Health, Education, and
Welfare, *Welfare in Review*, 7 (1969) : 43.

* Figures do not total since some recipients receive aid
under more than one program.

category of aid to the permanently and totally disabled (APTD) and have
added new dimensions to ADC, namely aid to families with dependent
children (AFDC) and AFDC grants to families in which the male head
of household is unemployed (ADC-U). Of these programs, the fastest
growing and the most controversial from the standpoint of social policy
is AFDC. This program deserves some special treatment. First, however,
it is useful to lay to rest one of the great, general myths of American
welfare policy.

One cannot discuss poverty and welfare very long before running into
the claim that the basic cause of poverty is the unwillingness of a significant segment of our population to work. Welfare payments are frequently
viewed as public subsidies for the lazy. There is little available evidence
to support this position. Even a cursory glance at Table 14–2 reveals that
the vast majority of recipients of maintenance payments are effectively
outside of the labor force and are likely to remain so for the foreseeable
future. Of the present recipients of maintenance welfare, 32.3 percent are
aged, blind, or permanently and totally disabled. While some of these
people can and do work, we do not usually expect them to do so, and any
policy designed to push them into the labor force is likely to be easily
frustrated. Another 50.6 percent of the recipients are minor children
whom society normally expects to remain in school and outside the labor
force, although this is an unrealistic expectation in many cases. This
would leave only 17.1 percent of the recipients as short-run potential
members of the work force, and this figure is high since some of those
receiving aid under general assistance and as head-of-household under
AFDC may well be receiving aid under other categorical programs as well.
Of course, the presumption is that by employing heads-of-household we

can relieve the public of the necessity for supporting dependent children. Such an assumption is warranted only to the degree that employment can be found which raises the total family income above the poverty level.

A second difficulty with the assumption that our welfare recipients are deadbeats and free loaders hinges upon the level of support possible under existing programs. While there are great variations from state to state in the level of support, it is safe to say that in the vast majority of states that level is below the level of subsistence which we use to define poverty. This factor tends to place great burdens upon the poor:

> In comparison with his counterpart in the general population, the recipient of aid must be a more capable money manager in order to survive. The assistance grant, while viewed as a bonanza by many critics, is actually sufficient only to provide the absolute necessities, and it must be managed well even to do that.[17]

Life on welfare is not a life of ease. It is filled with tensions and anxieties. Only those with a limited knowledge of the problem could claim that it is easier to live on welfare than to work.

Another frequent criticism voiced by opponents of welfare in general and of existing programs is that welfare recipients use subterfuge and outright fraud to get placed on the roles. This belief is so widespread that we actually spend 20 percent of our welfare budgets on policing eligibility requirements.[18] The picture revealed by careful study of welfare administration is quite different.[19] A check in California, for example, revealed that fraud was suspected in 1 percent of the cases in children's programs and in .02 percent of the cases in adult programs. Out of these suspected instances of fraud, only 28.5 percent in children's programs and 43.9 percent in adult programs were found to be well-founded enough to be referred for prosecution. While there is surely some welfare fraud that goes undetected, all of the available evidence indicates that this is not a significant problem. In fact, it is probably less significant than the fraud that occurs in the filing of middle- and upper-class income tax returns. The difference between fraud and behavior of which the general public does not approve is significant. It is possible for people to do things which many of us would condemn and for these same people to remain eligible for welfare. The concept of the deserving poor has not yet been carried to its ultimate extreme.

The AFDC program is the largest and fastest growing of the welfare programs which were inherited from the New Deal. As Table 14–1 dem-

---

[17] Clegg, *The Administrator in Public Welfare*, p. 192.

[18] Gladwin, *Poverty U.S.A.*, p. 70.

[19] The data presented are drawn from Clegg, *The Administrator in Public Welfare*, pp. 126–128.

onstrates, AFDC payments constitute nearly 30 percent of all public assistance payments and nearly 50 percent of maintenance payments. The general public has upon occasion expressed alarm over the growth of this program. However, such expressions have usually been for the wrong reasons. A significant number of those who are alarmed over the growth in AFDC view the program in much the same way as the Illinois state legislator who was recently quoted as describing AFDC as a program for supporting bastards. This is not really the case. While illegitimate children can be supported under AFDC, only 21 percent of the caseload can be traced to illegitimacy.[20] Most illegitimate children are in fact supported by natural or adoptive families, and there is strong evidence that AFDC families do *not* deliberately invite illegitimate children in order to receive greater welfare payments. Any poor mother would be able to testify that the costs of such behavior patterns far outweigh the benefits.

What are the reasons for concern about AFDC? Obviously, it is alarming that an increasing number of families should find themselves reduced to accepting government support and even more disturbing that these families should include a large number of children. These children cannot help but suffer from the adverse effects of living on welfare. In the first place, they are in almost every instance required to exist below the subsistence level. This not only affects their comfort and health, but it also has a serious impact on their ability to perform well in school. Perhaps even more importantly, welfare in general and AFDC in particular has a broader impact on the poor:

> Welfare has created a world which tends to perpetuate itself and is thus self-defeating. It does this for two reasons. First, it creates a set of economic relationships which often makes the continuance of welfare advantageous and preferable to the available alternatives. Second, its clumsy forays into the morality of individual citizens violate the dignity of welfare recipients and reduce them to pawns of the bureaucratic state.[21]

The economic relationships referred to here are the provisions of the law which reduce welfare payments by the amount that any recipient earns through working. This means that unless the recipient finds a job that pays more than the welfare check, it does not pay him to work. The second part of the demeaning combination is provided by the welfare workers who must check to make sure that no one is getting money who does not deserve it. This frequently involves nighttime "raids" of the homes of the poor without legal basis, in an effort to catch them doing something they are not supposed to be doing. The penalty is withdrawal

---

[20] Clegg, *The Administrator in Public Welfare*, pp. 163–165.
[21] Herbert Krosney, *Beyond Welfare: Poverty in the Supercity* (New York, 1966), p. 141.

of welfare. The problem here is that they are being punished largely because they are poor. The same tactics used in other portions of the community would undoubtedly reveal as much illegal and immoral behavior. Even the innocent among the poor are subjected to the same demeaning treatment which cannot help but damage their self-esteem. The fact that the courts have recently limited some of the bases on which welfare payments can be stopped is of some consolation. No longer is the presence of a man in the house of AFDC recipients during the nighttime hours sufficient grounds for stopping payments. However, the general practices continue. It remains a matter of public policy to try and starve families into compliance with the prevailing social mores of the time. The policy has not been an overwhelming success.

A final category of program attempts to deal with a major contributor to poverty rather than to deal directly with distributing money to the needy. This category includes government efforts to provide employment training for those who are poor because they cannot find a job. The number of people who fall into this category is increasing each year. Our developing technology has resulted in a diminished demand for unskilled labor, and an increased demand for certain types of skilled labor and for employees in the service industries. Federal, state, and local governments have developed a wide variety of training programs in a wide variety of agencies, all designed to train the poor. Most of these programs must be considered unsuccessful. Technological unemployment of the unskilled has rarely been solved by retraining, and the remedial education of school dropouts has produced few results in terms of employment.[22] Our past experience appears to indicate that there is little hope of retraining as long as the unemployed are steeped in the culture of poverty. Even the incentive payments offered to those who participate in training programs are not enough to provide the requisite motivation.

THE WAR ON POVERTY. On March 16, 1964, in recognition of the fact that traditional welfare and employment programs were not eliminating the problems of the poor in this country, President Lyndon Johnson declared war on poverty. The War on Poverty or the Economic Opportunity Act of 1964 received a great deal of attention as a major breakthrough in the attempt to permit every American to enjoy the economic and social benefits of our society. The war was to be fought on many fronts. The program provided for Head Start projects, designed to help children who were growing up in poverty become better prepared for their experience in the public schools. Upward Bound projects were developed to encourage the underachieving poverty-stricken student to raise

---

[22] Clegg, *The Administrator in Public Welfare*, pp. 227–230.

his sights toward a college education. The Neighborhood Youth Corps was to help provide short-term employment for poor youths within their own cities, while the Job Corps had the task of providing remedial education and job training for young men and women in order that they might take their place among the gainfully employed. Volunteers in Service to America provided a domestic Peace Corps that was designed to provide technical assistance to the poor in developing a better pattern of living. The Legal Services program was established to provide competent legal counsel to the poor in civil cases and to act as their advocate before the various government agencies with which they had to deal. Finally, the Community Action Program provided overall local coordination for the War on Poverty, developed new ideas and approaches to poverty and its problems, and established a decision-making mechanism relatively independent of existing local government agencies in which the poor themselves could participate and thereby share in some way in shaping their own destinies.

Because of the political complexities of the Community Action Program, it will be explored in some detail as an example of politics and participation in welfare programs. Before entering into this discussion, let us make a few general statements about the efficacy of the War on Poverty. In the six years it has existed, this program has developed both its impassioned defenders and its severe critics. On balance, in spite of its pretentious title and the grandiose rhetoric which characterized its announcement, the programs and their sponsoring agency do not appear to have won many battles in the war. Some relatively friendly critics have emphasized that the major problem with the program was that it was oversold:

> When in moments of realism and troubled conscience we find . . . generalizations untenable, we turn in a mood of anxiety to one or another nostrum that allegedly will melt away the trouble with fairly little effort and in a relatively short time; thus, much of the war on poverty is patent medicine, a public policy equivalent of reducing pills and faddish diets that promise major results without any serious change in our values or alteration of our modes of conduct.[23]

What began as radical and innovative social doctrine in the Mobilization For Youth and HARYOU experiments in New York City inevitably bogged down as a government program. The Office of Economic Opportunity and its local counterparts found themselves struggling just to stay alive in the jungle of government programs. System maintenance goals frequently replaced welfare goals at least in short-run situations. The pro-

---

[23] Bloomberg and Schmandt, *Power, Poverty, and Urban Policy*, p. 11.

gram became characterized by conflict-avoidance strategies that were designed to minimize opposition or to stifle and discredit all those who were critical of the failure of the program to make a real dent in the problem of poverty.[24]

Taken as a whole, the War on Poverty probably deserves a somewhat more mixed review than these criticisms imply. We have learned a great deal from its mistakes. It has helped to focus public attention on poverty as an area of vital national concern. Furthermore, it has encouraged a certain humility and uncertainty on the part of some with respect to easy answers to problems of poverty. It has effectively demonstrated the interrelationship between poverty and such other factors as health, education, family size, welfare history, and feelings of political inefficacy. Finally, the war has suggested a constructively critical skepticism that can in the long run encourage more imaginative approaches to old problems. However, the three most serious shortcomings of the War on Poverty have yet to be mentioned. In the first place, it clearly demonstrated the unwillingness of Congress and, quite probably, of the American people to adequately support any broad-scale and expensive effort to eliminate poverty in the 1960s. It also clearly showed the absence of coordination in dealing with the problems of the poor and the great shortage of the kind of leadership necessary to mount a truly effective battle against poverty. Finally, it retained the punitive and myopic character of the traditional welfare programs in dealing with the poor.[25]

POLITICS, POVERTY, AND WELFARE. Welfare as a function is no different than any other function when it comes to political activity. On one hand, the administrators piously decry the necessity for political activity:

> Public welfare should be completely devoid of politics. The public pressures and controversies surrounding welfare are sufficient to keep the program aware of public sentiment. Political pressures from parties and groups add nothing constructive to the proper administration of a program involving the welfare of thousands of people and the expenditures of millions of dollars.[26]

On the other hand, the practical necessities of making decisions as to how much in the way of resources should be allocated to welfare and as to who the recipients should be obviously render the administrators' statements meaningless. There is no question that welfare and its administration are political. The question is, "What kinds of politics characterize welfare decision-making?"

---

[24] Warren C. Haggstrom, "On Eliminating Poverty," in Bloomberg and Schmandt, *Power, Poverty, and Urban Policy*, pp. 518–521.

[25] Arthur B. Shostak, "Old Problems and New Agencies: How Much Change?" in Bloomberg and Schmandt, *Power, Poverty, and Urban Policy*, pp. 73–104.

[26] Clegg, *The Administrator in Public Welfare*, p. 70.

In the first place, it is helpful to recognize the nature of the so-called enemies of welfare. There is little evidence to support the contention that there is an identifiable, organized group of people in this country who are devoted to keeping a portion of the population in a state of poverty. Those who oppose governmental action to alleviate poverty usually do so out of a failure to understand the causes and consequences of poverty. They not only have no objection to everyone being well-off; they are firmly convinced that anyone who works hard can obtain not only the necessities of life but many of its luxuries as well. The people who make up this group are not just the industrialists and upper classes. All indications obtainable from the survey research conducted in the late 1960s suggest that the working classes and the great, middle class accept this general view as well. The prevalence of our ignorance about poverty leads almost inescapably to the conclusion that simple majority rule on questions of welfare will mean that nothing is done about poverty.[27]

To make matters worse, the forces arrayed to do battle in support of programs to eliminate poverty are remarkably weak. The major professional organization of welfare workers, the National Association of Social Workers, has a decidedly nonpolitical orientation. It is a small organization that includes many untrained welfare workers in its ranks—workers whose appreciation of the problems of poverty is limited. It is oriented toward the status quo, and its major programs consist of selling the existing welfare effort to the public and of persuading Congress to allocate more money to existing programs.[28] Obviously, no real breakthrough in welfare policy should be expected from this source.

Compounding the lack of professional initiative, the workers in the welfare bureaucracies have extended their control over their clientele group to the extent that decision-making within the context of present programs is highly unresponsive to the needs of the poor.[29] The same conservative tendencies that prevent welfare professionals from being an effective force for change of welfare policy act to insure stability in their relationships with their clients. The welfare bureaucrats have been charged with using a variety of strategies to maintain this stability. They emphasize consolidation of both expertise and benefits into single agencies and making benefits conditional upon the use of their controlled expertise. They attempt to phrase political policy problems as purely technical problems that are amenable to their expertise, and to reach accommodations with political leaders that minimize change. They attempt to control

---

[27] Bloomberg and Schmandt, *Power, Poverty, and Urban Policy*, p. 14.

[28] Gilbert Y. Steiner, *Social Insecurity: The Politics of Welfare* (Chicago, 1966), pp. 148–153.

[29] Richard A. Cloward and Frances Fox Piven, "Welfare for Whom?" in *Urban Government*, ed. Edward C. Banfield, rev. ed. (New York, 1969), pp. 666–681.

clients by emphasizing their isolation from major social roles, making the award of benefits contingent upon individual case circumstances, and responding to client organizations with policies of containment, direction, and manipulation of benefits which are designed to discourage organizational activity. Finally, the bureaucracy engages in a type of political socialization of welfare recipients by using conditional benefits as rewards and punishments and by exercising its discretion in such a way as to increase feelings of inefficacy among the poor.

These bureaucratic strategies are not really conscious attempts to victimize the poor. Like the socialization efforts in public housing administration discussed in Chapter 12, they are attempts at organizational maintenance. They appear to be perfectly rational strategies to most welfare administrators in the absence of clearly defined welfare goals and of programs and policies designed to satisfy those goals. Organizational maintenance becomes a way to do the best they can with what they have, and administrators have undoubtedly convinced themselves that the long-run interests of the poor are best served by these strategies. Perhaps this is so, but the point is at least debatable.

This situation has particular significance because it leaves the welfare and antipoverty agencies without a constituency to serve as a base for its political operations.[30] Without such a constituency all indications point to a rocky road ahead for major innovative programs in dealing with poverty. At the very least, new programs will find it difficult to avoid leaning heavily upon some of the old, shop-worn assumptions about the nature of poverty and the poor. They must clearly contain the element of self-help and the idea that the poor can work their way out of poverty without major reallocation of the general resources of the American public.

There is, however, one alternative that has burst upon the welfare scene with the advent of the War on Poverty. That alternative is the breaking down of the barriers to political activity on the part of the poor themselves and the formation of a client-based constituency for welfare programs which could provide the political base for innovation. The Community Action Program of the War on Poverty calls for "maximum feasible participation" by the poor in the boards which govern CAPs. This program, more than any other single factor, has spurred the populist rhetoric of participatory democracy in the urban America of the 1960s.

The participation of the poor can be justified on a variety of grounds.[31] In the first place, participation has some value as a positive democratic end in itself. Participation of one kind or another, or at least a very real opportunity to participate, is an essential characteristic of democratic so-

---

[30] Haggstrom, "On Eliminating Poverty," p. 515.
[31] Warner Bloomberg, Jr. and Florence W. Rosenstock, "Who Can Activate the Poor?" in Bloomberg and Schmandt, *Power, Poverty, and Urban Policy*, pp. 315–316.

ciety. Then too, it may be possible for the poor to obtain more goods and services—a greater level of support—by virtue of the persuasive powers of their participation. Third, there is little doubt that the image of a concerned, civic-minded poor working hard to better their lot will attract more support from the public at large. To the extent that their participation is in any way successful, it can serve as useful therapy for alienation and can help to pave the way back into society for the impoverished. Finally, it is entirely possible that, because of their intimate association with the problems of poverty, the poor may well be able to make some substantive contributions toward the design of programs which will indeed abolish poverty.

Whether or not one judges the participation of the poor in CAPs to be a success or failure clearly depends upon the criteria one uses. However, almost every observer has recognized the problems inherent in the community action concept. It is the problem that was raised in Chapter 11 of this book with respect to participation and comprehensive planning.

> Community action was trying to promote both a new freedom of initiative and the mutual reinforcement of disciplined cooperation; to rationalize the planning of policy through the insights of social science, and yet make it more immediately responsive to the demands of those the policy was to serve; to assimilate the poor into the opportunity structure of American education, yet to emancipate schools from the middle class prejudices which often reflected honestly enough the structure's demands.[32]

Measured in terms of the development of a careful, rational strategy for dealing with poverty, those CAPs that enjoyed true participation of the poor are quite likely to have been least successful programmatically. Even if such crude measures of programmatic progress as the amount of money actually given to the poor are used, participation did not appear to improve the picture much. The Chicago CAP was one of the most successful in getting money to the poor, and this program was controlled almost exclusively by the regular governmental organization of Mayor Daley.[33] In most instances the bulk of CAP money was tied up in administrative expenses and planning costs in a manner that made traditional welfare administration appear efficient by comparison. To be sure, a significant number of administrators under the community concept were drawn from the poor themselves, but the total, short-run cash results for the poor were disappointing to the poor, the designers of the program, and especially to Congress.

---

[32] Peter Marris and Martin Rein, *Dilemmas of Social Reform: Poverty and Community Action in the United States* (New York, 1967), p. 226.

[33] Daniel P. Moynihan, *Maximum Feasible Misunderstanding* (New York, 1969), p. 145.

The character of the programs and their impact on the urban political environment have been the subjects of a great deal of debate. Opponents have pictured the CAP as a training ground for radicals. They have feared the kind of assault on the power structure which might be mounted once the poor were sufficiently organized to provide a base for political action. The history of some CAPs and the rhetoric of many community organizers did little to console the established holders of power. A careful study of the actual operation of CAPs reveals quite a different picture.[34] The programs involved giving power to the poor and an overt strategy of confrontation with the power structure in only a few communities. In half of the communities studied, the CAP chose to focus its attention on attempts to break the cycle of poverty by changing the poor. Even in the other half of the communities, where the programs paid some attention to problems of the system as well, the results were far from revolutionary. One-third of these programs focused on inadequate and uncoordinated services to the poor, one-third on changing current institutional practices, and one-third on broad community changes. Only this final one-sixth of the sample could in any sense be considered revolutionary. In spite of the rather benign form which the participation of the poor took for most urban governmental institutions, the public officials in enough cities were alarmed by the prospects of an independent body, controlled by the poor, operating in their city to force some changes in the program. The result was an amendment to the Economic Opportunity Act that guaranteed that one-third of the seats on a CAP board would go to governmental officials, one-third to the poor, and the remainder to the community at large. This change was supposed to render the CAP less dangerous to the establishment.

The exact nature and extent of the participation of the poor in welfare politics through CAPs is also the subject of some disagreement. Most observers agree that participation has not been widespread. Attempts to elect the representatives of the poor to governing boards were almost uniformly participatory disasters. The accumulated apathy and alienation of generations was difficult to overcome simply through the announcement of another governmental program.[35] Although it is clear that the quantity of participation has not been great, it is more difficult to consider the quality of participation. On the one hand, we find those who claim that the poor are educationally not qualified to deal with the problems of poverty.[36] Yet others have found that the representatives of the poor on CAP governing boards have become increasingly effective

---

[34] Howard W. Hallman, "The Community Action Program: An Interpretative Analysis," in Bloomberg and Schmandt, *Power, Poverty, and Urban Policy*, pp. 285–311.

[35] Krosney, *Beyond Welfare*, p. 127.

[36] Krosney, *Beyond Welfare*, p. 127.

with practice.[37] Of course, much depends upon how effectiveness is measured, but there does seem to be some evidence that the poor have been able to work within the institutional and political environment of the CAP and to produce some results.

In the absence of spectacular policy changes, it is easy to dismiss the results of participation as insignificant and to predict doom for such efforts in the future. Cloward and Piven feel that the entrenched bureaucracy will prove to be too strong for the poor to overcome:

> We see no evidence that government's involvement of the poor will generate a force for social change by nurturing their political capabilities or by activating them with the promise of benefits. Rather, governmental programs for the poor are likely to diminish whatever collective political vitality the poor still exhibit.[38]

Daniel Moynihan, President Nixon's advisor on urban affairs, carries this argument even further when he suggests that participation demonstrates clearly the absence of community and that the resultant conflict might well result in the end of both participation and democracy.[39]

It is easy to carry this argument too far, and Cloward, Piven, and Moynihan have overstated the deficiencies of participation by the poor in our welfare system just as the proponents of participation tend to overstate its benefits. There is a middle ground for participation and community action that appears to be far more functional from the sociological point of view. If, as an earlier portion of this discussion claimed, most CAPs have not adopted a strategy of direct confrontation and conflict, it is possible for many of them to work with other interests in the community using existing mechanisms of compromise to resolve conflicts and to change in some manner the way in which government deals with the problems of poverty. The result may be what Bloomberg and Rosenstock call the "community action model"—a type of community action which focuses on the vulnerable spots in the existing system and which is, therefore, quite successful.[40]

Other indirect benefits of Community Action Programs are no less important from a political point of view. Moynihan himself recognizes this when he points out:

> Very possibly, the most important long run impact of the community action programs of the 1960s will prove to have been the formation of an urban

---

[37] Hallman, "Community Action Program," p. 301.
[38] Cloward and Piven, "Welfare for Whom?" p. 618.
[39] Moynihan, *Maximum Feasible Misunderstanding*, pp. 163–164.
[40] Bloomberg and Rosenstock, "Who Can Activate the Poor?" p. 344.

Negro leadership echelon at just the time when Negro masses and other minorities were verging towards extensive commitments to urban politics.[41]

Any program that serves to encourage the formation of leadership positions in an unorganized group, or to increase the number of such positions in an underorganized group, most assuredly will have some important impact on policy. No matter how small the immediate policy gains and how low the level of the actual participation by the great bulk of the poor, the political game of welfare is no longer the same. These changes have had an impact on welfare policy in the sixties, and they will continue to have an impact in the future.

The final important characteristic of the politics of welfare is their intergovernmental nature. As the interest of mayors in the poverty program indicates, the policy decisions made in the welfare program are of vital importance to the politics of the city. However, in most cases the local government agencies that administer welfare programs are at the county level and are rarely linked to the mayors of major cities in any meaningful way. Specific welfare programs are designed at the state level and, in the case of categorical aid programs, must be within federal guidelines. The result of the involvement of so many levels of government in welfare policy is a lack of coordination both within the welfare establishment and between welfare agencies and other governmental programs. This confusion also permits each level in the welfare establishment to blame someone else for the shortcomings of the program. Local administrators claim that the major faults in welfare policy can be traced to the federal bureaucrats, while those at other levels claim that the inefficiency of local administrators created the major difficulty. While this fragmentation does create multiple points of access for those who would change policy, it also serves to make clear responsibility for policy decisions next to impossible.

THE REFORM OF WELFARE. The War on Poverty and the emphasis on participation have obviously changed the welfare system to a degree, but as the 1960s drew to a close it was all too clear to most observers that the welfare system was itself essentially the same system that had emerged from the 1930s, and that this system was still not doing the job. The result has been a series of proposals for sweeping reforms. President Nixon's revision of the welfare system which he proposed to the nation on March 8, 1969, was perhaps one of the more modest of these suggested reforms, but it was designed to significantly alter some of the worst aspects of the present system. The attempt to put a federal "floor" under each of the

---

[41] Moynihan, *Maximum Feasible Misunderstanding*, p. 129.

categorical aid programs would guarantee minimum levels of welfare payments and would introduce greater equality of benefits among the states. Any increase in benefits that might result in the poorer states because of such a floor must be viewed as an improvement over the present state of affairs in simple, human terms. It also should serve to meet the criticism frequently voiced in northern, urban areas that the poor are flocking to these areas from the rural South in order to enjoy the greater welfare benefits available. This criticism has been particularly loud since the United States Supreme Court voided residency requirements that delay the receipt of public assistance under categorical programs. The criticism may be without foundation, but benefit floors help to remove it as a possibility.

Perhaps the most radical element of the president's proposal was the elimination of AFDC and the substitution of a Family Assistance program which appears to have a broader basis of eligibility. The biggest element of change is centered upon the relationship between work and welfare. Present programs reduce welfare benefits by the amount earned by wage earners so that it frequently does not pay to work. Under the new program, it would always pay to work in the sense that a portion of the income increment could always be maintained by the worker, and welfare benefits would be gradually scaled down as the worker worked his way back into society. These additional benefits are not without cost, however, since all welfare recipients who are physically and mentally able to work including the mothers of school-age children are required to seek employment and/or job training in order to maintain their eligibility. This obviously retains the old assumptions that only those who are willing to work are deserving of subsistence payments and that such payments are appropriate devices for motivating people to work.

In order that the Family Assistance program might work, several changes were proposed for other programs as well. All federally assisted job-training programs were to be consolidated and returned to state and local governments for administration. This was designed to reduce the duplication, inefficiency, and red tape that characterized the traditional programs. In addition, the President asked for a central job bank that would maintain data on jobs available and on the work force in order to insure that the poor were being trained for existing jobs. A system of day care centers, operated under many of the principles which characterized Operation Head Start, were proposed to enable female heads of household and other mothers to participate in job training and to enter the labor force.

Finally, the President proposed to change the Office of Economic Opportunity into a research and development agency that would experiment with new programs and approaches to poverty. Some of the most perceptive commentators have viewed innovation and experimentation as the strongest argument in favor of Community Action Programs in the War on Poverty.[42] The proposed changes in OEO might well maximize this capability of CAPs and similar agencies at the local level.

For many students of the problems of poverty, proposals like those of President Nixon represent improvement but simply do not go far enough.[43] They significantly reduce eligibility requirements, but they do not eliminate them entirely. The assumption that those who refuse to work *must* be relegated to an outcast's role is at least open to question. The further assumption that the act of societal rejection will serve to motivate the poor to accept work as an appropriate solution to their problems is seriously naïve in the light of our present understanding of the psychology of motivation. The absence of eligibility requirements implies some concept of a guaranteed annual income which is available to everyone as a matter of right. While the idea was radical when it was first proposed, it appears to be less and less so to careful observers of the problems of poverty in both liberal and conservative camps.

A second shortcoming of the proposed reforms, including in many instances those for a guaranteed annual income, is that they are tied too closely to the subsistence concept. The definition of poverty suggested earlier in this chapter indicated that the poor did not possess sufficient resources to participate in the economic life of society. They may be supported at the subsistence level and still lack adequate resources. In modern American urban society a man must have cash for down payments and deposits and access to credit before he can participate fully in economic life. These assets are denied the poor or are rendered so expensive as to make their full utilization impossible. They are not provided by a system of subsistence support that is aimed only at adequate food, clothing, and shelter. It is undoubtedly possible that a poor man, supported at the subsistence level and adequately trained for significant employment in the labor force, could work his way into a position in which such benefits were available. However, the gap between subsistence and full participation is great, and the task would take a long time. Thomas Gladwin has proposed a program of low-interest loans like those that have frequently been made available to the middle class as a workable solution to this problem.[44] The proposal is attractive enough to merit further consideration.

---

[42] Marris and Rein, *Dilemmas of Social Reform*, p. 232.
[43] See for example Gladwin, *Poverty U.S.A.*, p. 72.
[44] Gladwin, *Poverty U.S.A.*, p. 73.

Public Health in an Urban Environment

THE NATURE OF PUBLIC HEALTH. One problem that has been particularly
difficult for urban man has been the tendency of disease to spread more
rapidly with increased population densities. Were it not for the development of preventive measures, mankind would have long ago killed itself
off through urbanization. As a matter of fact, the verdict is not yet in,
and there are many ecologists who predict that we may yet achieve that
end. Public health problems are those that cannot be solved by individual
action,[45] and it is clear that the number of these problems increases significantly with urbanization. Urban man has a biological as well as a
sociological interdependence.

A number of specific local health programs are devoted to protecting
the urban dweller.[46] Programs dealing with vital statistics provide data on
births and deaths, individuals with tuberculosis, leprosy, and other diseases, the prevalence and the degree of disability incurred in certain
diseases, morbidity, the availability of health personnel and facilities,
and health needs and services. This information provides public health
officials with a means of evaluating the status of the health of the community, the kinds of problems which exist, and the ability of existing
resources to deal with those problems. In addition to collecting data,
public health officials also conduct positive environmental health programs
that include water protection, waste disposal, air pollution control, radia-
tion control, milk and food sanitation, vector (animal and insect) control,
housing and city planning efforts, and occupational health problems. Some
of the most pressing urban problems are centered on the environmental
health area. There seems to be little doubt in the mind of layman and
expert alike that if air pollution continues unabated our cities will soon
be uninhabitable. The air will be so foul that we will no longer be able
to breathe it. The massive pollution of our lakes and streams with human
and industrial waste has not only ruined the water from an aesthetic
point of view, it has also contributed greatly to an already alarming
shortage of potable water to support a highly concentrated population.

The list of public health functions also includes programs concerning
communicable disease control, maternal and child health, adult health,
chronic diseases such as arthritis, rheumatism, mental illness, cardiovascular-
renal disease, cancer and diabetes, laboratory services, and general health
education. Many of these programs, like those which focus on communicable diseases, have been in effect for years without engendering much

---

[45] Barbara M. Osborn, *Introduction to Community Health* (Boston, 1964), p. 6.
[46] Osborn, *Introduction to Community Health*, pp. 137–170.

controversy. However, programs that focus more on the diagnosis and treatment of individual health problems seem to many to suggest some type of socialized medicine and to present a threat to the private practice of medicine. The opponents of diagnosis and treatment programs suggest that the problems they are directed toward can be met through individual action and are, therefore, private rather than public in nature. They view such public practice as competitive with the private practice of medicine, and fear the results. However, this position fails to take into account the fact that the private practice of medicine has failed to reach large numbers of people and that many chronic illnesses go undiagnosed and untreated. The work that public health officials have done in the diagnosis and treatment of tuberculosis, for example, has been accepted by the general public as appropriate and has supplemented rather than supplanted private efforts in this area. There would seem to be no reason why other chronic diseases might not be handled in the same way.

HEALTH AND POVERTY. There is little doubt that many of the most serious public health problems are closely related to poverty in our cities.[47] The poor suffer greater and more frequent health problems than do those who are more fortunate. This problem is particularly acute in the cities where congestion and slums make it possible for the poor to receive less treatment than their rural counterparts, even though medical care is relatively more available to them. The efforts of public health sanitarians, visiting nurses, and a variety of clinics have been inadequate to the tremendous tasks that faced them. These programs have been seriously understaffed and underfinanced.

Other programs of aid to the indigent and medically indigent have partially relieved the problem. Clearly such categorical programs of public assistance as Aid to the Blind and Aid to the Permanently and Totally Disabled serve to provide some medical assistance by their very nature. Old Age Assistance programs also provide some medical care funds to the aged poor who are even more likely to suffer health problems than their more youthful fellows in poverty. In addition, general assistance payments that can be used for medical purposes are available from the states. Frequently, the medical expenses of the poor are paid directly through welfare funds under these general assistance programs. Both private and government hospitals provide some care for the poor at no cost or reduced cost in outpatient clinics, poor wards, or entire hospitals for the poor. In spite of all of these efforts, the health problems of the poor remain. A variety of factors contribute to these failures. Eligibility requirements and

---

[47] The section draws heavily from Milton I. Roemer and Arnold I. Kisch, "Health, Poverty, and the Medical Mainstream," in Bloomberg and Schmandt, *Power, Poverty, and Urban Policy*, pp. 181–202.

the demeaning red tape of welfare applications reduce the number of individuals who wish to battle the system to enjoy its benefits. Besides, in most instances there are few doctors, treatment facilities, or even welfare offices within reach of the poor. Finally, lack of education and apathy appear to contribute as much as lack of money to the poor health of those in poverty. Many do not understand the need for physical examinations or the early treatment of disease, and many others have accepted the "fact" that they are doomed to die an early death.

The period 1964–1966 was characterized by a significant number of new programs designed to improve the quality of medical care received by the poor. The War on Poverty authorized the operation of neighborhood health centers under the Office of Economic Opportunity, designed to bring health care closer to the poor. However, few of these centers have been established. Medicare was developed in 1965 to provide an insurance program as part of the Social Security system which would establish health benefits for those of the aged population who qualified for Old Age and Survivors' Insurance payments. In addition to this, the Medicaid provisions of the same bill attempted to revitalize state medical aid programs through expanded federal grants, and to extend those state programs to the poor and medically indigent as well as the aged. The Medicaid program has been almost too successful. The amount of money expended has astonished state and federal officials alike, and some programs are in both financial and political hot water. Although individual doctors have been reported to have received large sums of money under Medicaid, there is no indication that doctors have brought the plan to the brink of ruin by overcharging. As a matter of fact, investigations have proven that the per case cost of Medicaid treatments have not been particularly high. The problem of medical indigence or the inability to pay for adequate medical treatment is obviously bigger than government had foreseen.

Finally, the federal government established grant programs to aid in the construction and operation of neighborhood diagnostic centers for heart disease, cancer, and stroke in 1965, and, in 1966, consolidated a variety of grant programs under the Comprehensive Health Planning and Public Health Service Amendments that were designed to improve coordination and planning in the public health field. Both of these programs could have a strong impact on the quality and availability of health services for the poor.

THE POLITICS OF PUBLIC HEALTH. The politics of public health are not unlike those of welfare.[48] Although a vast number of public and private

---

[48] For an excellent discussion of the issues in a particular program context see Robert H. Connery, et al., *The Politics of Mental Health* (New York, 1968).

agencies are concerned with health problems, there is really no single constituency that can serve as sponsor for community health programs. The professional groups are fragmented and concerned with narrow, parochial interests of the organizational maintenance variety, and there are certainly few, if any, clientele groups that can serve to exert pressure on policy-makers. The clientele of public health agencies seem able to exert some political influence only to the degree that they can make common cause with the poor. Since the two groups frequently coincide, it is natural that many pressures for change in public health policies are coming from organizations of the poor. However, an emphasis on community-based organizations for dealing with health problems and on citizen participation has achieved less in the public health area than in any other policy area. The end result is that government officials have greater freedom in this area because of the general lack of public and group interest.[49]

There are also serious problems in the intergovernmental coordination of policy which are as relevant to public health as they are to welfare. Once more, the basic administrative unit is likely to be the county. As is true in the case of welfare, an area-wide public health policy that serves the needs of the county may be a long way from the kind of policy which serves the needs of the impoverished and ill in the central city. It is also clear that when federal, state, local, and private programs for public health and community health in general exist side by side in an urban environment the biggest single problem is once again likely to be one of coordination.

Suggested Readings

Advisory Commission on Intergovernmental Relations. *Intergovernmental Relations in the Poverty Program*. Washington, 1966.

Bloomberg, Warner, Jr., and Schmandt, Henry J., eds. *Power, Poverty, and Urban Policy*. Beverly Hills, 1968.

Clegg, Reed K. *The Administrator in Public Welfare*. Springfield, Ill., 1966.

Connery, Robert H., et al. *The Politics of Mental Health*. New York, 1968.

Gladwin, Thomas. *Poverty U.S.A.* Boston, 1967.

Hanlon, John J. *Principles of Public Health Administration*. 5th ed. St. Louis, 1969.

Harrington, Michael. *The Other America: Poverty in the United States*. New York, 1962.

Krosney, Herbert. *Beyond Welfare: Poverty in the Supercity*. New York, 1966.

---

[49] Connery, et al., *The Politics of Mental Health*, p. 566.

Marris, Peter, and Rein, Martin. *Dilemmas of Social Reform: Poverty and Community Action in the United States.* New York, 1967.

Moynihan, Daniel P. *Maximum Feasible Misunderstanding.* New York, 1969.

Osborn, Barbara M. *Introduction to Community Health.* Boston, 1964.

Seligman, Ben B. *Permanent Poverty.* Chicago, 1968.

Steiner, Gilbert Y. *Social Insecurity: The Politics of Welfare.* Chicago, 1966.

chapter **15**
Urban Education

([Many of the problems facing urban areas—integration, poverty, juvenile crime, large expenditures for public protection, extensive public assistance—focus on education. Perhaps we expect too much from our school systems, but they offer the only practical hope at the present time for long-range solutions to the most pressing social and economic problems facing urban society.[1]

Politics, Schools, and the City

A close examination of most of the traditional textbooks in urban politics or municipal government would reveal that the educational process is almost completely ignored. Even some of the newer texts in the field avoid this explosive subject. This omission has traditionally been justified on two grounds. In the first place, most of our public schools are operated by special purpose districts that are separate units of government, only remotely connected with the traditional institutions of municipal government. The second justification is clearly more fundamental and forms the basis for the first:

> The dogma has evolved that public education must occupy a position above the political conflicts that are waged over other public services, and educators

---

[1] T. Edward Hollander, "Fiscal Independence and Large City School Systems," in *Educating an Urban Population*, ed. Marilyn Gittell (Beverly Hills, 1967), p. 103.

are supposed to abide by the maxim that politics and education do not mix. In the eyes of the public, schools and their operations are removed, or should be removed, from the arenas where other governmental decisions are made.[2]

The logic of the argument was inescapable, given the major premises. Schools were considered to be apolitical, therefore, books about politics need not concern themselves with education. Furthermore, since the schools maintain their apolitical purity by separating themselves from the traditional institutions of municipal government, those books dealing with municipal government could also safely ignore education.

The fact that a chapter dealing with the subject appears in this particular textbook clearly demonstrates that there are at least some who do not accept the major premises of the traditional argument. As earlier chapters in this book have demonstrated, there is a strong tendency to confuse the particular form of partisan contests for power with the essence of politics. In education as in other public policy areas, interests attempt to control or influence the decision-making process so that they might better enjoy the distribution of rewards and deprivations in the system. The fact that the decisions are complex and that some of the contestants for power are technically "better qualified" to understand the complexities of policy which are involved does not make the contest any less real, nor does it render the contest inappropriate in what passes for a free and democratic society. Slowly but surely both educators and the public at large are beginning to realize that educational policy-making is highly political.

Even if one could not justify a discussion of urban education by virtue of its inherent political character, it could be supported on the basis of the close relationship between education and the other vital urban policy areas outlined in the opening statement of this chapter. No matter what the urban problem, it is impossible to discuss either its cause or its remedies without focusing a great deal of attention on the schools. In Chapter 1, we saw that some sociologists connected the urbanization process with the decline of the family as a relevant unit of socialization and social control. To the extent that this connection is valid, it is possible to trace a concomitant shift of socialization responsibilities to the schools. In addition, the schools have also been given the primary responsibility for insuring that future generations are adequately equipped to face the challenge of seeking employment in a world that is becoming increasingly complex and demanding from a technological point of view. The schools are charged both with vocational training and with the preparation of a sufficient number of individuals for the type of higher

---

[2] Nicholas A. Masters, Robert H. Salisbury, and Thomas H. Eliot, *State Politics and the Public Schools* (New York, 1964), p. 3.

education which tradition, if not necessity, requires in such a complex world.

Reasoning of this sort has led many to conclude that the schools have an obligation to community development as well as to individual development.[3] Richard C. Lonsdale has listed four contributions the schools can make to metropolitan area development. These contributions are certainly appropriate in nonmetropolitan urban areas as well:

1. The provision of information to adults and children with respect to the metropolitan (urban) area
2. The development of attitudes of metropolitan (urban) unity
3. The organization of and participation in metropolitan area study groups
4. The provision of assistance to people in formulating metropolitan (urban) goals

However, Lonsdale is quick to point out that the schools cannot fulfill this obligation and make these contributions in the face of the traditional isolation of the schools from community life. Obviously the involvement of the schools in community life would have first priority in such programs.

The metropolitan environment that was described in Chapter 4 creates some special problems for the urban schools and provides a sound basis for Lonsdale's emphasis on metropolitan development.[4] A variety of financial problems have beset the schools of most of the central cities of our metropolitan areas. The movement of the more wealthy, better-educated citizens, of commerce, and of industry to the suburbs has, to a degree at least, eroded the available tax base for the schools. To complicate the problem, the culture of poverty which is increasingly characteristic of our major cities creates an environment in which the costs of educating a child to meet the challenge of urban living are significantly higher than the costs of a comparable task in the suburbs. Equal facilities and per capita expenditures do not produce equal results. There is a third level of metropolitan educational disparity which renders simplistic central city versus suburbs analyses unsatisfactory. In terms of financial capacity "differences among suburban areas . . . are of the same order of magnitude as the differences between central city and suburb."[5] While most experts today are willing to rely upon the redistributive effects of

---

[3] Richard C. Lonsdale, *The School's Role in Metropolitan Area Development* (Syracuse, N.Y., 1960), pp. 38–50.

[4] See Alan K. Campbell and Philip Meranto, "The Metropolitan Education Dilemma: Matching Resources to Needs," in Gittell, *Educating an Urban Population*, pp. 15–36.

[5] Seymour Sacks and David C. Ranney, "Suburban Education: A Fiscal Analysis," in Gittell, *Educating an Urban Population*, pp. 75–76.

TABLE 15–1: Percentage of Superintendents and School Board Members
Exposed to Specified Pressures

Pressure	Superintendents (N = 105)	School Board Members (N = 508)
1. Demands that the schools should place more emphasis on the three R's.	59	53
2. Demands that the schools should teach more courses and subjects.	64	47
3. Protests about the use of particular textbooks.	19	19
4. Protests about the views expressed by teachers.	49	41
5. Demands that teachers should express certain views.	13	12
6. Protesting school tax increases or bond proposals.	73	70
7. Demanding more money for the general school program.	66	52
8. Protesting the introduction of new services (in addition to academic instruction) for pupils	39	35
9. Demanding the introduction of new services (in addition to academic instruction) for pupils	63	49
10. Demands that school contracts be given to certain firms.	46	24
11. Demands that teachers be appointed or dismissed for reasons other than competence.	46	24
12. Demanding the introduction of new teaching methods.	29	35
13. Protesting the introduction of new teaching methods.	43	28
14. Demanding that greater emphasis be placed on the athletic program.	58	52
15. Demanding that less emphasis be placed on the athletic program.	40	38

SOURCE: Neal Gross, *Who Runs Our Schools?* (New York, 1958), p. 50. Reprinted by permission of John Wiley & Sons, Inc.

state and federal aid to overcome these disparities, it is clear that there will have to be a change in the political climate of the metropolis before sufficient influence can be amassed to convince state legislatures and Congress to alter their distribution formulas. It is in encouraging this change of political climate that the contributions of politically aware school systems suggested by Lonsdale can be most valuable.

The successes and failures of the schools as agents of socialization and as vocational educators can either make or break urban society. All else seems to hang upon the ability of the schools to respond to current needs. Given our present assumptions as to appropriate norms of behavior and as to appropriate levels of training for employment, and given the absence of alternative institutions willing and able to share the burden, the schools are "it." This is what Hollander meant by expecting too much of our schools. It is obviously impossible to ignore the process by which decisions are made in such an important urban institution. Who sets the priorities and goals? Who decides which behavioral norms to enforce? What criteria are used in making these decisions? All of these questions are crucial.

TABLE 15–2: Percentage of Superintendents and School Board Members
Who Said They Were Exposed to Pressures from the
Specified Individuals and Groups

Individuals or Groups Who Exert Pressure	Superintendents (N = 105)	School Board Members (N = 508)
1. Parents or PTA	92	74
2. Individual school board members	75	51
3. Teachers	65	44
4. Taxpayers' association	49	31
5. Town finance committee or city council	48	38
6. Politicians	46	29
7. Business or commercial organizations	45	19
8. Individuals influential for economic reasons	44	25
9. Personal friends	37	37
10. The press	36	19
11. Old-line families	30	26
12. Church or religious groups	28	18
13. Veterans organizations	27	10
14. Labor unions	27	5
15. Chamber of commerce	23	5
16. Service clubs	20	11
17. Fraternal organizations	13	9
18. Farm organizations	12	4
19. Welfare organizations	3	1

SOURCE: Neal Gross, *Who Runs Our Schools?* (New York, 1958), p. 51. Reprinted by permission of John Wiley & Sons, Inc.

Group Politics and the Schools

The inherently political nature of local educational decision-making is clearly revealed in an examination of attempts by various groups to affect policy outcomes.[6] Tables 15–1 and 15–2 demonstrate the nature of pressures exerted upon school decision-makers and the sources of such pressures. With such a broad spectrum of issues and with such a wide variety of interest groups, school officials inevitably experience some cross-pressures. That is to say, the officials are presented with competing demands for contradictory policies. Even the same general group, parents for example, may embody a variety of interests and present competing demands. Such pressures are not usually welcomed by either administrators or the school board and are frequently viewed as an interference with the orderly process of running the schools in the best interests of the entire community. They must also result in some anxiety and insecurity for even the most well-adjusted administrator or board member.

---

[6] Neal Gross, "Who Applies What Kind of Pressures?" in *Governing Education*, ed. Alan Rosenthal (Garden City, N.Y., 1969), pp. 86–104.

School officials react to group pressures in different ways. If they do, in fact, view them as an interference, they may attempt to turn them aside or ignore them altogether. This possibility, which appears to be most attractive to the "nonpolitical" administrator, will be discussed in greater detail later in the chapter. Another possibility is that school officials will recognize competing group pressures as an inevitable result of a pluralistic and heterogeneous environment and will attempt to perform a conflict resolution function as part of their policy-making activities. In order to perform such a function, officials would have to take steps to insure that all points of view are represented and articulated, that the vocal leaders of groups are adequately representative of their groups, that all participants are willing to listen to the views of others, that there exists sufficient motivation and good will for consensus, that the school staff is adequately prepared to participate in meetings with the groups, and that the objectives sought by the various groups are in fact attainable.[7]

The most interesting aspect of pressure group activity in school politics is the frequency with which highly articulate and active groups fail to significantly affect school policy. As David Rogers has pointed out in his highly critical study of New York school politics, many protest groups have failed because of their inability to marshal active support from other groups including big business, the administration of the city government, universities, foundations, and labor.[8] The data reported in Table 15–2 tend to bear Rogers out since fewer than 50 percent of the school superintendents and an even smaller percentage of the board members covered in that study reported contacts from such groups. The reputation enjoyed by these groups for political clout and general effectiveness as pressure groups clearly indicates that they would be impressive allies in an attempt to influence school decisions. However, there are indications that these groups do not consider school issues worthy of their involvement. Most of them have yet to be shown what they have to gain by participating in school politics and by using their scarce political resources in influencing school policies.

PARENTS AND SCHOOL POLICY. Educational policy questions are likely to be of prime importance to parents of school-age children. It is hardly surprising that Table 15–2 reports that over 90 percent of the superintendents studied received direct contact from parents and parents' groups and over 70 percent of the school board members received similar contact. What seems puzzling about these figures is that 100 percent of the school officials surveyed did not report some sort of parental contact on school

---

[7] Bert E. Swanson, "Two Strategies For Power," in Rosenthal, Governing Education, pp. 199–224.
[8] David Rogers, 110 Livingston Street (New York, 1968), pp. 494–497.

policy. It is difficult to believe that there is a school district anywhere in this country that has experienced absolutely no organized parental pressures directed toward changing school policies of one kind or another. However, the pervasiveness of parental concern should not be construed as indicating that all or even most parents attempt to influence school policy, or that those who attempt to influence policy usually do so in a well-organized and concerted effort. The most careful study available of parental participation indicates that less than 16 percent of the parents in a given district are even involved enough in school politics to attend board meetings.[9] Even this minimal level of attention on the part of parents is not constant. Attendance at board meetings ebbs and flows with the presence or absence of policy issues which appeal to parents; most meetings are sparsely attended. The fact remains that parents constitute the largest single potential interest group in school politics, and if their attention can be focused on a common interest they can exert a massive amount of influence over policy.

Any discussion of school policy which ignored the existence of the one continuing group which encourages parental participation in school policy would be incomplete. The Parent-Teacher Association or its equivalent is undeniably involved in school politics. There is little evidence to indicate that this organization frequently initiates or vetoes policies that are ultimately considered by superintendents and school boards. It attempts to bring parents and teachers together on the basis of their common interest in providing the best possible education for the children of the community. At worst such organizations involve parents and teachers in minor fund-raising activities to support peripheral school programs. Most frequently, the PTA operates as an adjunct of the school administration and the board of education and serves to place the stamp of legitimacy on policy decisions and to assist in selling these decisions to the community at large. There are, of course, occasions on which the PTA presents issues to the board and the superintendent for their consideration, but these are the exception rather than the rule.

TEACHERS AND SCHOOL POLICY. Teachers and their professional organizations do not seem to be very significant in formulating school policy.[10] The impact of teachers is greatest in determining their own salaries. While influence in this area may not be of great importance in terms of the whole fabric of educational policy, it achieves special significance when the taxpayer realizes that these salaries represent the largest chunk of direct

---

[9] Basil G. Zimmer and Amos H. Hawley, *Metropolitan Area Schools: Resistance to District Reorganization* (Beverly Hills, 1968), p. 292.

[10] Alan Rosenthal, "Pedagogues and Power: A Descriptive Survey," in Gittell, *Educating an Urban Population*, pp. 185–204.

instructional costs and are probably instrumental in determining the size of his tax bill. There is some indication that teachers, especially those who are unionized, have a desire to become more actively involved in the decision-making process. They appear to desire major participation in decisions governing salaries and curriculum and appear to be satisfied with a less important role in the areas of school organization and personnel.

INFORMAL POWER STRUCTURES. There are those who claim that the policies of the schools are set by a few individuals who occupy top positions in an informal power structure and that formal officials are often used to legitimate informal decisions.[11] Such claims are largely the result of oversimplified extrapolations from the power elite theories explained in Chapter 6. In the absence of clear empirical support for this position, it appears to be accepted as a matter of faith. In fact, the empirical studies that attempt to describe the operation of politics in our school systems offer a different picture, as we shall see later. However, to recall an argument presented in Chapter 6, the data do not indicate that there are no communities in which school politics are dominated by an informal elite. All we can say at this point is that there is no indication that such domination is the usual pattern of school politics.

School Boards and Policy

If you were to ask average citizens who was responsible for establishing school policy in their community, those able to answer at all would probably point to the school board. For those who place heavy emphasis on statutory job descriptions and on institutional arrangements, it is obvious that the school board is charged with making educational policy, just as the city council has the policy-making responsibility for more general governmental concerns. This simple view is no more appropriate here than it was in our earlier examination of municipal governments and their structure.

> The fact that any sharp dichotomy between policy and administration is unreal makes it all the more difficult to implement the notion that the board should function in a purely policy-making or quasi-legislative capacity and keep itself aloof from the administrative processes that give full meaning to programs, policies, and standards. The very complexity and elusiveness of this question underlines a significant need for rethinking and restating the respective responsibilities of the . . . Board and its general superintendent.[12]

---

[11] Ralph B. Kimbrough, "An Informal Arrangement for Influence over Basic Policy," in Rosenthal, *Governing Education*, pp. 105–136.
[12] Joseph Pois, "The Board and the General Superintendent," in Rosenthal, *Governing Education*, pp. 427–454.

Despite the obvious complexity of the question, it is possible to make some general statements about the role school boards play in the making of policy.

For some observers, the social characteristics of school board members have provided an important clue as to the role these members might play in the making of policy and as to the kind of policies they might favor.[13] Most school board members are selected from among the socially and economically advantaged. The business and professional communities are disproportionately represented on almost all school boards. This is particularly so where members are directly elected. Where the board is appointed by the mayor, there is a greater tendency to balance the members according to the characteristics of the general electorate, since this is frequently viewed as a productive political tactic for the mayor. However, nonpartisanship, at-large elections, and elections that are separate from those conducted for other local offices all contribute to a low level of interest and a low turnout. The process works here as it was described in Chapter 5. It tends to benefit the higher social and economic groups in the community who turn out in greater numbers. These people tend to vote for candidates who most nearly reflect their own values and prejudices. To make the process even more heavily loaded in favor of these groups, slate-making and other quasi-partisan activity have had a tendency to exclude all but the most "acceptable" of the representatives of low-income and low-status groups and, in most cases, totally exclude such representation. To many people, the dominance of the school board by members of a formal socioeconomic elite is no better than the kind of informal dominance discussed earlier in this chapter. However, it is important to ask whether such dominance makes any real difference in the policy decisions that the board reaches. The results of empirical studies are mixed, and there is no unambiguous link between the social characteristics of school board members and their performance of their roles as board members.[14]

The most significant finding with respect to the role performance of school boards centers upon their general abdication of representational roles in favor of roles which legitimate decisions made elsewhere.[15] These decisions originate not with an informal elite as the power structure theorists would have us believe, but with the formal, professional staff of the school system which is personified by the superintendent. Figure 15–1 demonstrates the process by which this abdication of representational roles

---

[13] Roscoe C. Martin, "School Government," in Rosenthal, *Governing Education*, pp. 260–290.

[14] Norman D. Kerr, "The School Board as an Agency of Legitimation," in Rosenthal, *Governing Education*, p. 137.

[15] See Kerr, "The School Board," pp. 137–172.

Figure 15–1:

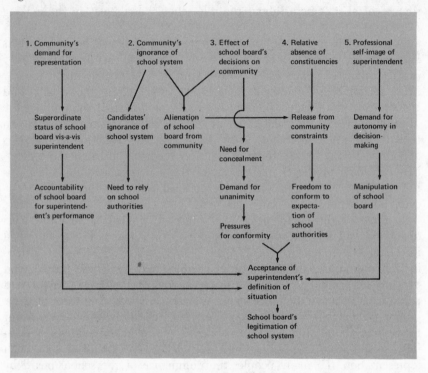

SOURCE: Norman D. Kerr, "The School Board as an Agency of Legitimation," *Sociology of Education* 38 (1964): 58. Reprinted by permission of the author and the American Sociological Association.

takes place. Nowhere is the mystique of professionalism more powerful than in school policy. Since few members of the board bring with them a command of the basic policy issues which face public education, the board is dependent upon the superintendent to define its roles for it. The general apathy and inattention of the public further alienate the board and deprive it of any real sense of constituency. Some of us who have approached school board members as parents and voters have found them truly disturbed by the thought that they had any real obligation to represent the people who had voted for them.

Two of the ways in which board members can insulate themselves from the increasingly unwelcome attention of those who would demand a constituency relationship are concealment and conflict avoidance.[16] Concealment can best be achieved through the device of the unanimous vote.

---

[16] Arthur Vidich and Joseph Bensman, *Small Town in Mass Society* (Princeton, 1958), pp. 171–197.

Board members iron out their disagreements prior to regular meetings and are able to present a united front to the public in open meetings. All actions become board actions rather than those of individual representatives. Boards achieve conflict avoidance by simply refusing to recognize the legitimacy of public challenges to school policy or, in extreme cases, by refusing to admit that the challenges even exist. The emphasis is on consensus in the community as well as consensus on the board. Such board meetings bring to mind Voltaire's Dr. Pangloss in *Candide* who persisted in claiming that this is "the best of all possible worlds."

If Norman Kerr is correct in his suggestion that candidates for positions on school boards know very little about the important issues and have a very vague concept of the role of a board member, then it is quite obvious that someone must socialize new board members. As Kerr points out, this function is performed admirably by the superintendent of schools and old board members. The major emphasis is placed upon conformity to established patterns of legitimation rather than upon representational roles.[17] The board becomes particularly dependent upon the superintendent, and outside criticism tends to have the effect of forcing the board and the superintendent together in order to present a united front against those who would challenge the sanctity of the public schools.[18]

Like most generalizations, this view of the school board admits to many exceptions. There are obviously some issues of such public importance that even a consensus-oriented board with no conception of representative roles cannot successfully ignore those interests that would affect policy. There are also some school boards that are more sensitive to their representational responsibilities and less dependent upon the superintendent than others. The major point is that most school boards usually do not play an active role in the formulation of school policies.

Domination by Professional Staff

The superintendent of schools and his professional staff are, therefore, the crucial decision-making agencies. Nearly every study of school policy has found these professionals at the heart of the decision-making process. In fact, the common description of educational subsystems is that they are "highly centralized, bureaucratic systems insulated from the public." [19] Many are quite satisfied with this state of affairs. Any attempt to challenge the dominance of the professionals is met either with the cry of

---

[17] Kerr, "The School Board," pp. 152–163.
[18] Pois, "The Board," p. 432.
[19] Marilyn Gittell and T. Edward Hollander, *Six Urban School Districts* (New York, 1968), p. 196.

"politics" or with the claim that the important process of setting educational policy is too complex to trust to inexpert laymen.

The first of these charges is quite obviously true. Any attempt to democratize the educational decision-making process is clearly political. But if the understanding of politics used throughout this book and emphasized at the beginning of this chapter is at all accurate, the decisions of administrators are equally political. The charge of inexpertise is, however, more serious. There is no doubt that even the most interested citizens know little about education. Most of us have some vague and highly inaccurate recollections of the process we experienced as children, and we use this as the pattern by which we judge the quality of the education our children are receiving. In education as in other public policy areas, the specialization that accompanies urbanization is taking its toll in terms of the ability of the average citizen to make intelligent judgments about the performance of his public servants.

The critics of professional dominance in education use the same sort of reasoning that is used in other policy areas to justify some minimal level of meaningful participation by the public in the decision-making process. Inexpertise with respect to specific techniques and processes does not prevent the average citizen from stating general preferences as to the goals toward which the professionals should be working. Just as one does not have to be an automotive engineer to know whether or not he is satisfied with the way in which his automobile meets his needs, a citizen does not have to have a professional degree in education in order to be able to intelligently express his satisfaction or dissatisfaction with the products of the public schools. The fact that many of the products of our urban school systems are unable to take their place as productive members of society and are unable to enjoy all of the benefits of society stands, for many critics of the schools, as a ringing indictment of the policies which the professionals have been following.

Most of the highly critical studies of decision-making in public education have focused on the inability or unwillingness of the dominant professionals to act as agents of innovation and change.[20] What is most impressive about much of this criticism is that it shifts its focus in such a way as to be utterly confusing to any policy-maker who attempts to take it seriously. After building a strong case indicting bureaucracy and professional dominance in educational policy-making, some critics trace the absence of innovative policies to the participation of groups of parents and teachers who are interested in the status quo, and who tend to counter

---

[20] See Gittell and Hollander, *Six Urban School Districts;* Rogers, *110 Livingston Street;* Marilyn Gittell, "Decision-Making in the Schools," in Gittell, *Educating an Urban Population,* pp. 205–239; and Peter Schrag, *Village School Downtown* (Boston, 1967).

the strong demands for change made by other groups in the community. The school board and the professional administrators end up being roundly criticized for vacillating and compromising on important policy questions.[21]

As the earlier discussions of interest groups and school boards indicated, the politics of school policy-making depend upon the kinds of issues raised and the importance of these issues to various segments of the community. Under normal circumstances the superintendent and his professional staff are the dominant forces. Neither the board nor any group in the community choose to challenge the policies that they establish. On the rare occasions when a policy decision strikes a nerve in the body politic, public reaction can achieve significant dimensions and successfully challenge this administrative dominance. The normal defense mechanisms of the superintendent (professionalism) and the board (concealment) are no longer adequate. They are then forced to face political reality. There are no studies that indicate that they do not do so in a relatively open and democratic way. The problem is that here, as in other policy areas, democracy does not always produce the policy results that many of us would hope for.

Citizen Participation and Community Control

The obvious failures of the urban educational system and the apparent dominance of administrative officials in many areas of decision-making have led many modern critics to seek a solution in significantly increased citizen participation, in spite of the complications outlined above. Some have proceeded on the assumption that participation in school politics should be particularly broad-based because of greater public interest in school policies and because of an ideological commitment on the part of administrators to public involvement in policy-making.[22] The foregoing discussion clearly revealed the shortcomings of the second assumption. The abstract commitment to the principle of participation is a long way from an acceptance of widespread citizen involvement in policy-making. School administrators, like other American citizens, can be expected to have serious reservations about the practical application of principles to which they generally subscribe.

The first assumption, that of greater public interest in school politics, and its corollary which posits greater public knowledge of school issues are both questionable. Few policy issues excite much public interest. Most members of the public appear willing to accept the argument that school

---

[21] See particularly Rogers, *110 Livingston Street*, pp. 401–407.
[22] Marilyn Gittell, *Participants and Participation: A Study of School Policy in New York City* (New York, 1967), pp. 2–3.

policies are really matters for the experts. Certainly there does not appear to be a significantly higher level of interest in school politics than in urban public policy generally. Financial and tax issues are the most salient,[23] and these are frequently matters of interest for reasons that have nothing in particular to do with school policies. Public involvement frequently takes the form of opposition to tax increases and bond issues without consideration of the merits of educational policy decisions which underlie increased expenditure levels. The level of knowledge with respect to schools and school politics is really quite low. A study of metropolitan area schools in six areas revealed a general lack of knowledge about schools on the part of residents, slightly greater knowledge in the suburbs than in the central cities, a decrease in knowledge with an increase in size of the district, and the paramount importance of the educational level of the citizen as a correlate of his knowledge of the schools.[24] The fact that the college-educated resident of a small suburb is more likely to be informed about his schools is not surprising to most, nor is it of any great consolation to the proponents of greater citizen participation in school politics. When these people advocate greater participation, they are focusing their attention on the schools of the inner city where the failures of the school appear to be greatest and where disagreements over policy decisions appear to have greatest potential.

One of the most interesting aspects of school politics is the tendency to invite somewhat greater participation than would normally be the case in urban politics by virtue of referenda. State law requires most of our school districts to submit significant questions to the voters before action can be taken. Of course, most of these significant questions deal with tax increases and the sale of bonds. Voter participation in such referenda partakes of all of the problems suggested in our earlier discussion of nonpartisan elections conducted separate from other elections. However, current research has revealed some interesting and unexpected patterns in voter participation when such referenda are linked with other elections.[25] When the referenda are conducted with general elections, the turnout of white voters is proportionately greater than that of nonwhites, but the situation is reversed when referenda are linked to primary elections. In both cases, about 20 percent of the nonwhite voters failed to vote in the referendum even though they turned out to vote in the election itself. Except in cities that had recently seen racial conflict, the nonwhite vote supported the schools in their request for more money more than the white vote. This may be because the nonwhite population is less satisfied

---

[23] Martin, "School Government," p. 272.

[24] Zimmer and Hawley, *Metropolitan Area Schools*, pp. 291–292.

[25] Louis H. Masotti, "Patterns of White and Nonwhite School Referenda Participation and Support," in Gittell, *Educating an Urban Population*, pp. 240–255.

with the present product of the schools and sees increased expenditure levels as a way to improve the schools.

However, dissatisfaction with the existing state of affairs is apparently not always enough to guarantee electoral participation in school referenda. Robert Agger's study of a Eugene, Oregon, referendum for the establishment of kindergartens indicates that it is possible to have a low turnout on the part of proponents of change.[26] Such low levels of participation can be explained in several ways. Some of the potential voters may be resigned to defeat and may lack a clear sense of efficacy even in the face of an opportunity to participate directly in the decision-making process. Others may be so confident of victory that they do not go to the polls. No matter what the explanation, the fact remains that participation does not always result even where interest and knowledge are fairly high and where clear opportunities and channels of access exist.

Some of the advocates of citizen participation in school politics seem willing to limit this participation to traditional electoral roles and interest representation before elected officials. Others appear to seek a more direct form of citizen participation, while still others demand community control of the schools in an absolute sense. Those who favor a more comprehensive form of participation usually view parents of school children as legitimate spokesmen for community interests, and seek a more active role for them in setting school policy.[27] They argue that the professional administrators should offer sound policy alternatives to the parents and allow the parents to choose between these alternatives. This process is recommended as one that will lead to greater responsibility among the parents, to greater respect for the problems facing educators, and to greater support by parents of the educational process.

Certainly, the more radical elements in school politics can find much to criticize in such prescriptions for parental participation. There is no guarantee that parents will prove to be the proper group to represent the community in educational politics. While parents are all too aware of the fact that citizens who have no children in the public schools frequently are not on the side of the angels when it comes to policy decisions, there seems to be little excuse for developing a decision-making process that either excludes them or weighs their contribution lightly. A more important objection to such a system from the radical point of view might well be that it runs the serious risk of encouraging an illusory participation. A mechanism that is designed to greatly increase parental support of the

---

[26] Robert E. Agger, "The Politics of Local Education," in Rosenthal, *Governing Education*, pp. 44–85.

[27] See for example Mario Fantini, "Community Participation," in *The Politics of Urban Education*, ed. Marilyn Gittell and Alan G. Hevesi (New York, 1969), pp. 323–337.

existing regime in the schools and that gives participants a choice between professionally acceptable alternatives may sound to many like cooptation. The radical alternative would be a school system in which community participants could initiate policy and could impose it upon the professional staff both in the headquarters and in the classroom. This would involve true control of the éducational process; the community could control personnel, budget, curriculum, and pupil policy. While the more sober academic critics of the existing mechanism of policy-making wish to stop short of a town meeting approach to school politics, it is clear that activist elements in the ghettos of our major cities anticipate just such a total control of the schools. Some members of the radical right also appear to favor a similar approach to school politics, especially in areas where they might reasonably hope to control the process.

Alternative Organizations

In many of our largest cities, the sheer size of the bureaucracy and of the school system itself has been singled out as a major factor in the lack of innovation. Critics of the school systems in these cities have frequently recommended some type of decentralization as the most promising remedy. The type of decentralization which these critics favor varies from the simple administrative decentralization of decision-making through the creation of subdistrict boards of education to the establishment of nearly independent neighborhood schools.[28] In each case the justifications for decentralization of large city school systems are roughly equivalent to those offered for the maintenance of a federal system of government in this country. That is to say, the proponents of such changes favor greater local control, the multiplication of points of access to the system, and the use of decentralized units as experimental laboratories in the development of new techniques. The interesting difference is that many observers have linked a defense of the federal system with social conservatism, while those who are now advocating school district decentralization might more accurately be cast as liberals or even radicals.

Each of these types of decentralization has been tried, but with little apparent success. The proponents of decentralization attribute this lack of success to the hesitancy of the central bureaucracy to release any of its substantive decision-making authority to subdistrict administrators, subdistrict boards of education, or to independent, parent-controlled schools. The participants in the struggle for control of the schools all appear to be

---

[28] Robert J. Havighurst and Daniel U. Levine, "The Quality of Urban Education," in *The Quality of Urban Life,* ed. Henry J. Schmandt and Warner Bloomberg, Jr. (Beverly Hills, 1969), pp. 341–342.

seeking some clearly defined division of powers between the central administration and constituent units that will achieve the desired policy results. Experience with our federal system demonstrates that such a clear division is probably not feasible. The theory of school district organization has apparently not progressed far enough to permit the advocates of increased decentralization to think in terms of the sharing of functions by design, politics, and professionalism which is characteristic of our federal system.

Some of the more extreme attempts at decentralization of the schools have served to bring the operation of the entire educational establishment to a halt. For example, the attempt to establish a pilot program of neighborhood control in New York City resulted in a great deal of acrimony and in a strike by teachers that was one of the most serious in our history.[29] The independent neighborhood school raises many significant questions of public policy. Because of the continued segregation evident in the housing patterns of our major cities, neighborhood schools are segregated schools, and the existence of such schools clearly contravenes both national and local policy. The maintenance of segregated schools sharpens existing racial and ethnic tensions. Furthermore, the concentration of the allegedly disadvantaged pupils which inevitably occurs under patterns of social and economic segregation makes it difficult to attract competent, not to mention talented, teachers to some schools. The criteria established by local groups for judging the performance of teachers and administrators may be at variance with those established by the central administration and the state. All of these problems lead inevitably to a politics of conflict for the schools, and there is little evidence that most Americans are willing to accept this type of political environment for education as a reality. The proponents of decentralization generally consider the conflict worth the price, since they assume that the new system will produce students better capable of dealing with life in an urban environment.[30]

Decentralization is not the only alternative available to existing educational structures in our cities.[31] Some of the other alternatives appear to be such departures from traditional approaches that they have gained few adherents. One such proposal, espoused by such unlikely bedfellows as Milton Friedman, William F. Buckley, Jr., and Paul Goodman, is the establishment of competing school systems under private auspices. Such competing systems would be organized so that any parent could choose to use his children's share of the educational resources of the community either in public or in private schools. The presumption is that a truly com-

---

[29] For detailed accounts of this dispute, see Maurice R. Berube and Marilyn Gittell, eds., *Confrontation at Ocean Hill-Brownsville* (New York, 1969).

[30] See for example Rogers, *110 Livingston Street*, pp. 478–492.

[31] Rogers, *110 Livingston Street*, pp. 486–488.

petitive environment will force continuous improvement in both public and private systems. Other reformers have suggested that private managers could be hired on a contract basis to operate the public schools. While such a scheme might improve the efficiency with which the schools are operated, there is little indication that it would improve the responsibility and responsiveness of the decision-making machinery. Finally, some have suggested the abandonment of existing physical plants in favor of giant educational parks which would serve children from all social and economic groups, including those who presently live in the suburbs. However, there appears to be little support from the general public for any of these schemes. At present, there is little chance that either decentralization or any of the more radical approaches will become widely used in our major cities. None of the relevant political groups are attracted in sufficient numbers to such structural reforms to make them a reality on a city-wide basis.

Schools and City Government

One of the recurrent themes in political scientists' discussions of school systems, particularly urban systems, is the necessity for establishing a closer relationship between decision-making activities in the schools and those in other urban governments. Given the political nature of educational decision-making and the link between the educational system and other important areas in urban public policy, the traditional attempts to isolate the schools from other urban governmental agencies are both senseless and harmful.

For many years, educators have been defending the independence of the schools on the grounds that fiscal independence would result in more money to spend on the schools. The traditional arguments favor special purpose districts as devices for evading the tax and debt limits established by state legislatures. However, an examination of the patterns of expenditure in large cities whose schools are dependent upon the city government for their money seriously undermines the case for fiscal independence. In big cities, higher expenditures appear to be tied to a dependence upon city government and its broader taxing powers which involve a decreasing dependence upon the real property tax as a source of income and upon voter approval for tax increases.[32] The validity of these findings is underlined by the experience of school districts in states like Illinois which find themselves caught when the state adopts an income tax and then attempts to deliver long-promised relief for property taxpayers. Under such circumstances, independent school districts frequently

---

[32] Hollander, "Fiscal Independence," p. 115.

are not compensated for their loss of tax base. In Illinois, the municipalities share in the revenue from the income tax and find themselves in a stronger financial position as a result of the changes.

Some of the critics of the present urban school systems have sought a partial solution to their problems in the closer control of the schools by other agencies of the urban political system.[33] The general thesis presented by these critics is that direct political-system control of the schools might help to make the schools more effectve instruments of social change. This implies something more than a formal structure in which the mayor appoints the school board and the city council passes on the school budget. Both of these structural arrangements are present in New York City, and the school system has been largely autonomous there. The term "control" as it is used here implies the willingness to impose the sanctions that are available under such a structure in order to effect basic policy changes. Under such an integrated urban political system, three kinds of benefits might accrue. The schools might well benefit in that the organized element controlling the political system could provide them with the political power necessary to generate support for educational programs and with the protection they need in order to survive in an increasingly pluralistic and tension-filled community. Secondly, such control might well force the schools to compete openly with other governmental functions for scarce public resources and to clearly justify their importance relative to those other urban programs. Finally, control by a political system overtly responsible to a pluralistic community might increase the degree of differentiation available in educational programs and undermine the basic operational myth of educators, the myth of the unitary community.

Those who favor a closer policy link between the schools and other urban governments frequently stress the role of the mayor in developing such a relationship and making it effective.[34] Closer involvement in the making of school policy on the part of the mayor may lead to policies that are more closely coordinated with policies in other problem areas. This view assumes that mayors have the political ability to achieve such coordination. Even in cities where the mayor possesses great institutional and informal powers, and even in the largest cities where the mayor's role as a political coordinator is most clearly recognized, the mayor cannot work miracles. The compromises that are inevitable in the heterogeneous urban environment may result in educational policy decisions that are unsatisfactory to vocal critics of the establishment and that are not fully compatible with decisions made in other program areas, even when the

---

[33] Robert H. Salisbury, "Autonomy vs. 'Political Control' of Schools," in *Urban Government*, rev. ed., ed. Edward C. Banfield (New York, 1969), pp. 628–644.

[34] Hollander, "Fiscal Independence," p. 116, and Rogers, *110 Livingston Street*, pp. 429–434.

mayor exercises vigorous policy leadership in the schools. The mayor may have an important role to play in developing policy for urban schools, but many current observers appear to expect more of him than he can deliver.

Two Illustrative Policy Problems

A cursory examination of two widely publicized problems will underline the dilemma in which superintendents, school boards, and their critics find themselves.

INTEGRATION AND/OR DESEGREGATION. Ever since the Supreme Court of the United States declared that separate school facilities for black and white students were inherently unequal [*Brown* v. *Board of Education* (1954)], there has been a continuing debate over the kinds of policies necessary at the local level to satisfy the requirements of the United States Constitution. For some years, many local school officials consoled themselves with the view that all that was required was a policy which was neutral—one which did not actively promote segregated facilities. However, the efforts of some federal government officials in enforcing civil rights legislation and some court decisions in the late 1960s have indicated that neutrality and inaction are not enough, and that a positive program of integration must be developed. As school officials have struggled with the problem, they have been led to face two relatively unpleasant facts: 1) mere token integration does not meet the standards established by the courts, especially in the South; and 2) the segregated pattern of urban housing makes it nearly impossible to maintain traditional neighborhood schools while attempting to establish integrated facilities.

In response to the uproar which greeted the announced intention of some federal officials and some courts to enforce integration standards which would force the bussing of pupils to obtain integration outside the South, President Nixon offered a statement in April, 1970 which was designed to clarify national policy in this area. The results of this clarification were mixed at best. On one hand, the President indicated that he did not interpret the decisions of the courts as dealing directly with the question of *de facto* segregation of the schools and that he saw no federal requirement for integration plans which necessarily involved the bussing of pupils. On the other hand, he reaffirmed his support of the *Brown* decision as humanly and constitutionally right, and this decision declares separate facilities to be inherently unequal. Local school officials may be forgiven if they view the President's statement as less than helpful in dealing with the real problems which face them. If the President is not backing off on the provision of equal educational opportunity—and he says that he is not—then bussing may be the only short-run policy which will produce the requisite racial balance consistent with the *Brown* decision, given our segregated living patterns.

Earlier students of the politics of school desegregation concluded that it was a mistake to expect serious community conflict over this question since there was no evidence that civil rights leaders were really demanding major concessions from school officials or that there was massive white opposition to school integration.[35] Such conclusions are no longer warranted—action by the federal government has bypassed the more moderate demands of civil rights leaders, and the threat to the neighborhood school has mobilized more members of the white community to oppose integration plans. In many school districts, bussing of pupils has replaced integration itself as the main issue. To make matters more complicated, the demands for community and neighborhood control of the schools, especially in the black community, have added some black groups to the ranks of the defenders of the neighborhood school.

This particular policy dilemma clearly illustrates the internal inconsistencies of many of the critics of the school system. Most of these critics[36] began their assault on school decision-makers because of the failure of the schools to develop a satisfactory policy on the integration of facilities. For the critics, the solution was greater participation in the decision-making process by parents and other interested groups in the community, participation that might lead to neighborhood control of the schools. However, if a significant portion of the potential participants are now opposed to any plan that destroys the neighborhood school, and if there is no way to satisfy integration requirements by maintaining neighborhood schools, there is obviously no way for the superintendent and the school board to satisfy both criteria.

One solution to the dilemma lies in the constitutional principle which holds that there are some policy areas in which participation and majority rule are irrelevant. The constitutionally protected rights of individuals may not be denied even by an overwhelming majority. Under this approach school boards have no choice but to integrate the schools even if this renders the concept of participation less viable and the concept of neighborhood control impossible. As Alexander Bickel has pointed out, the centralization of school control is an inevitable result of attempts to achieve fully integrated educational facilities.[37] There are problems with this solution in that it will still be possible for those who are wealthy enough to send their children to private schools or to move far enough

---

[35] Robert L. Crain and David Street, "School Desegregation and School Decision-Making," in Gittell, *Educating an Urban Population*," pp. 137–138.

[36] See Rogers, *110 Livingston Street*, in particular.

[37] Alexander M. Bickel, *The Supreme Court and the Idea of Progress* (New York, 1970), pp. 134–136.

from the center of the city or other black communities so as to render any efforts at integration futile. The end result would be the integration of the poor and the continued segregation of the rich and poor from each other.[38]

Another solution may lie in the acceptance of the principle of decentralization of control of the schools into neighborhood units and/or the establishment of a system of government tuition grants to individuals enabling them to send their children to the schools of their choice.[39] This approach is akin to what President Nixon suggested in his April, 1970, statement alluded to earlier in this section. It has the advantage of political "realism" although it does suggest that separate facilities can be equal as long as they are not separate by government decree. Such a position only makes sense if one is willing to accept the proposition that equality does not entail "sameness." This would clearly require a serious rethinking of the justification for public education in our society. No one has yet been willing to carry this argument to its logical conclusions and to examine its impact upon our social and political institutions.

This last dilemma is clearly revealed in the position which has been taken by educators themselves with respect to school integration. In the early debates over the question, superintendents and other educational professionals were willing to leave such policy decisions up to the board of education since they did not view it as a professional or technical question.[40] This is no longer the case. Careful examination of the impact of educational environment on the learning process has demonstrated to many teachers and administrators that integration and the dissolution of the neighborhood school are sound educational policies which will result in a generally higher level of performance in the schools.[41] However, those who support neighborhood schools and freedom of choice are clearly implying that many of the performance criteria utilized by educators are no longer acceptable to them. This returns us squarely to the questions of professional domination, citizen participation and community control considered earlier in this chapter. These are questions for which there appear to be no ready answers.

SEX EDUCATION. While matters of curriculum are usually left entirely up to the professionals, the general public occasionally becomes sufficiently interested in something that is being taught in the schools to attempt to

---

[38] Bickel, *The Supreme Court*, pp. 136–137.
[39] Bickel, *The Supreme Court*, pp. 140–150.
[40] Crain and Street, "School Desegregation," p. 141.
[41] James E. Kent, "The Coleman Report: Opening Pandora's Box," in Berube and Gittell, *Confrontation*, pp. 83–88.

influence educational policy. The development of sex education as a regular part of the school curriculum in many districts has generated such interest. Heated public debates, school board elections, and direct attacks on individual teachers and administrators have all characterized the public participation focused on this issue.

It is difficult to characterize positions on this issue as "minority" or "majority" positions. As is true of most public policy questions, sex education probably generates an opinion among members of several minorities. School boards and administrations that have adopted programs of sex education are particularly vulnerable to the criticism of such programs which some well-organized groups have directed toward them. The parents and groups who might support the programs are not so easily mobilized. The result is that an articulate minority can frequently frustrate the professional judgment of teachers and administrators. Many sex education programs have been abandoned, and still others have been seriously modified.

The disputes over sex education programs illustrate an important point about the politics of school policy. Whenever a group of citizens has strong feelings about a policy decision, it can force a reexamination of policy and, in many cases, force a change in policy. Even though the educational establishment and its powerful professional bureaucracy are arrayed against such changes, and even though school boards are oriented more toward legitimation than they are toward representation, the schools are vulnerable to participatory democracy. However, sex education disputes also illustrate clearly that citizen participation in the making of school policy can be a mixed blessing for those progressive critics of the school system who are its greatest advocates. For most of these critics, the abolition of sex education is a step backward.

Conclusions

Most evidence points to an enlarged set of participants in educational decision-making:

> The current "quality-equality" educational revolution, set in motion by the 1954 school desegregation decision of the U.S. Supreme Court and the 1957 launching of Sputnik, has had the effect of diminishing the relative influence of the schoolmen and made education politics more "public" as it shifted into the mainstream of the legislative, administrative and judicial processes at the local, state and national levels.[42]

---

[42] Michael Decker and Louis H. Masotti, "Determining the Quality of Education: A Political Process," in Schmandt and Bloomberg, *The Quality of Urban Life*, p. 370.

At the same time, educational politics have achieved even greater importance in urban society. In fact, it is possible to claim that educational
politics are central to the future of urban life:

> Ultimately the issue of urban education is also the issue of the morale and
> life of the city itself. . . . They [the schools] . . . tie the city together. If they
> fail—as they are failing—then the community will disintegrate into a con-
> geries of suburbs and renaissance baronies separated by ghettoes and vio-
> lence. If they fail, then the public weal will forever be committed to an
> uneasy division between warfare and welfare, while those sectors of public
> activity that make life rich and meaningful—the arts, recreation, education,
> the beauty of the city and country—will become even more privately glorious
> and publicly neglected. If they fail, then urban life fails, too.[43]

Suggested Readings

Berube, Maurice, and Gittell, Marilyn, eds. *Confrontation at Ocean Hill-
Brownsville.* New York, 1969.

Dahl, Robert A. *Who Governs?* New Haven, 1961.

Gans, Herbert J. *The Levittowners.* New York, 1967.

Gittell, Marilyn, ed. *Educating an Urban Population.* Beverly Hills, 1967.

————. *Participants and Participation: A Study of School Policy in New York
City.* New York, 1967.

————, and Hevesi, Alan G., eds. *The Politics of Urban Education.* New York,
1969.

————, and Hollander, T. Edward. *Six Urban School Districts.* New York,
1968.

Henry, Nelson B., and Kerwin, Jerome G. *Schools and City Government.* Chicago, 1938.

Lonsdale, Richard C. *The School's Role in Metropolitan Area Development.*
Syracuse, N.Y., 1960.

Masotti, Louis H. *Education and Politics in Suburbia: The New Trier Experience.* Cleveland, 1967.

Masters, Nicholas A.; Salisbury, Robert H.; and Eliot, Thomas H. *State Politics and the Public Schools.* New York, 1964.

Rogers, David. *110 Livingston Street.* New York, 1968.

Rosenthal, Alan., ed. *Governing Education.* Garden City, N.Y., 1969.

Schmandt, Henry J., and Bloomberg, Warner, Jr., eds. *The Quality of Urban
Life.* Beverly Hills, 1969.

Schrag, Peter. *Village School Downtown.* Boston, 1967.

Vidich, Arthur, and Bensman, Joseph. *Small Town in Mass Society.* Princeton,
1958.

Zimmer, Basil G., and Hawley, Amos H. *Metropolitan Area Schools: Resistance
to District Reorganization.* Beverly Hills, 1968.

---

[43] Schrag, *Village School Downtown,* p. 184.

chapter **16**

Public Works
and Public
Utilities

 [An important test of the adequacy of government in metropolitan areas is its ability to meet the contemporary challenge of population growth, suburban development, and rising service demands. Local governments provide a broad range of services. . . . The impact of metropolitan development extends to all these functions, and an adequate level of performance implies meeting increasing needs across this entire range of services.[1]

Public works and public utilities are subjects that many consider entirely too pedestrian to be included in a book on urban politics. However, as the above quotation indicates, the adequacy of any given set of governmental institutions can be judged in terms of its ability to meet service demands. For many if not most of the citizens of our cities, these service demands are centered upon the more mundane and routine functions that fall under the headings of public works and public utilities. Their satisfaction with and support of the mayor, the council and the government in general is likely to depend on their perception of how well the more traditional municipal services are performed and upon how well urban governments provide new services in the public works and utilities area.

General Functions

A list of functions performed by urban governments under the heading of public works includes most of those which have traditionally been consid-

---

[1] Advisory Commission on Intergovernmental Relations, *Metropolitan America: Challenge to Federalism* (Washington, 1966), p. 29.

413

ered to be in the domain of municipal governments. Street improvement and maintenance, street cleaning and snow removal, street lighting, refuse collection and disposal, sewerage and sewage disposal, waterworks, and airports all fall under the heading of public works.[2] Any urban government official, especially at the municipal level, can testify to the importance of these services to citizens. In the era of the motor vehicle it is virtually impossible for poorly maintained streets to go unnoticed by the public. Streets and surfaces that were once entirely adequate can no longer handle the volume of traffic which is generated even in smaller cities. Mayor John Lindsay of New York can offer detailed testimony on the degree of dissatisfaction stimulated by failure to collect garbage or to quickly remove snow from the streets, and on the political consequences of this dissatisfaction. Many political observers traced a portion of the difficulty which Mr. Lindsay experienced in gaining reelection in 1969 to a prolonged strike of garbage and refuse collectors and to the inability of the City of New York to rapidly remove the accumulation of snow following a particularly heavy storm. Many voters obviously have come to expect relatively quick and efficient performance of the more routine municipal services.

Water Supply

Some of the public works functions are deserving of more detailed attention because of the particularly serious problems they present. One such function is the supply of water. While this function is performed by private companies in a few areas, it is a predominantly governmental activity. Most citizens in urban areas take this service for granted. One of the characteristics of modern urban man is that he turns on a tap and expects an immediate supply of clean, potable water. There is no thought of wells, cisterns, or pumps. Somehow we expect the water to be there. However, the increased level and density of population which accompanies urbanization may well have rendered such expectations unrealistic in some urban areas. Many cities, large and small, have been faced with serious water shortages, especially during the dry summer months.

Man uses prodigious quantities of water in order to support his existence on earth.[3] Most of this water is presently used for such activities as irrigation and power generation, rather than for consumption by urban man. In fact, municipalities used only 25 billion gallons per day out of the 370 billion gallons per day used in 1965. The problem does not appear to be one of a total water shortage, at least for the foreseeable future. Much of

[2] International City Managers' Association, *Municipal Public Works Administration* (Chicago, 1957).
[3] Abel Wolman, "The Metabolism of Cities," *Urban Politics and Problems*, ed. H. R. Mahood and Edward I. Angus (New York, 1969), pp. 228–238.

the water used is not consumed, and therefore it can be returned to the supply for reuse following treatment in some cases. Insofar as urban governments are concerned, the major problem is one of obtaining a share of the total supply adequate to the needs of the cities. While there is plenty of water available to meet urban demands, much of it is not close at hand. Cities must plan and construct facilities that will get the water where it is needed. In those urban areas where the problem has been recognized largely because of its peculiar severity, as in Southern California, the facilities have been constructed and water is relatively plentiful. Others have not been so fortunate. Thus it is possible for residents of the semidesert to fill their pools and water their lawns profusely in the heat of the summer, while residents of areas more generously blessed with rainfall are suffering under water rationing.

In addition to providing expanded supply facilities for water, our cities must also enlarge their treatment facilities in order to make this increased volume of water usable. The water must be treated with such chemicals as alum and potassium permanganate to encourage the settling out of foreign matter, and then filtered to prevent any foreign matter from entering the distribution system. Because of the major threat to public health presented by bacteria in the water supply, the water is chlorinated in order to reduce these bacteria to acceptable levels. These treatment processes add significantly to the already considerable costs of supply.

While many experts assure us that the costs of providing adequate urban water systems can be met through long-term financing and the application of user fees, the diseconomies of small-scale operations are most evident in this service area. It is not only inordinantly expensive but also physically impossible for each small city and suburb to construct its own supply and treatment facilities. Intergovernmental remedies of the variety mentioned in Chapter 4 have been effectively applied, however. Smaller communities can, with the requisite consultation and prior planning, purchase water from large neighboring cities that have excess capacity. The major shortcoming with this approach is that few major cities have engaged in enough prior consultation and planning with surrounding communities to guarantee sufficient long-run excess capacity in water supply and treatment facilities to serve the entire area. The alternative is the formation of a special purpose district or other cooperative enterprise designed deliberately to meet the long-range water needs of an entire metropolitan area or urbanized area. This is the approach that has enabled residents of Southern California to provide for their present and future water needs through the Southern California Water District. Such intergovernmental agreements and special districts can focus entirely on supply, on treatment alone, or ideally on both the supply and the treatment of water. In this manner, each community can be guaranteed clean, potable water at the lowest possible cost to its citizens.

THE CASE OF FLUORIDATION. So far, the political aspects of water supply and treatment have appeared to center on the simple question of whether or not government was performing the service. If the citizen turns on his tap and nothing comes out, he is angry with City Hall. However, water treatment has developed into a major public policy question in many of our communities. In fact, some have suggested that the chemical treatment of drinking water by government may be the single biggest issue of city government in recent years.[4] The conflict has centered upon the question of whether or not to add sodium fluoride compounds to the water supply of communities in order to reduce the incidence of dental caries or tooth decay. Fluoridation, like other types of water treatment, is primarily a public health measure, and therefore could have been discussed in Chapter 14. Unlike other public health measures, those taken in conjunction with the supply of water have a particularly far-reaching impact, and no citizen can easily escape them. This fact has made the issue particularly explosive, and the overlapping of public health functions with public works and utilities functions has rendered normally routine governmental activity controversial.

It is sometimes difficult to fully appreciate the intensity of the furor over fluoridation. Surely no one is in favor of tooth decay, and surely anyone would favor such a simple way to deal with a serious health problem. Life is not that simple, however. Some of the objections to fluoridation have come from those who felt, at least initially, that there had been insufficient testing of the chemicals and processes involved before proponents of the process sought to introduce it into water systems on a large-scale basis.[5] Still others were firmly convinced that fluoridation constituted medical treatment that was being supported out of general tax revenues (in this case really user fees) and, therefore, was a giant step down the road to socialized medicine. (In all fairness, one should note that this view was not particularly widespread among dentists.) Another group, including some Christian Scientists, fought fluoridation on the grounds that it was compulsory medical treatment and a violation of the freedom of religion guaranteed by the First Amendment of the Constitution. This argument was all the more seriously proposed since the health hazard in question was highly individualized and was not, unlike others for which compulsory immunization had been approved, either contagious or infectious. Other opponents of fluoridation focused their attention on the fact

---

[4] This entire section draws heavily from Robert L. Crain, Elihu Katz, and Donald B. Rosenthal, *The Politics of Community Conflict: The Fluoridation Decision* (Indianapolis, 1969).

[5] For example, see F. B. Exner and G. L. Waldbott, *The American Fluoridation Experiment* (New York, 1957), and Robert M. Buck, *The Grim Truth About Fluoridation* (New York, 1964).

that fluorine as a chemical element was not safe for human consumption. They reasoned that, since fluorides are derived from fluorine, the fluoridation process was manifestly unsafe, and that fluoridated water was poisoning the citizens of those communities in which it had been introduced. These fears were heightened when scientists reported that laboratory animals were adversely affected by fluorides when ingested in sufficient concentration. Those who recall the more recent furor over the addition of such chemicals as cyclamates and monosodium glutamate to foods can appreciate both the impact and the importance of such findings in the minds of many.

What makes the fluoridation controversy unique is that there were a significant number of highly vocal opponents who carried the argument even further. They started with the proposition that fluorides were "obviously" poison and would have the most horrible effects on the population of any community which used them. In the face of this "fact," they said, there were still many who advocated the use of fluorides in the drinking water. The only explanation for such behavior was that these individuals were either conscious agents or dupes of powers—the international Communist conspiracy—who wished to poison the American people for their own nefarious ends. While there is no direct evidence available that would link the American Dental Association and the vast majority of its members either wittingly or unwittingly to the international Communist conspiracy, this argument has persuaded a significant number of Americans.

Because of the nature of the issue, once an opposition has formed to fluoridation a relatively rancorous conflict is almost certain to follow. One important reason is that the issue is not amenable to compromise. Either enough fluorides must be added to do the job or none at all. In most communities, either all of the water supply must be fluoridated or none. If one side wins, the other obviously loses.

Perhaps the most interesting facet of the fluoridation controversy is the ability of a relatively small number of relatively powerless individuals to veto governmental policy. In this instance "relatively powerless" means that these people possess few of the resources linked to power in most of our communities—wealth, social position, group affiliations, or institutional leadership roles. They are frequently ordinary citizens. The success of the opposition appears to be centered upon their ability to force a referendum and to create enough controversy over the issue to implant doubts in the minds of a majority of those voting. Where both the law and local practice encourage referenda on public policy questions, the opponents of fluoridation are likely to be successful. The institutions of direct democracy appear to work well for at least one nonelite group.

Another important facet of the fluoridation controversy is the impact of formal governmental structures and electoral systems. Nowhere has the significance of these institutional factors and their effect on behavior been more clearly demonstrated. This is particularly true when one examines the conditions and techniques that have led to the successful fluoridation of water supplies. Crain, Katz, and Rosenthal found that a referendum could be avoided and the water fluoridated if controversy could be kept at a low level, if the political leadership of the community was experienced and enjoyed high status, if fluoridation had the active support of health organizations and other important civic groups, and, most importantly, if the mayor adopted a favorable stand on the issue.[6] As earlier chapters in this book have indicated, there are institutional factors that bear upon the type of leadership enjoyed by a community. The executive centralization that characterizes both council-manager and strong mayor forms of government appears to be closely related to successful fluoridation attempts. The centralization and leadership is further strengthened by partisanship, which tends to render the conflict that does occur more manageable and, therefore, more acceptable to political leaders. Of course, communities that are partisan and have a high degree of executive centralization are likely to be communities that do not frequently resort to the encouragement of participation in the decision-making process through such devices as the referendum. Thus they avoid a short-run veto of a fluoridation decision. In the long run, in spite of the passions expressed, fluoridation is not likely to be a durable issue that could be used at election time. Institutional decision-makers run little risk of being turned out of office on the issue. Even if the issue were more durable, the absence of traditional power resources on the part of the opponents of fluoridation renders them unable to mount a successful campaign against the mayor and/or city council.

Pollution and Its Regulation

SEWAGE AND WATER POLLUTION. A government function that is closely related to water supply is the treatment of waste water or sewage. Urbanization has resulted in increased population densities that have made the natural treatment of human and other animal wastes insufficient to the task of protecting our water supply. Both the total amount and the degree of concentration of waste matter are so great that even the smallest towns are polluting the lakes and streams that serve as their own source of water and as sources for other communities as well. New products designed to make man's life easier result in new kinds of pollution for the water supply. An outstanding example is the detergent. Any housewife will testify that the new cleaning agents have made washing dishes and clothes much

---

[6] Crain, Katz, and Rosenthal, *Politics of Community Conflict*, p. 121.

easier than it used to be when we were wholly dependent on soap. However, many detergents did not break down under normal sewage treatment, and, in many places, they managed to find their way into the water supply. The result was that it was possible to draw a glass of water from the tap with a "head" of suds on it. New detergents have proven to be a partial answer to this problem.

Industrial waste has also contributed to the problem of water pollution. The concentration of industry in our major cities has brought a concentration of pollutants. Unlike most human waste, which is channeled through municipal sewage plants, much industrial waste is subjected to treatment only if the generator of the waste elects to do so. Untreated human waste presents a health hazard, and a detergent "head" adds nothing to the enjoyment of a refreshing glass of water, but industrial wastes can be far more noxious. Acids and other chemicals are poured into our streams in prodigious quantities. Oil and other hydrocarbons form a scum on the surface of the water in some locations in sufficient quantities to render the stream flammable. An example is Cleveland's Cuyahoga River.

Until recent years the attitude of local urban governments toward water pollution was highly parochial. The policy of many governments had been simply to obtain water upstream and dump wastes downstream. For a time it was possible for large numbers of local governments to maintain such policies with relative impunity. Two factors have ruled out this carefree attitude. In the first place, urban densities have reached the point at which the "upstream" point at which one town obtains its water is clearly another town's "downstream" point for dumping sewage, and it is getting more difficult to obtain water that can be rendered potable at a reasonable cost. In the second place, state governments and the national government have recognized that voluntary control of water pollution has not been satisfactory. Some communities choose to ignore the problem, while others are financially unable to amass the capital funds necessary to build adequate treatment facilities. As a result, many states have passed stringent legislation requiring the treatment of sewage. The legislation in conjunction with the Federal Water Pollution Control acts of 1954 and 1962 has rendered positive action by local governments imperative. In addition the federal government has established grant-in-aid programs and low-cost loans to help local governments meet the heavy capital costs of sewage treatment.

The politics of water pollution control have not received a great deal of attention. The general public finds the issue even less stimulating than most which characterize urban politics. Once more, individual citizens and groups are likely to attempt to influence policy only when they perceive an immediate and direct effect. For example, residents of an area close to an overtaxed sewage treatment facility are likely to take an interest in the development of policy governing the construction of new facilities and of policy governing new hookups to the old facilities when the smell of untreated sewage becomes too strong for them to stomach. In Carbondale, Illinois, just such a group became intimately involved in the political process when a low-tax group forced a referendum over the issuance of bonds for the construction of new sewage treatment facilities and the resultant increase in user fees. The successful defense of the bond issue in this case appeared to rest not so much upon a clear understanding of the problems of water pollution by the electorate as upon the desire of the residents of the affected neighborhood to reduce the nuisance of overtaxed facilities and the very real fear of the steep fine which could be levied by the state if the city continued to pollute area streams.

The problem of enforcing antipollution ordinances and laws directed at the generators of industrial waste is particularly great. Many industries have demonstrated a marked hesitancy to accept the standards embodied in local, state, and federal regulatory measures and to initiate voluntary compliance with the law. This has meant a slow process of inspection, warning, citation, and even prosecution by local governments. Even with a massive increase in the enforcement activities of local governments, this slow process, which must proceed pollutant by pollutant, company by company, and industry by industry, will take hundreds of years to achieve the desired results. This corporate civil disobedience is often justified on the grounds that present technology will not permit continued production if antipollution standards are met. It is difficult, however, to justify continued operation of industries whose by-products threaten the health and environment of urban man.

AIR POLLUTION. Much of the argument which has been presented with respect to water pollution is applicable to air pollution as well. Air is also a scarce and vital commodity for mankind. One has only to take a deep breath in any of America's major cities to recognize the degree to which our air is threatened by pollution. For many years cities cheerfully ignored air pollution in the mistaken belief that smog was a problem peculiar to the Los Angeles basin. In fact, the basin and the temperature inversion that trapped pollutants in the air of Los Angeles were only local peculiarities that brought the problem to light much earlier there than in other cities. The major difference between air pollution and water pollution is, quite obviously, that the supply of air is neither a public work nor a public utility. It is treated here only because of the close relationship it bears to water pollution in terms of developing patterns of regulation and enforcement problems.

The fact that air pollution, like water pollution, is no respecter of governmental boundaries, either municipal or state, has rendered the problem particularly difficult for local governments to control on their own. The federal government's Clean Air Act of 1967 and similar legislation at the state level have provided a firm basis for regulation and the establishment of enforcement standards. While many jurisdictions are suffering under some of the same limitations of corporate civil disobedience with respect to air pollution that they are suffering with respect to water pollution, some cities and states have experienced significant progress in controlling industrial pollution. In California, where Los Angeles' unfortunate early experience with smog brought earlier attempts at regulation, industrial pollution has been drastically reduced, and corporations have discovered that they can afford to control pollutants and that they have the technological know-how to do the job.

The major problem in the control of air pollution may be that industrial pollutants are not the primary cause of smog. Many experts suggest that the hydrocarbons emitted by the exhausts of internal combustion engines are the primary contributors to smog. Efforts to control these emissions through the installation of positive crankcase valves and other mechanical devices on all automobiles have not been notably successful. Experiments with automobiles powered by electricity and steam appear to indicate that such alternatives are inordinantly expensive at this time. As we shall see later in this chapter, attempts to persuade urban man to abandon the automobile or to restrict its use have been most unsuccessful of all. Until a method is found to control automotive pollutants, governmental efforts at air pollution control will remain frustrated. In most of our cities, however, much remains to be done in the control of industrial pollutants, and the primary enforcement effort today appears to be in this area.

Other Public Utilities

As Table 16–1 indicates, a number of other utilities are owned and operated by municipal governments in this country, but it is clear that outside of water and sewage facilities there is very little governmental activity. Some of the activity which does exist is highly localized. For example, in 1967 nearly half of the municipal gas systems were located in just five states—Alabama, Tennessee, Georgia, Louisiana, and Texas.[7] However, most communities of any appreciable size are involved in some way or another in the ownership and operation of utilities: 80 percent of the cities that responded with a complete negative to the survey reported in Table 16–1 had populations of less than 25,000.

There does not seem to be a trend toward increasing government

---

[7] T. R. Jacobi, "Municipal Public Works and Utilities," in *Municipal Yearbook, 1968*, International City Managers' Association (Washington, 1968), p. 318.

TABLE 16–1: Ownership and Operation of Utilities in Cities over 5,000

Type of Utility	ALL CITIES OVER 5,000		Over 500,000	250,000 to 500,000	100,000 to 250,000	50,000 to 100,000	25,000 to 50,000	10,000 to 25,000	5,000 to 10,000
	Number	Percent of Cities Reporting							
W Water supply and distribution	1,917	66.7	22	24	73	133	280	638	747
S Sewage treatment plant	1,738	60.5	19	20	75	109	243	605	667
E Electric generation and distribution	304	10.6	8	0	13	15	39	97	132
D Electric distribution only	243	8.5	0	1	4	9	23	81	125
V Water distribution only	261	9.1	1	0	6	26	38	95	95
F Gas distribution only	141	4.9	1	1	5	3	16	44	71
B Transportation systems	61	2.1	8	2	7	9	22	8	5
G Gas manufacture and distribution	44	1.5	4	0	2	2	4	14	18
None of the above	454	15.8	0	1	4	24	59	193	173
Cities not reporting	282		2	0	3	22	57	131	67

SOURCE: International City Managers' Association, *Municipal Yearbook, 1966* (Chicago, 1966), p. 97. Reprinted by permission of the International City Management Association.

ownership of such utilities as gas and electric production and distribution systems. Certainly, there has been no appreciable decrease in the public interest involved in the provision of these vital services. However, in most urban areas, privately owned utilities are able to profitably provide gas and electricity under a system of controlled rates which protects the consumer. These circumstances do not lead to an expansion of government owner-ship. Only where the service cannot be provided at a cost the citizen can afford and at a profit for the ownership do privately owned utilities become impractical.

The Special Problem of Transportation

Table 16–1 indicates that only 2.1 percent of the reporting municipalities operate transportation systems. Why then should the remainder of this chapter be devoted to the subject of governmental transportation policy? At least two reasons can be given. First, urban transportation, while not frequently publicly owned, is frequently subsidized in some way or an-other by the taxpayers in our cities. Second, policy decisions with respect to transportation are of vital importance to the urban area as a whole:

> Transportation made the modern metropolis possible; almost everywhere it is the preeminent metropolitan concern. No other urban problem causes such widespread public frustration, irritation, and preoccupation with inade-quacies. . . . Most important, transportation decisions have a crucial impact on the shape and the future of the metropolis, involve vast public outlays, and require difficult political choices. As a consequence, debates over the transportation system ultimately affect the totality of interests in a metro-politan area.[8]

Although there appears to be general agreement that subsidies and an all-encompassing public interest in the policy effects of transportation decisions have raised transportation to the status of a public utility, there is less agreement on the nature of the problems that face policy-makers. For some our problem is simply one of insufficient transportation facili-ties to handle the large numbers of people who must be moved from place to place in our cities. As George Smerk has pointed out, "no American city today enjoys a modern, smoothly operating, congestion-free system of individual or mass transport."[9] Other transportation experts have focused their attention more upon the manner in which existing facilities are allocated and used, claiming that "there seems to be

---

[8] Michael N. Danielson, *Federal-Metropolitan Politics and the Commuter Crisis* (New York, 1965), p. 9.

[9] George M. Smerk, *Urban Transportation: The Federal Role* (Bloomington, Ind., 1965), p. 4.

little immediate justification for the view that the present supply of urban transportation, taking all modes into consideration, is grossly inadequate." [10] Although the latter experts may be statistically correct, one must recognize, as most of them do, that problems in allocation and utilization may be even more critical than undersupply. The fact that many of the unemployed living either in the central city or in suburban slum areas have no way to get to where the jobs are has been a major source of dissatisfaction in recent years. Such a shortage of transportation among the urban poor may merely reflect the fact that other segments of society enjoy a surplus of facilities, not that there is a total shortage. It is equally true that the conjestion cited earlier as a major component of urban transportation problems reflects only the fact that too many people want to use existing facilities at the same time. The total supply may indeed be adequate if the use of these facilities can be spread out throughout the day. A closer look at the modes of urban transportation and the policy decisions that governments must make should better reveal the complexity of these problems.

THE AUTOMOBILE AND THE CITY. Urbanization and motor vehicles have fed upon one another in one of the most disturbing reciprocal relationships in modern society. Much of the rapid growth of our cities and much of their rapid displacement in urban and suburban sprawl can be traced directly to the development of the automobile and the truck. Chapter 1 has already given the devil its due in this respect. The relationship is reciprocal because urban growth and sprawl and the consequent diffusion of origins and destinations of urban travelers have made the automobile the only feasible method of movement in many cities.[11] As the population of major urban centers increases, the number of cars and trucks increases as well. To make matters worse, the one-car family is fast disappearing in favor of the two- and even three-car family.

The result of this growth in the use of the automobile is a problem of space. Where do we put them all? "Much of the street and highway system of the average city is obsolete in design, inadequate in capacity, and inefficient in operation." [12] While governments have devoted a tremendous amount of attention to building streets and highways in recent years, the problem of capacity still haunts us. Part of the problem can be traced to the fact that much of the construction has been devoted to the interstate highway system which has less impact on the cities than one

---

[10] J. R. Meyer, J. F. Kain, and M. Wohl, *The Urban Transportation Problem* (Cambridge, Mass., 1965), p. 82.

[11] Wilfred Owen, *The Metropolitan Transportation Problem*, rev. ed. (Garden City, N.Y., 1966), pp. 27–28.

[12] Owen, *The Metropolitan Transportation Problem*, p. 37.

might hope. For example, in 1967, 47.8 percent of the nation's driving was being done on the 14 percent of the streets which lay in the urban network.[13] Efforts to provide adequate space for the automobile in the city, where any major efforts have been made, have drastically affected the physical appearance of the city. In Los Angeles, where the automobile has achieved primary importance as a method of transportation, two-thirds of the central business district is devoted to motor vehicles in the form of streets, parking, loading, and service areas.[14]

One of the major difficulties experienced by urban governments in any attempt to provide or encourage the provision of adequate facilities for motor vehicles is that those who use automobiles as their primary means of transportation do not follow clear and consistent use patterns so that corridors and terminals can be predicted with any degree of certainty. Research has revealed that the public uses its cars primarily for shopping, social-recreational, and personal business trips rather than for commutation from home to place of work.[15] While it is possible to designate some arteries as more heavily used than others, the development of an adequate pattern of multilane, limited access highways is almost impossible. To relieve peak-hour congestion, it would be necessary to pave massive areas within the city in circumferentials and radials. The best that most cities are able to do is to relieve a portion of the pressure through the construction of freeways and the widening and resurfacing of other major arterial highways. This is clearly not the solution to the rapid and inexpensive movement of urban residents. At least, it is not the whole solution.

MASS TRANSIT. Some contemporary analysts focus their attention on mass transit as one of the solutions to urban transportation problems. By mass transit they mean buses, streetcars, subways, and elevated railways. Historically, governments have played a limited role in mass transit. In most cases, they have been primarily concerned with regulation of privately owned utilities. Such regulation has usually been focused upon the rates charged and upon the issuance of franchises to guarantee that the operation was in the public interest. Real public responsibility for mass transit has been assumed when financial crises demanded intervention.[16] The number of cases calling for such intervention has been increasing rapidly in recent years. Unfortunately, many mass transit companies have been unable to provide adequate service at prices that the traveler can afford. As a result, state, local, and national governments have had to intervene.

---

[13] Jacobi, "Municipal Public Works," p. 315.
[14] Smerk, *Urban Transportation*, p. 70.
[15] Meyer, Kain, and Wohl, *The Urban Transportation Problem*, p. 106.
[16] Owen, *The Metropolitan Transportation Problem*, p. 66.

A variety of approaches might be taken to the problems faced by mass transit, and not all of them involve government activity.[17] Privately owned companies have successfully attempted to boost revenues in some cities by chartering buses to groups during off-hours. This policy has a tendency to reduce the tremendous costs of providing equipment which is fully used during rush-hours only. In some cases, governments can provide assistance here by chartering school buses at appropriate rates rather than demanding reduced fares for students on regular routes as many cities do today. To be sure, such policies are of little value to the operators of subways and elevated trains, but few of these are private.

A second action that might be taken by private mass transit owners is the development of improved services. There is some indication that it is possible to stimulate demand for mass transit and to increase revenues by providing faster and more frequent service. Many passengers object to long rides and long waits and seek alternative methods of transportation. Such policies are particularly helpful on major commutation lines.

In most instances, purely private efforts will not be enough to revive mass transit. Some government assistance will be necessary at a minimum. Such assistance can take a variety of forms. In many jurisdictions, transit companies are subjected to heavy taxation, which can mean the difference between profit and loss for the ownership. A significant number of communities have found it advantageous to reduce the tax burden as a form of subsidy for transit operations. For example, in 1967 Nebraska and New Jersey exempted transit companies from the state sales tax, and the state of Washington and the city of Washington, D.C. exempted such companies from the gasoline tax.[18] Governments can also assist mass transit by planning and coordination of such services with other transportation systems and with the development of the community as a whole.

When all else fails, or when the subsidization of private transit companies is deemed unacceptable, government may have to take more drastic steps. In most instances, such steps would include some form of public ownership. The governmental transit operator may either be a municipality or a special purpose district or authority with wider jurisdiction. Thus, while Table 16–1 indicates that only 2.1 percent of the reporting cities own and operate transportation systems, an urban government owns and operates some portion of the mass transit system in many more than the sixty-one urban areas reflected in that data. Such a step serves to relieve the transit system from many of its tax burdens, and also relieves the system from the necessity of showing a profit. Once such relief has been provided, it is theoretically possible for transit fares to be based

---

[17] See Owen, *The Metropolitan Transportation Problem*, pp. 98–110.
[18] Jacobi, "Municipal Public Works," p. 316.

more closely upon the direct costs of providing transportation. While such savings and the resultant fare stabilization or reduction may not stimulate large numbers of people to leave their cars in favor of mass transit, they undoubtedly do serve to keep the costs of transit closer to what the poor citizens who are dependent upon public transportation can afford to pay.

Finally, the federal government has developed a series of grant and loan programs designed to improve mass transit services in the cities. The Housing Act of 1961 provided for demonstration grants for cities that were trying to improve their transit systems as well as for loans, and the Urban Mass Transportation Act of 1964 includes a grant program designed to provide two-thirds of the net capital costs for developing transit systems.[19] While these programs have encouraged the development of many imaginative programs for mass transit, they have not managed to significantly slow the slump into which such transportation systems are falling. Only when such grants and loans are combined with government ownership or heavy subsidy, more frequent and faster service, and the leasing of idle buses during off-hours is there any hope of making a real contribution to urban transportation problems. Even then, there appears to be little hope of replacing more than a small portion of the present automobile traffic with mass transit.

COMMUTER RAIL SERVICE. Some major urban centers continue to be dependent upon commuter trains operating on regular rail lines as a major source of transportation within the urban area. There has been ample evidence in recent years that cities such as New York are almost completely choked off when commuters are no longer able to use the trains. This is true even though the use of commuter railroads has been declining. Although urban population has been rapidly increasing, the number of commuter passengers has fallen off drastically, and the number of passenger-miles traveled has declined significantly in the last forty-five years.[20] In spite of the fact that railroads have sharply increased commuter fares in order to provide greater revenue per passenger-mile, commuter services are no longer profitable. Railroads are reducing and discontinuing such services as rapidly as they can receive permission from the appropriate governmental regulatory bodies. Such reductions in service obviously place an even greater load on alternative forms of urban transportation.

In those cases in which the railroads have been unable to discontinue their commuter services, they have frequently resulted in reducing the

---

[19] Smerk, *Urban Transportation*, pp. 148 and 168.
[20] Owen, *The Metropolitan Transportation Problem*, p. 245.

quality of service provided. Erratic schedules and improperly maintained equipment are familiar to nearly every rail commuter. In response to these problems, local, state, and national governments have attempted to subsidize the commuter service of the railroads in the realization that this service must be maintained in the absence of feasible alternative transportation methods. In some cases the subsidies have come in the form of assistance in meeting the operating costs of commuter services, while in others they have been assistance in the form of purchase of such capital equipment as new cars for commuter runs. Such subsidies have enabled the Penn Central and Reading railroads to provide fast, comfortable, and relatively inexpensive commuter service in the Philadelphia area while receiving aid through the Southeastern Pennsylvania Transit Authority (SEPTA).

Clearly there are some significant limitations to the use of commuter railroads for urban transportation. They are only of real importance in cities that enjoyed established rail service prior to suburbanization. Given the losses involved in commuter operations, railroads are certainly not laying new track to establish service where none now exists. As our major metropolitan areas increase in size, suburban communities are established farther and farther away from rail lines, and many commuters are unable to use existing facilities. Finally, it is obvious that commuter rail services benefit only a small portion of urban residents. They are designed primarily to move commuters from the suburbs to the central city. Extensions and improvements of commuter services "hardly will befit the needs either of many nonwhites or, for that matter, of most low-income groups." [21] This is a crucial point. While many major cities must take steps to insure the continuation of commuter services if they are to survive, the plight of the poor in the central city may be of greater significance to more cities.

TRANSPORTATION COSTS AND FINANCING. One of the more difficult tasks facing policy-makers in urban transportation has been the development of materials related to the cost structure of urban transportation. In order to make intelligent decisions, public officials must know the capital and operating costs of each method of transportation, as borne both by the traveler and by government. Even a cursory examination of the literature in this area leaves little doubt that the automobile is the most expensive method of commutation transportation presently in use in our cities, particularly since it is used to transport an average of 1.7 passengers per trip. Unfortunately, few drivers bother to take all of these costs into consideration. For example, almost none of the drivers on our urban

---

[21] Meyer, Kain, and Wohl, *The Urban Transportation Problem*, p. 107.

streets know that it costs at least 6.1¢ per vehicle mile to build and maintain highways.[22] In addition, while transit and railroad fares include capital and operating costs, the average motorist considers only his out-of-pocket or operating costs when making comparisons. A systematic comparison indicates that bus or rail transit is clearly cheaper than cars when meeting peak-hour needs, where the density of traffic along particular corridors is high, and where the routes are relatively long.[23] The advantage of mass transit and rail service can be overcome by increasing the number of passengers per car to a sufficient density under the above conditions, but governmental policy-makers have not found an acceptable device for achieving this end.

The second problem with such cost-based conclusions is that, despite rush-hour appearances, most urban traffic does not conform to peak-hour, corridor density, and route length qualifications. A portion of this discussion has already pointed out that most urban travel is diffuse in origin and destination and devoted to some purpose other than home-to-work travel. In addition it tends to ignore the noneconomic preference patterns of urban travelers, many of whom prefer to operate their own automobile for reasons of comfort, flexibility, and convenience, or sheer psychological satisfaction.

It is possible, of course, for urban governments through the careful use of comprehensive planning and development controls to alter this state of affairs. Should government officials and the public in general decide that the massive expanses of concrete necessary to support automotive traffic are destructive of the desired urban environment, then they may take action to alter the distribution of homes, shopping centers, and places of work either to minimize the amount of travel necessary for urban man or to increase the corridor density of that travel. While many urban theorists may recommend such drastic action as desirable, there is no evidence to indicate that it has received widespread public acceptance.

The generally accepted norm with respect to financing urban transportation is that, like other public utilities, it should primarily be supported by user fees. This norm is honored more in the breach than in the observance by most major cities in this country today. There is heavy subsidization of highway transportation by local, state, and national governments. Although the gas tax is considered by many to be a user fee, it does not adequately cover the cost of building and maintaining public highways and streets. The disproportionate allocation of revenues from the gas tax to governments that are not primarily urban further reduces its effectiveness as a device for allocating the capital costs of streets and highways

---

[22] Meyer, Kain, and Wohl, *The Urban Transportation Problem*, p. 244.
[23] Meyer, Kain, and Wohl, *The Urban Transportation Problem*, p. 243.

to their primary users—much of the money contributed by urban users is allocated to building rural roads. Urban governments further subsidize automobile travel to the extent that they continue to provide free parking or even low-cost parking at the destination for urban travelers.

To make matters worse, the fares charged by most mass transit operations and some subsidized commuter trains discriminate against riders who make only short trips. Most of these fares are flat-rate fares. For example, a ride on the SEPTA-subsidized Chestnut Hill line of the Pennsylvania Railroad in Philadelphia costs thirty-five cents whether the passenger boards at the end of the line, which is over eight miles from center city, or at some point much closer to downtown. The same is true of most city bus lines. This discrimination is doubly troublesome because the short-haul riders who are forced to pay significantly higher fares per mile are most frequently the poorest riders who live in the slums closest to the center city. Such flat-rate fares are neither true user fees, nor are they particularly productive social policy if urban governments intend to relieve the plight of the poor significantly.

Many experts have argued for a scheme of financing urban transportation which would result in fares and pricing that adequately reflect the costs involved. Such pricing policies would, no doubt, be extremely difficult and expensive to administer.[24] Perhaps the best that can be hoped for is a more rational set of policies toward governmental subsidization of urban transportation. Under these circumstances, governments might be forced to consider clearly which types of transportation they were subsidizing and why. In many cases, this might lead to an increasing demand for a greater share for the cities of gas tax revenues and perhaps ultimately to the imposition of higher gas taxes which are more closely related to the costs of urban highway construction and maintenance. In other cases, under demonstration grants from the federal government, it has already led some cities to establish special bus routes with subsidized fares—routes that lead from the slums to places of employment for the poor. While the latter type of subsidy will no doubt prove to be expensive, it should not be much more so than the subsidies already given to automobile travel, and it should produce results consonant with health, welfare, and housing policies designed to help the urban poor.

TRANSPORTATION ALTERNATIVES. The preceding discussion clearly demonstrates that no one solution to urban transportation problems is available. There seems to be little hope of altering the dependency upon the automobile as the major form of transportation in an urban society. However, in most cities there is also a need for continuing alternative modes of

---

[24] Smerk, *Urban Transportation*, pp. 223–226.

transportation. Where social and economic patterns indicate that origins and destinations are sufficiently concentrated and travel corridors are sufficiently dense, then public transportation, whether it be bus, subway, or train, should be maintained. The key appears to be a balanced approach to urban transportation in which each type of transportation is used for what it does best.[25]

THE POLITICS OF TRANSPORTATION. One of the leading studies of the politics of transportation has found that they are characterized by functional cooperation and interfunctional conflict.[26] In other words, there is a tendency for the supporters of the automobile to band together to combat the supporters of mass transit. In neither case are the participants drawn from the general public. They are primarily public agencies that band together with private interests to affect public policy. In New York City, for example, the highway coalition includes the Port of New York Authority, the Triborough Bridge and Tunnel Authority, county and state highway agencies, the United States Bureau of Public Roads, bus companies, automobile associations, and so forth. The supporters of rail commutation are a much looser coalition of railroads, central-city groups, and suburban interests.[27]

In general, the supporters of governmental policies which encourage the use of highways rather than mass transit and rail commuter service have been more successful in influencing public policy. This is particularly evident in the development of federal highway policy, where the major successful political pressures for federal subsidies and the nondiversion of highway funds to other transportation means has come from "automobile users, truckers, manufacturers and suppliers, highway builders, and state and local road officials." [28] The fact that the same groups have been particularly effective at the state level as well has insured that the disproportionate subsidization of highways is a general governmental policy. In the absence of adequate resources, local governments could not, even if they wished, overcome the impact of this influence.

If the opposition to the highways groups is loosely organized at the local level, it is practically disorganized at higher levels where increasing numbers of subsidization decisions are being made. Danielson's study revealed little effective organization of commuters and found that what pressures were exerted on Congress reflected particular, localized interests

---

[25] B. R. Stokes, "The Progress of Rapid Transit in the Bay Area," in *Urban America: Crisis and Opportunity*, ed. Jim Chard and Jon York (Belmont, Calif., 1969), p. 128.

[26] Jameson W. Doig, *Metropolitan Transportation Politics and the New York Region* (New York, 1966), p. 232.

[27] Doig, *Metropolitan Transportation Politics*, pp. 21–22.

[28] Danielson, *Federal-Metropolitan Politics*, p. 25.

rather than an attempt to develop broad policy. The most general emphases were on the elimination of subsidies to competing forms of transportation, the maximization of subsidies to railroads for carrying mail,
and the insuring of adequate passenger facilities.[29] In most of these areas,
the railroads have carried the ball and have been amazingly unsuccessful.
Highway subsidies are bigger and better than ever, and the Post Office
has discontinued the use of railroads as prime carriers of mail. Passenger
facilities have continued to deteriorate in spite of sporadic efforts by commuter organizations to improve them. Finally, commuters have rarely
been able to mount enough pressure to prevent the railroads from discontinuing service on many of their more unprofitable lines. This last
aspect of transportation politics is, perhaps, the most telling. Commuters
and railroads are not really allies. They are much more frequently cast
in the role of adversaries. Thus divided, they are relatively easy for the
highway interests to conquer.

One of the more frequent complaints voiced about the nature of the
politics of transportation is that local governments and local participants
have little control over expenditures and over the location of transportation routes, particularly those involving highways.[30] There is little doubt
that this complaint is well-founded. Federal and state highway officials
control the lion's share of the money spent on roads in this country, and
they frequently pay little attention to the problems that their route
selections engender for cities. In city after city, new interstate highways
have drastically reduced the supply of already scarce housing. Freeways
have effectively cut neighborhoods in half and have isolated one part of
the city from another. Many observers mentioned the isolation of the
Watts section of Los Angeles by the freeways as a major factor in the
riots that took place there in 1965.

There are some cities in which the feeling of local impotence has
proven to be unwarranted. Particularly when the middle class and the
business community have become sufficiently aroused, local groups have
frustrated the highway builders. Both New Orleans and San Francisco
experienced conflicts in which local groups forced the abandonment of
partially constructed freeways which would have had a significant impact
on the nature of the city. In both cases, a sufficient number of people
were aroused to opposition to win the day for the defenders of the city.
Such successful action is, of course, less likely when the affected group is
a collection of slum residents who will lose their homes if the freeway is
constructed, but there is hope for even such relatively impotent groups if

---

[29] Danielson, *Federal-Metropolitan Politics*, pp. 62–68.
[30] See for example Committee for Economic Development, *Developing Metropolitan
Transportation Policies: A Guide For Local Leadership* (New York, 1965), pp. 14–15.

they protest loudly enough and if they can attract sufficient allies to their cause. All of this successful protest carries with it a heavy cost, however. Failure to complete a federally aided highway project may result in the curtailment of funds for future highway projects that are badly needed by the city and that involve routes acceptable to the entire community.

Current studies have presented a mixed picture as to the source of innovative urban transportation policy.[31] Most observers agree that policy changes are highly dependent upon sources outside the urban area in question. The most important of these forces is frequently the federal government, although state governments, and particularly governors, are becoming increasingly important. On the other hand, in some communities central city actors appear to provide a stimulus for innovation. These central city figures, the mayor for instance, are able to attract supporters from the ranks of regional planners and other officials interested in the solution of area-wide problems.

GOVERNMENTAL ORGANIZATION AND TRANSPORTATION POLICY. Most students of urban transportation problems have concluded that the policy decisions able to effectively produce the desired results must be made on a regional or area-wide basis.[32] In only a few instances are the means and routes for urban transportation concentrated within the jurisdiction of a single governmental unit. Where the problems are the greatest, several governments are involved in making decisions even at the local level. Therefore, great emphasis is placed upon the need for regional arrangements in the establishment of transportation policy. The most frequently used device is the regional transportation authority, which can at least serve to coordinate the operation of public transportation within the urban area. However, such authorities do not have the ability by themselves to coordinate public transportation policy with the control of automotive traffic and the location and utilization of urban streets and highways. In order to achieve a truly effective transportation effort, they must work with municipal, county, state, and federal governments. The planning requirements in federal grant programs in the mass transit area and the further development of the Department of Transportation in the national government may encourage more cooperation in the future. Without such coordination, it is difficult to see how the movement of large numbers of people in urban areas will be possible in the years to come.

---

[31] See Doig, *Metropolitan Transportation Politics*, p. 238, and Frank C. Colcord, Jr., "Decision-Making and Transportation Policy: A Comparative Analysis," in Mahood and Angus, *Urban Politics and Problems*, pp. 199–214.

[32] See Owen, *The Metropolitan Transportation Problem*, pp. 165–187.

Suggested Readings

Committee for Economic Development. *Developing Metropolitan Transportation Policies: A Guide for Local Leadership.* New York, 1965.

Crain, Robert L.; Katz, Elihu; and Rosenthal, Donald B. *The Politics of Community Conflict: The Fluoridation Decision.* Indianapolis, 1969.

Danielson, Michael N. *Federal-Metropolitan Politics and the Commuter Crisis.* New York, 1965.

Doig, Jameson W. *Metropolitan Transportation Politics and the New York Region.* New York, 1966.

Fitch, Lyle C., and associates. *Urban Transportation and Public Policy.* San Francisco, 1964.

International City Managers' Association. *Municipal Public Works Administration.* Chicago, 1957.

Meyer, J. R.; Kain, J. F.; and Wohl, M. *The Urban Transportation Problem.* Cambridge, Mass., 1965.

Mumford, Lewis. *The Highway and the City.* New York, 1953.

Owen, Wilfred. *The Metropolitan Transportation Problem.* Rev. ed. Garden City, N.Y., 1966.

Smerk, George M. *Urban Transportation: The Federal Role.* Bloomington, Ind., 1965.

Part Four
Concluding
Observations

In this final chapter, some of the discussions of the previous sections will be brought together and focused upon what may be the two basic considerations in urban politics—the concept of the ideal city as a physical unit and the tension between the city as a political unit and as a provider of services. Once again, no firm conclusions will be found. Perhaps all that we can hope for is to understand what it is we are discussing in the seemingly endless battle over the quality and form of urban life and its relationship to inherently political questions.

chapter 17
The Future
of Urban
Governments

❲Enthusiasm for the American city has not been typical or predominant in our intellectual history. Fear has been the more common reaction. . . . We have no persistent or pervasive tradition of romantic attachment to the city in our literature or in our philosophy, nothing like the Greek attachment to the polis or the French writer's affection for Paris.[1]

Views of the City

One of the most significant problems facing anyone who attempts to offer some general statements in conclusion to a book about our cities and their government is the variety of perspectives from which the city can be viewed. The leading student of urban imagery has pointed out that:

The city can be variously conceived, by its citizens as well as its students: as a place in which to get ahead; a place where anonymity cloaks opportunities for fun, excitement, and freedom; perhaps as a place which undermines health and happiness but whose resources are usable from a safe suburban distance.[2]

The basic mental set or view of the city has had a considerable impact on judgments about the quality of life in today's cities and predictions

---

[1] Morton White and Lucia White, *The Intellectual Versus the City* (Cambridge, Mass., 1962), pp. 13–14.

[2] Anselm L. Strauss, *Images of the American City* (New York, 1961), pp. 12–13.

and prescriptions for the city of the future. While some elements of these urban views may have been empirically derived, they are often dependent upon the observer's emotional reaction to the city and to the urbanization process.

Views of the city and the resultant judgments as to its performance and predictions for its future are complicated to a significant degree by the definitional problems raised in Chapter 1. Many contemporary urban critics have reserved the bulk of their comments for our truly large cities with populations of 500,000 or more. This is *the* city, the metropolis, megalopolis that is bringing mankind to the brink of destruction. However, other more perceptive critics have directed their attention to the complexities of the urbanization process itself wherever it may occur. There is a tendency for those in the first group—and this group includes most current, popular critics of the city—to talk almost exclusively in terms of size and scale. Those who focus on the broader implications of the urbanization process might well find problems in smaller urban aggregations as well.

THE ANTI-URBAN TRADITION. The quotation from Morton and Lucia White that opened this chapter clearly identifies the intellectual foundation for much of the current anti-urban comment. It has always been fashionable for the American intellectual to be somewhat disdainful of urban life. The impressive list of anti-urban intellectuals which the Whites discuss in their excellent book may not include all of this country's greatest, but it certainly includes a sufficient number of our leading literary and philosophical luminaries to establish the existence of the anti-urban tradition. From Thomas Jefferson through Emerson, Thoreau, Hawthorne, Melville, Poe, Henry Adams, Henry James, and William Dean Howells to Frank Lloyd Wright and Lewis Mumford, the list of those who had serious reservations about life in the city in general and in American cities in particular is impressive. However, neither the Whites nor any other sensible observer would want to claim that these luminaries represented the typical American view of cities. At the very least we can say that there is no well-articulated, widespread dissatisfaction with the city among average Americans. But this does not mean that the anti-urban tradition is unimportant. As the Whites point out:

> [We] may regard this critical tradition as a repository of deep, though troubling, wisdom and as a source of sometimes justified, sometimes baseless, fear and anxiety about urbanization.[3]

---

[3] White and White, *The Intellectual*, p. 15.

A particularly pertinent example of the troubling wisdom and justified fear and anxiety can be found in the observations of Alexis de Tocqueville.[4] While this worthy gentleman was neither an American nor truly anti-urban, he did perceive some of the great problems facing American cities and some of their potential solutions. In 1835, Tocqueville observed that one of the great enduring problems of American cities would be to control the urban masses, especially blacks and immigrants, and he foresaw armed force as the only practical method of achieving this control. The point of this illustration is not to endorse Tocqueville's solution to racial violence in our cities. The significant fact is that a critic of American cities identified the problem over 135 years ago and correctly identified the unpleasant resolution of the problem which would result. For some this prediction and its accuracy has merely served as additional proof of the inherent decadence of the city. Others, weaned on the irrelevance of history, simply chose to ignore it and to be surprised and shocked at the new and unexpected problems of the mid-twentieth century. In neither case did Tocqueville serve as the source of insight or inspiration that the Whites apparently hope that the anti-urban intellectual will provide.

Perhaps the most interesting aspect of the anti-urban tradition as it is described by the Whites is the inability of all but the most virulent of the critics of the city to be wholly anti-urban. Some, like Jefferson, came to recognize the inevitability and utility of urbanization, even if they could not appreciate all aspects of city life. Others, like Emerson, Melville, Hawthorne, and Poe, did not share an empirical appreciation of the need for cities, yet found themselves drawn to the city for the intellectual and cultural advantages that it could provide. Even utopian intellectual communities were not an adequate substitute for the city. The Whites imply that the anti-urban rhetoric of the American intellectual tradition must not be confused with a true anti-urbanism which would result in the abolition of cities. They see the essence of the tradition as a fear of the city mob, an impatience with the unwieldy and corrupt political character of the city, and a distrust of commerce and the accumulation of money. The reaction of these earlier critics was either a romantic effort to abolish the objects of their fears or an attempt to establish a method of social control of their worst effects.[5]

Much of the current criticism of the city is in this anti-urban tradition. However, modern critics have learned their lesson well. They are not seriously concerned with dismantling the city and returning to a more agrarian way of life. As we shall shortly see, the major concern today, as

---

[4] White and White, *The Intellectual*, p. 35.
[5] White and White, *The Intellectual*, p. 217.

it was in the eighteenth and nineteenth centuries, is to make the city more livable according to the standards employed by its critics. Now, as then, these standards vary with the critic, and the prescriptions vary as widely as the diagnoses.

CONTEMPORARY VIEWS. For many critics of the city, its failures are functional. Part Three of this book discussed the functions that are not being performed to the satisfaction of many urban residents. It is possible to prepare a general indictment of urban transportation, air and water pollution, lawlessness, blight, diverging educational opportunities, and inadequate facilities for recreation and libraries. Even the experts in each of these fields are quite willing to admit that performance falls a good deal short of everyone's goals. In his ringing journalistic indictment of the cities, Mitchell Gordon details these failures and links them closely to the structural and legal problems of governmental fragmentation which were raised in Chapter 4. Gordon displays a marked impatience with the inaction that has characterized the approach to these functional problems and recommends immediate vigorous action:

> The shibboleths so often sounded, sometimes for political reasons and sometimes in all sincerity, which hold that "peculiar local conditions" or "special situations" make the solutions or approaches of one region totally inapplicable in any other, are rarely more than a shibboleth.[6]

Gordon's style of criticism is not new. Lincoln Steffens and other muckraking journalists at the turn of the century used it with some effect. The earlier effect took the form of structural reforms which did not strike at the heart of the functional failures of the cities and their governments. There is little reason to believe that the wholesale annexations and area-wide governments espoused by modern muckrakers would be any more effective.

Other contemporary critics are carrying on the tradition of Melville, Hawthorne, and Poe by focusing on the real or imagined impact of the city and urbanization on the human spirit. Lewis Mumford stands out clearly as the most articulate and the most widely appreciated member of this group.[7] Mumford's credentials as a critic are impressive. He is not a planner or an academic urbanist, but as a scholar his knowledge of the urbanization process and the planning profession exceeds that of most practitioners. Unlike Gordon, Mumford and many other critics are worried lest urban settlements become too large and subject their citizens to the depersonalization or even dehumanization of their environment. In

---

[6] Mitchell Gordon, *Sick Cities* (New York, 1963), p. 12.
[7] See for example Mumford's *The Urban Prospect* (New York, 1968) for some of his most recent thoughts on cities.

fact, Mumford charges that this has already clearly occurred in many, if not most, major American cities. He would reverse the process by using the basic concepts of Ebenezer Howard which call for regional clusters of urban settlements ranging from 30,000 to 300,000 people in each settlement. Thus Mumford would reintroduce the personal human element to the urban environment. Each settlement would at once be self-sufficient and linked to other settlements in the region and to the common core.

Mumford's defense of Howard may well be necessary only because of the danger that the regional city concept might be corrupted by planners with insufficient vision. There appears to be little danger that the concept will die out for lack of advocates. Leading planners continue to press for the acceptance of the basic Howard design as the future city. E. A. Gutkind has issued a call that is even clearer and more direct than Mumford's for the dismantlement of the city as we know it today.[8] Gutkind seeks to attain an inspiring and diversified environment by splitting up large masses into small, meaningful units, providing more living space, and the systematic dispersal and relocation of the entire urban region. Unlike many planners, Gutkind openly acknowledges some of the problems inherent in the regional city concept. Many of its objectives are to him "apparently incompatible." The challenge is to provide compactness and openness of settlement, order and flexibility, differentiation and homogeneity, as well as privacy and social intercourse. The stress here is on "apparently," however. The whole thrust of Gutkind's argument is that these contradictions can be resolved or at least handled in a more satisfactory manner. It is one of the standard arguments of urban critics stated most baldly. What planners like Gutkind and general critics like Mumford seem to be searching for is an urban environment that provides all of those things which they perceive as benefits of the big city without any of the characteristics which they see as prices of urban living.

These critics are not alone in their search for the ideal city. Their seemingly paradoxical goals may well express the basic ambiguity of modern man toward his urban environment. Gutkind and Mumford strike a responsive chord because many of us are seeking the same kinds of things. There is every indication that man "wants both Gargantua and the rural village, the advantages of urbanism and the freedom from its costs."[9] This is part of the age-old search for benefits without cost. One of the central problems in such a search is our inability to agree as to what constitutes a benefit and what a cost. For example, we have already seen

---

[8] E. A. Gutkind, *The Twilight of Cities* (New York, 1962), especially pp. 195–199.

[9] Henry J. Schmandt and John C. Goldbach, "The Urban Paradox," in *The Quality of Urban Life*, ed. Warner Bloomberg, Jr. and Henry J. Schmandt (Beverly Hills, 1969), p. 477.

that for some critics the city fails as a human container because it and
its institutions are too large, while for others the failure can be traced
to the fact that the city is not large enough. Is size a cost or a benefit?
The subsequent discussion of reactions to the Gutkind and Mumford
type of criticism will demonstrate this point further.

Before abandoning this admittedly small sample of critics of the modern American city, perhaps we should consider the position of a critic
who shares many of their concerns but whose conclusions are a little
different. William H. Whyte has presented an eloquent plea for preserving
the environment and landscape from the onslaught of the contractor and
urbanization.[10] The heart of Whyte's approach is the yearning for green
grass and trees which is shared not only by planners in the Garden City
tradition but also by the vast majority (95 percent) of the American
people according to a Harris poll taken at the close of the 1960s. There is
surely a strong sense of the desire for open space in all of the traditional
criticism of the city. However, Whyte differs from critics like Gutkind
and Mumford in two important particulars. In the first place, Whyte
clearly recognizes the need to work with existing urban forms. He dis-
misses attempts to establish self-contained, limited-size communities as
utopian since they are largely based on assumptions that would start
cities over from scratch. The second major difference lies in Whyte's
approach to the problem of density. While other critics worry about
problems of human scale and the enormity of high-density architecture,
Whyte is content to increase open space in our major cities by increasing
density. He is consoled by the fact that most other urbanized societies
have much greater population densities than we do without apparent ill
effect.

THE DEFENDERS OF THE CITY. The city has always had its defenders, those
who find the urban experience, on balance, a pleasant one and generally
worth whatever costs it entails. These supporters of the city have not
often found it necessary to publish their position abroad. It has only been
in recent years that anyone has taken criticisms of the city very seriously
and has threatened to act on them on a broad scale. The publicity and
concern devoted to undeniable social problems in an urban society and
the increased emphasis on planning has led some to fear the destruction
of the city as they know it. They feel that the city's rewards must be
protected from those who would seriously undermine all that is good
about city life in order to cure ills that may be as imaginary as they are
real.

One of the more eloquent of the modern defenders of the city, Roger

---

[10] William H. Whyte, *The Last Landscape* (Garden City, N.Y., 1968).

Starr, has mounted a frontal attack on what he holds to be the incorrect assumptions of urban critics.[11] Starr quite correctly takes the critics, both modern and traditional, to task for negativism and a failure to emphasize the positive contributions of cities to the lives of millions. For most urban Americans, the cities have not meant poverty and squalor. Most have found them a source of growth and enrichment in the past, and many continue to find them so. This does not deny the existence of the problems upon which the critics have focused. It merely attempts to place them in perspective. At the risk of destroying Starr's excellent point with an earthy analogy, it may be appropriate to suggest that it is misleading to characterize a football quarterback's performance by his fumble and two intercepted passes if he completed 75 percent of his passes and was responsible for total offensive gains in excess of 300 yards. The coach may elect to work on ball handling and passing accuracy, but he probably would not fire the quarterback. Starr suggests that we can work on the problems of the city without destroying it.

The second assumption that disturbs Starr is the assumption that urban Americans live in communities (or ought to). The stress that critics like Mumford place on "human," face-to-face relationships and the sense of community is clearly derived in part from the concern of sociologists with primary groups which was outlined in the first chapter of this book. This concern has received added impetus, in Mumford's case at least, from the intensely interpersonal I-Thou relationships recommended by theologian Martin Buber.[12] There are two problems with the community approach to cities. Even if the sociologists are correct and the modern city is characterized by a breakdown of primary, face-to-face relationships, such a breakdown is quite probably linked to the broader process of urbanization and cannot be reversed simply by physically reorganizing urban man into smaller groups. Intelligent urban critics would no doubt claim that this is a serious oversimplification of their position, but their conclusions lead one inevitably back to this assumption. The second problem occurs on the theological and normative level. Some reputable modern theologians have questioned the moral value of Buber's intense interpersonal relationships for urban man and have suggested less intense but not impersonal relationships that would be more compatible with Starr's concept of the city as a noncommunity.[13]

The most celebrated current champion of the city, particularly the large, metropolitan, central city, against its critics is Jane Jacobs.[14] Her work constitutes a vigorous defense of the life and form of the city as it exists.

---

[11] Roger Starr, *The Living End: The City and Its Critics* (New York, 1966).

[12] White and White, *The Intellectual*, p. 208.

[13] See particularly Harvey Cox, *The Secular City*, rev. ed. (New York, 1966).

[14] Jane Jacobs, *The Death and Life of Great American Cities* (New York, 1961).

She suggests that major alterations of urban living patterns would destroy much of what is valuable in the city. She is most disturbed by what she sees as a tendency for planners, spurred on by anti-urban critics, to attempt to create physical, social, and economic homogeneity in the city. Her reaction is an eloquent statement of a lover of the big city:

> In our American cities, we need all kinds of diversity, intricately mingled in mutual support. We need this so city life can work decently and constructively, and so the people of cities can sustain (and further develop) their society and civilization.[15]

Although she is talking here specifically about land-use diversity, Mrs. Jacobs' picture of the city she loves (New York) clearly indicates her preference for urban diversity of all kinds.

Jane Jacobs is not the only urban analyst who views diversity as a valuable and exciting characteristic of the large city. Building on existing urban forms, Kevin Lynch has developed a view of the future city which focuses on the essential value of its diversity:

> It is clear that the form of a city or of a metropolis will not exhibit some gigantic, stratified order. It will be a complicated pattern, continuous and whole, yet intricate and mobile. It must be plastic to the perceptual habits of thousands of citizens, open-ended to change of function and meaning, receptive to the formation of new imagery. It must invite its viewers to explore the world.[16]

Such pleas for diversity should not be construed as simple, conservative apologia for slums, poverty, and crime. Those who defend the big cities are protesting what they see as a sterilization of the urban environment in the name of eliminating slums, poverty, and crime. They view such a sterilization as a process that inevitably saps the city of its vitality and progressive force.

THE CRITICS AND SUPPORTERS JOIN FORCES. In spite of the harsh language which has been exchanged between modern exponents of differing views of the city, they are not so very far apart. Much of the dispute seems to be based upon misunderstanding. Mumford himself has seemed genuinely outraged that Mrs. Jacobs has so seriously misinterpreted his position and that of Ebenezer Howard on the subject of diversity in the city. Both place a high value on diversity, and Mumford considers the homogeneous garden city to be a planner's corruption of Howard's heterogeneous, self-sufficient urban settlements.[17] Mumford is clearly seeking diversity and

---

[15] Jacobs, *Death and Life*, p. 241.
[16] Kevin Lynch, *The Image of the City* (Cambridge, Mass., 1960), p. 119.
[17] Several of the essays in *The Urban Prospect* make this point most emphatically.

heterogeneity within some sort of a unified urban framework. Mrs. Jacobs implicitly and Lynch explicitly are attempting to establish a similar urban view. All of their discussions point again to two of Gutkind's "apparently incompatible" objectives—order with flexibility and differentiation with homogeneity. The main bone of contention between modern critics and supporters of the large urbanized area is one of physical organization, and this is an argument about means rather than a conflict over basic goals.

One final view of the city may be of some help in understanding the problem of diversity and integration. Scott Greer has linked the question most closely with our understanding of the social process of urbanization and with some of the major trends in current urban life.[18] Greer points out that the diversity which characterizes the city is based to a great extent upon different kinds of work, different life styles, and different ethnic backgrounds in the city. As the scale of society increases, these differences increase as well. Further specialization of labor continues the diversification of the job structure, a variety of choices for leisure time activity allows each man to "do his own thing" in his time off, and differences in wealth and education further distinguish between urban residents. But these forces for diversity do not go unchallenged. Modern urban society has at the same time experienced powerful forces for uniformity. The development of the powerful national state with general norms that are widely shared tends to pull urban society together under the vague but effective rubric of Americanism. The development of a mass market and a truly national economy have underlined an interdependency that can perform integrative functions. Finally, the establishment of mass communications and a mass education system have further increased the possibility that urban Americans will share experiences that can serve as a force to bind "communities" together. Greer concludes that "from variation among small groups segregated by region, class, race, and religion, we move to variations among segments of one integrated system." [19]

Governing the City

One of the questions which has begun to haunt students of urban politics is "Does it really make any sense to talk about governing the city?" The literature of the cities abounds with pessimistic statements:

> Never have American city officials held more executive power, and never have they had less political strength.[20]

---

[18] Scott Greer, "Urbanization and Social Character," in Bloomberg and Schmandt, *The Quality of Urban Life*, pp. 95–127.
[19] Greer, "Urbanization and Social Character," p. 101.
[20] Starr, *The Living End*, p. 22.

These are not boys sent on a man's errand. These are men sent on a superman's errand.[21]

The conclusion that one reaches with respect to this question clearly depends upon one's view of the primary functions of a government. There are currently two major emphases that result not only in different kinds of judgments as to the performance of urban governments, but also in radically different kinds of prescriptions for the future organization of urban governments and cities themselves. These prescriptions are often closely related to the views of the city discussed in the preceding section.

What is bothering an increasing number of political scientists is the apparent lack of emphasis on the traditional governmental role of the city:

> Classical urban theory explicitly recognized this responsibility by its emphasis on the role of the city or polity as an ordering and integrating agent of social control. Modern theory, however, rejected this notion by viewing local government as a service-providing bureaucracy and formulating its basic problems in terms of administrative efficiency. The result was a distortion of the role of the local polity and its significance for contemporary urban life.[22]

This modern theory leads to a view of urban life which has been described as "markedly apolitical." [23] The major emphasis is on the achievement of consensus through the narrowing of social and economic differences in an affluent and egalitarian society and through improved communications. The end result is often pictured as the bureaucratic control of a highly conformist majority. Ten years ago such fears would have been dismissed as the hopeless ravings of right-wing apologists for the establishment. Today they are taken quite seriously by conservatives and radicals alike.

GOVERNMENT AS A PROVIDER OF SERVICES. Those who emphasize the performance of urban services and who seek some modicum of economy and efficiency in government cannot wisely be condemned. After all, government is more than just an agency of social control. It must, inevitably, exercise some service responsibilities. There is also little doubt that these services are not now being performed either to the satisfaction of the general public (at least the attentive portion of it) or to the satisfaction of the professionals who provide the services. Besides, the sentiment that leads many to focus on consensus and the common good is one of the most popular urban images in existence:

---

[21] Jacobs, *Death and Life*, p. 407.

[22] Schmandt and Goldbach, "The Urban Paradox," p. 474.

[23] Warner Bloomberg, Jr. and Henry J. Schmandt, "The Problem of Contemplating the Quality of Life," in Bloomberg and Schmandt, *The Quality of Urban Life*, pp. 16–20.

> The vision of local communities composed of citizens working together in peace and harmony, dedicated to the general good, and closely attached to their city . . . has long intrigued man.[24]

For many who have been bothered by the failures of urban government, these failures have been largely the result of insufficient power and authority. For some, the power and authority are needed only for providing economical and efficient services. In these cases, the emphasis may well be on "rationalizing" the government of our urban areas, particularly those that are metropolitan in nature. These are the reformers who continue to look to annexation and consolidation of governmental units as the only hope for the creation of governmental units large enough to do the job. Their battle is against the evils of fragmentation, and they depend heavily on the standard critiques of government in the metropolis which were detailed in Chapter 4. The reformer of this school is primarily interested in getting the job done and in creating a government large enough and strong enough to do it. There is little awareness of the fact that reasonable men do disagree as to which jobs need doing, which jobs should be done first, and the standards for judging when the job is done. It is this group that is most markedly apolitical.

There are others who are more aware of politics and political constraints but who still are concerned lest city governments fail to get the job done. Such a concern serves as the basis for Roger Starr's complaint quoted earlier in this section that city officials lack political authority. Starr is clearly aware of conflict within the cities. He points out that:

> The contention of the colliding "we's" over the use of the physical space of cities—who shall live where, and how—is the central political fact in the present life of the cities.[25]

What bothers Starr is the tendency of this political fact to get in the way of accomplishing the great tasks that face the city. In the face of all this conflict, the common good, the public interest, are just not shining through. He recommends a more vigorous policy of pursuing the public good as perceived by public officials and a good deal less participation in the decision-making process by "special interests"—"humane city politics must depend on something other than the extent to which officials elected to office do what the people say they want." [26] Starr yearns for a return to the old-style political machine which insulated public officials from day-to-day pressures and which he perceives as being responsible to the people at election time rather than responsive to them during their term of

---

[24] Schmandt and Goldbach, "The Urban Paradox," p. 476.
[25] Starr, *The Living End*, p. 38.
[26] Starr, *The Living End*, p. 258.

office. While this may be a somewhat tortured view of the urban machine, it serves to underline the basic assumptions about the nature of democratic government which Starr shares with a great number of public officials both elected and appointed.

Others have gone even farther in recognizing the problems that conflicting views pose for the provision of services in the common good. At one point, Milton Kotler saw the problem as a failure to consciously view the city as an existential polity:

> Social judgement is unable to govern these contests of power because there is no municipal authority sufficient to rule and compose the dimensions of these conflicts. In the absence of sufficient authority there can be no pragmatic of social judgement to achieve consensus and govern for the common interest.[27]

Kotler concluded that the most satisfactory solution to this lack of authority was to turn to the federal government, which could provide what was necessary to achieve consensus and rule in the common interest. His emphasis is clearly upon the integrative forces that formed one portion of the dichotomy presented earlier in Scott Greer's view of the city.

As these activists who are concerned with solving the physical problems that plague the city come more and more to grips with the problems of the city as a political unit, they cannot avoid some treatment of the questions of integration and social control which Schmandt and Goldbach feared that they were ignoring. However, their emphasis on consensus and a common good for the city, which is appreciated by all right-thinking men, almost inevitably crowds us toward the kind of bureaucratic domination by experts that many other urban analysts find alarming.[28]

DECENTRALIZATION AND PARTICIPATION. Throughout the earlier chapters of this book, the subjects of decentralization and participation have been raised time and time again. It is not surprising that the leading opponents of large cities should view them as governmental monstrosities. Mumford's reaction to New York City may be taken as typical:

> Because they lack any integral organs for formulating policies or making decisions, or even contesting the proposals of the Mayor, the City Planning Commissioners, the Borough Presidents, or Mr. [Robert] Moses, the political pressure exerted by local areas is feeble and sporadic, and achieved only with

---

[27] Milton Kotler, "The Urban Polity," in *The American City: A Sourcebook of Urban Imagery*, ed. Anselm L. Strauss (New York, 1968), pp. 252–263.

[28] See for example Edward C. Banfield, "The Political Implications of Metropolitan Growth," in *The Future Metropolis*, ed. Lloyd Rodwin (New York, 1961), pp. 80–102.

great effort through *ad-hoc* organizations. The result has been a docile conformity by our governing agencies to other more powerful financial influences, unconcerned with the common good.[29]

This may not be a very accurate portrayal of politics in New York or any other large city, but it does indicate that there are consciously political motives behind the recommendations of those who would dismantle our largest cities. The argument appears to be that their very size renders them unable to govern in the common good and, therefore, ungovernable according to democratic criteria.

Even the defenders of the city have to grant much of this argument. As an ardent democrat, Jane Jacobs has also found the cities deficient from a governmental point of view. Her desire to keep the city intact leads her to offer a different prescription for returning the government to the people. She recommends a system of administrative decentralization which is linked to the central administration of the city and which provides the citizens with contact points at which they might influence decision making.[30]

One can read proponents of decentralization like Mumford and Jacobs, and still retain a vague feeling of uneasiness about the basis of their criticisms of urban government in our largest cities. Mumford, in particular, appears to view the problem as essentially one of size. He says that "democracy, in any active sense, begins and ends in communities small enough for their members to meet face to face."[31] Presumably his satellite communities in the regional city would better satisfy his criteria for democracy, although communities between 30,000 and 300,000 certainly have not been immune from criticism as democratic polities. When all of the undergrowth is stripped away, it is neither size nor procedural failures of the city as a democratic polity which bother Mumford and Jacobs. The substance of governmental decisions prompts their criticism.

Other commentators have concerned themselves much more directly with the process by which urban decisions are made. While this concern with the democratic process in the city was largely a manifestation of the 1960s, Frederic C. Howe recognized as early as 1914 that much of what passed for urban reform was based upon a distrust of mass government and democracy, and suggested that the real reform of the cities would have to be popular in nature.[32] Participation and involvement are key concepts in the rhetoric if not the practice of urban government today. This

---

[29] Mumford, *The Urban Prospect*, p. 201.
[30] Jacobs, *Death and Life*, pp. 418–422.
[31] Mumford, *The Urban Prospect*, p. 224.
[32] Frederic C. Howe, "The City: The Hope of Democracy," in Strauss, *The American City*, pp. 239–240.

is clearly true in small cities as well as large. These concepts may have even provided a meeting ground for the radicals of the central city and the conservatives of the suburbs, though neither group is likely to want to accept the logical consequences of their common interests. At every turn in this discussion of urban government we have found ourselves faced by problems of participation.

It should be clear by now that participation means many things to many people. For those who are oriented toward democratic formalism it means voting. For others, it means joining civic groups and becoming "involved." While these activities may be satisfying for a variety of reasons, there is no indication in earlier chapters of this book or elsewhere that they are really a very effective way for a man to change his environment.[33] A very few see participation only as a device to generate discussion of the problems which face our cities, and these people appear to be seeking only a consciousness or awareness of urban problems on the part of the general population and to be reserving true participation in the decision-making process for leaders.[34] While this latter view may well correspond most closely to the realities of present efforts for participatory democracy in an urban setting, it does not meet the democratic standards of many of our severest social critics.

The greatest shortcoming in most evaluations of the performance of urban governments in recent years has been the failure to recognize the implications of the findings which have been reported in the empirical studies cited in earlier chapters of this book dealing with functions and services. These findings indicate that there may well be an inherent contradiction between the emphasis upon urban government as a democratic polity in which there is broad-based participation by citizens in the decision-making process and the emphasis upon urban governments as providers of particular services and tangible rewards. Crain, Katz, and Rosenthal deal with this problem most explicitly in the introduction to their study of fluoridation politics:

> A major difference between political systems is the degree to which citizens are encouraged to participate in government; and, in general, the more "participative" a government, the more difficult it is to collect together the power to make a decision. Furthermore, some political systems are participative, but provide a structure that permits action despite citizen activity; other systems are immobilized as soon as a large number of voters become involved in an issue.[35]

---

[33] For a more complete discussion, see James Q. Wilson, "The Urban Unease: Community vs. City," in Bloomberg and Schmandt, *The Quality of Urban Life*, pp. 455–472.

[34] Jean Gottmann, "Environment and Ways of Life in Modern Metropolis," in Bloomberg and Schmandt, *The Quality of Urban Life*, pp. 90–94.

[35] Robert L. Crain, Elihu Katz, and Donald B. Rosenthal, *The Politics of Community Conflict: The Fluoridation Decision* (Indianapolis, 1969), p. 13.

If decision-making is in fact more difficult in a participatory environment, stalemate and indecision may well make the development of programs to alleviate poverty, hunger, poor housing, poor transportation, pollution, and so forth, more difficult as well.

CONFLICT AND SOCIAL CONTROL. Ultimately, critics of both those who focus upon urban government as a provider of services and those who focus upon the polity as a democratic unit must point to the failure of these groups to give adequate attention to the problems of conflict and social control. These critics strike at the heart of current urban governmental problems when they observe that "the important questions for political analysis . . . concern . . . the amount and intensity of conflict and the capacity of the government for managing it."[36] In recognizing that questions of social order are fundamental to any discussion of the city, many political scientists are now beginning to come to grips not only with the crises of modern cities in the United States but also with many of the standard criticisms and fears which characterized the approach of earlier scholars to the city. Matthew Holden, Jr. summarizes this position best when he says that:

> The policy objective cannot be the elimination of conflict (whence disorder springs), for that is an impossible task. It is rather to provide a conflict management structure (pattern) which most participants will regard as dominant (at minimum) and (preferably) acceptable, desirable, or legitimate.[37]

We have, in other words, paid insufficient attention to Tocqueville's warning that extraordinary armed force would be necessary to maintain peace in the cities and to prevent significant numbers of urban residents from taking to the streets in protest.

> There is, in the urban literature, virtually no attention to the conditions and processes of achieving domestic peace, the necessary basis for reducing the elements of coercion in the maintenance of order.[38]

In the absence of such attention, it is no wonder that urban government appears by almost any criteria to be ineffective. Urban services and democratic forms for the decision-making process may well be closely linked to the management of conflict and the achieving of domestic peace. How-

---

[36] Banfield, "The Political Implications," p. 97.

[37] Matthew Holden, Jr., "The Quality of Urban Order," in Bloomberg and Schmandt, *The Quality of Urban Life*, p. 434.

[38] Holden, "The Quality of Urban Order," p. 449.

ever, the confusion generated by the earlier chapters in this book should provide ample evidence that we know very little about the nature of this linkage. It merely serves to demonstrate that the simplistic assumptions of earlier reformers who chose to emphasize consensus, and the equally simplistic emphasis of many current reformers on the performance of services are inadequate.

Those who would find salvation for the cities in participation certainly do not come to grips with the question of social order either. Holden views this as an attempt to avoid the hard questions of urban politics:

> The present mood of thought actually impedes the responsible behavior of political elites, precisely because those who are currently in this position and those who soon will be (the student generation) lack the self-confidence and capacity to conceive what would be an appropriate and viable order. The response to this lack of self-confidence is a form of intellectual posturing in the romanticization of "participatory democracy" which means that no one is prepared to offer guidance and to be held accountable for the successes and failures of his guidance.[39]

Perhaps Holden is too hard on those who advocate participatory democracy. The application of democratic ideals to urban politics surely can be more than a cop-out. However, in many cases, Holden's diagnosis is correct. Slogans replace hard thought and careful analysis, and patent medicine programs are designed to divert the attention of urban Americans from their real problems.

All is not hopeless, however. Programs exist that may encourage us to take a more realistic look at the urban political process in all its forms. Communities that are participating in the federally funded Model Cities program have an unparalleled opportunity to come to grips with the design of a social order while at the same time facing some of the more obvious service failures. This process is being conducted in the context of both the traditional governmental and bureaucratic organizations and participatory democracy and is plagued by all of the shortcomings which characterize each. It is a decision-making environment in which conflict cannot be ignored. At the time of this writing, no Model Cities program has risen to the heights of Holden's challenge. The cynics among us suggest that none will. But it is only when an attempt is made to approach urban government and politics in its total context that there is any hope of dealing with the fundamental questions of social order, democratic decision-making, and the maintenance of an adequate if not superior urban environment.

---

[39] Holden, "The Quality of Urban Order," p. 450.

Suggested Readings

Bloomberg, Warner, Jr., and Schmandt, Henry J., eds. *The Quality of Urban Life*. Beverly Hills, Calif., 1969.

Cox, Harvey, *The Secular City*. Rev. ed. New York, 1966.

Gordon, Mitchell. *Sick Cities*. New York, 1963.

Gutkind, E. A. *The Twilight of Cities*. New York, 1962.

Jacobs, Jane. *The Death and Life of Great American Cities*. New York, 1961.

Lynch, Kevin. *The Image of the City*. Cambridge, Mass., 1960.

Mumford, Lewis. *The Urban Prospect*. New York, 1968.

Rodwin, Lloyd, ed. *The Future Metropolis*. New York, 1961.

Starr, Roger. *The Living End: The City and Its Critics*. New York, 1966.

Strauss, Anselm L., ed. *The American City: A Sourcebook of Urban Imagery*. New York, 1968.

———. *Images of the American City*. New York, 1961.

White, Morton, and White, Lucia. *The Intellectual Versus the City*. Cambridge, Mass., 1962.

Whyte, William H. *The Last Landscape*. Garden City, N.Y., 1968.

Index

Index